KENNETH BRANAGH

by the same author

THE CUBAN MISSILE CRISIS
MISSILES IN CUBA: KENNEDY, KHRUSHCHEV, CASTRO AND THE 1962 CRISIS
KENNEDY: THE NEW FRONTIER REVISITED (Ed.)
THE KENNEDYS AND CUBA: THE DECLASSIFIED DOCUMENTARY HISTORY (Ed.)

Kenneth Branagh

MARK WHITE

First published in 2005
by Faber and Faber Limited
3 Queen Square London WC1N 3AU

Typeset by Alex Lazarou, Surbiton, Surrey
Printed in England by Mackays of Chatham plc, Chatham, Kent

A CIP record for this book
is available from the British Library

ISBN 0–571–22068–1

2 4 6 8 10 9 7 5 3 1

For Reginald Horsman

Contents

Illustrations

Introduction

In the spring of 1990 I went to the Oriental Theater in Milwaukee, Wisconsin, to see a new film, *Henry V*, directed by and starring one Kenneth Branagh. Raised in Britain, I was at that time living in the United States, doing graduate work in history. There was a good deal of flattering talk in the American media about Branagh being the new Laurence Olivier, and he had already garnered Best Actor and Best Director Oscar nominations for *Henry V*. I was eager to see the picture. With an interest in theatre and in film, particularly in Olivier's career, I was curious about the comparisons being drawn between Branagh and the titan who had passed away the previous summer.

I arrived at the cinema to find it packed to the rafters. Surprising, I thought, for a movie of a play by Shakespeare. Then the film itself, and Branagh's performance as Henry. I was impressed – by the naturalism and the power of his acting, the calibre of the cast he had recruited, and by how well Branagh had made the play work cinematically. I recall thinking that here was a major talent. In retrospect, that initial response to *Henry V* was the original spark for this book.

The next was my surprise in discovering on my periodic trips home that the respect he received in America was not evident on the other side of the Atlantic. In the United States he was lauded for his audacity in combining directing and acting, and in undertaking projects that brought to mind the work of Olivier and Orson Welles. It was felt that he was carrying out a worthy public service in trying to enlarge the audience receptive to Shakespeare, and there was general admiration for the fact that he was doing these things at a young age. In England, by contrast, his rise had been accompanied by widespread criticism in the media. He had been castigated for his wedding, his autobiography, his appearance, his acting, his supposed arrogance in laying claim to Olivier's throne, and his character. A desire to explore this theme – the difference between how Branagh has been viewed in the United States and in England – was another impulse behind my interest in writing this book.

In undertaking this project, I have sought to utilise every source I could find. As a trained historian, my instincts are to spend a lot of time in the archives. Accordingly, I have examined the vast quantity of materials on Branagh's film and television career housed at the British Film Institute, including the special collection on his *Henry V* movie. Of great value were the papers of Branagh's Renaissance Theatre Company, deposited by London's Theatre Museum at the Victoria and Albert Museum archive in Blythe House. Other materials at the Theatre Museum, such as the files of newspaper clippings, proved useful. Consulting the papers of Laurence Olivier at the British Library, I found the letter Branagh had sent, whilst at RADA, to Olivier, asking for his advice. There were also some items in John Gielgud's papers at the British Library pertaining to his various collaborations with Branagh. In Stratford-upon-Avon I was able to examine the Shakespeare Centre Library's records on Branagh's work in 1984–5 and in 1992–3 for the Royal Shakespeare Company. The University of Birmingham's Shakespeare Institute, also in Stratford, had a wide range of materials on Branagh. I examined the papers of the Progress Theatre Company, the amateur group Branagh joined as a teenager, at the Berkshire Record Office in Reading. At the University of Hull I consulted the papers of Alan Plater, who wrote the screenplays for two of the television dramas in which Branagh appeared in the 1980s. I received from Branagh fan Jude Tessel various materials that will form part of the Branagh collection being developed at Queen's University, Belfast. In addition, I have read approximately one thousand newspaper, magazine and journal articles on Branagh, many of which are listed in the Bibliography. A biographer can learn simply by going to the places that have been important to his or her subject's life; hence I have visited Reading, Stratford, the Villa Vignamaggio, in Tuscany, where Branagh filmed *Much Ado About Nothing*, and the places in London, such as RADA, where he spent time.

I have, moreover, interviewed or corresponded with a good many individuals who have either worked with Branagh, or who have a certain status in theatre or film and have insights into his career. This is not an authorised work, but I was fortunate to be able to research it with some cooperation from Kenneth Branagh. In the autumn of 2003 he provided me with a letter, which he suggested I show prospective interviewees, saying that, although he would not be able to speak to me himself, he would be happy for his friends to talk to me if they were willing to do so. I would like to thank Kenneth Branagh for that, and for furnishing me with a copy of *Listening*, the short film he released in 2003. I would also like to thank the following interviewees and correspondents: David Parfitt, Stephen Evans, Patricia Marmont, Richard Briers, Julie Christie, Paul Scofield, Chris Columbus, Michael Grandage, Robert Altman, Oliver Parker, James Cellan Jones, Clare Peploe, Michael Kalesniko, Hubert Taczanowski, Michael Billington, Michael Coveney, Alastair Macaulay, Toby Jones, Alex Lowe, Simon Callow, David Hare, Alan Ayckbourn, Charlotte Jones, Christopher Hampton, Brian Friel, Jamie Payne, Al Senter, Simon Woodham, Frank Pierson and Stephen Goldblatt. So that the reader can distinguish statements made in these interviews and letters from quotes found elsewhere, my interviewees' and correspondents' comments in this book will be made in the present tense, whilst the past tense will be used for quotations from published sources. For longer quotes, the source is indicated – unless otherwise apparent – in the Notes section towards the end of the book.

I wish to express my gratitude to all of the archivists who assisted my work. I am also indebted to James Cellan Jones for allowing me to make use of his personal scrapbooks on the making of the *Fortunes of War* series, which he directed; Jamie Payne for providing me with a copy of *The Dance of Shiva*, the short film which he directed and in which Branagh appeared; Alastair Macaulay for furnishing me with his notes on Branagh's stage performance as Richard III; and Peter Durrant, County Archivist at the Berkshire Record Office, for granting me permission to examine press reviews for the Progress Theatre Company, which had not hitherto been processed, and an entry relating to Branagh in the Meadway School logbook, which was not due to become available to researchers for some years. I would also like to thank Reginald Horsman, Dinah Wood, Peggy Paterson, Amanda Armstrong, Jude Tessel, Guy Rose, Adam Mark and Mark Glancy.

I

Driven Youth

In early 1984, as the Royal Shakespeare Company was gearing up for its new season, a press conference was held to promote the productions that would soon be opening in Stratford-upon-Avon. There in attendance were Antony Sher, about to take on the challenge of Richard III, and a young Kenneth Branagh, who was rehearsing Henry V. Sher had been worrying about the legacy of Laurence Olivier; he had even had dreams (or was it nightmares?) about the great man. How to succeed in a part on which Olivier had left such an indelible impression – that was the question. Encountering Branagh away from the assembled throng of journalists, Sher anticipated a touch of empathy. 'I confided my fear to him, thinking I'd have a soulmate,' he recalled. 'After all, his role, Henry V, had the same warning sign hanging over it: *This is the property of Laurence Olivier – trespassers will be prosecuted.*' But Branagh seemed unfazed. 'Oh look,' he said, 'Olivier's performances exist, there's nothing we can do about them, may as well just get on with the job.'

Sher was taken aback:

> *Just get on with the job?* The fearlessness, the folly of youth, I thought, staring at the cherubic face topped with red-gold hair – he'll find out!
>
> Or not. As far as I know Branagh wasn't born with a cowl round his head – he just arrived with a written guarantee in his hand. It was from God and it said, 'You're gonna make it, kid.'
>
> The nonchalance, the certainty with which he'd spoken to me that day were the same qualities which graced his performance as Henry a few weeks later.[1]

That portrayal of Henry V was an important milestone in Branagh's rise to star status. The story of his ascent, however, begins twenty-four years earlier, in Northern Ireland.

It was on the afternoon of Saturday, 10 December 1960, that Kenneth Charles Branagh was born in Belfast. As with a number of prominent British actors who have emerged since World War II, his background was quintessentially working-class. His father, William, was a joiner by trade, and his mother, Frances, had worked in the local mill. William and Frances came from the York Street area of Belfast adjacent to the docks, growing up in large families that were headed up by fathers known for their hard-drinking exploits. Married in 1954, William and Frances had their first child, Bill, a year later. Kenneth was their second son.

Growing up in the 1960s in a council house at 96 Mountcollyer Street, Kenneth Branagh benefited from a strong sense of rootedness. Though money was scarce – he had to share a bed with his brother when he was seven years old – relatives and friends were not. Visits to family were the centre of young Branagh's social life, and he has spoken nostalgically about evenings in which his father would tell jokes, his mother would sing and everyone would recount episodes from the history of the family. On Mountcollyer Street Branagh was part of an extensive social network, knowing everyone his own age well. All of this furnished him with a sense of belonging. 'My time in Belfast was when I was most consistently happy,' he would say in later years. 'I think coming from a culture where people – individually and nationally – have a very strong sense of identity is not something I've enjoyed since.'

These early years were not altogether tranquil, for they took place against the backdrop of rising sectarian tension and violence. Branagh's family was Protestant, but only nominally attached to organised religion. His father did not join the Orange Order, and in an area where Protestants – though in the majority – lived alongside Catholics, he promoted a family attitude of toleration. 'He had a very basic belief that it was inappropriate to make distinctions,' recalled Kenneth Branagh. 'And if we ever did, it was a clip around the ear.' Initially the sectarian issue had little impact on Branagh's life. But as the 1960s unfolded it impinged with greater frequency. Periodically he would be stopped by groups of youngsters and quizzed as to his religious affiliation. He would try to guess their religion before declaring his own; and even if he guessed correctly he would often end up being hit anyway.

Branagh's years in Belfast bred in him a certain steeliness. Corporal punishment was meted out at Grove Primary School for misconduct, and strict academic standards were set. At home, as he explained in his 1989 autobiography *Beginning*, his mother was not averse to giving him a clip round the ear if he misbehaved. There was also something about life in the city that generated ambition and robustness in the young Branagh. 'I think Belfast made us driven individuals,' his brother Bill reflected. 'We're both extremely competitive – I don't like to be second best. Nor does Ken. He hates it. When we came to England, Ken and I were determined to be responsible for our own destiny.'

As for the performing arts and literature, Branagh's family had no tradition of involvement. There were neither regular trips to the theatre nor an accumulation of books in the house. But the movies sparked in Branagh an incipient interest in acting. He was gripped, in particular, by Burt Lancaster's performance in *The Birdman of Alcatraz*. That early fascination with film was sustained by family outings to the cinema. He also had his first experience in Belfast of the theatre, taking in a production of Dickens's *A Christmas Carol*, starring Joseph Tomelty, at the Grove Theatre. 'There was no other word for it,' recalled Branagh. 'Magic.' But it proved to be an ephemeral intoxication; his interest in the stage did not become deep and sustained until several years later.

Beginning in 1967, Branagh's father took work in England. Every third weekend he would return to see the family. That connection proved to be an important escape route when the Troubles began to affect the lives of his wife and children. One night, as Kenneth's brother was playing football down the road, a peculiar humming noise started. Bill Branagh dashed towards 96 Mountcollyer Street, shouting at Kenneth: 'Get in the house, get in the house!' A large group of Protestants had come from the Shankhill Road. The sound was caused by their smashing of iron draining grates from the gutters so that they could be used to break the windows of Catholic houses. Kenneth Branagh ran inside, where his mother put him under the dining-room table. 'I was hysterical,' he said later. When the mob had departed, people left their houses and began to erect a barricade at each end of the street. The next day soldiers were dispatched to the road. A new era in the life of the city was under way. At this juncture Branagh's parents decided to leave for England. With his mother expecting her third child, Joyce, the nine-year-old Branagh relocated with the rest of his family in the spring of 1970 to Reading, forty miles outside London.

It did not appear to be the most promising base from which a youngster could build a career as an actor. Two years before Branagh arrived, a group of local residents declared: 'Reading is dead, there is no professional theatre, no concert hall, and the town hall is so gloomy.' Yet Reading probably helped to develop the intense drive that Branagh would soon display. There was a great enough sense of suburban mundaneness (which Reading still evokes today) to generate a feeling of wanting to get out, and at the same time its proximity to London made it clear that getting out was possible. It is worth noting that the town has become something of a mini-conveyor belt for the performing arts in recent years: Kate Winslet and Ricky Gervais also hail from there.

Whatever its long-term consequences, the immediate impact on Kenneth of the move to Reading was profound, robbing him of the sense of secure identity that he had enjoyed in Belfast. The transition was smoothest for his father. With three years of work in England under his belt, he knew what to expect; but for the rest of the family, there was an acute sense of dislocation. Reports of the violence in Ireland dominated the television news in the early 1970s. As there were children in Reading with elder brothers in the army, fitting in was never going to be easy. Frances found the move the most disorientating. Detached from the strong support unit that was her family network in Belfast, she felt isolated. She also had to deal with two sons who worried that her strong Belfast accent would make them conspicuous. On one occasion, the day before his parents were to take him to pick up some schoolmates, Kenneth asked: 'Would you mind speaking a little more clearly tomorrow, Mum?' His humiliated mother was reduced to tears.

Kenneth, like his brother Bill, adapted to his new circumstances by acquiring an English accent. On his first day at Whiteknights County Primary, he had to repeat himself time after time as classmates and teachers struggled to understand him. For a while he led a double life – employing an English accent at school, and an Irish one at home. The connection between that development and his later life as an actor is clear. At an early stage he became adept at playing different roles. He was already acting.

The move to Reading caused Branagh to develop a keen appreciation of not only the linguistic differences between his new and old worlds but the social ones as well. Having been part of a working-class environment, he now had a greater connection with a middle-class milieu, and an accompanying sense of not quite belonging. 'I had to start listening to what was said with a kind of keenness that was new,' he recalled. Even a subject as banal as the food he had eaten at home meant learning different terminology. Copying what he had heard his schoolmates say, he would tell other kids that he had eaten a cold-meat salad for lunch, even though he was not certain what it was exactly.

It was only in later years that Branagh was able to understand fully the emotional consequences of the move from Northern Ireland to England:

> Fear, suspicion, whatever, a kind of innate protectiveness. I have been instinctively building layers of protection against the world, which I believe somewhere in my subconscious is going to fuck me over. When you move to a strange place where you talk funny, you immediately have to start being deceptive. I began speaking English at school, then coming home and speaking in an Irish accent. Not only was I doing that, but I was also wracked with guilt about it.[2]

In 1999 he elaborated on that assessment:

> The move to England felt at times like some kind of betrayal. The transformation from that very grounded Belfast life, with its comfortable and simple expectations, had a profound effect on me. But I didn't fight to get it out of my system the way [my brother] Bill did. And subsequently I carried much more baggage. Maybe the whole acting game was a way of hiding or escaping from it. When I try and do my psychobabble analysis of it, I feel that only now do I have a strong sense of who I am in the way that I did in Belfast.[3]

Torn between his Irishness and his newly acquired Englishness, subject to a spell of bullying on beginning his secondary school, Meadway Comprehensive, the young Branagh went into his shell. His talent at sports, which led to his selection as captain of the school football and rugby teams, gave him a certain credibility among his peers. But he became more reclusive, spending ever more time by himself in his attic bedroom.

As his personality developed, it became clear that he was akin to his self-contained father, while Bill and his mother shared a more fiery temperament. 'Ken looks like my mother, but in character he's more like my father – he doesn't wear his heart on his sleeve,' explained Bill. 'My mother's incredibly emotional, as am I. We have big arguments, and as a child I could make her cry, and she could make me cry. Ken and my father hide their feelings.' During their relationship, Emma

Thompson was also struck by this facet of Kenneth's personality, the self-protective coating he had developed that could be difficult to penetrate.

It was in these years of introspection, from the age of twelve to fifteen, that Kenneth found one of the keys that would unlock his imagination and open up the way towards a new, more exciting, more creative life: books. Having started a paper round, he had a little spare cash that he used to build up his own library. 'Spend your money on something else,' his father recommended, as his son's book-buying gathered pace. 'Once you've read a book, what can you do with it?' Kenneth ignored the advice. He derived immense pleasure from seeing, for the first time, a shelf full of books in the house. His father would recall in later years how, whenever he encouraged Kenneth to play football, he would stay inside, despite his passion for the game, with his head buried in a book. 'The world's knowledge is in books,' his father reflected, 'and he knew it.'

Furthering Branagh's love for the written word was a position, offered to him at the age of thirteen, by the *Reading Evening Post*, as reviewer of children's books. He was beginning to display a confidence and resourcefulness that would fuel his rise, and these traits were to the fore as he fired off a letter to his local newspaper complaining about the paucity of children's books among those they reviewed. What was required, he urged them, was to publish book reviews 'by kids, for kids'. Impressed, the *Reading Evening Post* responded by offering him his own column. Thus was born 'Branagh's Junior Bookshelf', and though no remuneration was involved, he was allowed to keep the books he reviewed. A proud family faithfully collected the newspaper cuttings. The degree of local celebrity involved in writing his own column can only have augmented Branagh's confidence. He would continue to write for the *Post* until, as a jaded, sixteen-year-old hack, he found himself concocting a review on the basis of the book's jacket notes. He realised it was time to resign.

Branagh was already searching for a way ahead. His stint on the local newspaper furnished him with his first plan of action: he would become a journalist. As he looked at it, journalism would provide a path to a more glamorous future, which optimally would culminate in his own television chat show. He clung to this conception of his future as the next Michael Parkinson until the watershed event of his adolescence: being cast in a school production of *Oh! What a Lovely War*.

Such was his aptitude and enthusiasm that he ended up accepting no less than four parts. At primary school he had played Dougal in *The Magic Roundabout* – a role he was never able to revisit at RADA or with the Royal Shakespeare Company – but this was his first sustained, meaningful involvement in acting. And he loved it. He was struck by the enormous camaraderie generated by the enterprise, and his talent was apparent from the start. Roger Lewis, the drama teacher, certainly thought he had what it would take. 'Have you ever thought of doing this professionally?' he asked his young charge. Performing in *Oh! What a Lovely War* had 'absolutely met me in the centre of myself,' Branagh said later. 'Everything clicked at once.' This was his road-to-Damascus experience. With complete certainty, he made up his mind about the future: he would become an actor. He immediately informed June Sparey, with whom he had worked at the *Reading Evening Post*, of his decision to forsake journalism for the stage. 'He said it was the most wonderful thing he'd ever done, and he was going to be an actor,' she recalled.

Branagh was fifteen years old when he acted in *Oh! What a Lovely War*. When he started RADA, at eighteen years of age, his fellow students noticed how he was more technically advanced than anyone else in his year. That transformation in such a short period, from a novice schoolboy actor to the most skilled actor at probably the most prestigious drama school in the land, represented the key achievement of his early life; it was the foundation on which his future success was based.

Regular trips to the theatre, an early immersion in the works of Shakespeare and Chekhov, and the development of a sense of the cultural landscape of the country were not integral features of Branagh's childhood experience. Inevitably he would soon find himself competing against young actors who did enjoy those advantages. He needed to learn quickly, and he knew it. He did so by embarking on a rigorous programme of self-improvement. Most important was the acquisition of as much actual acting experience as possible. Accordingly, he joined the Berkshire Shakespeare Players, for whom he played Cassio in a 1978 production of *Othello*. He also continued to perform in school productions, including *Toad of Toad Hall* in December 1978. The Meadway logbook, kept as a record of the school's activities, includes an entry on this production which reads '1st night. Excellently done: Ken Branagh, Ken Meadley ... and Chris Everett were outstanding. All four nights sold out.'

Most importantly, Branagh became a member of a local amateur company, the Progress Theatre, and its offshoot, the Progress Youth Theatre. This proved to be an invaluable part of Branagh's theatrical education. Progress was amateur dramatics at its most credible. Founded just after World War II, it had developed a cutting-edge reputation. Not only did it stage productions of the classics, it put on newer, more controversial work as well. As early as 1960 Progress had ruffled feathers by staging a play that dealt openly with homosexuality. A dozen years after Branagh had left Progress, a local journalist wrote, 'Many experts believe it to be the best amateur theatre in the country.'

By the time Branagh joined, in the late 1970s, Progress was indeed a lively, passionate company. A production of *Who's Afraid of Virginia Woolf?*, in which a group of actors refused to perform in protest at the leading man's inability to learn his lines, led to an extraordinary meeting being convened and threats of expulsion for the dissenting actors. During his time with the company, Branagh broadened his experience, appearing in plays by Christopher Hampton and by Tom Stoppard. Moreover, he almost certainly performed his first Shakespeare, with Progress, in the spring of 1978. On 27, 28 and 29 April Branagh, along with six other actors, presented a series of poems, dramatic speeches and other writings to celebrate Shakespeare's birthday and St George's Day. Branagh read poems by Robert Browning and Rupert Brooke, recollections by John Gielgud about the time when, still in his twenties, he played Lear, and speeches from *Hamlet* and *Measure for Measure*. The climax of the event was the delivery by Branagh of the 'Once more unto the breach' speech from *Henry V*. Even at this early stage, he was interested in the play. Who could have foretold on those three evenings that this teenager would become, a little more than a decade later, the most famous Shakespearean actor in the world, making his name a household word by filming that very play? And the local punters got to see this star-in-the-making for the princely sum of fifty pence.

Other work undertaken by Branagh for Progress was well received. In a Progress Youth Theatre production of Yevgheny Shvarts' *The Naked King*, in the 1978–9 season, he earned a rave from the local press: 'Ken Branagh gave a masterly performance as the Professor. His scene with the King in which the ancestral pedigree of the princess was divulged was brilliantly played.'

As well as giving him valuable acting experience, Progress also furnished Branagh with a useful sense of the more prosaic side of the theatre. Along with other actors in the company, he was put on a cleaning roster. One year, at 10 a.m. on Sunday, 10 December, his eighteenth birthday, he had to go in to mop and scrub the theatre's premises.

Branagh deepened his appreciation of the craft of acting not only by treading the boards himself but by watching outstanding professional practioners at work. A trip to Stratford-upon-Avon allowed him to see performances by Alan Rickman, Jonathan Pryce and Michael Hordern. Making an even greater impression on him was Derek Jacobi's Hamlet, which he watched in Oxford. He was utterly exhilarated by what he had seen. 'It was eleven at night on a Friday,' he recalled, 'I was taking the train back to Reading, and I could have walked home.' Over the years Branagh has consistently cited this experience as one of the seminal events of his early life. It left him with a sense of the excitement that theatre could produce, and triggered a fascination with the role of Hamlet, one that he would indulge periodically over the course of the next two decades.

Supplementing his acting and theatre-going was the teenage Branagh's extensive reading on the history of the stage. Hundreds of back copies of *Plays and Players* and other theatre magazines, which had been given to him as a present, were absorbed. Joining the Berkshire County Drama Library, he read books by Gielgud and Emlyn Williams, and biographies of Olivier, Irving and Garrick. He read with particular interest about the heady days of Olivier's reign as director of the National Theatre in the 1960s. He also began to buy paperbacks of Shakespeare's plays. Fellow actors would, in later years, comment on Branagh's encyclopedic knowledge of stage history. It was in this period that his theatrical education got under way.

As he mounted this multi-faceted campaign to give himself a fighting chance when it came to applying to the top drama schools, Branagh exhibited the characteristics that continued to be evident during his professional life: drive, focus, energy, imagination and – perhaps most importantly – confidence and intelligence. His intellect was a paradox. He was by no means an outstanding student at school, and would end up disappointing himself by the marks he achieved in his English, Sociology and History A levels; but he was blessed with a quick and highly retentive mind, and his concern was always with the practical application of knowledge. He knew that every hour spent acting or watching acting or reading about acting would help him get into drama school, while every hour reading about sociology or history would not, in any significant way. His confidence became more evident as his experience of performance increased. Somewhat reclusive in his early teenage years, he became more dynamic, audacious and outgoing as his adolescence unfolded. As with anybody, his confidence was not total, but it was considerable in a relative sense. Of all the traits making up Branagh's character, it is his formidable confidence that is the most difficult to explain. Given his humble beginnings and the elevated world to which he aspired, a 'chippiness', a deep well of insecurity, could have been expected; but that was not the case. Self-assurance was something he just had. It proved to be a major asset.

Branagh's self-belief was apparent not only in the way he pursued his professional aspirations, but in his personal life as well; he was confident with girls. 'They came in one after the other,' his mother recalled. 'I'd see one a few times, then another I didn't know would walk through the door. Mind you, he was never abrupt with them. They always stayed friends after he finished with them.'

As he entered his final year at Meadway Comprehensive, Branagh had one goal in mind: getting into the Royal Academy of Dramatic Art. He applied to the Central School of Speech and Drama, which Olivier had attended, and was offered a place there. But his heart was set not on Olivier's alma mater, but on Gielgud's. For the audition at RADA, in January 1979, Branagh practised speeches from *Hamlet* and Pinter's *The Caretaker*. The audition appeared to go well. The selection panel was keen to offer him a place, but Hugh Cruttwell, the principal of RADA, wanted to take a closer look, to make sure that beneath the theatrical pyrotechnics was an actor open to guidance and able to locate the truths of a character. Accordingly he invited Branagh to a special one-on-one coaching class at RADA. Putting him through his paces on a speech from Tennessee Williams's *The Glass Menagerie*, Cruttwell urged him to posture less and to allow 'the character to play you. You'll be surprised at the results.' By the end of their session Cruttwell had been reassured: 'You've absolutely convinced me of your potential to work in the way I think is important for you.' Branagh was offered the place he so fervently desired.

Winning a place at RADA attracted the attention of the local press. 'Ken treads the boards to success' was the title of an article devoted to the story, and included was a photo of a bearded Branagh, dressed neatly in shirt, tie and sweater, with a head seemingly so large it was difficult to work out how his narrow shoulders could support it, reading hammily from a script. 'I like comedy and Shakespeare,' he was quoted as saying, 'but I do not specialise in anything at the moment. I'll be quite happy if I finish my time at the academy with an Equity card and some parts in plays.' The main concern articulated by Branagh was financial: 'I desperately need the grant from the council because it would be impossible for me to afford the fees plus my lodgings in London. I am quite hopeful, however, that the council will give me the grant as this is quite an honour for the county.'

His optimism proved to be well founded. The Berkshire County Council did decide to cover his tuition fees and living expenses. No bar remained to his enrolling at RADA. On 15 July 1979 he appeared for the last time at the Progress Theatre, performing in three one-act plays. The company's newsletter invited members to attend so they could 'say goodbye to Ken Branagh'. In the autumn, he bid an emotional farewell to his family. He was off to London.

Though only forty miles separated Reading from the capital city, it was a new world for the young man who felt as though he was 'up from the country like a character in a Dickens novel'. He had never been in a London taxi or bus, nor had he used the Underground. The rich cosmopolitanism, the frenetic pace of the city, the intoxicating array of cultural delights stood in stark contrast to the humdrum suburbanism to which he had been accustomed.

Soon after his arrival in London, a couple of his friends gave Branagh a wonderful insight into what this city, which would be his home throughout the 1980s and beyond, had to offer. On one exhausting, exhilarating day they had a 'fry-up' breakfast, took in a matinee of *Peter Pan*, browsed in the bookshops of Charing Cross Road, ate chocolate eclairs at tea time, took in a Bertolucci film, *La Luna*, and capped it all off with dinner at L'Escargot, where Branagh ate his first snails. 'I ended the day back in my apartment after midnight,' he recalled. 'I just thought, "London is an amazing place, because as you go through the day, you hear every sound, every accent, see every colour." If you've lived in the suburbs until you're eighteen, it's quite a shock to the system.'

Not only did Branagh feel like a country bumpkin on his arrival at RADA, he looked like one. 'He was one of the worst dressed people [there],' recalled John Sessions, a classmate. 'He wore anoraks, bad jeans and the sort of shoes you'd buy from a chain store.' His haircut was old-fashioned, and his sense of style remained unaffected by contemporary British youth trends, such as the punk movement. 'The original young fogey,' is how Branagh described himself. But there was something about him that stood out. 'Ken wore that look he often does,' said Sessions about their first day together, 'like he's listening very carefully while looking down the barrel of a gun.'

Simon Callow, who was a good friend of Angus MacKay, the actor with whom Branagh stayed in Clapham during his first months at RADA, got to meet the new student when MacKay brought some friends, including his lodger, to see Callow in *Amadeus* at the National Theatre. After the show, recalls Callow,

> there was Angus and the friends and there was this young man in a rather long raincoat – a sort of gingery-blondy-haired young man, hovering at the back ... I shook his hand, said hello and nothing else. And then virtually everybody left ... Then the young man in the raincoat ... looking Jimmy Porter-like ... said, 'Look, excuse me, good evening. But would you mind if I ask you something?' I said, 'No, not at all.' He said, 'Do you think it's a really good idea to play the second act as quickly as you're playing it at the moment?' And I said, 'Yes, I do.' And he said, 'You don't mind my asking?' I said, 'I don't mind you asking at all. Goodnight.'[4]

With *Amadeus* Callow had been more accustomed to receiving fulsome praise than such objections.

Along with Angus MacKay, Callow took in a production of *The Barber of Seville* with Branagh, and met him on a few other occasions during this period. Callow's impression of Branagh from these encounters was that, 'He was shy and cocky at the same time. It was quite an interesting combination.'

Much to Branagh's delight, RADA provided the sort of all-consuming theatrical training he had sought. Formal classes would last from 10 a.m. to 6 p.m., and would be followed in the evenings by additional sessions, including rehearsals for RADA productions. Despite the school's image as a bastion of traditionalism, Branagh found himself exposed to a wide range of acting approaches, including the method.

In the account of his time at RADA written in his autobiography, Branagh lists a series of difficult experiences that he endured – criticisms of his overacting, his voice and his propensity for 'corpsing' (laughing inappropriately and uncontrollably) – as part of the process by which his rough acting technique was polished. Undoubtedly he did take great strides, but his contemporaries have testified to the skill he demonstrated at the start and throughout his RADA career. Sessions remembered a voice test, in their early days on Gower Street, in which 'listening to that amazing clarinet voice, I felt my jaw drop. Whatever emotions he wanted to show were there. It was soon obvious that he was light years ahead of the rest of us.' Geraldine Alexander likewise remembered a production of Chekhov's *Three Sisters* in which Branagh played Chebutykin: 'Everyone was astounded by his precocious technical ability.' In his fourth term he won the school's Edmund Grey Prize for high comedy for his performance as Sir Joseph Wittol in Congreve's *The Old Bachelor*. In a very strong year at RADA, Branagh was outstanding.

Branagh's boundless energy was also evident to his peers. 'I thought that everybody would be bright-eyed and Mickey Rooneyish, saying, "Why don't we do the show right here!" I was a funny old keenie,' he reminisced. 'It was rather uncool to be *that* ambitious and enthusiastic. I think a lot of people felt it was rather vulgar of me to be enjoying it so much. It's not cool.'

Helping Branagh during his RADA training were key sources of support. The first was Hugh Cruttwell, who became his mentor, a role he would continue to play long after Branagh had left drama school. It was a relationship based on mutual respect. Cruttwell could see the talent, while Branagh appreciated Cruttwell's pedagogical skills, particularly his ability to pinpoint shortcomings in his acting technique in a way that was candid but never mean-spirited. 'You want to produce great acting,' he counselled his pupil on one occasion.

> There are three major ingredients: passion, poetry and humour. You often have the humour, though not necessarily of the right sort. You have great access to passion, but you seldom find the heart of the poetry. For this you must surrender yourself much more to the part. Not indulge, but give away your technical awareness to a large extent. Not advice to give to every actor, but certainly to you.[5]

Branagh also developed great friendships with two fellow students, Mark Hadfield and John Sessions. 'They were inseparable,' a RADA contemporary recalled. All three were natural comics, which made for good banter. Together they immersed themselves in the professional theatre, catching all the major West End productions. After the shows they would ruthlessly dissect the performances they had seen. In later years both Hadfield and Sessions would act in Branagh's films.

Support also came from fellow student Katy Behean. Acting with her in a scene from *Richard III*, he realised that he was in love. 'It felt like the real thing,' he said. The relationship would continue throughout his time at RADA, and beyond. It was not without its vicissitudes. After living for a few months in Clapham, Branagh moved with Behean into a two-room flat in Willesden Green. The pressures involved in working and living together, however, became intolerable. Behean moved out and, not wishing to stay in the same flat by himself, Branagh likewise departed, finding for himself a dingy bedsit in Ealing. Given space, Branagh and Behean began to appreciate each other, and the relationship resumed. By the end of their second year at RADA they were, as Branagh put it, 'very settled and happy and spent as much time together as possible'.

Punctuating his time at drama school were the connections he established, even at this early stage, with the acting greats he idolised. After being offered a place at RADA, he had written to Derek Jacobi, the man whose Hamlet had done much to heighten his early interest in theatre, requesting a meeting. Jacobi had agreed. In his dressing room at the Old Vic, where he was reprising his role as Hamlet, Jacobi spoke of the importance of adopting a pragmatic approach to the profession. Asked by Branagh whether he regarded himself as a classical actor, he responded, 'No. I'm just an actor pure and simple. I have to make a living. I have to be prepared to do anything. Not just Shakespeare. Actors are still just beggars, really.' This would prove to be only the start of what would turn out to be a long and productive friendship with Jacobi. He would later direct Branagh's first professional stage Hamlet, and act in a number of Branagh's films.

Jacobi was not the only hero whose path Branagh crossed during his RADA years. To commemorate the academy's seventy-fifth anniversary, a visit by the Queen and Prince Philip was scheduled. As part of that event, it was decided that a number of students would perform before the royal couple. Branagh volunteered to deliver Hamlet's 'rogue and peasant slave' soliloquy. After rehearsing it with Hugh Cruttwell, he was given the opportunity to receive feedback from a legend. John Gielgud would be visiting RADA prior to the royal visit, and was willing to spare the time to hear Branagh's speech. Performing as Hamlet before arguably the greatest Hamlet of the twentieth century, Branagh rather crumbled, but Gielgud was charitable and helpful. 'Well done,' he said. 'There are some good things there, but you're really trying too hard. Don't over-colour the early section. You can be much straighter. Give yourself a breather in the middle. Don't stress "I *am* pigeon-livered" when "pigeon-livered" is much more juicy.' His performance for the Queen and Prince Philip was much the stronger as a result of Gielgud's advice. 'Oh, that's much better,' he told Branagh afterwards. 'Very good. You took all my notes.' As with Jacobi, Gielgud would subsequently work with Branagh – on radio productions, on an Oscar-nominated short film and on his 1996 screen version of *Hamlet*.

Branagh's connection with another legend, Laurence Olivier, was slighter, but meaningful nonetheless. Cast as the doctor Chebutykin in *Three Sisters*, he decided to seek advice from Olivier, who had directed a stage production of Chekhov's play and played Chebutykin in his film version. Seldom bashful, Branagh sent to Olivier, in January 1981, a letter that is now to be found in the Olivier papers at the British Library. 'Dear Sir,' he wrote,

> I have been cast as Chebutykin in a production of 'Three Sisters' opening here in March.
>
> I am writing to ask you for any thoughts, advice or comments you might have on the part having played it in your own film version. Simarlily [sic] I would be very interested in any sources of inspiration you might have found while working on it.
>
> In short, anything that you might possibly be interested enough to say about the part which you think might assist my own work.

A fortnight later Olivier dictated a response in which he assured Branagh that the part of Chebutykin was straightforward: 'Like Hotspur, Mercutio, etc., he is the plain man in all of Chekhov's plays.' 'I don't think you can go very wrong, basically, as the author has it all there for you,' he added. 'If I were you, I should have a bash at it and hope for the best – which I certainly wish you.' Just the notion that Olivier had given a moment's thought to a performance Branagh would give inspired the young actor.

In the autumn of 1981, as the end of his training at RADA approached, two pieces of good fortune came Branagh's way. First, Cruttwell accepted a request from him to take the lead in a production of *Hamlet*. Second, he was offered his first professional work, cast as the lead in *Too Late to Talk to Billy*, a BBC television 'Play for Today' written by Graham Reid and set in Belfast. Having not yet finished his course of study at RADA, Branagh had no Equity card. But the makers of *Billy* managed to procure one for him on a temporary basis.

October 1981, therefore, was a frenetic time. He rehearsed *Billy* during the day at studios in West London, jumped in a car provided by the BBC and headed off for Gower Street in the late afternoon, and then played Hamlet in the evening. He felt later that, as a result of this punishing schedule, the sharpness of his performance as the Danish prince had suffered. Hugh Cruttwell was on hand to highlight the areas where improvement could be made:

> Yes, Ken. Lots of work to do. Two fundamental points. First, comedy and humour. There is a difference. You give us comedy in Hamlet. What he has is a deep-seated melancholia producing a black, bleak humour. You give us a sort of gratuitous clowning. Secondly, passion. Hamlet is a haunted man, shaken to his very soul by the deep repulsion about his mother's marriage and horror at the arrival of his father's ghost. You give us a sort of lively irritability.[6]

Lessons to be absorbed for when Branagh revisited the role. Nevertheless, the reaction from the audiences at RADA had been enthusiastic. Moreover, the audience one night included Patricia Marmont, a former actress turned agent, who had been tipped off that there was a special talent at RADA. 'Tremendous verve and energy,' was what struck her about Branagh's performance. 'When they're inexperienced you don't expect them to come in and lift a scene and take command of it the way he could; and [he was] so relaxed in Shakespeare.' Marmont decided to take immediate action. Rather than going into her office the following day to send a formal letter, as was her customary practice when offering representation to a young actor, she scribbled a note to Branagh that same evening and left it for him at the stage door. Branagh responded immediately; they met and, as Marmont recalls, 'We got on very well from the word go.' She found him 'terribly easy. He was so uncomplicated. Utterly devoid of any chip at all.'

The competition for the role of Billy had been intense. Before auditioning Branagh, the director, Paul Seed, had cast an eye over more than fifty actors interested in the part. Branagh 'simply shone above the rest', Seed recalled. 'Even though this was his first professional part, he showed a confidence and intelligence you could not ignore.'

Set in Belfast in the late 1970s, *Too Late to Talk to Billy* told the story of a working-class, Protestant family in Belfast, torn apart by conflict. The historical source of that conflict was an episode in which the father (played with intimidating ferocity by James Ellis), catching his adulterous wife with another man, beats them both senseless. The play opens with the invariably drunk and belligerent father refusing to visit his wife, who is in hospital with cancer. Branagh's Billy is furious at his father, telling him he never appreciated his mother as her lover had. At the same time Billy feels a strong sense of responsibility towards his three sisters.

In addition to the pressure on Branagh to deliver a strong performance, the experience of making *Billy* also brought to the surface the long-standing Anglo-Irish identity issues that had affected him since the move to Reading. Rehearsals in London were followed by further rehearsals and filming in Belfast. With his English accent and short haircut, he was told to be careful not to be mistaken for an off-duty English soldier. He encountered, too, the confusion deriving from his being an Irishman with an English accent playing an Irishman. At the initial read-through Branagh re-adopted his Irish accent for the part of Billy. When the two Irish children cast in the television play heard Branagh speak afterwards in his usual, standard English, they asked, 'What's happened to your accent? What's *wrong* with you, mister?' Branagh enjoyed spending time with his relations, especially his eighty-year-old grandmother, but his approach to his home-town was wary. 'You can act tough,' he observed, 'so long as you've seen enough Clint Eastwood films and been convinced by them. In Belfast, I kept being Billy. People knew that Billy was a surly git, so I'd keep up that look as if to say, "I'll be just about civil but don't you come any closer."' It was not the sense of homecoming he would experience in Belfast when at the height of his fame.

Too Late to Talk to Billy represented an excellent start to Branagh's career. It was a meaty part in a meaty drama, the sort that is rarely to be seen on television nowadays. Writer Graham Reid had created a rich character in Billy – full of anger (towards his father), loyalty (to his sisters) and intelligence (never touching a drop of alcohol, having observed its effects on his father). Billy is also cleverly sardonic and quick-tongued, especially in his exchanges with his father. Branagh's performance did justice to the complexities of his character, and certainly pleased the writer and producers of *Billy*. When shortly afterwards the same team made *Easter 2016* for the BBC, a television play set in a teacher-training college in Northern Ireland's future, they asked Branagh to play a cameo role as a student militant. He had just one scene, but the story was intriguing, and the cast, which included the likes of Bill Nighy and Colm Meaney, was strong.

Billy developed Branagh's technical knowledge of film as well as his acting experience. One of the reasons he advanced so far so fast in his career was his ability to extract from each undertaking every possible benefit. Many rookie actors would have concentrated solely on their own performance in their first appearance in front of the cameras. But Branagh peppered the director with questions about the shooting script that was used. He carefully studied the moves made by the camera. 'I took in everything,' he recalled. When, seven years later, still in his twenties, he began directing his first film, *Henry V*, it seemed to be either a foolish or an audacious step into the unknown. In fact he had been learning the requisite skills for years.

Too Late to Talk to Billy went out on BBC 1 at 9.25 p.m. on 16 February 1982. Millions of people watched Branagh in action for the first time. *Broadcast*, the television industry's weekly newspaper, judged the performance by Branagh, along with those given by the rest of the cast, to be 'marvellous'. The part of Billy brought Branagh not only praise from the pundits, but also his first taste of fame. As he was taking the bus in London, shortly after *Billy* was aired, a group of schoolboys recognised him. An embarrassed Branagh reacted by trying to hide his face behind his newspaper.

After the making of *Billy*, Branagh returned to drama school to complete his course of study. He finished his RADA career by playing a servant in John Webster's *The White Devil*. Its final performance occurred on 10 December 1981, his twenty-first birthday. The relatively cosseted world of drama school had come to an end. He had an agent, and had already enjoyed his first professional experience with *Billy*. Now he was confronted with the prosaic but anxiety-inducing economic issue facing all young actors: finding work on a consistent basis – earning a crust.

Whatever the extent of the uncertainty felt by Branagh as he set out as a professional actor, it soon evaporated. Within a matter of weeks both the Royal Shakespeare Company and the West End were vying for his services. He was invited to audition for the RSC after Joyce Nettles, their casting director, saw his RADA Hamlet. Initially the idea was that he would receive a 'play-as-cast' contract, for which he would be given a number of minor parts; but Howard Davies offered him a good juvenile role in the production he was about to direct. Though Branagh's career trajectory did ultimately take him to Stratford, it would not be in 1982. He rejected the RSC in favour of an offer to star in a new play, written by Julian Mitchell and directed by Stuart Burge.

Another Country, a fictionalised account of the 1930s schooldays of the spy Guy Burgess, had opened in Greenwich, but on its West End transfer the decision was made to recast two of the parts – and it was at this point that Branagh came into the reckoning. After shining in his audition, he was asked to take the role of Judd, whose relationship with the Burgess character, played by Rupert Everett, is central to the play. A Communist who detests the English class system, Judd is a wonderfully rich character, and for a young actor just out of drama school, a dream part. Mitchell had based him on two people: Esmond Romilly, Jessica Mitford's husband, and the poet John Cornford, both of whom died fighting for the Loyalists in the Spanish Civil War. Branagh was intrigued by Judd's pure idealism, his belief that revolution in Britain was really possible.

The only problem for Branagh was that he did not yet have an Equity card. The issue was resolved, but only after the producer, Robert Fox, took the matter to arbitration, so determined was he to recruit this young actor. In the end Branagh signed a £150-a-week contract for a six-month run.

Rehearsals began on 1 February 1982 and, as would be the case throughout his career, Branagh left nothing to chance in researching the role. He read extensively, particularly on Cornford and Romilly, the Spanish Civil War, and the English public-school system. He even got to meet Jessica Mitford, who spoke affectionately about Romilly. In one sense, playing someone from the upper middle classes, a world so distinct from the one he had known, was a challenge for Branagh. In another, it was an excellent opportunity to demonstrate his range at the outset of his career, having portrayed an Irish working-class youth in *Billy*.

David Parfitt, a 1970s child television star cast in the part of Menzies, recalls the impression made by Branagh as rehearsals began:

> We'd heard there was this whizz-kid coming out of RADA, that he'd blown them away at the interview, that he'd already shot a television [show, *Billy*], which was incredible ... And he turned up on the first day of rehearsals word-perfect, which was pretty scary for a group [in their] late teens or early twenties [who] were pretty casual about the whole thing. We were a bit blasé. We had done the run [at Greenwich]. We were quite cool about it, and this guy came in and took it very seriously. So it was a little while before we really discovered the real Ken, as it were, because it was all about getting his head down.[7]

Branagh's general knowledge of the theatre, as well as his professional attitude, struck the other actors. 'I'm so impressed with this young man,' the experienced David William told Patricia Marmont. 'I can't fault him on his history of the theatre. He's read everything. He's read about everybody.'

Shortly before opening night, Branagh received two pieces of good news. The first was that the broadcast of *Too Late to Talk to Billy* in mid-February had been well received, particularly in Belfast. The second, delivered to him personally by Albert Finney, whose company was investing in *Another Country*, was that RADA had awarded him the Bancroft Gold Medal, its loftiest prize, given to the best student actor of the year. With *Another Country*, Branagh would be aiming for a hat-trick of triumphs within three months of his departure from RADA.

He achieved it. The opening night at the Queen's Theatre, on 2 March, turned out to be an emotional occasion for Branagh, with those nearest and dearest to him in attendance to urge him on. 'We'll never forget tonight, son,' a grateful paterfamilias told him afterwards, while his brother and mother were moved to tears. Hugh Cruttwell showed up, as did some old school friends. Adding lustre to the post-performance dressing-room celebrations were Albert Finney and Joan Plowright. 'He's not half bad,' declared Finney to Branagh's suitably impressed family.

The critics agreed. They lavished praise on Branagh, as well as on Everett and the production in general. 'Kenneth Branagh brings great flair to Judd's decent doomed doggedness,' judged Robert Cushman of the *Observer*. John Barber wrote in the *Daily Telegraph* of his commendably 'subtle performance', while Michael Coveney of the *Financial Times* felt compelled to elaborate on the impression made by Branagh: he is 'literally straight from RADA. His technique is assured and flawless. Especially good is the way he bestows unsullied affection on a bullied young fag, or sums up his predicament by confessing that what he hates about cricket is that it is such a damned good game.'

Leading figures in the theatre took note of Branagh's stage debut. 'He was a great discovery,' recalled Irving Wardle, 'appearing suddenly out of nowhere, fully formed.' David Hare was likewise struck by what he had seen: Branagh was 'like an orchestral conductor with an eerily prodigious gift for rhythm and beat'; while Simon Callow says, 'He was weirdly technically assured. It was uncanny. He was so on top of it ... It was weird – almost a bit shocking, almost a little lacking in modesty. It was so confident and certain.'

As the six-month run of *Another Country* proceeded, Branagh developed a friendship with David Parfitt, whose dressing room was next to his own, that would be of long-term significance to his career. In addition to the usual banter between actors, they began a dialogue on how little control actors exerted in the theatre, wondering how it was that they could be in a hit play yet be paid minimum Equity wages.

Feeling the sense of repetitive drudgery that can accompany a long run in the theatre, Branagh, Parfitt and the rest of the cast resolved to restore a sense of freshness and artistic challenge by mounting a lunchtime production of Gogol's *Gamblers* at the Upstream Theatre Club. The actors themselves supplied the props, those understudying or playing small parts in *Another Country* were given meatier roles, and David Parfitt conducted the necessary negotiations with the venue. This collaboration between Branagh and Parfitt in independent production was a sign of things to come. Five years later they would set up the Renaissance Theatre Company.

Putting on *Gamblers* was not the only thing to buoy Branagh's spirits during the run of *Another Country*. After one performance John Gielgud, who had been in the house, paid Branagh a visit. 'Very good,' he said. 'Didn't I see you at RADA?' To receive such praise from Gielgud was 'absolute magic for him', recalls Patricia Marmont.

After six months Branagh had had enough. He would probably have stayed on had Rupert Everett done so; but once Everett announced his departure Branagh declined the offer to renew his contract, deciding instead to look for other work. With *Another Country* his stage career had got off to a flying start. Not only had the notices been glowing, but he ended up garnering two prestigious prizes – the Society of West End Theatres Award for Most Promising Newcomer of 1982, and the Plays and Players Award for Best Newcomer. Only later did Branagh fully appreciate the importance of *Another Country* to his career. 'I was getting work from that part for some time to come,' he acknowledged. *Another Country* would turn out to be the launching pad for the career of not only Branagh but also Rupert Everett and subsequent cast members Colin Firth and Daniel Day-Lewis.

Branagh would devote the following year to television work. Ultimately he would be known best for his performances in film and on the stage, but the television roles he played in the 1980s were significant. First, he produced a body of work on the small screen commendable for its consistent excellence. Second, he cleverly secured parts in productions that did not diminish but in fact augmented the reputation he would develop through his stage work as a classical actor. He performed in television adaptations of work by Ibsen, O'Neill, D. H. Lawrence, and Virginia Woolf. It is difficult to imagine a young actor being able to utilise television in this way today.

In addition to starring in sequels to *Too Late to Talk to Billy*, Branagh worked on three other television productions in this period: *To the Lighthouse*, *Maybury* and *The Boy in the Bush*. *To the Lighthouse*, a Hugh Stoddart reworking of the Virginia Woolf novel, was one of those literary adaptations for which the BBC was famed. It explored the emotional politics of the Ramsay family, headed by an irascible patriarch, played by Michael Gough, and an altruistic matriarch, portrayed by Rosemary Harris, and their assorted guests during a summer vacation in Cornwall. Branagh was cast in the role of Mr Ramsay's student, Charles Tansley, described by Branagh as 'a wonderful, cravenly ambitious, snotty little loser. A small man, depressive, vulnerable, and with an enormous chip about his background.' As the story unfolded, Tansley would grouse about the lack of attention he received from Mr Ramsay.

Directed by Colin Gregg, the filming of *To the Lighthouse* took place in and around a farmer's house in Penzance in the autumn of 1982. Branagh was reprimanded at one point by the vastly more experienced T. P. McKenna when, during a dinner scene, he corpsed – a foible that would affect him throughout his career. But a sociable cast and crew made for what was in the main an enjoyable shoot. 'It was all so friendly,' recalled Rosemary Harris. 'At the end of the day everybody would eat together and there were always children about.' Branagh was able to sustain the friendship he had developed on *Another Country* with David Parfitt, who was cast as Andrew Ramsay. All of this was compensation for Branagh for his enforced separation from Katy Behean, who by this point was ensconced in Stratford-upon-Avon, acting for the Royal Shakespeare Company.

To the Lighthouse was broadcast in Britain in the spring of 1983, and in the United States a year and a half later. It could not and did not do justice to the subtleties of Woolf's novel, but was nonetheless a thoughtful and thought-provoking adaptation. Though it was in many ways a vehicle for Rosemary Harris, Branagh convinced in his supporting role, conveying well his character's smallness of spirit.

Next for this emerging presence on the small screen was *Maybury*, a series starring RSC stalwart and soon-to-be *Star Trek* icon Patrick Stewart as a psychiatrist. Branagh was up for a leading role in two episodes as Robert Clyde Moffat, an antisocial epileptic, whose character was based on the writer of the story, Douglas Watkinson. Reluctant to get his epilepsy under control, as he feels it would detract from the distinctiveness of his personality, Moffat is subject to intense mood swings. He is clever and sensitive but also aggressive and savagely sardonic. It was a juicy part, the physical mannerisms of which would allow an actor to shine, as Dustin Hoffman and Daniel Day-Lewis did later in the decade in *Rainman* and *My Left Foot* respectively.

Patrick Stewart, who attended Branagh's audition for the role, was struck by him. 'I had never seen anyone transform himself in an instant from a charming, rather modest individual into this highly strung, nervous person,' said Stewart. 'I thought, "He's a phenomenon. We'll be hearing a great deal from him."'

In preparation, Branagh researched the medical dimension of the role so that he could reproduce accurately the epileptic fits suffered by his character. The research paid off. His was a riveting portrayal, one that elicited praise from the critics. It was described in the *Listener* as 'a virtuoso performance', and as 'great' by *Broadcast*. Particularly effective were the scenes between himself and an authoritative Patrick Stewart. It was like watching two skilled boxers exchange blows. Most impressively, Branagh made an impact on Douglas Watkinson, the man he was in effect portraying. 'I was very moved,' acknowledged Watkinson, 'to the point where I felt ashamed.'

Branagh's work in television continued with *The Boy in the Bush*, based on the novel by D. H. Lawrence and Mollie Skinner, and adapted for television by Hugh Whitemore. Branagh played Jack Grant, whose wayward behaviour at college in England sees him banished to Western Australia. Tested by the jibes of the locals and the harshness of his new environment, Grant makes the journey from callow youth to manhood.

Already a devotee of D. H. Lawrence, Branagh was happy to be cast in the lead role. Filming took place over a three-month period in the summer of 1983, the Australian winter, during which time

Branagh was based in Sydney. On a personal level Australia was a tonic. He was struck by the marked sociability of the Australians he met, how – in a manner he described as very un-English – they went out of their way to make him feel welcome. The experience ignited a love affair with Australia, one he was able to indulge over the coming years with several return trips.

In a professional sense *The Boy in the Bush* was significant for the way it furthered Branagh's education in terms of acting in front of the camera. Quite simply he had never done so much before. This production was also noteworthy for the establishment by Branagh of what would be the *modus operandi* for his future career: if he was going to kick up a fuss, he would do it with people in authority. Unhappy with what they regarded as the overly cerebral approach adopted in the early days of the shoot by the director Ken Hannam, the producers sacked him and brought in Rob 'Rocket' Stewart, whose nickname reflected the speed at which he worked. Informed by the camera operator, Roger Lanser, of the new director's reputation, Branagh worried that the action-adventure dimension of the story would be highlighted at the expense of character development. He decided to make his feelings known in no uncertain terms. He told the producers that he would have to review his position with his agent, as the original arrangement had been for him to work with Hannam. When he did agree to continue on the production, he issued a blunt warning to them about the new director: 'Don't give me any sweet talk about this fellow's reputation. I know exactly what it is, and if I get any trouble from him, and if there is any attempt to interfere with my work, then I'm on the next plane home.' Once Stewart started directing, Branagh threw the odd sarcastic remark his way. 'I was the only one with sufficient professional status and power enough to challenge him,' he said.

The friendship that Branagh developed with Roger Lanser during the shoot endured. A decade later he hired him as the director of photography on his film of *Much Ado About Nothing*. This was typical of the way Branagh continuously built up an informal social and professional network – an artistic family, as he saw it. He worked with David Parfitt on *Another Country*, then five years later set up the Renaissance Theatre Company with him. Collaborating with Rosemary Harris on *To the Lighthouse*, he would go on to cast her as the Player Queen in his film of *Hamlet*.

In this period Branagh nearly transformed himself from a television and stage actor to star of the big screen. Milos Forman was casting around for someone to play the lead in his film adaptation of Peter Shaffer's play *Amadeus*. Branagh went up for the role of Mozart, and nearly got it. He was interviewed for the part, did several readings with Forman, and at one point was informed that he was on a shortlist of four. In the end the American actor Tom Hulce won the role, garnering an Oscar nomination for his performance. Had Branagh secured the part and the laurels that would probably have followed, his career might have taken a very different path.

With his movie career in abeyance and a year of continuous television work under his belt, Branagh was itching by the autumn of 1983 to return to the stage. He would do so in a one-man show, a dramatic interpretation of Tennyson's poem *Maud: the Madness*, but not before an important event had taken place in his personal life. After a love affair that stretched back to their early days at RADA, Branagh and Katy Behean parted. The demands of their respective careers had separated them geographically for much of their post-RADA relationship, culminating in Branagh's stint in Australia working on *The Boy in the Bush*. It was in the week following his return from Australia that the couple decided to call it a day. Branagh has said that the initiative for ending it came from Behean, but that deep down he knew it was a sensible decision.

The Madness told the story of a young man's thwarted love for a girl whose brother he ends up killing in a duel. The lines beginning 'Come into the garden, Maud,' constitute the most famous part of the poem. As much as anything, it would be a monumental test of Branagh's retentive powers. He would have to commit fourteen hundred lines of verse to memory. In Australia he had learned several lines a day, badgering his fellow actors to test him between takes.

Given that Branagh would make his mark later in the decade by running his own theatre company, *The Madness* was a seminal undertaking. He produced the show himself, financed it with the money he had made from his television work, negotiated a two-week run at London's 150-seater Upstream Theatre Club, and hired as director a friend from his Reading days, Colin Wakefield. In addition to rehearsing intensively with Wakefield, therefore, Branagh busied himself by trying to persuade the likes of *Time Out* to give the show publicity, and by sending out fliers to journalists. At only twenty-two he was already learning about the practicalities of independent production in the theatre.

The critics who made the effort to review *The Madness* picked up on what would become some of the hallmarks of his work on stage: his technical proficiency and his ability to extract the maximum comic potential from the work. Rosalind Carne wrote in the *Guardian* that Branagh had 'that quality shared by the greatest actors, of showing several faces at once, laughing with his wide mouth as his eyes look sad'. 'Almost every word, certainly every emotion,' gushed Christopher Hudson in the London *Evening Standard*, 'is made to count and Branagh charts this turbulent, emotional journey not only with passion but with illuminating clarity ... This is a chilling, exhilarating presentation of a masterpiece,' he added. Once the reviews were published, the venue sold out. The event generated interest from Branagh's peers, with Edward Petherbridge and Alec McCowen among the actors who came to see his performance.

Less successful was the second theatrical venture undertaken by Branagh in the autumn of 1983, *Francis*, a new play by Julian Mitchell, in which Branagh played the lead role of Francis of Assisi. No doubt Branagh and Mitchell hoped for the same sort of success as their previous collaboration on *Another Country* had enjoyed. Directed by David William at Greenwich Theatre, *Francis* flopped in the face of a barrage of press criticism. Branagh emerged with some credit, with the *Daily Telegraph* and *Financial Times* finding much to admire in his performance. But with the box office quiet the hoped-for transfer to the West End did not materialise. Branagh ascribed that disappointing outcome to the lack of scheduled previews, needed to smooth out the production's rough edges before opening to the critics.

In 1984 Branagh would take his stage career to new heights. He and the Royal Shakespeare Company had been wooing each other warily. The RSC wanted to have on board this young actor, with his evident confidence and precocious technical skills; but the offers they had made to Branagh after his leaving RADA had been rebuffed. Branagh had long envisaged working for the company, but he wanted to do it on his terms. He did not want to work his way up the RSC pecking order gradually. He was after a great part.

A conversation between Patricia Marmont and the RSC's Joyce Nettles, about a year after Branagh had left RADA, revealed this bone of contention. After Marmont explained that Branagh was not interested in the sorts of roles the RSC was offering, an exasperated Nettles asked, 'What would he come for?' 'If you want to know the part he wants to play,' replied Marmont, 'I can tell you that.' 'Yes, well what is it?' 'It's Henry V.' 'Oh, Pat, come on. He's got to work his way up in the company for that.' 'Not this actor, Joyce,' insisted Marmont. 'He's really now.'

The RSC, however, continued to keep an eye on Branagh. The turning point came with *The Madness*, to which Patricia Marmont took Jenny McIntosh, who had influence over casting at the RSC. 'We've just got to get him,' declared McIntosh after seeing the show. 'It's as simple as that.' Branagh was then invited to meet RSC directors Adrian Noble and Barry Kyle. He delivered the 'Once more unto the breach' speech for them. They were impressed. Branagh was offered work for much of the next two years, not only as Henry but as Laertes in *Hamlet*, the King of Navarre in *Love's Labour's Lost*, and as an athlete in *Golden Girls*, a new play by Louise Page.

The period spent by Branagh with the RSC in 1984–5 was a key phase in his career. It brought him his first professional Shakespearean roles. It initiated the process by which the public came to identify him with the Bard, culminating a few years later in the perception of him as the most prominent Shakespearean in the land. It facilitated significant new relationships with actors such as Brian Blessed, Jimmy Yuill and Frances Barber, friendships that would not only enrich his personal life but that he could draw on when casting his future projects. It helped him to establish the rationale for the subsequent launching of his own theatre company, namely that institutions such as the RSC had become unwieldy and were run by virtually omnipotent directors at the expense of creative input from actors themselves.

For Branagh, the main event of the RSC season was *Henry V*. This was the first but by no means the last instance in which Branagh did work that invited comparison with Laurence Olivier; such was the reverence in Britain for his 1944 film of the play that to many it was impossible to think of Shakespeare's *Henry V* without bringing to mind the imposing figure of Olivier. Not that this bothered Branagh. He simply pushed ahead regardless.

The assurance that would characterise Branagh's performance as Henry V reflected not only that fearlessness, but the ten weeks of rehearsals in which he honed his interpretation under the guidance of Adrian Noble. The director's influence was, of course, important, but

Branagh had strong ideas of his own, which he had developed since studying the part at RADA. Olivier's interpretation had been essentially heroic; but Branagh wanted to do it differently. His Henry would have something of Hamlet's psychological complexity about him, plagued by guilt over his father's seizure of the crown from Richard II as well as his own reckless past. This would also be a pious leader. All his decisions would be tortured ones, as he examined them under the microscope of his own strong religious convictions.

Branagh received the unique opportunity to discuss his ideas about the role with someone who had first-hand knowledge of royal life, Prince Charles. It was a contact at court of Julian Wadham, with whom Branagh had acted in *Another Country*, who served as intermediary between Charles and Branagh. As well as making use of the Wadham connection, Branagh wrote Charles a letter explaining why he wanted to see him. Charles consented to the meeting, which took place at Kensington Palace in March 1984. 'I'm not intending my Henry V to be an impersonation of you,' Branagh told Charles, 'but I simply wanted to explain some of my feelings about the character, particularly his role as king ... If you have anything to say about them,' he added, 'I'd be most grateful. You don't *have* to say anything.'

In a sense, the analogy that Branagh seemed to be making between Henry V and Prince Charles was inappropriate. Henry had a role as a political and a military leader; Charles did not. But Charles did know what it meant to be royal, and was able to confirm for Branagh certain realities of having that status, particularly the sense of isolation and the concomitant importance of having some sort of religious faith in order to cope. 'Prince Charles had enormously increased my understanding of many aspects of the role,' a grateful Branagh later wrote. For his part, Charles began to take an interest in Branagh's career. He came to Stratford-upon-Avon, with Diana, to see for himself this performance of Henry V at the Royal Shakespeare Theatre that he had helped shape. In a four-page, handwritten letter to Branagh a few weeks later, he indicated how much it had moved him. Patricia Marmont recalls that the letter ended with Charles saying, 'I'll be very proud in years to come that I will be able to tell my children that I saw you play Henry V when you were only twenty-three.' This was the start of what proved to be an enduring relationship. When Branagh set up his own theatre company in 1987, Charles agreed to serve as patron.

The *Henry V* that Charles had seen was stripped of the glamour and pageantry so evident in Olivier's film. Warfare was depicted as harsh, not heroic. As Branagh's Henry read the names of those killed at Agincourt, in the immediate aftermath of the battle, his voice trembled with emotion. The technical excellence that was becoming a hallmark of his acting was to the fore – a voice clear in diction, rich in tone, that could hit the back row with apparent ease. It was also a measured performance. Even in the show-stopping set pieces such as the 'band of brothers' speech before Agincourt, he resisted the temptation to be excessively operatic. What emerged was a multi-faceted Henry – restrained and bellicose, capable of cruelty but with a strong moral code, calculating but pious. His comedic gifts were again apparent. In the scene where Henry woos Katherine in his broken French, his timing was perfect when, having kissed her, he quickly interjected: 'Here comes your father.' In the performance recorded for the historical record by the Shakespeare Centre Library in Stratford-upon-Avon, he nearly brought the house down with that line.

This was not a one-man show, however. Brian Blessed was a robust Exeter, Richard Easton a formidable Constable, and Ian McDiarmid an expressive, engaging Chorus. But the overriding impression of this *Henry V* was of a young actor 'strolling around that famous stage', as Antony Sher put it, 'as if born on it.'

The virtues of Branagh's performance were not lost on the critics. 'No Henry has ever moved me so much,' Michael Ratcliffe wrote in the *Observer*. In the *Financial Times* Michael Coveney added his voice to those singing Branagh's praises: 'He speaks Shakespeare as well as anyone in recent years in Stratford and he does so without a trace of verbal or physical mannerism. He is undemonstrative, but powerful.'

Michael Billington, who told his *Guardian* readers that Branagh's portrayal of Henry 'betokens a rich Shakespearian future', recalls that it was the parallel between actor and part that made the performance especially rich, and how Branagh reminded him of a young Albert Finney:

> The play gained enormously from his youth. None of us had ever seen a twenty-three-year-old Henry V before, and what you saw on stage was a sort of strange correlation between the play and the actor. The play is about a young king obviously being given this awesome responsibility and to some extent being guided by older people than himself, and led into a war over which he has moral questions. And ... the part was being played by a young actor, also aware of his awesome

responsibility of carrying the Stratford season in a sense – or carrying the opening of it – and also being guided (not as manipulatively) by older, more experienced figures. It was the symbiotic connection between the play and the actor that made it very powerful ...

People always talk about Olivier and Branagh, but Finney and Branagh are quite interesting comparisons. Finney also had exactly the same quality of looking as if he owned the stage, as if the stage was his by right. Some actors take the stage by default and some actors take it by right. And Branagh had this extraordinary quality [with his Henry V] of seeming to be both in command of the stage but at the same time able to explore the character's self-doubt and self-awareness. The other parallel that strikes me is that both Finney and Branagh brought out the humour which there is in *Henry V*.[8]

Branagh's contribution to three other RSC shows that season demonstrated his versatility. In Louise Page's new play *Golden Girls*, which explored a multiplicity of issues in athletics, including race, gender, commercialism and ethics (drug use), Branagh played Geordie athlete Mike Bassett, the romantic interest for one of the sprinters in a women's relay team. It was a small part, which he dropped by the time Barry Kyle's production reached London, but one he took seriously. He went on a rigorous training routine, running and lifting weights three times a week, in order, he said, to become more muscular and so look the part.

Branagh played Laertes in a production of *Hamlet* starring Roger Rees and directed by Ron Daniels. At his own request he also understudied the role of Hamlet during the show's Stratford run. With Virginia McKenna as Gertrude, and Brian Blessed as Claudius, Branagh was part of a production that had box-office clout. In what was a clear, sensible rendering of the play, Branagh's Laertes combined a forceful personality with a deep love of family. His inveterate affection for his sister and father, played by Frances Barber and Frank Middlemass, manifest in the intensity of his grief on seeing Ophelia deranged, heightened the sense of tragedy when his entire family is destroyed by the play's end. His robustness, his implied physical threat, magnified the tension of his sword fight with Hamlet. The threat to Hamlet seemed all the greater. Absent from the action for a couple of hours, Laertes is not the easiest role in which to make an impression. But Branagh did so. Significantly, playing Laertes had given him a perspective on the play separate from Hamlet's. It was a salutary reminder that the play is about the demise of two families, not one. This would shape his approach when filming the play a decade later.

Following this was *Love's Labour's Lost*, Barry Kyle's enchanting production of one of Shakespeare's more obscure but most linguistically ornate comedies. As the King of Navarre, Branagh's role was an important one. His character drives the story in proclaiming at the start that he and his chums will avoid the company of women for three years so that they can devote themselves to study, only to fall head over heels in love when the Princess of France and her ladies-in-waiting turn up. Branagh's razor-sharp exchanges with Roger Rees, who played the sceptical Berowne, were a highlight of the show. Branagh suggested a King motivated in part to study with his pals rather than chase girls because he was a swot who went to an all-boys' school and whose inexperience with women meant that he was more comfortable in the company of men. Branagh's King stuttered badly when simply mentioning the word 'woman' and did so again on meeting the Princess of France. As he had in the wooing scene with the French princess in *Henry V*, Branagh showed a flair for comedy. In *Love's Labour's Lost* he was perhaps too broad at times. Yet it often paid off. When Berowne overheard the King's acknowledgement that he was in love and thus in breach of his own edict, Branagh fell backwards in Charlie Chaplin fashion – and the audience loved it. Branagh's performance was complemented by other fine ones from a cast that included Amanda Root and Josette Simon.

This cluster of supporting roles attracted uniformly positive comments from the critics. Of his Laertes, Rosemary Say of the *Sunday Telegraph* said it placed the *Hamlet* production on 'a surer footing', while Christopher Edwards wrote in the *Spectator* that it was 'outstanding'. John Barber of the *Daily Telegraph* said he 'delighted' in Branagh's King of Navarre, and Michael Billington felt Branagh's performance in *Golden Girls* had been an asset to that production.

These approving notices were consistent with the general press coverage of Branagh since the start of his career in 1982. As early as *Another Country*, his work had elicited excited and extensive assessments, and not just in the theatre-review sections. 'Singular star', proclaimed *The Times* in March 1982. 'Talent triumphs in *Another Country*', declared the *Daily Mail* that same month. Joining the RSC intensified the media attention. A huge picture of Branagh in Henry V garb was published in the spring of 1984 in the *Sunday Times*; and the panegyrics spread from the national newspapers to the locals. The enthusiasm with which Branagh's emergence was greeted would turn out to be in sharp contrast to the ambivalence and even downright hostility that accompanied the establishment of his film career after 1989.

It was during this period in the 1980s that Branagh and Olivier began to be compared. Finding the new Olivier had long been the Holy Grail for observers of British film and theatre. Every so often a new candidate would be identified, something, Joan Plowright reports, which always brought a faint smile to the face of Olivier. Triumphing in *Henry V* for the RSC established for some a connection between the careers of Branagh and Olivier, and soon the parallel was being drawn. 'Mr Branagh,' wrote J. C. Trewin in the *Illustrated London News*, 'reminding me sometimes of the young Olivier in his Old Vic performances, appears to be as valuable a recruit as the RSC has had for a long time.' In the *Mail on Sunday* Nicholas de Jongh went further in an article entitled 'Pretender to the Crown', suggesting that Branagh was outstripping his august forebears. 'His career is less than three years old,' explained de Jongh, 'but he seems marked out already as a candidate for theatrical glory. Henry V is only the latest, highest rung in his flight up the ladder quicker than Lord Olivier or Sir John Gielgud, who at his age were merely touring in the Constant Nymph.'

These flattering comparisons must have been music to Branagh's ears, but in the end the accolade of being the new Olivier proved to be invidious. When the backlash set in five years later, one of the charges levelled at him was that he had had the gall to compare himself to Olivier. To be sure, Branagh had always conveyed the sense that he had a clear plan of action designed to make himself one of the acknowledged leaders in his field, and it may well have occurred to him that a success as a twenty-three-year-old on the great Stratford stage in the role of Henry V would cause some to consider his performance alongside Olivier's. However, it is worth making the point that it was various critics, rather than the actor himself, who originally spoke of the arrival of a new Olivier.

As well as providing several excellent roles and glowing coverage in the media, the 1984–5 RSC season furthered Branagh's theatrical education in a general sense. He was the proverbial sponge, soaking up every good idea that came his way. Octogenarian Sebastian Shaw, who was playing Charles VI in *Henry V*, emphasised to Branagh the importance to an actor of conserving energy when working hard. 'Don't stand when you can sit down,' he counselled, 'and don't sit if you can lie down.' Branagh took the advice on board.

As for his personal life between the end of his relationship with Katy Behean and settling down with Emma Thompson, Branagh was having fun. 'I had a great time in my roaring twenties,' he said later. 'That was what you might call my ... rogue phase,' he added. 'I think it had something to do with the pace at which I was working. Things tended to happen in quite pressurised and intense ways. One went through emotions and intensity in a different kind of way. I think working so hard gave one excuses to be more of a rogue than one would have wished to have been.' His name was linked with the likes of Amanda Root and Joely Richardson. His personal life inevitably suffered as a result of the demands of a career that was now motoring along at full throttle. One sensible thing he did do in this period was buy a flat in Camberwell, South London.

Challenging roles, skilled directors, camaraderie with his fellow actors – Branagh's stint at the RSC fulfilled so many of his expectations. His one bone of contention, however, was the vast and stifling bureaucracy that he felt the RSC had come to represent. Indeed the company had become a gargantuan operation. As Branagh rehearsed *Henry V* in early 1984, the plan was for the RSC to mount no less than thirty-four productions that year. The corollary, in Branagh's view, was that the RSC had become impersonal, inattentive to the needs of its actors. 'I went expecting a family enterprise where you could always knock on someone's door,' he recalled. 'Well, you could knock on a door, but there was not usually anyone on the other side of it.' In his autobiography Branagh expressed dismay that Trevor Nunn, on sabbatical from his responsibilities as joint artistic director of the RSC, did not see his Henry V until its penultimate performance.

Branagh's fractious relations with the company management were also manifest in a pay dispute. He was happy to sign an initial contract for the Stratford run of £300 a week, comfortably below the top rate for a lead actor at the RSC. He was young, not yet a household name, and his salary would have to reflect that. As *Henry V* was about to transfer to the RSC's London base at the Barbican, Branagh and Patricia Marmont decided that a pay rise would be appropriate. It wasn't just that he had been good at Stratford; it was that he had established a following, particularly with a younger audience, a good many of whom would wait for him in large numbers at the stage door.

'Already he was the pop idol of the kids,' says Marmont. Accordingly, she insisted on £350 a week for her client. At first the RSC balked at the proposition, preferring a figure of £315, and even threatened to pull the *Henry V* production from the Barbican. In the end Branagh and Marmont prevailed. But the situation had been tense.

It is important to note that a mood of dissatisfaction was permeating the ranks of actors in general, not just at the RSC, in the mid-1980s. In his book *Being an Actor* Simon Callow had articulated the feeling among his peers that the emergence of omnipotent non-acting directors and hierarchical theatre companies had eroded the creative input that actors could make. For years – indeed centuries – actors ran the show, whether it had been Shakespeare or Garrick or Irving or Olivier. But no more.

Branagh took note of the prevailing mood, including Callow's specific arguments. In a published interview in the winter of 1984 Branagh applauded him for 'opening up the debate', expressing agreement that 'actors can do almost anything. It's a question of igniting their imagination.' Other RSC actors were similarly convinced of the need to fight back. Ian McDiarmid, who would go on to help run the Almeida in one of theatre's great success stories of the 1990s, decided to take action. He chaired a committee in charge of organising a fringe season, during the RSC's visit to Newcastle in the spring of 1985, in which actors would be able to display the range of their interests.

It was under the auspices of this fringe programme that Branagh made his debut as a writer and director. He penned a one-act play, *Tell Me Honestly*, based on the end-of-year interviews that RSC actors had with Terry Hands. In it a director, Largewit, conducts interviews with two actresses, Neuroza and Assinina, who are concerned about their standing in a large theatre company. The aim of the piece, as Branagh put it, was to explore the desire shared by actors 'to be more involved on every level and the frustration felt at not being able to achieve this in co-operation with the management'. The original casting included Nicholas Woodeson and Amanda Root, and with the assistance of David Parfitt, foreshadowing the role he would play in Branagh's independent theatre productions in later years, the play transferred to London for the 'Not the RSC Festival' at the Almeida and then for a limited season of lunch-time shows at the Donmar Warehouse. Reviewing the production in the *Guardian*,

Billington wrote, 'It pins down amusingly the mutual insecurity, the subterranean eroticism, the nervous bonhomie ... that doubtless attends all such encounters [between actors and directors]. What it also does is bring into the open the frustration and remoteness from power felt by actors in big ensembles.'

In conversations with David Parfitt, who had visited him frequently at the house in which he lived during the Stratford season, Branagh poured out his feelings of frustration. He began to think more and more in terms of leaving the RSC and launching his own theatre company, one in which actors would be at the forefront, not consigned to the role of underlings. As early as 1984 he spoke openly of his desire to set up his own company. It may well have been the case that Branagh had ideas for such a venture before joining the RSC, perhaps while still a student at RADA; but his season with the RSC strengthened that inclination. A year and a half after leaving the company he made good on his promise to himself to set up his own.

Despite the simmering tension between Branagh and the RSC management, the 1984–5 season was a triumph for the young actor. Many who watched him that season were left with a lasting impression. Charlotte Jones, one of Britain's most gifted young playwrights, who has enjoyed enormous success with *Humble Boy*, had her first theatregoing experiences at Stratford, taking in various productions, including those in which Branagh starred. 'I just remember his wonderful clarity as an actor – his ability to make Shakespeare totally accessible – so that to my teenaged ears sometimes I thought he must have "made it up" – it sounded so modern and fresh,' recalls Jones. 'He has great charm as an actor – and great dignity – a rare combination, perfect for those tricky Shakespearean kings. And he's a great comedian ... When I write I always write for actors – and Kenneth Branagh was one of my earliest inspirations – an example of what alchemy a great actor can perform with a script.'

2

Renaissance

Kenneth Branagh spent most of the eighteen months that followed his season at the Royal Shakespeare Company working in television. In the same period he made his debut in the world of film, which would become, by the middle of the 1990s, his preferred milieu. The television shows and movies raised his public profile, thereby enhancing the box-office appeal he needed to make the theatre company he set up in 1987 commercially viable.

In addition to acting in a fourth instalment of the *Billy* television plays, Branagh appeared in two prestigious small-screen projects. The first was *Coming Through*, written by Alan Plater and directed by Peter Barber-Fleming for Central Television, which examined D. H. Lawrence's elopement with Frieda Weekley, the aristocratic German wife of a professor at University College, Nottingham. Running parallel to that plot line was the contemporary story of a mature student, Kate, played by Alison Steadman, who found herself wooed by a local Lothario when visiting the University of Nottingham to research about Lawrence. A Lawrence aficionado, Branagh had even thought about writing and performing in a one-man show about his life. So he was delighted to be offered the lead role in *Coming Through*, playing opposite Helen Mirren's Frieda.

He added to his knowledge of Lawrence by visiting Eastwood, from where Lawrence hailed, reading all of his writings from this period, and paying a visit to the British Sound Archive to listen to recordings of Frieda Weekley reminiscing about Lawrence. Branagh undertook the necessary physical as well as intellectual preparations for the part. Determined to display Lawrence's gauntness, he lost around thirty pounds of weight in an act of bodily transformation of which Robert De Niro in his *Raging Bull* period would have been proud.

Filming took place on location in the Midlands in September and October 1985, and when the programme was broadcast, just after Christmas, viewers were able to watch a compelling portrayal of Lawrence. With his emaciated appearance and convincing Nottinghamshire accent, Branagh both looked and sounded the part. He was able to convey Lawrence's keen intelligence, his directness and his ardour for Frieda. There was an unadorned truthfulness to his acting, no ham or histrionics. He also succeeded, as he had intended, in presenting a Lawrence that confounded expectations – not sullen or tortured, but sociable, witty and charming. 'Refreshing and probably very near the truth,' is how the *Listener* judged Branagh's characterisation of Lawrence.

Branagh was also cast in *Ghosts*, a BBC adaptation of Ibsen's play. Director Elijah Moshinsky was a fervent admirer of Branagh's work, saying he had 'a razor-sharp quality, unlike any other actor in the English theatre. His characters seem possessed by a terrific driving force ... Everything about him reminds me of what you read about Olivier at the same age,' added Moshinsky, making the analogy that was becoming commonplace. 'He's probably the most dedicated, serious performer of his generation.' It was no surprise, therefore, that Moshinsky asked Branagh to play the doomed Oswald, who inherits venereal disease from his dissolute father, and falls for the maid (played by Natasha Richardson) who, unbeknown to him, is his half-sister, the offspring from one of his father's extramarital flings.

One of the attractions for Branagh in playing Oswald was the opportunity it afforded to work with two distinguished actors: Judi Dench, cast as Mrs Alving, and Michael Gambon, who portrayed that defender of traditional morality, Pastor Manders. Branagh's experience with Dench and Gambon comprised periods of impressively committed acting on the one hand, and bouts of uncontrollable corpsing on the other. The connection with Dench proved significant: she would go on to play a major role in Branagh's Renaissance Theatre Company.

Branagh delivered an intense performance as Oswald. Intriguingly, he hinted at a Hamlet-and-Gertrude-type quasi-sexual relationship between Oswald and his mother, as Branagh shared one very passionate kiss with Dench. Heightening the resonance of the story in general and Branagh's performance in particular was AIDS, which had become such a salient issue of public concern in the 1980s. As he had in many of his previous small-screen projects, Branagh had shown with *Ghosts* that he was able to use television, and not just the stage, to build his reputation as a classical actor.

In May 1986 Branagh's career entered a new phase; for that month principal photography began on *High Season*, his first feature film. Scripted by siblings Mark Peploe and Bernardo Bertolucci's wife Clare Peploe, *High Season* was to be directed by the latter. Set on the island of Rhodes, it explored in a light-hearted way the deleterious impact of modern tourism on an ancient culture through the interlocking stories of a number of curious characters.

Branagh was up for the role of Rick, ostensibly an archetypal tourist, who turns out to be an agent sent on a mission to deal with an English art historian found to have been working for Moscow. Jack Nicholson had been keen on the part, phoning Clare Peploe himself to say he was interested. Casting Nicholson would have meant changing the script and, Peploe assumed, making Rick's character an American. On the other hand, Nicholson's involvement would have resulted in a bigger budget. In the end Peploe decided against altering the story, and so it was that Branagh found himself on his way to Peploe's flat to be interviewed for the role. At this point she had someone else in mind for the part. 'Then Kenneth Branagh walked in,' she recalls, 'and I thought, "Oh, James Cagney." He has that big head and small but powerful stature ... And this kind of magnetism also ... I knew at once: "I've got to have him."' Peploe says that she was attracted to the idea of fitting the heroic dimension of Branagh's acting persona into a comic character, believing that this would make for a funnier performance. For Branagh, the appeal of the part seemed clear: it would allow him to get a feel for the movie world, to enjoy seven idyllic weeks on the island of Rhodes, where the shoot would take place on location, and to rub shoulders with a group of prominent actors that included Jacqueline Bisset, James Fox, Robert Stephens and Sebastian Shaw.

Once filming began Clare Peploe noticed the efficiency of Branagh's work: he required little directorial guidance and few takes. She also observed his chivalry when, in what can only be regarded as one of the perks of the job, he had to do a nude scene with Jacqueline Bisset. She was uncomfortable about doing that scene but, reveals Peploe, 'He was great with her.' When the film was released, in 1987, the negativity that characterised many of the reviews was not directed at Branagh's performance. Those who commented on his contribution did so favourably.

The shoot in Rhodes in the summer of 1986, however, was not a happy time for Branagh. A self-confessed winter person, the heat made him irritable. All the good things about the experience, he has admitted, 'didn't stop me moaning'. When the cameras weren't rolling, he kept himself to himself. 'I thought he was rather snooty about film-making,' states Clare Peploe.

The time spent alone did not go to waste, for Branagh used it to plot his return to the stage. He was now determined to direct and star in *Romeo and Juliet*. This would serve as preparation for the formal launching of his own theatre company. Accordingly, he decided on cuts to the text, the roles that could be doubled and the budget required for the production. He asked David Parfitt to help organise the show, and found a venue – the Lyric Studio, Hammersmith.

Paying for the production was problematic, and so Branagh was forced to dip into his own pockets. It was this factor, alongside the artistic merit of the piece, that persuaded him to accept a part in his second movie of the summer, *A Month in the Country*, co-starring Colin Firth and directed by Pat O'Connor, even though filming would take place in the same weeks as he was treading the boards as Romeo. By ensuring that his scenes were the first to be shot each day and that the makers of the film laid on a car to get him to the theatre on time, Branagh was able to work on the play and film simultaneously.

Simon Gray's screenplay for *A Month in the Country*, based on the novel by J. L. Carr, tells the story of two traumatised World War I veterans, Birkin (Firth) and Moon (Branagh), who have come to a remote Yorkshire village on separate assignments. Birkin has been hired to uncover a medieval mural in the village church, while Moon, working out of a tent pitched next to the church, is digging for the remains of an ancestor of a local benefactress. Completing archaelogical and restorative tasks are the immediate objectives of Branagh's character and Firth's, but at a deeper, spiritual level they are searching for a balm for their emotional wounds, and the tranquillity of their rustic surroundings and the eccentric charm of most of the locals help provide one.

A quietly elegiac quality suffused *A Month in the Country*. The work of cinematographer Ken MacMillan had made for a beautiful-looking movie, something Branagh would remember when recruiting a director of photography for his film of *Henry V*. There was no pacey narrative, riveting climax or intricate dialogue: this was a film of quiet pleasures – of memorable moods, suppressed feelings and a rich subtext.

As for Branagh's contribution, he conveyed well the charm of his character that at the start contrasts with the taciturn sadness of Colin Firth's Birkin. But as the story unfolded, Branagh removed the external layers of Moon's personality to reveal the pain at its core. Like Birkin, he suffered from nightmares, haunted by a secret from the war: he had been removed from the fighting in 1918 for sodomising a subordinate. Not a single reviewer expressed any reservation about Branagh's performance, and a good many sang his praises. 'Astonishingly sure-footed', gushed the *Guardian*; 'immaculate', agreed the *Daily Telegraph*; 'outstanding', opined the *Daily Mail*; while the *Sunday Times* said that he now merited a major film role.

Branagh's stage production of *Romeo and Juliet* proved less successful, despite the energy he poured into it. His manifold responsibilities included casting, and in that he made good progress, securing the services of Samantha Bond as Juliet. In what was, to say the least, an economical production, several actors would be asked to double up. Hence Mark Hadfield would play Mercutio before returning to a no doubt surprised audience as Friar Laurence. Branagh also put in place a quality-control mechanism. Knowing that his energies as producer, director and actor would be dispersed, he recruited two consultants, his RADA mentor Hugh Cruttwell and Russell Jackson of the Shakespeare Institute in Stratford-upon-Avon. Cruttwell would keep an eye on Branagh's performance and the production in general; Jackson would serve as text adviser. With little more than three weeks scheduled for rehearsals, the assistance of these two men would be invaluable.

As director, Branagh needed to crystallise his thinking on his overall approach to *Romeo and Juliet*. He resisted the idea of a single overarching concept, feeling this would constrain rather than liberate the actors, and likewise did not encourage the designer to create an elaborate set. He wanted a paçey production, 'to create the effect of fate *rushing* the lives of these two people to their tragic ends', and so made substantial cuts to the text. Above all, he hoped that a feeling of freshness would permeate the show, a strong sense of the youthful impulses that drive the story; and there would be nothing antiquated about the actors' technique. 'All that cobwebby Shakespearean acting is out of the window,' he told the press before opening night. 'People might hate it but they won't think it's boring ... We are going for raw emotion,' he added. 'I want to capture that feeling of being in love when your knees buckle and your whole life changes. It should be earth-shattering.' The heat between the two lead characters would be mirrored by the representation of a sun-baked Verona. Branagh hired from the RSC one of the best lighting designers in the business, who borrowed extra lights from contacts all over London to create a sense of white heat.

The boldness exhibited by the twenty-five-year-old Branagh in putting on and starring in his own production of *Romeo and Juliet* was clear to see, but on this occasion the critics thought he had bitten off more than he could chew. The general feeling was that a cheerful amateurishness had marred the show. Martin Hoyle of the *Financial Times* admired Branagh's portrayal of Romeo, but most other reviewers were enamoured of neither his performance nor the production as a whole. 'Kenneth Branagh ... seems to think that Shakespeare's poetry alone will waft us to Verona,' wrote Milton Shulman in the London *Standard*, 'since little in his acting, direction or décor suggests the steamy, lustful, violent atmosphere of Latin families obsessed by a blood feud.' Eric Shorter of the *Daily Telegraph* said: '[Branagh] has a pleasant, boyish, honest-seeming personality but it would take a more persuasive, lyrical performance to bring that lover to life.' It was the least flattering set of notices he had ever received.

For Branagh and the rest of the cast, however, the enterprise had been fun. 'Lovely time,' recalls David Parfitt. 'Fantastic group of people. A lot of laughing, general drunkenness and bad behaviour, and all the things that happen around a tight company.' More importantly, the production proved educative for Branagh, even if critical acclaim had eluded him. Determined to establish his own theatre company, he knew there was a learning curve he needed to experience if he were to do that successfully. As a result of *Romeo and Juliet*, he was more knowledgeable about the practical aspects of putting on a show, such as negotiating with theatres and making the financial equation work. His partnership with David Parfitt was stronger; they now had a clear sense of how to divide up responsibilities. In Hugh Cruttwell and Russell Jackson he had established a support team that would be of long-term benefit to his work. Branagh had profited, moreover, from the directing, his experience of which had been limited hitherto. He would soon be doing a good deal more of it.

During the run of *Romeo and Juliet*, the RSC's Terry Hands paid a visit. 'Well, have you got this out of your system now?' he asked Branagh. 'When are you going to come back and join us?' The answer would turn out to be: not for another six or seven years. Branagh had his heart set on launching many more productions by his own company. *Romeo and Juliet* had been merely a dry run.

Before establishing a new company, Branagh had one substantial piece of television work to undertake first. He had been cast in a major BBC television series as one of the leads in *Fortunes of War*, based on Olivia Manning's novels about the impact of World War II on a newly married English couple, Guy and Harriet Pringle. An English lecturer in Bucharest when war breaks out, Guy is forced into a nomadic existence as he and Harriet keep one step ahead of the German army, fleeing to Athens, then Cairo. The Pringle's partnership is problematic. Harriet yearns for the sort of exclusive devotion from a husband whose keen interest in the lives of everyone else in his social and professional circle means that he cannot provide it. That personal drama plays out against the backdrop of the monumental political and military events of the war in southern and eastern Europe. Enlivening the story is the fascinating assortment of characters whose paths cross those of the Pringles. The sense of nuance and authenticity was amplified by the autobiographical inspiration behind *Fortunes of War*: Olivia Manning had been married to a British Council lecturer R. D. Smith, with whom she travelled to Bucharest at the start of the war.

It was James Cellan Jones, whose credits included *The Forsyte Saga*, who would direct this series, for which Alan Plater had produced a consummate adaptation of Manning's novels. Branagh was hired after an interview with Jones in which he turned up, as he himself recalled, 'as Guy Pringle: bulky, teddy-bearish and distracted'. The other crucial piece of casting was Guy's wife. 'I'm determined this time not to fall in love with whoever it is,' Branagh told Patricia Marmont. 'That had been his Achilles' heel,' she recalls. 'He always fell in love left, right and centre with whoever was playing opposite.' Jones had already considered the likes of Fiona Shaw and Joanne Whalley as

Branagh's co-star when Emma Thompson, sporting what the director described as 'monumentally disgusting' dyed-orange hair, came for interview. 'Something struck me about her,' recalls Jones, 'and I offered her the part on the spot.' Anxious that her client's co-star be of the right calibre, and unfamiliar with Emma Thompson's work, Patricia Marmont called the producer of *Me and My Girl*, the West End musical in which Thompson had been performing. Marmont and Branagh would have been reassured by what she was told: 'She's absolutely marvellous, and she's very intelligent. Don't just write her off because this is a musical comedy.'

Born in 1959, a year and eight months before Branagh, to stage and television director Eric Thompson and the actress Phyllida Law, Emma had grown up in north London before reading English Literature at Cambridge University. There she had performed for the Footlights, carving out a reputation as a comedienne. She had appeared in *Alfresco* and *Tutti Frutti*, television comedy shows, as well as doing stand-up. She was talented, highly intelligent, confident, versatile and politically active.

The filming of *Fortunes of War*, which began in September 1986 in Ljubljana, Yugoslavia, lasted nine months, and it was during this period that Branagh and Thompson became involved. Both of them spoke subsequently about their initial wariness, their mutual concern that emotions manufactured on behalf of their characters were being confused with the feelings they had for each other. Of the two, it seems that Thompson was the first to fall in love. 'I didn't know his work,' she recalled, 'but I did know that he was sort of a young lion in the British theatre. It was sort of keen interest at first sight.' Branagh's recollection differed. 'We didn't exactly go *doiinngg*,' he said; but as the filming of *Fortunes of War* continued, taking in the cultural delights of Egypt and Greece, his affection for Emma Thompson deepened. 'I think Emma fell totally in love before Ken did,' one acquaintance revealed. 'Then quite suddenly – unlike the rest of them [previous girlfriends] – this one came up behind him and whacked him on the head, so to speak. And he suddenly thought – "Oh my God – yes, this is the one!"' The Valley of the Kings, the Pyramids at Giza, the Acropolis, and Venice (which was visited by the cast though not used for filming) – not bad settings for a love affair with the woman who would become his wife.

Despite their very different backgrounds – one working-class, one middle-class; one from a family immersed in the performing arts, the other from a family with no involvement in that world at all – Branagh and Thompson had a good deal in common: a lively intelligence, prodigious confidence, a strong sense of humour and considerable ambition. In retrospect, they bring to mind Bill and Hillary Clinton or Tony and Cherie Blair – modern couples whose careerist aspirations are intimately woven into the fabric of their relationships. Branagh and Thompson would develop a professional partnership, as well as a romantic attachment.

If not initially head-over-heels in love, Branagh was by the time the shoot for *Fortunes of War* was over. Directing John Sessions in his one-man show *Napoleon* in the summer of 1987, Branagh took time out to pour out his emotions on the back page of his copy of the script. I came across this remarkable document among the records of the Renaissance Theatre Company, held by the V. & A. archive at Blythe House, in London. It represents a rare glimpse into Branagh's inner world. Alongside his affability, there is a wary, self-contained side to his personality, as he himself has acknowledged. This document represents the man at his most raw and exposed. Sounding like Orsino in *Twelfth Night*, Branagh scribbled down his heartfelt emotions, revealing not only surprising doubts about his just-launched Renaissance company and a possible tiff with Thompson, but also the anguished ardour of his feelings for her. At no point did he mention Thompson by name. But given that the document dates from the period immediately following the *Fortunes of War* shoot, it would seem a safe assumption that he was referring to her. Set down in small segments at varying angles on the page, he wrote:

> Besotted – agonized – hysterical – weepy – strong – brave – feeble – serene – completely in it! – I miss you so much.
>
> Agony. That's what this is. – Wonderful agony. – I miss you so much. – Agony. Wonderful agony. – I miss you so much.
>
> I miss you so much it hurts. – Renaissance is a shambles. – Instead of working on budgets – I spend all day thinking – of you, – wonderful. – Agony.
>
> Slightly weepy. – Slightly hysterical. – Very besotted. – This is Agony. I miss you – so much. – Don't be cross.
>
> Agony – Thinking of – you 25 hours a day. – I miss you so much – Wonderful agony.
>
> This is agony. – Wonderful yes. – But agony nonetheless – I miss you so much. – Love from very besotted – person.

Falling in love was not the only important offscreen development for Branagh during the filming of *Fortunes of War*. The other was making concrete his theatre company plans. Mulling over the plays to perform, directors to hire, venues to book, and the right name for his company, Branagh had a lot to think about during the winter of 1986–7. As for the name, he settled on Renaissance: 'It seemed to reflect our youthfulness and express some sense of rebirth that was going on in the British theatre,' he said. As for the company patron, he persuaded Prince Charles to serve in that role after another meeting at Kensington Palace.

Branagh's thinking on the programme of plays to be staged by his nascent company had crystallised by the spring of 1987. Renaissance would make its debut with *Public Enemy*, a new play set in Belfast that Branagh had written himself. Next would come *Napoleon*, a one-man show penned and performed by John Sessions, and *Twelfth Night*, with Richard Briers as Malvolio. Branagh planned to follow all of this with a repertory season of Shakespeare plays: *Hamlet*, *Much Ado About Nothing* and *As You Like It*. The original intention had been to put on *Macbeth* as well, with Anthony Hopkins directing Branagh in the lead role; but Hopkins was uncertain. He said yes, then no. To resolve matters, Branagh met him at the National Theatre for a chat. They then embarked on a very long walk – David Parfitt recalls that it ended up in Clapham – continuing their discussion along the way. 'I think I've got him,' Branagh told Parfitt afterwards. But he hadn't. Hopkins pulled out at the last moment.

In fashioning his plans for the Renaissance Theatre Company's 1987–8 season, Branagh was able to give expression to his longstanding ideas on the need for actors, and not non-acting directors, to be given a chance to run the show. Accordingly, Branagh would direct *Napoleon* and *Twelfth Night*, while Derek Jacobi, Judi Dench and Geraldine McEwan agreed to direct, respectively, *Hamlet*, *Much Ado* and *As You Like It*. Money would be a problem. Public funding from the Arts Council was sought but not forthcoming. He would need to be resourceful.

While falling in love and planning his own theatre company, Branagh still had the little matter of sustaining a cogent portrayal of Guy Pringle. As the broadcast of the *Fortunes of War* series on BBC television in the autumn of 1987 showed, Branagh had done a good job at making Pringle sympathetic despite his selfishness towards his wife. 'It's very interesting because he's not conventionally handsome,' reflects James Cellan Jones. 'But he managed to convey an intelligence, a physical attraction, a certain bravery ... and a certain pig-headedness ... and I don't quite know how he did it.' Jones adds:

He was, in a sense, very young for his age – had a very open, childish sense of humour, which was very infectious. And it was a weird combination because [at the same time] he knew exactly where he was going. He was very determined. He wasn't about to admit to failure ever ... He's a much calmer person than many I've worked with. I've worked with Tony Hopkins, who's not calm, Alec Guinness, who wasn't calm, [and] Rex Harrison who was extremely bad tempered.[1]

As the filming of *Fortunes of War* drew to a close, Branagh began to focus ever more on what would be one of the watershed events of his career: launching the Renaissance Theatre Company. A press conference was scheduled for the Covent Garden Gallery in April 1987 to announce the venture. With Judi Dench, Derek Jacobi, Richard Briers and Geraldine McEwan present to show their support, Branagh addressed the throng of journalists, explaining the rationale for his new company: the restoration of the actor to the heart of the creative process. The Renaissance season for 1987–8 was unveiled, and information packs distributed. There was now no turning back. Branagh had attached his credibility to the success of Renaissance.

How was Branagh now looked upon in the world of theatre as the Renaissance experiment got under way? Christopher Hampton recalls 'a sense that people slightly had it in for him because he was so young, which I felt sympathetic towards because I started when I was twenty; and you do feel that you're making your way against a certain kind of prejudice.' However, some admired Branagh's initiative. A number of critics at that time were hostile to the big institutions, especially the RSC, believing that they absorbed an inordinately high proportion of the public funding for theatre. From that perspective, the new company seemed a good thing.

With the establishment of Renaissance, Branagh showed himself to be a man of action. As Michael Billington observes,

What is extraordinary about him is this entrepreneurial spirit ... The thing is, he *does* it and other actors talk about it. That's the key fact, it seems to me. The RSC – and the National – is always full of actors who sit in pubs or green rooms whinging about the institution and saying if only we could set up our own company. Actors in my experience are nearly always discontented with whatever company they're working in, and they always have these pipe dreams like Eugene O'Neill characters of running their own show ... The point about Ken Branagh is he did it and he did it [at a very young age]. That is what is so extraordinary; and it says a lot about ... his practicality, self-determination, entrepreneurial spirit.

> And one of the things that has always struck me about him: his awareness of theatre history. I have never met any other actor ... who knew as much about the past of the theatre. Most actors always assume that the theatre began with them. And you could talk to Branagh – this is partly why I like him so much – you could always talk to him about the theatre of the previous generation ... He could talk about old critics, that was what even more impressed me actually. He would know about the reviews of James Agate. The point of that is because he knew so much about theatre history, he was aware that there was a tradition in England of actors [such as Gielgud and Olivier] trying to take control of things or set up companies ... The difference is that he was in his twenties where ... Gielgud [for example] didn't set up his own company until he was in his thirties or forties. I think he learned a lot from this studious attitude towards the theatrical past.[2]

Public Enemy blended Branagh's fascination with old Hollywood, and particularly the films of James Cagney, with his perspective on contemporary life in his home-town. It centred on the character of Tommy Black, an unemployed Belfast youth who squabbles with his more responsible brother, adores his mother, and spends much of his time watching Cagney's movies on television. The play opens with Tommy Black reprising Cagney's 'Yankee Doodle Dandy' dance routine in a pub talent contest, and as the story unfolds, Tommy Black's fixation with the Cagney gangster persona reaches the point of dangerous obsession. Desperate to endow a life made empty by unemployment with greater excitement and significance, and to take revenge on the paramilitaries responsible for his father's death, he ends up unable to distinguish himself from Cagney's screen personality, and kills a video-shop owner before staging a shoot-out that results in his own death and that of his girlfriend. *Public Enemy* would provide fast-paced entertainment, with a multiplicity of short scenes; but Branagh also wanted to explore some serious issues, particularly the impact of sectarianism and long-term unemployment on Belfast.

With the help of feedback from friends, including Emma Thompson and Alan Bennett, Branagh had converted a rough draft into a polished version of *Public Enemy* by early 1987. A lot seemed to be riding on this enterprise. For one thing, Branagh cast himself in the lead role of Tommy Black, though he would leave the directing to Malcolm McKay (who had directed his Hamlet at RADA). For another, he wanted *Public Enemy* to be the Renaissance Theatre Company's debut production, to open at London's Lyric, Hammersmith, in July 1987. That decision was made despite opposition from David Parfitt, who worried about a possible backlash from the critics against what could be construed as Branagh's brazenness at launching his new company with a play written by himself, starring himself and opening with a show-stopping dance routine performed by himself. 'You sort of knew,' says Parfitt, 'that the de Jonghs [theatre critic at that time for the *Guardian*] of this world would be gunning for you ... Who are these people setting up this company? Who is this guy who thinks he can write it and star in it and he can sing and he can dance ... It was one of those things where you sort of knew that the cynical press would have a go at him; and we weren't disappointed.' Safer to start with *Twelfth Night*, Parfitt told Branagh, and then open with *Public Enemy* later in the year to demonstrate the breadth of the company's work. Sound advice, in retrospect, but at the time Branagh decided to stick to his original plan: he pressed ahead with *Public Enemy* regardless.

As Branagh prepared for his new play, his workload escalated, reaching the energy-sapping levels where it would remain for the next decade. He arrived for rehearsals an hour and a half before the other actors in order to practise his dancing with a choreographer. On evenings and at weekends he busied himself redrafting the play. Moreover, he was now saddled with the administrative and financial chores involved in running a company. In spare moments he would fire off letters to actors to beg for money to keep Renaissance afloat. The generosity he encountered was gratifying. Parfitt recalls Branagh and himself being amazed when Ian McKellen responded to just such a plea by promptly sending them a cheque for £500. But the administrative demands increased the pressure on Branagh. The extent to which these sorts of additional responsibilities affected his acting was an issue Branagh had to consider not only with *Public Enemy* but on many of the projects he would accept in the years to come.

On the press night of *Public Enemy* the critics witnessed Renaissance's debut as Branagh launched into the 'Yankee Doodle Dandy' dance routine. In a way, it was an apt demonstration of the audacity he had shown in creating this company. David Parfitt recalls the moment, and the response he divined among the critics: 'The opening was a sort of theatrical conceit, and it was Ken saying I can do this and actually ... [it was] almost irrelevant to the rest of the plot. But it was still beautifully done. He pulled it off amazingly. There were almost gasps on the press night, [the sense of which were] (a) how dare he? And (b) actually he can.'

Jack Tinker of the *Daily Mail* liked *Public Enemy* a good deal, as did Charles Osborne of the *Daily Telegraph*, who felt compelled to comment on the Olivier–Branagh analogy: 'For his work at Stratford, Branagh has been hailed as a young Olivier. But there is only one young Olivier, and he is the chap who is now the old Olivier. Kenneth Branagh deserves to be assessed without reference to a great actor whom he in no way resembles, physically or temperamentally. His Henry V at Stratford owed nothing to Olivier's, and his Tommy Black in *Public Enemy* is a remarkable creation.' The Olivier comparison, Osborne was suggesting, could end up being used to diminish Branagh.

The reviews by Osborne and Tinker must have pleased Branagh, but they were hardly typical of the general response from the critics. Noah Richler of the London *Standard* argued that 'the whole adventure is a bit soulless and, for all its action, flat and unexciting.' 'Everything about the play – and indeed his performance – suggests to me that Branagh is playing with fire,' wrote Nicholas de Jongh. 'He emerges nastily singed.' Branagh later ascribed the play's disappointing impact to the lack of scheduled previews, but Parfitt feels there was another dynamic at work. If one decodes the reviews, he argues, 'it's more about how dare he [Branagh]? than it was about the play … It was just the undertow of what they would try and do to him later.'

Public Enemy was a setback not only in terms of how the critics judged the company's new work, but financially as well; the production failed to make its money back, and some of its investors decided against supporting Renaissance's forthcoming shows. Still, it provided Branagh with his first publication, the playtext coming out with Faber and Faber. He dedicated it to his parents. Seven years later, moreover, the play was revived in a New York production. In the short term, Branagh had the opportunity to make amends for *Public Enemy*'s lack of commercial and critical success with Renaissance's next production, *Napoleon*, which he would direct. John Sessions had written this one-man show himself, and now turned to his old RADA chum to help him shape the production. Branagh barely had time to catch his breath. Rehearsals for *Napoleon* commenced the morning after *Public Enemy* opened.

Branagh's chief contribution to Sessions' comic account of the life of Napoleon was to rein in his friend's penchant for improvisation, and to remind him of the importance of making the show accessible; no point in providing impressively obscure references if no one knew what he was talking about. His direction was effective. *Napoleon* turned out to be a hit, earning strong notices and a transfer after its run at the Riverside Studios to the West End's Albery Theatre.

It was during the rehearsals for *Napoleon* that a crucial addition was made to the Renaissance team. At that time the company's financial situation was parlous. The money for *Twelfth Night*, the next scheduled production, was not in place. Then, out of the blue, Stephen Evans, a stockbroker with a keen interest in the arts, phoned the Riverside Studios to offer a helping hand. Branagh was not available, but Evans tried again several times. None of his calls were returned. When Evans phoned for the final time, Branagh took the call as he happened to be passing the box office. Evans said he had been reading about Renaissance in the papers, and wanted to give the company financial support. Branagh agreed to meet Evans at the Riverside.

When Evans turned up, Branagh was immersed in a particularly demanding rehearsal for *Napoleon*; so he asked Parfitt to take the meeting. During their discussion Evans was direct, lucid and proactive. 'I work in the city,' he told Parfitt. 'I'm a stockbroker. How much money are you looking for?' £12,000 divulged Parfitt. 'Done,' Evans responded. 'So when do you need it?' 'Now!' Parfitt declared. 'OK, I'll get you a cheque by Friday.'

Parfitt reported all of this to a suspicious Branagh, whose response was pithily dismissive: 'Bollocks! He's a bullshitter.' To find out if that was the case – to ascertain whether Evans was a crank or a potential saviour – a sort of background check was conducted. 'We made some phone calls to people,' Parfitt recalls, 'and said can you find out who this man is? ... People said, "Well ... he is a member of the Stock Exchange. He does exist. The company is there. They're real." And the money arrived.'

What cemented Evans's interest in becoming part of the Renaissance enterprise was the impression Branagh made on him. 'Once I got to know him a bit,' recalls Evans, 'he was, at that point in time, absolutely amazing ... He knew how to use that charm, which is critical. He was very gung-ho – lot of chutzpah about him. I thought he was amazing, which he was ... I really wanted to back him in any way I could ... I've met a lot of bright people around twenty-seven or eight, but no one with that level of ability and energy.'

A diarchy thus became a triumvirate; and an effective division of labour was established. Branagh would retain responsibility for

Renaissance's artistic choices. Parfitt would run the company from an administrative point of view. Evans would provide the financial acumen. The long-term future now looked a good deal rosier.

Between the Renaissance productions of *Napoleon* and *Twelfth Night*, Branagh played Thomas Mendip in a television adaptation of Christopher Fry's 1948 play, *The Lady's Not for Burning*, broadcast to celebrate Fry's eightieth birthday. Branagh put in a solid enough performance. He was more powerful in another piece of television work, filmed earlier in the year, Eugene O'Neill's *Strange Interlude*. Adopting a convincing American accent, he portrayed Gordon Evans, a young man disturbed by the close relationship between his mother (played by Glenda Jackson) and a family friend, who, unbeknown to Evans, is his biological father. Branagh's performance added to the strong body of television work that he had produced during the 1980s.

Branagh directed but did not act in *Twelfth Night*, a play that had long fascinated him. He envisaged a production (scheduled for a December 1987 opening at the Riverside Studios) that highlighted the play's melancholia. He would still try to get the big laughs, but the anguish experienced by many of the characters – the heartache felt by Viola and Olivia, the breaking of Malvolio, the treatment ultimately received by Andrew Aguecheek at the hands of Sir Toby Belch – would be to the fore. To provide a visual metaphor that would unlock the play's harsher themes Branagh set his production in a snow-covered Victorian garden. The winter season made clear that a high-spirited frivolity would not be this *Twelfth Night*'s dominant emotion.

The artists recruited by Branagh boded well. Paul McCartney, no less, agreed to assist Renaissance's musical director Patrick Doyle, providing a song for the show. Frances Barber would play Viola; Anton Lesser would tackle the role of Feste; and, most intriguingly, Richard Briers was cast as Malvolio.

In developing his interpretation of Malvolio, this veteran of television sitcom was much influenced by his director. 'Malvolio is often portrayed as simply a clown,' Branagh told Briers, 'but ... he's a megalomaniac – and quite a dangerous man if he got any power. Not a pleasant person at all. But on the other hand you must remember that Malvolio holds the household [of Olivia] together because you've got ... Aguecheek and Belch, who are a couple of drunks. You've got a clown who is also a bloody drunk.' Briers' performance, therefore, would acknowledge the necessary responsibilities assumed by Malvolio, while making clear that his gulling, at the hands of Belch, Aguecheek *et al.*, is not wanton but vital in order to clip the wings of a man with dangerous, dictatorial tendencies.

At the time Briers described Branagh as 'the best director I've worked with in twenty-five years.' Years later his gratitude for Branagh's impact on his performance as Malvolio remained undiminished. He recalls the cleverness of the direction. In the scene where Malvolio is released from his confinement, it is customary for the humiliated steward to rant and rave. But Branagh encouraged Briers to do exactly the opposite: 'Don't move at all. Just don't move at all. Just say the lines.' As a self-confessed fidget, Briers found it difficult to follow Branagh's advice. In performance, however, he could see that this approach mesmerised the audience. When the scene was underplayed, Briers discovered, the audience did the work for the actor by imagining the powerful emotions coursing through Malvolio. 'So that was a very sophisticated piece of direction from still a very young man,' observes Briers. 'One began to realise very early that he wasn't an ordinary young man.'

Branagh's production of *Twelfth Night* earned rave reviews. Richard Briers and Frances Barber received a good deal of praise, as did Branagh's direction. Especially pleasing for him must have been the observation by Jack Tinker of the *Daily Mail* that there was a difference between this show, directed by an actor, and those directed by non-acting directors. 'It is a distinct plus of Mr Branagh's Renaissance Theatre Company's season,' he wrote in his review, 'that, in allowing actors to direct, we are able to see the wood of the play instead of the interpretive trees which so often obscure it.' That represented an endorsement of the whole rationale behind Renaissance. Branagh's *Twelfth Night* was a box-office success, compensating financially for the fact that *Public Enemy* had lost money, and that *Napoleon*, though doing well, did not show a profit.

1987 had finished with a flourish for Branagh; 1988 would see a continuation of his attempt to put Renaissance well and truly on the theatrical map. A Shakespeare season at the Birmingham Repertory Studio would open with *Much Ado About Nothing* and follow with *As You Like It* and *Hamlet*. Three months honing those productions at that small venue would be followed by more lucrative runs at larger theatres across the nation, in Ireland and in Denmark's Elsinore

Castle, before arriving in the West End for a brief run at the Phoenix Theatre.

Before starting work on *Much Ado About Nothing*, the director, Judi Dench, threw a party at her Elizabethan home in Surrey to alleviate the nerves felt by this group of mainly young actors, which included Samantha Bond, James Larkin and Emma's sister, Sophie Thompson. A champagne-induced state of relaxation was ideal preparation for the rehearsals, which began in London the next day.

Dench did not have an overarching directorial concept for the play, but she did have a clear sense of how the production should look: a Regency setting but an appropriately Italianate feel. Dench, along with Renaissance's other directors, Geraldine McEwan and Derek Jacobi, brought to bear their own particular strengths. With Dench, it was the scrupulous attention she paid to the proper speaking of the verse. In her own acting career Dench had received advice on how best to handle the verse from Peter Hall, John Barton and Trevor Nunn, all of whom had in turn been influenced by an approach passed on by George Rylands, Edith Evans and William Poel. Carrying on this rich tradition, Dench handed down this precious fund of technical knowledge to the young Renaissance cast.

Derek Jacobi's production of *Hamlet* benefited from his encyclopedic knowledge of the text, which came from the countless performances he had given as the Danish prince, and his innovative approach to the women's parts. Determined to make Ophelia and Gertrude less peripheral than they can often appear, Jacobi insisted that Branagh's Hamlet deliver the 'To be or not to be' speech not alone but directly to Sophie Thompson's Ophelia. Hearing Hamlet's meditation on suicide, it would be suggested, helps explain Ophelia's subsequent decision to take her own life. In directing Branagh, Jacobi had to put their friendship aside so that he could be candid. An American television documentary on the rehearsals for *Hamlet* showed a frank though diplomatic Jacobi ticking off a chastened-looking Branagh for not listening carefully enough when the other actors were saying their lines.

The key to Geraldine McEwan's approach to *As You Like It* was her decision to set it in the Edwardian era. 'It's such a delicate and romantic comedy that the period works very well,' she explained, 'with Rosalind and Celia emerging as New Women and Touchstone as a music-hall comedian.' Branagh was cast in the supporting role of

Touchstone, a clown who can appear more bizarre than funny to a modern audience. McEwan's concept of the play, however, allowed Branagh to draw on the personae of Max Miller, Archie Rice and others in developing an exuberant portrayal of Touchstone.

Full houses, enthusiastic audiences and strong reviews made for a contented and close-knit company; but there was more to the group's cohesiveness than that. They really did believe that having actors direct actors created a different, less ego-driven atmosphere. 'While directors who *only* direct tend to stamp their ego onto the show in some way,' said David Parfitt, 'these three [Dench, Jacobi and McEwan] do not feel the need to do that. Their careers do not depend on the production being *theirs* in the same way. All three directors are much more concerned with getting the best performances out of the cast, and telling the story clearly.'

Having an actor as the leader of the company also created a different dynamic – the sense that the usual division between those who run the company and those who act had been blurred, so that everyone was in the trenches together. 'In all my years as an actress,' reflected McEwan, 'the happiest time I have ever had was at the National with Olivier from 1965 to 1972; there was something about having Larry himself as head of the company on stage with us every night in different plays that gave a kind of buoyancy and enthusiasm to the actors ... Renaissance has also begun to achieve the same feeling.' For Branagh's part, he relished the duality of his role: both leader of a company and part of a team.

After completing its three-month run at the Birmingham Rep, Renaissance went on tour, beginning with Branagh's home-town. By this point Belfast had taken note of the success achieved by one of their own. They had read of Branagh's accomplishments in the newspapers, and seen his performances in the series of *Billy* television plays and in *Fortunes of War*. Hence there was a tangible sense of pride as Branagh brought his company into town for a brief run at the Grand Opera House. 'I cannot recall a visiting company generating such excitement and enthusiasm among what is normally a fairly non-committal theatre-going public,' observed one local journalist. For Branagh, it became a whirl of activity. He spent time with relatives, spoke to numerous journalists wanting to write their 'local boy makes good' stories, attended parties thrown by sponsors, conducted a workshop at the Old Museum, and found himself stopped and congratulated by strangers he bumped into on the street. He could see how thrilled people were by his success – and he appreciated the warmth of their support. 'There was no denying his own personal relishing,' wrote one Belfast journalist, 'of a week which brought him back into the bosom of a family and a community from which he has been absent for many years.'

If Belfast proved the most poignant leg of the Renaissance tour for Branagh, then Denmark was the most prestigious. Following in the footsteps of Olivier, Gielgud, Burton and Jacobi, Branagh would play Hamlet where Shakespeare had actually set the play, in the castle at Elsinore. Branagh's burgeoning reputation preceded him; it took only two days to sell 10,000 of the 15,000 tickets available, breaking previous box-office records in the process.

It was during the run at Elsinore that Prince Charles showed his continued support for Branagh and Renaissance by attending a performance of *Hamlet*. Before he went backstage to offer his congratulations, the rest of the cast asked Branagh how best to address him. 'You call him Sir. Just like me,' Branagh quipped.

'That was a wonderful, tremendous evening,' Charles told Branagh. 'I found it very moving.' At the time of this royal visit Branagh spoke appreciatively to the press about Charles, touching on the discussions that had taken place about their shared passion for Shakespeare: 'He is widely interested in the arts and, along with music and poetry, he finds it a solace from all the pressures. He said about *Hamlet* that it was very like listening to a piece of music. It acts on the senses and he responds in that way. The thing he found about *Hamlet* is that it speaks to many people. It is a kind of spiritual comfort-blanket to the Prince and to everyone else.'

Charles's visit to Elsinore was but one example of what was a significant interaction between Renaissance and its patron. The Prince threw a morale-boosting party at Kensington Palace just for company members, while Branagh organised a show in which the likes of Judi Dench, Derek Jacobi and Emma Thompson performed scenes from Shakespeare for a private party given by Charles at Windsor. Reflecting on the role played by Charles as patron of the company, David Parfitt is positive: 'He was incredibly supportive ... All the dealings that we had with him were incredibly intelligent and thoughtful.' There was almost certainly an element of sensible self-interest in the relationship that developed between Prince Charles and Branagh. For

Charles, his link with Renaissance allowed him to keep his finger on the pulse of at least one branch of the performing arts in Britain. From Branagh's point of view, to have Charles serve as patron endowed the enterprise with a certain prestige. But beyond those considerations, the two men simply got on well.

After Elsinore, Branagh brought to London's West End, in late August 1988, three Shakespeare productions polished by six months of performance. There was a feverish sense of anticipation. Renaissance had been attracting a lot of publicity, and Londoners were keen to catch the work of Branagh and his company. The first week of booking for the run at the Phoenix Theatre resulted in advanced ticket sales of £250,000.

The critics were as enthused as the public. Jack Tinker spoke for many of his peers in declaring: 'Of Mr Branagh's Benedick it is impossible to speak too highly. He offers the words as if they had just tumbled into his consciousness; lifts phrases with the bafflement of a nimble wit suddenly out of its own depth.' If anything, the critics admired Branagh's comic turn as Touchstone in *As You Like It* even more. 'A performance of massive invention,' stated Tinker, 'definitive', asserted Nicholas de Jongh, 'a minor miracle', according to the London *Standard*'s Milton Shulman. The reviews for *Hamlet*, including Branagh's performance, were more mixed. While some critics thought that Branagh had failed to illuminate the prince's interior world, that there was a superficiality to his performance, Michael Billington wrote in the *Guardian*, 'It is the best Hamlet we have seen since Jacobi's own.' In later years Branagh came to feel that his Hamlet for Renaissance lacked maturity, that he had battled with the part and in the end had lost. Nevertheless, the experience of simply playing the role was an asset, helping him four years later to produce what many felt was an outstanding Hamlet.

The only real negative for Branagh in 1988 was the potential problem of overexposure. The enormous attention paid by the press to the Renaissance experiment in general and to Branagh in particular seemed a good thing. Indeed it was something Branagh had sought in order to raise the profile of the company. But there were inherent dangers. David Parfitt explains:

> Part of this comes down to money, because when we were starting up the theatre company the only publicity we could afford was the free publicity that the press could give us. Peter Thompson, who [was in charge of relations with the press for

Renaissance and] is a master at that, got us everything ... There was no publication that we didn't have something in at some point. We were totally overexposed. I think that what we didn't know was you *could* be overexposed. We just thought, this is fantastic. The more we talk to the press the more coverage they give us. We were very naïve. We were selling a tour. We had thousands of seats to sell, and we talked to everybody.[3]

The press coverage of Branagh would reach even more saturated levels a year later.

Dark clouds might have loomed on the horizon, but the Renaissance repertory season had been a triumph nonetheless. Just keeping the company afloat, given its lack of public subsidy, was no small achievement; but Renaissance had done more than survive: it had – in an artistic sense – prospered. Branagh's instincts about the potential of his fellow actors to direct had proved sound. He himself had performed outstandingly as Benedick and as Touchstone, and had proved to be at least an able Hamlet. Moreover, the 1988 season had increased the identification of Branagh, in the public mind, with the plays of William Shakespeare. With his work for the RSC and then for his own company, Branagh had acted in and directed a total of eight Shakespeare productions – *Henry V*, *Love's Labour's Lost*, *Romeo and Juliet*, *Twelfth Night*, *Much Ado About Nothing*, *As You Like It* and two *Hamlets*. The association of Branagh with the Bard would only increase in the months that followed the end of the Renaissance theatre season, for he had hatched a bold plan: to make a film of *Henry V*.

3

King

Perhaps it was the wine talking, but when Stephen Evans asked about his plans once Renaissance's Shakespeare theatre season ended in the autumn of 1988, Kenneth Branagh responded audaciously: 'I want to make a film of *Henry V*. I will direct and play the leading role.' Evans enquired as to Branagh's experience for such an undertaking. 'Have you directed a film before?' 'No,' Branagh conceded. 'How many films have you acted in?' 'Two,' was the candid reply. Evans cut to the chase: 'Do you think it's possible for you to do it?' 'Absolutely,' asserted Branagh, 'with your help.' In selling the idea to Evans, Branagh stressed the potential of *Henry V* as a popular film. Short scenes, a riveting linear plot, and the elements of action, humour and romance made Shakespeare's play about the military victory of a young English king over the French at Agincourt ideal for the big screen. Branagh and Evans clinked glasses. The plan had been hatched.

Exploring the origins and impact of the film of *Henry V* is crucial to understanding Branagh's rise to fame. It was the seminal event of his career. Prior to *Henry V* Branagh had been a presence in television and a rising force in British theatre. After *Henry V* Branagh was fêted with Oscar nominations, courted by Hollywood, splashed over the covers of *Time* and other prestigious magazines. With *Henry V*, he became an international star.

Branagh did not want *Henry V* to be his first movie of a Shakespeare play. Rather his heart was set on filming *Hamlet*, as David Parfitt confirms. The trouble was that with the Franco Zeffirelli *Hamlet*, starring Mel Gibson, already in the works, it would be impossible in the short term to gain the financial backing needed to make another *Hamlet*. So it was that Branagh turned his attention to *Henry V*. 'You're making a big mistake,' warned David Parfitt, who worried about the unflattering comparisons that would inevitably be made with Olivier's classic 1944 film of the play.

Branagh resisted such objections. He had long considered a film of *Henry V* feasible. 'Even in the days I was working on the play for voice classes at RADA,' Branagh has revealed, 'I thought that a film could be made. It has a cracking narrative, the visual possibilities are immense and it has a greater psychological depth than is often supposed. It is full of ideas – about politics – about war.'

This conviction had been fortified by Branagh's experience in 1984–5 of playing Henry V for the Royal Shakespeare Company. In that production Branagh had steered clear of a simplistic portrayal of Henry as a knight in shining armour. In the aftermath of Britain's war against Argentina over the Falklands, the battle against the French was depicted as more brutal and tragic than heroic. With large numbers of people coming to see the show, Branagh became convinced that a successful film of the play could be made. On leaving the RSC, he began to produce a mental 'storyboard' for the film. His conversation with Stephen Evans in 1987, therefore, was the culmination of years of intermittent consideration of the merits of *Henry V* as a movie.

Branagh's overall conception of the film, influenced heavily by Adrian Noble's RSC production, rested on two ideas. The first was the notion that this version must not be jingoistic. On a superficial level *Henry V* seems to be a hugely patriotic story: an heroic victory over the French against all the odds. Certainly Laurence Olivier's film of *Henry V* adhered to this line. In the context of World War II, Olivier's interpretation made eminent sense. At a time when patriotism and commitment to martial glory were moral requirements – necessary to defeat Hitler and to save Britain and indeed the whole of Western civilisation – a film of a great English military victory was a tonic to the nation.

In the Cold War era in which Branagh formulated his ideas about *Henry V* the notion of war as good was more problematic. Conflicts such as Vietnam had been messy not glorious, and the moral imperative behind them often questionable. In the nuclear age, furthermore, any war involving the major powers could spell the destruction of everything. Shaped by these post-World War II sensibilities, Branagh resolved to highlight what he identified as the anti-war aspects of the *Henry V* story.

In analysing the text, Branagh found ample evidence to support the idea that Shakespeare's play was as much about the dangers and the tragic loss of warfare as about the potential for heroism in military conflict. 'Pray take heed how you impawn our person,' Henry warns the Archbishop of Canterbury when soliciting his advice on whether to fight France, 'for never two such kingdoms did contend without much fall of blood.' 'There are few die well that die in a battle,' Henry is reminded by one of his soldiers on the eve of Agincourt. The horrors rather than the glory of war, then, would be one salient theme in Branagh's film.

The second was a subtle psychological exploration of leadership. In Olivier's film Henry came across as dashing, fearless, and inspirational – in short, a flawless hero. (It is interesting to note, however, that when first tackling the role on stage in 1937 Olivier himself was reluctant to play Henry heroically before being convinced otherwise by the director, Tyrone Guthrie.) Branagh's aim was to produce something more nuanced. He wanted to display in Henry 'the qualities of introspection, fear, doubt and anger which I believe the text indicated: an especially young Henry with more than a little of the Hamlet in him'. Branagh's Henry would be multi-faceted and self-critical. His guilt over his father's seizure of the crown from Richard II and over his own reckless past would be made clear, as would his piety and his concerns over the justness of his quarrel with the French. In his portrayal of Henry, three dimensions would be the aim, not two.

As well as exploring the ambiguity of war and the complexity of leadership, Branagh had one other, overriding objective – box-office success. His earlier career, particularly his decision to launch Renaissance, had been driven by the conviction that Shakespeare must not be regarded as the preserve of a cultural elite but should be accessible to all. The enthusiastic public response to the plays performed by Renaissance convinced him a potentially vast audience existed for a Shakespeare film that was genuinely entertaining. Before the opening of *Henry V* Branagh was candid about his commercial ambitions: 'I believe that it could be a truly popular film, that the audience that wants to see *Rambo III* could also be stimulated to see *Henry V*, not just because it's a splendid narrative that some people think is sort of *Boys' Own*, but because it's a very thought-provoking piece which says a lot in a complicated and ambiguous way, it seems to me, about war.'

Branagh's populist instincts shaped his view of the acting style to be adopted in his film. The declamatory, stylistically heightened traditional technique – an approach felt by Branagh to have alienated countless numbers from Shakespeare – was to be avoided at all costs. Instead he would insist that his cast sound naturalistic, real. 'What one is after', he explained, 'is an under-the-skin effect, whereby one astonishes people with how naturalistic the verse seems.' This outlook would inform other aspects of Branagh's film. His actors would not be wearing tights, and the haircuts would be contemporary rather than what to modern sensibilities seem the somewhat risible pudding-bowl style of Olivier's *Henry V*.

With the conceptual and stylistic approach of his film settled, Branagh turned his attention to practicalities: assembling a cast, securing a film studio, and – most important of all – obtaining the necessary financial backing. In order to move on these fronts, Stephen Evans advised Branagh, it was vital that a script for the film be written. At the start of 1988 Branagh typed away furiously, editing the text of the play and formulating stage directions. In order to ensure the commercial viability of his film, he resolved to produce a lean script, one that would result in a movie far shorter than his RSC *Henry V*, which had come in at over three hours.

With the first draft of the script finished in January 1988, Branagh's *Henry V* was up and running. It was only a rough draft, though, and would be much changed by the film's completion. For instance, in this first draft the film opens with the 'hollow crown' speech from Shakespeare's *Richard II* spoken as a voice-over as the camera pans along the English coastline before settling on the pensive face of Branagh's Henry. Originally Branagh had even thought of asking Olivier to do the speech, putting the idea to close friend and collaborator Richard Briers. 'No, no, love,' a sceptical Briers warned Branagh, 'he'll upstage you, love, before you've even started, no he'll nick it, love. He's had the first one; he'll have the second one.' Ultimately Branagh abandoned the whole idea of this opening scene.

Branagh succeeded in assembling an exceptional cast. For a first-time director, this coterie of acting talent represented a safety net. 'If I discovered that I couldn't direct on film,' he calculated, 'I would still have to go a long way to obscure the talents of this remarkable group.' By the start of 1988 Derek Jacobi and Judi Dench had agreed to play Chorus and Mistress Quickly respectively. Over the course of the year

Branagh gradually completed the cast, drawing heavily on two sources. The first was Branagh's own Renaissance company, the majority of whom were hired for the film. The second was the 1984–5 RSC production of *Henry V*. Brian Blessed reprised his role as Exeter, while Richard Easton would again play the French Constable. For Branagh, the benefit in dealing with actors with whom he had an established rapport was significant. As the period between the end of the Renaissance season in the West End and the start of filming for *Henry V* was a matter of days, the ease of communication and overall speed of work that a close-knit group of actors could provide would be essential.

Branagh supplemented the ranks of these actors with the cream of British theatre. Alec McCowen, Ian Holm, Robert Stephens and Charles Kay signed up. Perhaps the greatest coup of all for Branagh was that he persuaded Paul Scofield to play the French king. In the pantheon of theatre greats and winner of an Oscar for his performance as Thomas More in *A Man for All Seasons*, Branagh was in awe of the man but thrilled to have him on board. Though she encouraged him to choose someone else, arguing that a French actress would be more appropriate, Emma Thompson bowed to pressure from Branagh to play Katherine, the French princess. Not everyone succumbed to Branagh's charms. Ian McKellen, for one, declined to participate. Nonetheless he had succeeded in bringing together a strong cast.

As with the actors, Branagh looked to previous collaborators in assembling the crew. He hired those with whom he had worked on either the *Fortunes of War* series or *A Month in the Country*, including Tim Harvey as production designer and Ken MacMillan as director of photography. Branagh also surrounded himself with his own tried and trusted support unit in the form of Hugh Cruttwell and Russell Jackson. Cruttwell's main job would be to ensure that Branagh's responsibilities as director did not detract from the quality of his acting. Jackson would advise the cast on the text, alerting them to the rhythm of the language, places where they should pause, and sometimes the actual meaning of phrases. Together, Cruttwell and Jackson would strive to guarantee the technical proficiency of the performances. Branagh hired Patrick Doyle, who had studied at the Royal Scottish Academy of Music and Drama, and had already provided the music for Branagh's Renaissance theatre productions, to write the score. He would become a long-term Branagh collaborator, composing the music for many of his subsequent films.

Despite the assembly of a strong cast and crew, the shooting of *Henry V* could not proceed until the financing was in place. Branagh had originally told Evans that the film would cost £2.5 million. But once Bruce Sharman, recruited as the producer, used an accountant to calculate the sum more accurately, it turned out to be £4.5 million. The problem now was how to get it. This proved difficult, partly because of Branagh's status as a first-time movie director, and also because of the lack of time to arrange the finances – Branagh insisted that shooting begin at the end of October 1988, only two days after Renaissance completed its Shakespeare season in the West End. Evans hit a brick wall in his attempts to court the traditional providers of film finance. 'When they heard who was going to direct, the room would go quiet,' recalled Evans. 'When I admitted that he had never directed a film before, they would open the door for me.' Head of the British Screen Advisory Council Simon Relph, whose responsibility it was to dispense government funds for British films, was equally unsympathetic. 'He put forward the familiar arguments,' according to Branagh. 'The budget would overrun. It was a ridiculously ambitious project for a first-time director. No one would want to finance it, no one would want to be in it, no one would want to buy it and no one would want to see it.' Though civil at the meeting, Branagh later vented his fury: 'I was in a rage for days. I mean fuck! British Screen – *Henry V*! Use your fucking imagination. You couldn't have a better flagship. Take a fucking risk! I will finish the fucking thing on time. I won't go over budget.'

By June 1988 even Evans believed the financing could not be secured in time for shooting to start in October. After a Renaissance performance of *Much Ado About Nothing* in Manchester he urged Branagh to take a break after his theatre season ended in London, and to wait until the New Year to start work on the film. Performing in eight shows a week in the West End, argued Evans, was hardly conducive to proper preparation for the film. But Branagh disagreed. The public interest generated by Renaissance's theatre season, he contended, had to be sustained. Moreover, he was convinced that if the film were delayed it would never materialise. 'In the weird world of movies,' Branagh later explained, 'it would ensure that once people had enough time to think about its drawbacks, the film would never be made.'

Nor was Branagh deterred by the scepticism of David Puttnam, the celebrated film producer whose credits included *Chariots of Fire*. When, in the summer of 1988, Puttnam offered to ask Warner Brothers for money in return for the distribution rights in the United States, he emerged as a potential saviour of the project; but when Warner Brothers began to procrastinate, Puttnam decided that the film could not be made in the short term. He conveyed that view to Branagh in no uncertain terms: 'I'm sorry to have to say this, Ken, but it is my absolute belief that this film will not be made. I've been in this situation before. Every warning signal is flashing. I believe totally in you, and I believe totally in Stephen. What I don't believe is that you have enough time. With the best will in the world, and with the best skills in the world, it just will not be possible to do the paperwork in order to get this money into place.' 'I am convinced,' Puttnam concluded, 'that this film will collapse either two weeks before or two weeks after shooting begins.' Despite the caveat, Branagh remained resolute. Renaissance partner David Parfitt recalled the thrust of Branagh's response: 'Either it happens now, or it doesn't happen at all.'

In the end, Evans delivered the goods. First of all, the BBC put up £400,000 in exchange for the television rights. Curzon cinemas paid £300,000 for distribution. A Business Expansion Scheme generated additional finances. Evans also contacted old friends in the City, encouraging them to underwrite the film for sums of £100,000 and upwards. Still, it went down to the wire. At 10.50 a.m. on the very last day on which the deal had to be sealed if the money were to be released for shooting to commence on time, Branagh found himself at Shepperton Studios surrounded by eleven lawyers and with a wad of documents the size of a telephone directory. He signed everything put in front of him. 'I still don't know what I was signing,' admitted Branagh at the time of the film's release. 'I could be in slavery if this doesn't make money. I just signed anything to get the money.'

'Stephen [Evans] was absolutely fundamental to that [film] happening,' says David Parfitt. 'It could not have happened without him, whatever energy Ken had at this point.' But Branagh's role was important too. When the venture seemed on the verge of crumbling, he talked to Evans about mortgaging their properties to keep it alive – though it never came to that. Despite having to perform no less than eight shows a week in the theatre, right up to forty-eight hours before the start of filming, he somehow managed to attend countless meetings either to woo potential investors or to work on pre-production for the film. Drawing on his innermost resources of energy, driven by his belief in the potential merit of the *Henry V* project, refusing to be deterred by obstacles and detractors, he achieved his objective: to earn the opportunity to make a new film of *Henry V* before the year was out.

Stephen Evans would later pay tribute to Branagh's efforts. 'We felt like slitting our throats a couple of times,' he confessed, 'and I lost my nerve once or twice in putting it all together. But Ken is like a Henry V leading his troops into battle – he's a great enthuser.'

Rehearsals started on Tuesday, 18 October, at Westminster Cathedral Hall. As it was the one occasion when virtually the entire cast would be together, it was a vital opportunity for Branagh to make clear his ambitions for *Henry V*. In his directorial address he emphasised his desire to make a 'company' film, to foster an authentic team spirit. To convey a sense of the ambience he envisioned for the film, he played Patrick Doyle's demo tape of the stirring score. He also asked the cast for a read-through of the entire screenplay. 'The atmosphere', Branagh recalled of that day, 'was thick with a rare sense of occasion.'

The next few days were taken up with rehearsals. Even though he was able to schedule only one rehearsal of each scene, Branagh attached great importance to this. 'Rehearsals break down everyone's nervousness,' he once explained. 'It is a place to establish a trust and rhythm with the actors. You can settle all the arguments over interpretation and character before the cameras ever start rolling. For me, it is like putting a flame under things to get them hot, but not quite to the boiling point.' As he knew rehearsal time was limited, he was forthright and decisive in explaining to his cast exactly what he wanted.

At 7.15 a.m. on Monday, 31 October 1988, Branagh arrived at Shepperton Studios to begin shooting the film. Fifteen minutes later he went for his costume-fitting and make-up. By 8.30 he was on set, ready to start work. He had to be on his mettle. John Sessions, who played Macmorris, recalled the mood of expectation on set: 'The crew saw this whipper-snapper making his own version of a famous film and a lot of them were feeling, come on, then, let's see you.' The pressure was on in more fundamental ways too. Branagh had reached an understanding with Evans whereby he would be replaced as director if after a week he was behind schedule.

Branagh, however, rose to the occasion. He approached the filming of *Henry V*, as he himself put it, 'scene by scene and page by page. If I ever thought about the whole thing, I couldn't sleep.' Remaining on schedule, he completed the first scene of the conspiring clerics, played by Alec McCowen and Charles Kay, by midday. Come the afternoon Branagh was acting as well as directing, delivering his opening speech before the English court. Branagh finished work at 6.50 p.m. He had made it through his first day.

By the second day of shooting Brian Blessed was deflating any remaining tension with his larger-than-life personality and sense of humour. 'You can't direct for toffee, you big pouf,' he bellowed at Branagh. The entire cast and crew keeled over laughing. Filming continued to go well. Branagh had prepared very thoroughly and now that preparation was paying off. By the third day, Sessions recalls, he had won the confidence of a crew initially sceptical of such a young director. 'The whole unit were on an adventure and everyone was pulling together.'

Though Branagh was more comfortable and experienced as an actor than a director, it was the latter task to which he attached more importance in the making of *Henry V*. His chief interest was in shaping the film as a whole. 'If I'd had to give up one of them,' he revealed, 'I'd have given up the acting in it, because I wanted to decide the whole atmosphere. The whole attitude to battle, to the telling of the story, the historical detail – it all had to be of a piece.'

In assuming his responsibilities as director, Branagh had to draw on his previous screen work as an actor, which had been confined to various television dramas and two feature films. He had familiarised himself with the basic moves of the camera, and then used this information in directing *Henry V*. He made up for gaps in his knowledge simply by questioning. He would explain to the crew the effect he wished to create and then ask how they could help him achieve it. On other occasions he would delegate. If uncertain about how to make best use of the second camera unit, he would respond to queries from the unit's main operator about what to do with set-ups by advising, 'Anything you like, love. As long as it's exciting.' Certainly his direction found favour with the cast and crew. 'Ken's got the general's gift of being the man you automatically follow,' said Richard Briers. 'His instructions are clear, and he's positive he's right.'

Branagh pushed his team on through a punishing schedule. The opening English court scenes were followed by the conspirators' scene, the night-time shooting of the English siege at Harfleur, the English camp on the eve of Agincourt, the Boar's Head scenes involving Henry's old drinking cronies, the Battle of Agincourt itself, and the scenes of the French court. Branagh was resourceful as well as driven. As he approached the shooting of the Boar's Head scenes, in which the death of Henry's dubious mentor Falstaff is reported, he became convinced that a flashback scene involving Falstaff had to be inserted. This would make clear Henry's reckless past, his subsequent journey to maturity, and the sense of loss felt by the Boar's Head set on Falstaff's death. Having got ahead of schedule, Branagh went back to the *Henry IV* plays, quickly constructed a scene, persuaded the gifted Scot Robbie Coltrane to play Falstaff, and then shot the new segment. This flashback scene worked well, adding poignancy to the story.

Part of Branagh's success in directing *Henry V* was his understanding that with a cast of such experience and ability it was important at times *not* to impose himself, but simply to stand back and let things happen. Paul Scofield explains this in connection to his own performance as the King of France:

> He was for me an exemplary director, open to the impulses of his actors – for instance I was loth to follow the accepted view that my role was a half-crazed royal, but saw him as tragically worried to the point of neurosis. Ken accepted this reading without demur, and after careful consideration.
>
> He was remarkably concise in his methods of direction, sensitive to the balance and importance of each scene, and in the many scenes in which he was himself involved as an actor, he blended the necessities of both subjectivity and objectivity with truly amazing discretion and skill.[1]

Branagh was cutting the mustard on the acting as well as on the directing front. It would have been easy for him to allow his directing duties to diminish the focus he brought to his portrayal of Henry V, but his performance was powerful and subtle, technically assured and emotionally engaged. His friends believed that his acting on *Henry V* showed the depth felt by some critics to be lacking from his previous performances.

The responsibility of both acting and directing was exacting an immense personal toll, however. The stress afflicting him had escalated during Renaissance's theatre run, and peaked during the making of *Henry V*. 'He was appalling,' a friend revealed. 'He was completely exhausted. He became a monster – especially to those closest to him –

treating them totally thoughtlessly, almost cruelly.' Branagh himself has confirmed this: 'I was pretty close to a total breakdown. It was ongoing deep, deep thoughtlessness to the people around me, which was very wounding to them. Emma, particularly, suffered at the hands of it.' Despite Branagh's self-assurance, he harboured nagging doubts about his ability to get the job done on *Henry V*. The journalist, Al Senter, had been hired to write the production notes for the film. He recalls standing next to Emma Thompson on the set as they watched Branagh in the midst of directing a scene: 'I remember saying to Emma that Ken seemed full of boundless self-confidence, considering it was the first film he'd ever directed.' 'I wouldn't be so sure,' she replied.

Branagh's diary of the making of the film describes the anguish he felt during this period. After supervising the long tracking shot that powerfully records a contrite Henry carrying the corpse of the Boar's Head boy, played by Christian Bale, the entire length of the Agincourt battlefield amidst the carnage caused by his own ambition, a shattered Branagh returned home. 'Somehow defeated and, for no good reason, [I] burst into tears. I felt as if I had come back from the war.' By the end of the film, Branagh found himself quarrelling with his script supervisor over the most appropriate way to fold a map. 'What had happened to me?' a perplexed Branagh asked himself.

Fortunately for him, friends such as Brian Blessed were tolerant and supportive. But it was Emma Thompson who played the key role. Theirs was a relationship which had had its ups and downs, but her selfless support helped get him through this demanding period. She cradled him in her arms after each day's filming. On Sundays she would encourage him to rest, watch television, enjoy a good lunch. Emma, a grateful Branagh acknowledged, brought 'wisdom and understanding and peace and love and became the centre of my life'. The backing she gave him cemented their relationship. Since the making of *Fortunes of War*, they had been an item. But the period encompassing *Henry V* made Branagh appreciate the extent to which he had come to rely on her emotionally. This made the wooing scene in *Henry V*, when an uncharacteristically shy Henry tries to win the hand in marriage of the French princess, portrayed by Thompson, especially touching. Their playing of these prospective lovers was clearly enriched by the emotional realities of their own relationship. It was a case of art mirroring life.

The stress affecting Branagh during the making of *Henry V* did not prevent a strong sense of collegiality developing among cast and crew.

For his part, Branagh was struck by the high level of commitment and the quality of performance of his fellow actors. Robert Stephens's Pistol was definitive, he felt, and Robbie Coltrane's Falstaff was both comic and moving. Ian Holm, as Welsh Captain Fluellen, likewise impressed the director with his mastery of film technique.

Branagh was fascinated in particular by Judi Dench and Paul Scofield. He noticed how they both combined unassuming demeanours with exceptional acting. Dench, he wrote in his diary on the day of her first appearance on set, was 'nervous and vulnerable but, as always, ready to plunge in and trust her director and fellow actors'. When technical problems necessitated the reshooting of one of her scenes, she proceeded to deliver what Branagh felt was an even better performance.

Branagh greeted the arrival on set of Paul Scofield with unconcealed reverence. 'Enter Paul Scofield,' reads Branagh's diary entry for 9 December. 'If ever anyone was born to play kings, then it was this Titan, with his regal frame and haunted majestic face. I was more in awe of him than of any of the other legends working on the film, and yet he was the shyest of them all.' Scofield went on to give an impressively dignified performance as the French king. How he was later overlooked by the Oscars in the best supporting acting category is hard to fathom.

The respect Branagh felt for his cast was reciprocated. 'There is already something of the spirit of Henry's happy few in the cast and crew behind the camera,' reported the *Daily Mail*; 'every member of this film unit would go to the wall for Kenneth Branagh.' Prince Charles was able to observe this team spirit first-hand when he visited the set on 15 November. As patron of Renaissance, Charles was interested in the making of *Henry V*. Indeed one newspaper went so far as to describe Charles as 'the silent producer' behind the film. His involvement was significant. He gave Branagh special dispensation to film the Battle of Agincourt on royal land at Bodmin Moor in Cornwall, though it was ultimately decided to use an empty field at Shepperton. He put Branagh and David Parfitt in touch with Lord Brabourne, who gave them some tips on how to tackle the making of *Henry V*. And Branagh and Charles made sure there was a meeting of minds on the overall objective for the film. 'The Prince shares our view that this should be accessible and not museum Shakespeare,' revealed Branagh. 'He wants it to be the sort of film he can easily take his sons to when they are old enough.'

When Prince Charles visited the set, he took a look at the design department and watched some of the rushes of what had been filmed. That day Branagh reshot the soliloquy delivered by Henry the night before the Battle of Agincourt. Charles listened as Branagh repeated the speech until he had got it right:

Upon the King! Let us our lives, our souls,
Our debts, our careful wives,
Our children, and our sins lay on the King!
We must bear all. O hard condition,
Twin-born with greatness, subject to the breath
Of every fool ... What infinite heart's ease
Must kings neglect that private men enjoy! ...

It was reported that Charles wept openly. 'That speech was a very personal thing for Prince Charles,' Branagh explained. 'It is about the isolation of leadership and it is the emotional centre of the film.'

Charles chatted with Branagh at the end of the day's filming, emphasising his own backing for the project. True to his word, Charles kept close tabs on the making of the movie. In September 1989, a month before the film's release, it was reported that Charles had headed for his holidays at Balmoral with the original print of *Henry V* in his possession. The making of the film thus cemented the bond between Branagh and Charles. Apparently Charles even kept a photograph of Branagh in his rooms at Kensington Palace, and tried unsuccessfully to persuade the government of Margaret Thatcher to give Branagh a knighthood. Downing Street thought him too young for such a lofty honour.

With the support of patron, cast and crew, Branagh was set by mid-December to finish the film on schedule; but he felt ambivalent as the end of shooting approached. 'My insides were screaming out, "Only a few days to go,"' Branagh wrote in his diary on 14 December, 'but I also felt a growing sadness that this marvellous family atmosphere on the set was about to be broken up.' The following day Branagh had to bid farewell to the many members of the cast who had completed their parts, including Paul Scofield and Geraldine McEwan. The unit photograph was taken amidst feelings of euphoria. On 16 December Branagh journeyed to Beachy Head to shoot a Chorus speech delivered by Jacobi. The next day he indulged in a little Christmas shopping. Sunday, 18 December, was the final day of shooting. Branagh shot the Jacobi speech that would open the movie. Stephen Evans arrived to watch the final take. By 4.45 p.m. it was all over. Branagh had finished the film under budget, and in only seven weeks, a day ahead of schedule. It had taken Olivier eight weeks to film just the battle scenes. Jubilant but exhausted, Branagh celebrated with champagne.

With the shooting of the picture complete, Branagh's attention turned immediately to post-production issues. A mere five days after filming had finished, the editor, Mike Bradsell, was able to present a rough cut of the entire movie to Branagh, senior members of the crew, and a small group of Branagh's friends. They liked what they had seen. To be sure, the film was too long. From a running time of two hours and forty minutes, more than twenty minutes would have to be pruned, calculated Branagh. Sans soundtrack, moreover, the film had a rather stark quality.

Branagh attached great importance to the music for *Henry V*. He knew it could play a vital role in heightening the film's emotional impact on the audience, and in clarifying the meaning of the language. To ease Patrick Doyle's task, Branagh cast him as Court so that he would be more involved in the making of the film, invited him to Shepperton for the duration of the shoot, and allowed him to watch the daily rushes. Usually the composer becomes involved after the film has been made; but the alternative approach by Branagh and Doyle, in the words of the latter, 'gave me a unique insight into the characterisation, construction and requirements of the film'. This first-hand knowledge enabled Doyle to compose what Branagh wanted: a series of highly melodic tunes that were classical but not identifiably medieval in tone. Branagh was happy with Doyle's score: 'I intended the film to move people to every possible extreme of emotion, and what Patrick Doyle produced surpassed my wildest expectations.'

When it came to recording Doyle's music, Branagh turned to the best in the land. Simon Rattle, who had single-handedly transformed the fortunes of the City of Birmingham Symphony Orchestra (CBSO), was always Branagh's first choice; but he assumed Rattle would have neither the time nor the interest. A mutual friend managed to put the two men in touch, though. As things turned out, Rattle was very keen to come on board. A devotee of movies, he was excited by the prospect of entering, as he put it, 'a new, uncharted world'.

Rattle and the CBSO recorded Doyle's score at studios in north London in March 1989. John Sessions kept Rattle and his musicians entertained with an impression of Olivier as he would have been if cast in the television soap *EastEnders*, and of Pat Doyle reading the Bible in twenty seconds. Branagh, who also attended the recording sessions, was pleased with the results. 'I didn't know the difference between an orchestra and a great orchestra until I saw those people,' he explained. 'It was almost the most exciting part of the movie, the three days of recording the music.' Rattle and the CBSO did justice to Doyle's music, producing a powerful, passionate performance. This was important. Olivier had enlisted the services of the illustrious composer William Walton for his *Henry V*, and it was inevitable that the music of the movies would be compared.

As well as keeping an eye on the production of the soundtrack in early 1989, Branagh supervised the editing of the film. He reduced it from 160 to 137 minutes, making the film more commercially orientated in the process. To do so, he had to be ruthless in cutting some fine acting. Later on Branagh overheard Robert Stephens at a reception grousing about the fact that one of his major speeches had ended up on the cutting-room floor. 'Pay no attention,' an unapologetic Branagh declared. 'Scofield was cut. Emma Thompson was cut, so was Jacobi, so was Branagh. Why should Stephens complain?'

By the spring of 1989 everything seemed set for success. Then came Cannes. The backers of the movie felt that the Cannes Film Festival would be the ideal forum for introducing *Henry V* to the film world; and on 3 March a cut of the film was screened in Paris for the festival's director Giles Jacob. In what appeared to be a major setback, however, Cannes barred the film from its annual competition. It was rumoured that Jacob deemed a story about an ignominious French military defeat at the hands of the English to be inappropriate for a French film festival celebrating the bicentennial of the French Revolution. Another report claimed that this story was a canard, the real reason for the decision being that when Jacob first saw *Henry V* it was in its original, uncut form, and so did not seem ready for the festival. Either way, the press coverage back home did not help. 'Henry banned from the Cannes Festival,' boomed the *Daily Mail* in early April. The decision left Branagh crestfallen for a time. 'I remember thinking that my baby had just been born,' he recalled, 'and here it was being rejected at the first possible stage.'

Branagh and his backers were bruised but unbowed. They went ahead and screened the film at Cannes, outside the formal competition, for potential buyers who were impressed but worried about how to market it. Recalling their reaction, Branagh said, 'If a film is unusual – in other words, if it's Shakespearean, or foreign, or off-beat in any way; in fact, if it doesn't have Tom Cruise – the distributors get nervous about how they're going to sell it.'

Some British journalists caught *Henry V* at Cannes. Their mixed response was a portent of the reviews that would greet the film's official release in Britain in October 1989. The *Financial Times* described *Henry V* as 'disappointing' and 'dismayingly claustrophobic'. 'Worse still,' the article continued, 'one keeps suspecting that Henry's army is really a band of thirty-odd British actors rhubarbing away in a bid to persuade us that they are several hundred. We are not convinced. Good moments. A goodish Battle of Agincourt. Otherwise, once more unto the drawing board, dear friends.'

Alexander Walker of the London *Standard*, by contrast, used a pen dipped in honey rather than acid. 'Here and now,' he wrote, 'let me whet your appetite by saying that Kenneth Branagh, as star, director and producer, has achieved the most any mortal could hope for ... Branagh has bravely broken the spell that made us beware of all imitations. He has set his own boldly original version alongside Olivier's innovative breakthrough in filmed Shakespeare. He has dared us to judge him against that Imperial measure. That took guts. The result looks it.' Walker closed by lamenting the exclusion of *Henry V* from the competition at Cannes: 'If Henry V had been shown at Cannes, it would have done more than redeem our national cinema's absence from the main event. It would have confirmed that all Laurence Olivier taught us about filming Shakespeare has not been forgotten – only boldly revised to fit a crueller world of kingship and power, mercifully one still tempered by magnificently spoken poetry.'

By the summer of 1989 Branagh was poised to make a splash in the world of film. He had succeeded in creating an outstanding, accessible version of *Henry V*. The film's release was only a matter of months away. With it, he would show that his talent encompassed the cinematic as well as the theatrical medium. He *was* poised for a great success – but also for a backlash of staggering proportions.

4

Backlash

He could have been a national hero, a sort of Steve Redgrave for the performing arts. Prior to the release of *Henry V* Branagh had dazzled. He had won the top acting prize at RADA. He had shone in a West End hit, *Another Country*, while barely out of drama school. He had been the youngest actor in RSC history to play Henry V. He had been the youngest actor-manager of the century. When he filmed *Henry V* he was eight years younger than Olivier had been at the equivalent stage in his career. With the release of *Henry V*, he was garlanded with laurels: New York Film Critics' Best First Time Director, Chicago Film Critics' Best Foreign Film, European Actor of the Year, not to mention Oscar nominations for Best Actor and for Best Director. The speed and enormity of his accomplishments were breathtaking. Paradoxically, Branagh's achievements opened up a Pandora's box of complaints about his acting, directing, writing, ambition – even his appearance. 'The British press, bored with the Ken-worship it invented, has lately gone in for Branagh-bashing,' reported *Time* magazine in November 1989. Actually it was the English press. In Northern Ireland journalists took pride in his achievements, and in the Scottish media there was nothing comparable to the onslaught that was so in evidence south of the border.

The *Sunday Telegraph*, for instance, published an article entitled 'More deserving of heckle than of hype' in mid-September. In the same period Branagh was called 'wally of the month', Emma Thompson 'ET', and the couple 'a pair of spoilt brats'. While a sarcastic piece in the *Tatler* talked of 'Clever Ken, Confident Ken, Cocky Ken, Canny Ken, Calculating Ken and Campaigning Ken', the *Independent* carried a cartoon in which a teacher, pointing to the blackboard, instructed his class, 'OK, repeat after me ... Kenneth Branagh ... Kenneth Branagh.' In her *Daily Mirror* column, Anne Robinson ridiculed the decision of *GQ* to promote its magazine by announcing it would devote five pages to an article on Branagh. This, she maintained, was bound to reduce sales. The thoughtful title of Robinson's piece? 'Oh no – it's Bran...aargh!'

Taking the prize for the most gratuitous attack was politician Roy Hattersley. In a 23 September article in the *Guardian*, he constructed an article, the logic of which was elusive:

> Kenneth Branagh is, as far as I can tell, an engaging as well as talented chap, who holds radical opinions and plays football. He does, however, suffer from one terrible flaw. He is fashionable. By that I do not mean that in matters of food, clothing, motor cars and political opinion he follows the mood of the moment. He *is* the mood of the moment. He is in; the man of the year, the flavour of the month, the spirit of the age. In consequence, I find a raspberry irresistible. You may well argue, rational reader, that such an attitude is silly as well as self-destructive. Granted. But it is impossible to overcome.

What is striking is that these sorts of attacks, in 1989, were not, as one might assume, triggered by the release of *Henry V* in October. Many of them were made before the film had even opened.

As early as September 1989 there appeared articles not only bashing Branagh but reflecting on the bashing. On 9 September Peter Lewis noted in the *Sunday Times* that 'a good deal of knocking [of Branagh] has been heard. Sarcastic comments about "the greatest living Englishman" have taken the place of the equally gratuitous question, is this the next Olivier? It all sounds like another example of the English "too-clever-by-half" syndrome, the grudging suspicion of those who do too well.' 'Such is his fame', wrote Ian Christie of the *Daily Express* on 4 October, the day before the première of *Henry V*, 'that backstage murmurs of disapproval are now starting to be heard around the thespian parish.'

What factors explain the backlash against Branagh? Different people have different theories. Playwright, screenwriter and director Christopher Hampton highlights the media's need for narrative, and relates the phenomenon to his own experience:

> I think it's quite an English thing. People are perceived to be too big for their breeches ... They'll weigh in. Anyway it's a sort of automatic response, which I became familiar with very early on. My first play got wonderful reviews, then my second play, which was much, much better, got absolutely slaughtered. And it was

very, very puzzling because you thought, 'I know the play is better – how come it's got unanimously terrible reviews?' And the answer is because you're a journalistic item, and in journalism there's only two stories: he comes, he goes ... You just have to hope that eventually they'll say, he comes back.[1]

Julie Christie identifies an animus among journalists against Branagh's enthusiasm:

It's very British that, anti-enthusiasm, and Kenneth has all that in spades. He has enthusiasm and effusion and eagerness. That's not cool, being eager. Not to that mindset. [He has] terrific confidence, overwhelming confidence, and I think they only like confidence in sexy women ... and probably in blatantly macho men ... What surprises me about it most of all is that they [journalists] won't let themselves be seduced by him because he is so utterly seductive and deeply attractive ... The press sometimes do that; they absolutely gird themselves against charm, and in the business of girding themselves produce some sort of matter which is even more malevolent than it would be otherwise – in the reaction against this enormous charm.[2]

Distinguished director John Schlesinger maintained that the vilification endured by Branagh was the result of an ingrained cultural trait: 'I don't know why we sit on this island and look at each other with such great suspicion. It may have something to do with how we're brought up from the cradle with words like: "Don't get excited," and: "Don't get above yourself." And people who do get off their asses and do things, like Kenneth Branagh, are unpopular because of it.' Britain's most prolific playwright, Alan Ayckbourn, argues that Branagh's ability to do his work with apparent ease is significant. 'I think his problem – if problem it be – is that his talent is *effortless* and the British love to see their artists *working* for their success, preferably very hard indeed.'

My view is that a number of factors account for the attacks on Branagh. The first, as Schlesinger suggested, is what can be regarded as a traditionally English suspicion of success, a cultural trait that contrasts with the American ethos of cherishing ambition, drive and achievement above other attributes. This tendency to build people up and then knock them down is evident in other walks of national life, such as the sporting arena. In the case of Branagh, his career had always generated publicity, and especially so after the launch of Renaissance. But in the summer and early autumn of 1989 a cluster of developments – the promotion of *Henry V* as the release of the film approached, the opening of *Look Back in Anger* in the West End, his marriage to Thompson, and the publication of his autobiography *Beginning* – sent it rocketing to stratospheric levels. Anyone reading the press during this period could not fail to be struck by the avalanche of publicity not only about Branagh as an individual artist but also about his partnership with Emma Thompson. As a phenomenon they were the Beckham and Posh Spice of their day, *the* celebrity couple at the centre of popular culture. At a certain stage this publicity surge reached the critical point of overload, and the backlash inevitably followed.

In the months preceding the film's release, both local and national newspapers devoted a good many column inches to *Henry V*. A *Daily Telegraph* journalist waxed lyrical in July after catching a sneak preview of the film, and a *Daily Mail* article previewing the movies to come out in the autumn of 1989 dwelt most on *Henry V*. To whet the appetite of critics and film-goers, Branagh permitted a number of pre-release screenings of his movie. It was shown in Belfast in early June, and then at film festivals in Brighton, Birmingham and Dublin. All of these events received extensive coverage in the press.

Branagh's trip to the United States to promote the film likewise sparked media interest. On 19 July he jetted off with Emma Thompson to Los Angeles for what was ostensibly a well-deserved eleven-day holiday. The following day the *Daily Express* carried a big picture of the couple in relaxed mode at the airport. But the trip involved work as well as play. Meetings were scheduled with Hollywood moguls in order to interest them in what must have seemed a movie with slender commercial prospects. An exasperated Branagh found himself lecturing them: 'Why do people make films? What is the point, if everything you tell me suggests that I might as well not come out the door in the morning.' Reflecting a few weeks later on this encounter, Branagh tore into the film industry: 'There's crap being made left, right and centre and people lie through their fucking teeth, creating mythical rules as they go along about what will and won't work. I'd say to them: "What were you saying about [*A*] *Room With a View* at this stage? Were you saying, of *course* it'll be marvellous, of *course* people want to go and see an E. M. Forster story?" ... Of course, they bloody weren't.'

Branagh succeeded in securing an American backer for the film, nonetheless. It was announced that the Samuel Goldwyn Company had acquired all North American rights to the film. They were taken with the dark, brooding feel of the movie, and the basic story of a young, uncertain leader struggling to find maturity.

If the press coverage anticipating the release of *Henry V* was one factor behind the publicity surge partly responsible for the backlash, the second was the attention paid to his major theatrical venture in the summer of 1989: a new production of John Osborne's landmark play *Look Back in Anger*. Branagh had originally planned to direct Emma Thompson in Ibsen's *Hedda Gabler*, but jettisoned the idea as the scheduled dates clashed with the opening of *Henry V* in October. He did find time to redirect John Sessions in an expanded version of his one-man show *Napoleon*.

His main theatrical enterprise that summer, however, was tackling the role of Osborne's quintessential angry young man, Jimmy Porter. Originally performed at George Devine's Royal Court in 1956 with a cast that included a young Alan Bates, *Look Back in Anger* had been a path-breaking piece of theatre. Railing against his bourgeois wife, the hapless Alison, and much else besides, the character of working-class Jimmy Porter paved the way in British theatre for a new approach. As one observer has put it, Osborne 'achieved a revolution in attitude: theatre suddenly became a spitting-ground, a forum for bad manners, an excuse for breaking with the past and coming to terms with the mediocrity of the present'.

Branagh had long been interested in playing Jimmy Porter. Though the National Theatre had reportedly asked him to take on the role, he decided to do it with Renaissance, launching his own production of *Look Back in Anger* in June 1989. He recruited Judi Dench as director – an innovative choice, as she was associated with the classical repertoire, but a logical one, given the fine job she had done for Renaissance in directing *Much Ado About Nothing*. Emma Thompson would take the role of Alison Porter. All took place at breakneck speed, with the rehearsals lasting a mere seven and a half days. 'We were all reeling a bit,' Branagh admitted, 'but we went on with a lot of high-voltage adrenalin.' It played for five nights at the Grand Opera House in Belfast, raising more than £50,000 for the Northern Ireland Council for Voluntary Action and for the Ulster Youth Theatre, followed by one London performance in the presence of Prince Charles at the Coliseum, the profits from which went to the Friends of the Earth. No commercial West End run could take place, as Osborne strictly controlled the rights to the play. Having seen the

Coliseum performance in person, however, Osborne decided to permit a longer London run. Branagh's *Look Back in Anger* thus ended up playing for a month at the Lyric in the late summer, before moving on to Newcastle. It was also filmed for Thames Television, the broadcast taking place in August.

This theatre production became infamous for an incident that took place at the Lyric. When Branagh's Jimmy Porter was in the middle of a misogynistic diatribe, a woman in the audience got up and shouted, 'Absolutely disgraceful. This is disgraceful. The worst performance I've ever seen.' She then walked out. Observing the incident from his seat in the audience, David Parfitt immediately thought the disgruntled theatre-goer was a plant of some sort. He rushed from his seat and caught up with her in the foyer. 'I want to talk to you,' he said. 'Do you want your money back?' 'No, no,' she replied. 'I just have to leave.' To Parfitt, her response did not ring true. It confirmed for him his initial suspicion.

The episode elicited much comment in the press. The general view was that it had diminished Branagh. But all the attention given to this one incident obscured the fact that the initial reaction to the show was positive. Michael Billington of the *Guardian* said of Branagh's 'superb central performance': '[He] does not ask us to like Jimmy Porter. What he presents us with, unforgettably, is a man driven to madness by the unresponsive cool of those around him.' 'The great thing about Branagh's blistering performance', wrote Michael Coveney in the *Financial Times*, 'is that it works as a self-destructive comic turn.' Damian Smyth waxed lyrical in the *Independent*, saying Branagh had succeeded in developing 'a characterisation of sweet subtlety, with a large repertoire of gesture and intonation', and that the entire production had been commendably powerful. The *Daily Mail* and the *Daily Express* echoed these sentiments, with the latter referring to Branagh as 'the hottest young actor in Britain today'.

A common theme in the reviews was the success enjoyed by Branagh in highlighting the comedic aspects of the play. This reflected not only Branagh's vaudevillian instincts, but the advice he had received from John Osborne, who had sent Branagh and his colleagues a note encouraging them to play *Look Back in Anger* as a comedy. Perhaps the most appropriate final judge on the merits of Branagh's Jimmy Porter is Osborne himself. He regarded it as the finest since Peter O'Toole.

Branagh's marriage to Emma Thompson, as well as the imminent release of *Henry V* and the production of *Look Back in Anger*, fuelled the media blitz. He had proposed to Thompson in New York City, and she had accepted.

The next thing was to organise the wedding. Determined to avoid a showbiz media event, Branagh and Thompson did all they could to keep their plans under wraps. To that end, the press was fed misinformation. 'Yes, it's on,' Branagh told reporters in early August. 'It will happen by the end of September. It can't be any sooner because we are in the middle of a run [of *Look Back in Anger*].' The wedding ceremony, in fact, was set for Sunday, 20 August, whilst the play was still on.

As he approached marriage, Branagh hoped to find the contentment evident in his parents' relationship. 'My parents' marriage was an inspiration to me,' he explained, 'and the right kind of marriage gives the centre to your life.' He also viewed it as a salutary counterweight to his relentless professional drive: 'It is lovely to work and to accomplish things. But even *Henry V* does not comfort you if you are alone in the wee small hours of the night. Work is not the be-all and the end-all for me. It does not replace all the other things. You need someone else to be interested in. You have to protect yourself against the costs of self-absorption because otherwise you don't realise how selfish you may have become.'

While Branagh's hopes for his marriage were inspired by his parents' example, his conception of the wedding itself was on an altogether grander scale. At one point he and Emma Thompson considered having a modest, quiet wedding in order to make sure the paparazzi were kept away. In retrospect that would have been a good idea. But in the end they decided to splash out £30,000 on Cliveden House as the historically vibrant setting for their special day. Previously owned by the Astor family, it was where Minister for War John Profumo had met Christine Keeler in the scandal that had rocked the government of Harold Macmillan in the early 1960s. It was now operating as a plush Buckinghamshire hotel. The fact that the wedding service was to take place in a country mansion may have reflected Branagh's antipathy for the Church. Raised in sectarian Belfast, he had been appalled by its divisive impact on the community. 'I hate organised religion,' he once declared.

A few days before the wedding the press revealed the closely guarded twin secrets of the Cliveden location and the date of the ceremony.

But this did not prevent Branagh from enjoying his stag night. Meeting up with his mates at Jo Jo's, a Soho transvestite club whose drag artist Ruby Venezuela was popular with the theatre crowd, Branagh drank champagne until 3 a.m. The wedding day itself would provide glamour of a different sort.

It was estimated that as many as two hundred friends and relations attended the wedding ceremony. Ben Elton, Stephen Fry, David Puttnam and John Sessions were among the celebrity friends in attendance. Judi Dench and Richard Briers did the readings. Thompson's godfather, playwright and director Ronald Eyre, gave away the bride, who wore a knee-length, multicoloured dress. Brian Blessed served as best man. After the twenty-minute ceremony, guests feasted on a banquet of smoked salmon and roast lamb. Later on they went out to the terrace to enjoy a lavish firework display before returning inside to dance to a jazz band and disco. The feelings of bride and groom included relief as well as jubilation. 'I feel wonderful now it's all over,' revealed Thompson. 'It was very nerve-racking and was much worse than being on stage,' Branagh added, 'but much more fun.'

Despite their assiduous preparations, the couple's day did not pass without mishap. The National Trust, which ran the estate, refused to close the grounds to the public, thereby allowing a stream of day trippers to flock to the mansion. The wedding service had to be delayed for two hours as a result, and moved from the rose garden to the roof terrace.

It also transpired that at the end of the day's events Branagh and Thompson were not legally married, as the service had taken place in neither a church nor a registry office. The Reverend Malcolm Johnson, the rector of St Botolph's Church in Aldgate, London, controversial for his support of gay marriage, had agreed to perform the ceremony only after receiving assurances from the couple that they would get married legally anon. This they did a week after the Cliveden festivities, at Camden Town Hall. Still, for Branagh and Thompson it was the Cliveden ceremony that represented their authentic wedding day on an emotional level.

Professional commitments meant that the honeymoon had to be postponed. The couple spent their wedding night at Cliveden House, but the following afternoon had to return to London to resume their West End roles as Jimmy and Alison Porter. Bizzarely, Branagh and Thompson spent the evening after their wedding abusing each other publicly in the vilest terms. 'Yes,' Branagh observed, 'there was a moment when the oddity of the situation struck me – we'd had such a fantastic day, then there we were in full flow in *Look Back in Anger*. In a way, it was a wonderful discipline to do it.'

Despite being unable to escape the pressure of work, even as a newly-wed, the early days of his marriage provided Branagh with a rare period of genuine peace and contentment. In the days after his wedding he spoke of the desire brought on by his marriage for a quieter life, one where his marriage took precedence over his career. 'She's more important to me than my work,' he said of his wife. 'That's where my life is right now. And marriage has had a stabilising influence on me. It helps me keep the lid on.'

Such an obvious milestone could have brought about a period of salutary introspection. This did not occur, as the intensity of his professional life did not diminish in the months and years ahead. The Renaissance company diaries reveal the frenetic schedule he maintained. On 17 October 1989, for instance, he returned from Paris in the early morning, did an interview with the *Christian Science Monitor* at 10 a.m., saw Stephen Evans an hour later and Patricia Marmont at 1 p.m., held further meetings at 3.30 and 5.50, before dining with Richard Briers, presumably to discuss the forthcoming Renaissance production in which he would direct Briers as Lear. Juggling the demands of his career with the obligations of his personal life would continue to be a tricky matter.

His marriage to Emma Thompson generated immense publicity. Some of the comments by the press were to be expected. The obvious comparisons with Olivier and Vivien Leigh, and with Richard Burton and Elizabeth Taylor, were made. The nexus between the life and the art of the young couple was highlighted. Getting married was something for which they had ample preparation, it was observed, having played newly-weds in *Fortunes of War*, Jimmy and Alison Porter in *Look Back in Anger*, and Henry V and Princess Katherine of France as they became betrothed in Branagh's upcoming film. But much of the press coverage of the Branagh–Thompson union was uncharitable. Even before the wedding, knives were sharpened. 'Should he or should he not reward the nation's indifference,' a *Daily Express* article asked on 10 August, 'and announce his long-awaited engagement to the multi-purpose Emma Thompson?' Another publication was even more derisive: 'We trust that their own married life will not prove as boring as that of Guy and Harriet Pringle – the couple they play in the saga *Fortunes of War*.'

The reporting of the wedding itself was no less cutting. Much attention was given to the fact that the proceedings at Cliveden did not represent a legal marriage. Branagh and Thompson, it was suggested, had duped their guests and the British public. 'Our Phoney Wedding, by Emma' – the view articulated in *Today* – was representative of the tabloid coverage. The *Daily Mirror* not only pulled no punches but hit under the belt in an article published four days after the wedding: 'Even this clever-clogs couple came unstuck at the weekend. The shenanigans over their wedding will be remembered as the eccentricities of an immensely talented, superstar couple. They were the cavortings of a couple of spoilt brats. The joke is on them. Not on us. But then, perhaps we should have guessed it was [a] joke the minute we saw the wedding photographs ... I mean, did you see that dress?' The extensive and disparaging coverage of his wedding contributed to the sense that Branagh was hitting the headlines too often.

Following hot on the heels of the wedding was publication of Branagh's autobiography, *Beginning*. The superficial reason for writing the book was money, the underlying factor a determination to sustain the Renaissance Theatre Company. In early 1988 a small room in Branagh's Camberwell flat served as Renaissance's business office. Committed to moving the company into proper offices, and left to his own entrepreneurial devices in the absence of state subsidy, Branagh consulted his literary agent when Chatto and Windus approached him with the idea that he write a book. He decided to auction the idea of an autobiographical work with an emphasis on the development of Renaissance. No less than seventeen British publishing houses bid for the book. Chatto and Windus prevailed, offering Branagh a £50,000 advance. That sum did facilitate the acquisition of new offices.

Beyond funding Renaissance, an autobiography appealed to Branagh for other reasons. He relished the idea of displaying his versatility, and this provided him with the opportunity to be a man of letters, not just a star of stage and screen. He had already enjoyed writing plays for the theatre, a good sign for the work to come. In addition he thought a certain freshness would suffuse an autobiography written at twenty-eight rather than decades later. 'I didn't want to end up writing one of those books by seventy-year-old actors which are always a bit "lovey",' he explained. 'Besides, I thought it would be interesting to write about what it's like starting out as a young actor, as well as the things I'm doing now with Renaissance.' Branagh much admired *Early Stages*, a work written by a young John Gielgud, and this served as a model for his own book.

Writing his autobiography proved to be a mixed experience. On the one hand he found it therapeutic, forcing him to be uncharacteristically reflective. But the writing was also accompanied by a good dose of fear – fear as to whether he could complete the manuscript on time, and fear of revealing too much of himself for his own comfort. The stress was immense. 'Writing the book itself ... cost me my social life, my sleep, my normally OK temper,' admitted Branagh. 'By the end, I felt I was living on borrowed time. It was as if the blue touch paper had been lit and I might blow up at any minute.'

For the title of his book, Branagh turned to a trusty friend: Shakespeare. *Beginning* was culled from a passage he had noted in *As You Like It*: 'I will tell you the beginning, and if it please your ladyships you shall see the end, for the best is yet to do.' He toyed with the idea of adding the subtitle *Revelations of a Renaissance Man*, before thinking better of it.

With the manuscript complete and a title chosen, Branagh considered the likely reaction to his book. While he could not have expected the criticism of his wedding, he did anticipate the flak accompanying the publication of *Beginning*. He knew that writing an autobiography at only twenty-eight would appear inappropriate. 'I suspect the book will be savaged,' he told an interviewer. 'People will be asking: who the fuck does he think he is? I knew they'd bring it out the week before the film [of *Henry V*] opens. I'd rather not be set up as young Sir Kenny O'Lovey giving you his memoirs at the same time as he flogs his movie. It's like saying: can you take the piss now, please?'

Portions of *Beginning* were serialised in the *Observer* in late September, whetting the appetite of his fans. It was published in Britain on 28 September. To promote the book, Branagh did newspaper interviews, as well as talks and book-signings in London and Manchester. All this activity sustained the public interest that had engulfed Branagh since the early summer.

Then came the reviews. Some were gentle, with the *Sunday Times* finding Branagh's writing lively; but many were not. The *Independent* called *Beginning* 'a strange book', chiding Branagh for a lack of rigorous self-analysis: 'It is all agreeable, but a shade too conventional, as though real introspection might be dangerous.' The *Listener* was even less impressed. Though describing Branagh as a major talent, it derided him for believing his own hype, again for a paucity of self-analysis in the book, and for a decline in the quality of his acting since establishing Renaissance. The criticism that was part and parcel of life at RADA and the RSC was better for his acting, it was argued, than was the 'ego-massaging ambience of Renaissance'. Nothing, however, could match the vitriol of *City Limits*:

The introduction describes this as 'a story of a particular talent': why invite someone else to contribute a preface when you can shamelessly eulogise yourself? Completely written by, and completely concerned with, Kenneth Branagh, *Beginning* is a book infused with self and vain conceit.

Reeking of self-promotion, this is the book most actors wait until they are nearly dead to write. Indeed, as mediocre memoirs go, it is rather unsatisfying, since someone who is interested in no one but himself makes a poor storyteller. The tone throughout is one of a self-deprecation which you are not to take seriously, concealing huge arrogance, but equally vast insecurity.

Few people can make the process of acting or directing seem so dull.

Nor were the reviewers the only ones to take umbrage at Branagh's literary efforts. Trevor Nunn, joint artistic director of the RSC during Branagh's stint with the company, was very vexed. In *Beginning* Branagh told the story of his alienation from the RSC hierarchy, including his disappointment at the detachment of Nunn, who had taken a sabbatical at the time. Included was an account of a meeting between Branagh and Nunn shortly after a performance of *Henry V*. According to Branagh, a fawning Nunn declared passionately that he had found the performance '"Huuuuuuuuuuuuuuuugely enjoyable".' When this record of events was included in the *Observer*'s serialisation of *Beginning*, Nunn retaliated. He penned a letter to the newspaper alleging that Branagh's account was largely inaccurate. 'Instead of giving him the obsequious adulation he recalls,' wrote an indignant Nunn, 'I spoke about his achievement in the context of the two previous performances of the role I had most admired.' He concluded his letter sardonically:

As more extracts from *Beginnings* [*sic*] appear, I imagine many of Kenneth's professional colleagues will discover that they must share the collective guilt of having held him back; and many more will make sure they don't do so in the future because they will wind up in his life story Part 2.

Now that Part 1 is out of his system, perhaps the 'extraordinary and genuine humility' he attributes to the Prince of Wales will be a quality he can find in himself.

Onlookers were intrigued by the spectacle of these two robust personalities locking horns. 'The fight among two unequals is mesmerising theatre people,' reported the London *Standard*. 'One RSC faction insists that Branagh was right to criticise Nunn's lofty distance from the company. A larger group point out that Nunn's contribution to the stage vastly outweighs Branagh's, and that the actor's main grievance seems to be that Nunn did not rate him highly enough.'

For all the criticism it provoked, *Beginning* succeeded on a number of fronts. It was highly readable and breezy. The account of Branagh's early years in Belfast was written with genuine affection, and its character sketches of prominent personalities in British theatre were colourful. An authorial guardedness prevented it from being truly revelatory, and it lacked the intellectual depth of, say, Antony Sher's masterful 1985 study *Year of the King*; but *Beginning* did explore some important issues, particularly the growth in the power of non-acting directors in the theatre. Ultimately it achieved its objective: to keep the Renaissance Theatre Company afloat.

For a variety of reasons, then, Branagh received extensive media coverage during the summer and early autumn of 1989. A much-awaited film due for release, a hit West End play, marriage, the publication of an autobiography – any one of these by itself would have guaranteed attention. But the four together meant that coverage of Branagh became saturated. For some of those ill disposed towards the rising star, he was hitting the headlines too often; and the feeling developed that he needed to be taken down a peg or two.

Another factor was the hostility caused by Branagh's apparent attempt to seize the mantle of Laurence Olivier as Britain's greatest actor. From the early days of his career, critics had spoken of Branagh as a possible heir to Olivier. But when the news broke that Branagh was making a film of *Henry V*, just as Olivier had done, the comparisons multiplied. They would not have to the same degree had Branagh filmed any Shakespeare play other than *Henry V*. Despite the cluster of Shakespeare films associated with Olivier, as star or director and star – *As You Like It*, *Hamlet*, *Richard III*, *Othello* – it was his *Henry V* that had made the greatest impact on the public and on the critics. It truly established Shakespeare as credible film-making material and sealed Olivier's reputation as a great artist. In filming *Henry V*, therefore, Branagh made it inevitable that parallels would be drawn with Olivier. And so they were, again and again during 1989. The

Observer described Branagh as the 'new Olivier', the *Sunday Times* as 'pretender to Olivier's throne', while the *Sunday Mirror* wrote that he was 'widely hailed as the new Olivier'. Some believed that this obsession with searching for new Oliviers, evident in the sort of attention paid previously to the likes of Peter O'Toole, Albert Finney, and Ian McKellen, was a fatuous national exercise. 'Bring down the curtain on calling Ken the next Olivier,' urged a *Daily Express* journalist in mid-August. 'The notion of the "next Olivier" really is very silly,' he insisted, 'though Branagh has not exactly helped to distance himself from it.'

Fatuous or not, the comparison with Olivier invited by the new film contributed to the backlash against Branagh. In part this was because Olivier's *Henry V* had acquired a special cultural and political significance in Britain. With its lush romanticism and a visual gorgeousness to match the gorgeousness of Shakespeare's poetry, the patriotic resonances of Olivier's *Henry V* have echoed down the years. Made during World War II, and with input from Winston Churchill himself, Olivier's film had been part artistic venture, part propaganda. Elements of the play reflecting ill on England, such as the treason of Henry's nobles and his cruel threats to the Governor of Harfleur, were cut. Olivier's story of an heroic victory against all the odds was a tonic to the nation, and its timing, released as it was in 1944, the year of the D-Day landings, when the British and their American allies began to push Hitler's forces in France back towards Germany, was perfect.

Olivier's version became no less than an important strand in the tapestry of British patriotism. Challenging it, as Branagh appeared to do by making his own, thus appeared unpatriotic, equivalent to throwing eggs at the Queen or burning the Union Jack. Branagh's perceived lack of respect for what had become Britain's cinematic national anthem was enlarged by the justification he gave the press. Time and again in 1989 he was asked why make a film version of *Henry V* when it had been done so well by Olivier. To answer that question Branagh had to identify weaknesses in the Olivier film – its jingoism, the lack of naturalism in the speaking of the verse, the failure to explore the psychological complexity of Henry. He told *Vogue* magazine, for instance, that Olivier's *Henry V* did show the great man 'at his best and deserves its classic status as a piece of pioneering film-making. But the movie is resolutely of its time, reflecting values, politics and even acting styles that have undergone great shifts. I was convinced that a screen *Henry V* for the nineties and beyond must reflect our very different world ... A political thriller that eschewed historical pageantry and presented a gritty blood-stained campaign,' Branagh continued, in explaining how his version would differ from Olivier's. 'A complicated and ambiguous debate about war that could endow the central character with some of the Hamletian despair that Olivier's hero could not portray in wartime Britain.' Compelled to justify himself, Branagh made what could be construed as disrespectful criticisms of Olivier's patriotic masterpiece.

Contesting the merits of a film regarded as sacrosanct was one reason why Branagh's *Henry V* ruffled feathers; challenging Olivier himself was another. It was not difficult for observers to believe that making the film was a deliberate attempt by Branagh to seize Olivier's crown; and this was viewed as no less than an assault on a national institution. *Henry V* had made Olivier a symbol of England, and the consensus among critics was that he had been the finest actor of the century, perhaps any century. He stood with Richard Burbage, David Garrick, Edmund Kean and Henry Irving in the pantheon of acting greats, the men who had dominated an age and had passed on the Shakespearean baton from the Bard's own day to the present. This esteem for Olivier meant that any attempt to usurp his crown would be met with scorn.

What happened on 11 July 1989, however, served to enlarge both respect for Laurence Olivier and disdain for any pretender to his throne. For on that day Olivier, having endured a terrible sequence of illnesses, including cancer, pleurisy, pneumonia and thrombosis, passed away in his sleep at his home in West Sussex, surrounded by family and friends. He was eighty-two years old. At his funeral three days later, in Ashurst, West Sussex, the mourners included Alec Guinness, John Mills, Douglas Fairbanks Jnr, and Maggie Smith. Elizabeth Taylor sent the largest bouquet of flowers, along with a simple message, 'Adieu'. Anthony Hopkins, who had recently been the lead in *King Lear* at the National's Olivier Theatre, read from the play. After the service Olivier's body was cremated.

While the funeral was a private affair, plans were made for a public celebration of Olivier's life. A memorial service was set for Westminster on 20 October. A mood of frenzied expectation developed as the event approached. Newspapers reported that touts, who could apply for the seats set aside for the public in the Abbey, were planning to charge £500 for a ticket. By late August the London *Standard* was reporting that the memorial service was 'rapidly becoming The Greatest Show on Earth'.

The day itself lived up to expectations. Distinguished actors who had collaborated with Olivier processed with souvenirs from his career. Michael Caine carried Olivier's Oscar for Lifetime Achievement, Paul Scofield a replica of the National Theatre, Derek Jacobi the crown worn by Olivier in *Richard III*, while Peter O'Toole bore Olivier's script for *Hamlet*. A eulogy from Alec Guinness and readings by John Gielgud and Peggy Ashcroft added lustre to the occasion. The Dean of Westminster announced that Olivier's ashes would be interred alongside those of Henry Irving and David Garrick, fittingly only a few feet from the grave of King Henry V.

The theatrical world reacted to Olivier's demise with intense grief. On the day of his death the National Theatre replaced its huge advertising lights on the Thames with a sign, visible for miles, reading simply: 'Laurence Olivier, 1907–1989'. West End theatres switched off their outside neon lights for an hour as a mark of respect. Actress Felicity Kendal wept openly as she and other cast members of a production of *Much Ado About Nothing* paid their respects to Olivier. In Stratford-upon-Avon the flag at the Royal Shakespeare Theatre flew at half-mast.

Outpourings of praise as well as grief accompanied Olivier's death. Michael Caine remarked that Olivier was 'great in all things that he did – acting, directing, theatre and film. He was a unique man and undeniably irreplaceable.' Peter Hall, the man who had succeeded Olivier as artistic director of the National Theatre, was even more rhapsodic: 'It is not too much to say that Larry Olivier was perhaps the greatest man of the theatre ever. He was a great actor, a great film director and a great impressario. His genius shaped the last fifty years.' The press no less than the theatrical community remembered Olivier by glorifying his name. 'The death of Laurence Olivier', asserted the *Daily Telegraph*, 'robs British theatre of its greatest actor, and the theatrical profession of its most resounding name.' The *Daily Mirror* went further: 'The greatest actor the world has ever seen.'

With the passing of such a titan, the question arose as to whether there was a worthy successor in the land. Writing in the *Guardian*, Michael Billington identified a cluster of actors who possessed many of Olivier's virtues, but acknowledged there would probably never be anyone with his technical ability or his capacity to see himself as a symbol of the nation. This group of actors, Billington argued, included Ian McKellen, Antony Sher, Anthony Hopkins, Derek Jacobi and Michael Gambon. But the actor judged by Billington to be most reminiscent of Olivier was Branagh:

> If any one actor has recently proved that the Olivier spirit is not dead it is surely Kenneth Branagh. At the age of 28 he has already formed (with David Parfitt) the durable-looking Renaissance Theatre Company, directed, starred in, and adapted a film version of *Henry V* and written his autobiography. Branagh told me recently that as a teenager he was given a set of back numbers of *Plays and Players* and used to pore over every detail of the golden Olivier years at the National. It was that, as much as anything, that led him into a passionate awareness of what he calls 'the great tradition' in British theatre.
>
> There is however another, little noted, respect in which Branagh follows in Olivier's footsteps. Sybil Thorndike once said perceptively of Olivier that 'he is a comedian by instinct and a tragedian by art'. I suspect the same may be true of Branagh: the best performances I have seen him give to date are his incredible cheeky chappy, Cockney wide-boy Touchstone and his Jimmy Porter in which authentic pain was blended with a vaudevillian sense of comic timing.

While Billington was prepared to speak of Branagh as a credible successor to Olivier, others were not. The general sentiment was that it had been hubristic of Branagh to imply that he was the next Olivier by making *Henry V*. 'Should "Sir" Ken, as he is flippantly known in theatrical circles, lay claim to the throne vacated so recently by the sad demise of Laurence Olivier?' asked the *Daily Express*. 'Some of Branagh's colleagues are wondering if this is the diplomatic time for him to release his film of Shakespeare's *Henry V* as a successor to Olivier's version.' At Olivier's memorial service Alec Guinness declared: 'Sometimes we have read in the press of a young actor being hailed as "a second Olivier". That is nonsense, of course, and unfair to the actor ... there may be imitators, but there is no second Olivier. He was unique.' Decoded, that statement could be taken as an attack on Branagh.

This resentment of Branagh's apparent attempt to be acknowledged as the new Olivier can only, therefore, be fully understood in the context of Olivier's death, for it heightened reverence for Olivier and distaste for putative successors. The extent to which harsh assessments of Branagh were linked to the worshipping of Olivier would become clearer with the reviews accompanying the release of *Henry V* in October 1989.

In the end, the critics proved to be more obsessed with Olivier than was Branagh. With some of them attacking him simply for attempting to make *Henry V*, regardless of its artistic merits, one would have thought it was Olivier's play not Shakespeare's. As Branagh himself argued, it is a given in the theatre that new productions of Shakespeare plays that have been done well in the past should be staged. No one was criticising Daniel Day-Lewis for playing Hamlet, Branagh remarked, just because it had been done before. If this were true for Shakespeare on stage, then surely it was also the case for Shakespeare on screen.

What might be called the Michael Caine factor was another possible reason for the backlash. Defenders of Branagh often suspected that one cause of Branagh-bashing was class, that coverage of him had been biased because of his humble origins. It could be argued that his geographical as well as his social background was relevant: he was not only working-class, but Irish working-class.

It was Michael Caine who, in February 2000, drew attention to this issue. In a remarkable interview with *The Times* he claimed to have been mistreated in Britain, especially by the press, though revered in America. The root cause of this phenomenon, Caine alleged, was class. 'I'm every bourgeois' nightmare,' he asserted. 'A Cockney with intelligence and a million dollars. They think they should have done it – but then why didn't they, if they were so much smarter and more intelligent than this stupid Cockney git? So their revenge is to say, "He's not a real actor, he's a Cockney actor." It's like calling Tony Hopkins a Welsh actor or Sean Connery a Scots actor. Why am I a "Cockney actor" and they are just actors?'

Nor did Caine let the matter rest there. Two months later he returned to the subject when receiving a British Academy of Film and Television Arts (BAFTA) Fellowship for Lifetime Achievement, only days after winning an Oscar for Best Supporting Actor for his performance as a kindly doctor in *The Cider House Rules*. At the BAFTA ceremony in London Caine stunned the audience by rounding on the British film industry:

> I have never really felt that I belonged in my own country and in my own profession. I have been what's known as a loner. I became an actor in a youth club in South London. I never went to drama school – not because of any snobbery but because I came from a section of the community that never knew that there was such a thing as a drama school.

> I had an awkward voice and a duff accent when people were writing plays about chaps coming through French windows in cricket jumpers shouting, 'Bunty's having a party,' so my life in the theatre was extremely turgid, as I didn't master those accents and play those parts.
>
> It's an honour to be invited in from the cold by an organisation as illustrious as the BAFTA. It is a great honour for me. It has been cold out there; maybe I will feel more welcome in my own country than I have up until now.[3]

Caine's outburst triggered a lively debate on class. Jane Horrocks, the multi-talented Lancashire-born actress who had starred with Caine in the film *Little Voice*, leapt to his defence. 'There is a lot of snobbery in the British film industry,' she insisted. 'A lot of people in the lower classes are all ignored. Juliet Stevenson, Judi Dench and Maggie Smith will always get the nominations and the awards. That isn't to say they don't deserve it, but it is much easier for them.' Bob Hoskins agreed: 'There is still a class aspect in this country. It is ridiculous. The industry is so full of lunatics. The Americans show much more respect to Michael and I.'

Branagh himself never concealed his working-class background, discussing it with pride in interviews with the press. 'I remain steeped in a working-class Protestant Belfast philosophy,' he told a journalist on one occasion. Enlarging Branagh's working-class image were his allegedly left-wing political views. It is difficult to speak with certainty on this issue, as Branagh was no Vanessa Redgrave in wearing his political heart on his sleeve. Periodically, however, he made statements suggesting that he was left-wing. In July he told the *Tatler* that he had not only refused to permit publication of his autobiography in South Africa but had allowed it to be serialised in the *Observer* even though the *Sunday Times* had offered twice the money. He also revealed to the press his distaste for organised religion, and for the 'everyone-for-himself mentality' of Thatcher's Britain. He would go on to reject a CBE in 1994, thereby showing his aversion to the honours system. In September 1989 the *Sunday Telegraph* linked Branagh's political inclinations with the interpretation of *Henry V* in his forthcoming film: 'Mr Branagh is said to be a supporter of the greens, and one theory is that he will somehow create a green Henry. It will be interesting to see how he does it. Mr Branagh is also said to have pro-CND leanings. It will be even more interesting to see whether he will set about making Henry a pacifist.' What this article had picked up on was that the anti-war theme of Branagh's *Henry V* was consonant with his political views. This sense of Branagh as a radical was accentuated by his relationship with Emma Thompson, well known as a left-wing activist. As early as 1983 she had participated in a Reagan Out CND rally in London.

Magnifying Branagh's proletarian image further was his quest to make Shakespeare accessible to as many people as possible, rather than accepting it as a middle-class entertainment. With *Henry V*, for example, he had no qualms about expressing his hope that it would attract the fans of Sylvester Stallone. 'I don't like anything that rounds home this class superiority,' he asserted, 'including the appropriation of certain types of art or culture.'

Did class bias mean that Branagh's background and artistic objectives offended the sensibilities of some onlookers? It is impossible to prove the point. Still the suspicion persists. In a *Daily Mail* article in October 1989 Geoffrey Levy insisted that class was an important factor behind the backlash. All of Branagh's accomplishments, he argued,

> might just be acceptable if the young Branagh carried the princely air of a young Olivier, for we must not delude ourselves that 'class' (even of the assumed variety) doesn't still play a major role in British life.
>
> But outwardly Branagh is such an ordinary bloke, coming from the back streets of Ulster by way of Reading, Berks. Overweight, untidy, spotty. You see people like him every day standing at bus stops.
>
> Ordinary people, particularly those who, like Branagh, make a point of reiterating their ordinariness, are expected to know their place. They are not expected to create a whirlwind in a well-ordered society.

The emphasis in the press on Branagh's background suggests that class was a factor in its coverage. This becomes apparent from the relative perspective of the treatment by the American media of its stars. As one observer has noted, in the United States 'No one can place Tom Cruise or Julia Roberts and no one would try: do they come from Iowa or Atlanta or New Mexico or Duluth? Where did they go to school? Who knows? Who cares?' By contrast, 'The British like to be able to place people and once they start they won't let up.' This proved to be the case with Branagh, with virtually every article on him emphasising his Belfast working-class origins. The counter-argument to this line of reasoning would be that a good many working-class actors, such as Tom Courtenay and Roger Moore, have been successful without enduring the treatment meted out to Branagh. The key difference, however, is that unlike any other working-class actor in the twentieth century Branagh became the chief possessor of the Shakespearean tradition in the public mind; and this seemed to grate with those who perhaps regarded Shakespeare as a middle-class preserve. The other difference between Branagh and most other actors, as theatre critic Michael Coveney perceives, is that 'they haven't set themselves up, as it were, as a leader of their profession in the way that he has'. It is reasonable to conclude that class, to a degree impossible to calculate, did play a role in changing attitudes towards Branagh.

Whatever the origins of this change, having his reputation kicked around like a football left Branagh perplexed. At times he brushed aside the criticism with apparent ease. His skin was thick, he would point out; he had anticipated the backlash, and he would not allow 'uninformed resentment' to bother him. He also believed or hoped the attacks would prove ephemeral. 'They can go off and build somebody else up [now],' he stated. 'And I can get on with my work.'

The criticism, though, did hurt deeply; and in October 1989 Branagh began to fight back. 'I haven't gone around saying I'm the new Olivier, nor would I,' he declared. 'I've just read a[n] article from somebody saying, "Who does he think he is?" and this was a person who had written six months ago, "It's only a matter of time before he deservedly becomes Sir Kenneth Dah-De-Dah." It was a graphic example. It says more about the desire for heroes than it does about any poor sod who gets stuck with it.'

The sense of being under siege did not diminish the genuine thrill felt by Branagh at the time of *Henry V*'s release. The première, which took place on 5 October at the Odeon Cinema, Leicester Square, was a glittering occasion. Prince Charles, as patron of Renaissance, attended, as did other luminaries. The next day pictures of Branagh and Emma Thompson in conversation with Prince Charles were splashed over the newspapers.

Given the slings and arrows he had suffered prior to the release, Branagh feared the worst as the reviewers got to work. As things turned out, the critics were divided. Some hailed Branagh's film a masterpiece, some judged it a disappointment, others felt ambivalent. Whatever their position in this spectrum of opinion, reviewers showed their fixation with Olivier, as they invariably used his 1944 film as the benchmark for assessing Branagh's.

Alexander Walker of the London *Standard* lavished praise on Branagh's efforts, as he had in the spring after attending a Cannes screening of *Henry V*. Branagh 'carries it off magnificently', he enthused. 'This is a production that runs on a young man's adrenalin as well as a scholar's imagination. If it has less chilly aristocracy than Olivier's, it has more, much more physicality. It is steeped in blood, battle mud and realism.' Olivier's throne 'may still be vacant', Walker concluded, 'but the claimant has announced his arrival.' Though less ecstatic, Derek Malcolm of the *Guardian* was impressed too. The cast was generally excellent, he thought, and though Branagh's was 'perhaps not a great performance ... it is a good and fresh one that will last the test of time as any portrayal on film has to. It is of the earth rather than the air (which is the opposite of Olivier) but more or less rock solid.' Hugo Davenport of the *Daily Telegraph* objected to the hype surrounding Branagh, but still regarded *Henry V* as 'a considerable achievement'. In the *Mail on Sunday* Tom Hutchinson argued that the film was 'as definitive for our time as Olivier's was for his'.

Other reviewers were less convinced. David Robinson eschewed judgement in *The Times*. While commending the cast's naturalistic style of acting, he said Branagh's own performance was 'entirely a matter of taste'. Some pundits were more negative. Branagh's *Henry V* did not 'hold a flambeau to Olivier's', contended Nigel Andrews of the *Financial Times*. He berated Branagh's performance, essentially, for not being like Olivier's:

> When not out-braying Olivier or delivering (his best moment) a moving 'O God of battle, steel my soldiers' hearts,' he proves a curiously anodyne screen presence. Blond-mopped and doughy-featured, he resembles – Nature's fault not his, but one magnified on screen – a schoolboy who has eaten too many buns during the tuck-box break. Shorn of Olivier's physical charisma and reserves of sullen, glowing mystery, Branagh tries to compensate with a pugnacious modernism. But all one feels is a talented adjutant desperately grabbing at officer status.

In the *Sunday Telegraph* Christopher Tookey wrote in a similar vein, believing the film suffered by comparison with Olivier's. '*Henry V* is a movie for those who don't like movies,' he concluded. 'But it will not have much impact on sections of our population which have not yet succumbed to Branaghmania.'

Tookey's review prompted an angry riposte from Paul Olliver of Shepperton Studios. 'Has the *Sunday Telegraph* sunk to the tabloids' standards, joining in the British disease of knocking successful people?' Olliver asked in a published letter to the newspaper the following week. He accused Tookey of being obsessed with Olivier's film, and of being 'motivated by dislike of Emma Thompson and Kenneth

Branagh'. What Olliver implied was that the mindless Branagh-bashing evident prior to the release of *Henry V* was continuing now that the film had opened. In his response Tookey said Olliver was being naïve if he did not think Branagh was deliberately courting comparisons with Olivier's film. As an artist, he claimed, Branagh was not in the same league as Woody Allen, never mind Olivier.

Henry V did reasonable box office for a film of its type, despite the mixed reviews. A week after its première the *Guardian* reported that it had 'opened in London to huge audiences at Mayfair and West End Curzons, where advance bookings are easily a record'. In its first week it made almost $100,000 from those two screens alone. When it opened around the country, it did particularly well in towns where the Renaissance Theatre Company had played. However, a tactical mistake was made: its initial release was limited, and by the time it went wide to a greater number of screens the buzz of the opening weekend had died down. A wide-scale release on the opening weekend would probably have made a substantial difference to its commercial success in Britain. That mistake would not be repeated when *Much Ado About Nothing* was released four years later.

Henry V, regardless of its impact at the box office, was an exceptional film and the most important achievement of Branagh's career. Other directors, including Olivier, Orson Welles and Franco Zeffirelli, had made major contributions to the development of the Shakespeare film. My view, however, is that Branagh's *Henry V* is the outstanding example of the genre. For one thing, it was a milestone in terms of its naturalism, and this accounts for its ability to connect with a modern audience. Branagh had established as one of Renaissance's guiding principles a commitment to an absolute clarity when speaking the verse. In terms of stage performance, this was not exactly a new development: actors at the RSC had not spent the 1980s turning in hammy performances. But in terms of cinematic Shakespeare Branagh's claim to an unprecedented naturalism was more than just rhetoric. In a relative sense, previous Shakespeare films did seem stagey. Compare, for instance, Paul Scofield's King of France and Ian Holm's Fluellen in Branagh's film to the performances given by their counterparts in Olivier's, Harcourt Williams and Esmond Knight. Of course there were other Shakespeare films more naturalistic than Olivier's *Henry V*. Nonetheless, Branagh's was path-breaking for the way it offered its audience performances that were realistic, truthful.

The film was also special in terms of the balance it struck between text and visual image. In the making of Shakespeare films, this has always been the key issue: the extent to which fidelity to Shakespeare's language should be honoured, and the degree to which the exciting visual possibilities offered by cinema should be explored. Different directors have handled the visual–textual conundrum in different ways. In his 1996 version of *Romeo and Juliet* with Leonardo DiCaprio, Baz Luhrmann fashioned a fast-paced, visually dazzling interpretation of the play. It functioned almost as an extended pop-music video, a feeling accentuated by its use of contemporary songs in the soundtrack. It was clever and original, but the sense of the textual complexity and poetic beauty of what Shakespeare had written was limited.

Welles, too, veered towards a similar approach albeit with a different, essentially film-noir sensibility. Both his *Othello* and *Chimes at Midnight* were replete with the sorts of striking visual images one would expect from his fertile imagination. For example, the battle scenes in *Chimes at Midnight*, Welles' examination of the triangular relationship between Falstaff, Prince Hal and Henry IV, were remarkable, providing a far more authentic sense of the realities of war than Olivier had in his depiction of Agincourt in *Henry V*. Indeed Welles' film was probably more of an influence on the way that Branagh shot *Henry V* than Olivier's, contrary to what the critics tended to assume. The combination of austere interior shots of the court and an uncompromising portrayal of the brutality of battle was common to *Chimes at Midnight* and Branagh's *Henry*. On the other hand, Welles was no great respecter of the text. He had no qualms about removing huge chunks of it in order to realise his cinematic vision.

Even Olivier, though more committed to a textual integrity than either Welles or Luhrmann, was more cavalier than one might assume. Consider his *Hamlet*. Such were his incisions that there was no Fortinbras, no Rosencrantz, no Guildenstern. This was no trivial matter: it weakened the play's political theme of dynastic struggle and our understanding of what Hamlet had been like prior to his father's death. In his *Hamlet* Olivier did present a coherent interpretation of the play, but it was narrowly focused.

With the exception of his *Love's Labour's Lost*, filmed a decade after *Henry V*, Branagh has shown a respect for both the textual richness of Shakespeare's plays and the visual possibilities of cinema.

More than his predecessors in the making of the Shakespeare film, Branagh succeeded in striking the appropriate balance between the textual and the visual. This was evident from the outset with his *Henry*. Lucid speaking of the verse with a screenplay that did justice to Shakespeare's text was combined with a series of memorable images, such as the dramatic, backlit appearance of Branagh's Henry in silhouette in the doorway, as a way of introducing the character to the audience, and the long tracking shot of Henry at the end of Agincourt as he carries the corpse of the boy across the breadth of the body-strewn battlefield. Branagh's ability to make his movies dazzling to the eye and pleasing to the ear would continue, peaking in his film of *Hamlet*. Not only did he use an uncut version of the text, he presented a visual extravaganza, from the opening scene in the opulent state room with confetti raining down as Claudius (Derek Jacobi) and Gertrude (Julie Christie) depart, to the shot with Hamlet (Branagh) on the plains as Fortinbras advances with his army.

Not only was Branagh's *Henry V* noteworthy for these reasons; it was manifestly the most influential Shakespeare movie in terms of its impact on other film-makers. After the initial attempts to film Shakespeare during the silent era and the early years of sound, it was Olivier, beginning with his *Henry V* in 1944, who ushered in an exciting period, lasting about a quarter of a century, in which major directors including Welles, Zeffirelli, Peter Brook, Peter Hall and Akira Kurosawa were inspired to film Shakespeare. Following Roman Polanski's 1971 version of *Macbeth*, however, the Shakespeare movie became moribund. Few films of his plays were made. It took Branagh's *Henry V* to reinvigorate the genre. Such was its impact in encouraging other film-makers to tackle the Bard that the following decade turned out to be the most productive in the history of the Shakespeare film; and it was Branagh who made the difference. As Al Pacino explained, 'Branagh opened it all up with *Henry V*. Now you say Shakespeare on Film in Hollywood and people listen.'

The impact of *Henry V* means that it is a film of importance in the history of British cinema. That the British Film Institute's list of the top hundred British films ever made does not include it is risible, and a prime example of the way his achievements have been underestimated in his home country. It is difficult to believe that *The Full Monty* (no. 25) or *Brassed Off* (no. 85) is a better, more important, more artistically credible film.

One other claim that can be made for *Henry V* is the outstanding quality of its central performance. Indeed it is more compelling, more nuanced than Olivier's Henry. Olivier did provide a strong centre to his film, and an impressive sense of heroism at a time when Britain needed heroes. More than Olivier, however, Branagh illuminates the complexity of Henry's character – his doubts about the validity of his claim to France, his guilt over his misspent youth and the high-handed seizure of the crown by his father, and his religious convictions. The crucial scene is the night before Agincourt, when Henry examines his soul before God. As Olivier had presented such a strongly heroic personality, the concerns his Henry articulates in this scene come across as ephemeral, as not reflecting the fundamental nature of his character. But with Branagh the doubts expressed reinforce the picture presented earlier in the film of a complex monarch whose ability to declare and prosecute war sits alongside his Hamletian self-questioning – hence Branagh's playing of the scene is more poignant than Olivier's.

Evidence of the quality of what Branagh had achieved with *Henry V* can be seen in how some of the greatest actors of the twentieth century responded to it. In a private letter John Gielgud wrote of Branagh, 'His *Henry V* film was shown last week and impressed me very much – a terrific feat of direction which he has evidently taken to like a duck to water. I have never cared much for the play, and he has really done wonders with it and it compares very favourably even with Larry's fine film version.' 'The evolution of English theater came to full flower in Kenneth Branagh's production of *Henry V*,' wrote Marlon Brando in his autobiography. 'He did not injure the language; he showed a reverence for it, and followed Shakespeare's instructions precisely. It was an extraordinary accomplishment of melding the realities of human behavior with the poetry of language. I can't imagine Shakespeare being performed with more refinement.' Paul Scofield also had a high opinion. 'I admired the resulting movie with something like awe,' he recalls.

With *Henry V* up and running in Britain, the question for Branagh was whether America would judge his film kindly. The *Daily Mail* set the scene: 'When King Ken arrives in New York this weekend to launch his film *Henry V*, he plays one of his toughest roles ever. Can this ordinary-looking young Briton … actually conquer a society saturated with its own stars.' The film's Stateside première was set for

10 November at the Paris Theater in New York, but Branagh busied himself immediately by embarking on a gruelling promotional tour. In one three-week period, he visited no less than fifteen cities. The *Houston Chronicle* defined Branagh's mission thus: 'to bring Shakespeare to the mall rats of America'. Despite the fatigue, Branagh enjoyed his encounters with American journalists, finding them an agreeable contrast to many of their British counterparts. It did not strike Americans 'as remotely odd', he once explained, that he should try to achieve so much so quickly. 'They were just rather interested in what it was like. That was the question. Not "Who do you think you are?" but "What's it like?"'

Branagh could have been no less gratified by the American reviews. Vincent Canby, in the *New York Times*, declared enthusiastically: 'Kenneth Branagh has done it ... [transforming] what initially seemed to be a lunatic dare into a genuine triumph.' His Henry had 'psychological heft and intellectual weight'. Hal Hinson of the *Washington Post*, describing the film as 'audacious, resonant, passionate', said of Branagh that 'a more auspicious, more thrilling debut could not be imagined', and closed by arguing: 'While his work doesn't supplant Olivier's, it is worthy of a place beside it. He has made a *Henry V* for his time, and a masterful one. The king is dead, long live the king.' In the *New Yorker*, august critic Pauline Kael judged Branagh to be 'an intensely likeable performer, with a straightforwardness that drives the whole film ahead'. She was particularly struck by his technical gifts, noting the quality of his voice: 'This actor's earthy, doughy presence is the wrapping for his beautiful, expressive voice. Emotion pours out of it with surpising ease; he's conversational without sacrificing the poetry. His readings are a source of true pleasure. Listening to him, you think, With an instrument like that, he can play anything.' 'What a stunning debut!' declared the *Village Voice*, while *Rolling Stone* magazine said of Branagh's voice that it was 'the most exciting and distinctive since Richard Burton's ... Branagh is a marvel. You can't take your eyes off him ... His film is more than a promising first try: It's thrilling.'

At the start of 1990 Branagh turned his attention from impressing Americans with his cinematic accomplishments to showing them his gifts on stage. It was time for the Renaissance Theatre Company to hit the road again. Branagh's theatrical vision of taking Shakespeare to the masses had expanded. It was now global rather than national; and the plan was to take *King Lear* and *A Midsummer Night's Dream* to Japan, across Europe, and to Chicago, before returning to Britain in the summer of 1990. But the world tour would kick off with a two-month stint in Los Angeles, beginning in January. Richard Briers would play Lear, encouraged by Branagh to forsake his middle-class inhibitions in order to show the intense anger needed for the part; and in an innovative piece of casting Emma Thompson would play the Fool. Branagh would not only direct both productions, but play Edgar in *Lear* and Peter Quince in the *Dream*.

Ensconced in Los Angeles for the Renaissance theatre run, Branagh was close at hand as Oscar fever built in the early weeks of 1990. His decision to take Renaissance to LA resulted in considerable interest, with advanced ticket sales setting new records. That Branagh's *Lear* and *Dream* were hot tickets in Los Angeles could not have failed to catch the attention of Academy voters on the west coast. To ensure that it did not go unnoticed by east-coast voters, a large advertisement was placed in the *New York Times* announcing that Branagh's productions had 'Sold Out Before We Open!' His media appearances, as well as his theatrical endeavours, kept him in the public eye. He was a guest on the *Tonight* show, exchanging banter with Johnny Carson, who liked him so much he invited him back for a second appearance three weeks later. Branagh's life was now beginning to change, as the inevitable concomitants of stardom came his way. For his appearances on the *Tonight* show, a limousine was sent to pick him up. Not what he had been accustomed to back in Britain.

Though he was not nominated for a Golden Globe, an awards ceremony often viewed as a guide to the Oscars, Branagh was hopeful of recognition from the Academy as its president, Karl Malden, along with Geena Davis, announced the nominations at 5.30 a.m. on Valentine's Day. 'We were living in the Oakwood Apartments in Burbank,' recalled Emma Thompson. 'Rain was coming in through the ceiling and we had the four posts of the bed set in water-filled ashtrays to keep the ants out of the sheets.' Her husband was 'up all night on the couch waiting for news ... There was a receiver-shaped dent on the side of his head.' For Branagh, the news turned out to be magnificent. He had received Oscar nominations for Best Director and for Best Actor, and in so doing made a bit of Oscar history. Orson Welles, Woody Allen and Warren Beatty were among the few to have achieved the same feat of being nominated in both categories in the same year. 'It took all morning to get him off the ceiling,' said Thompson.

The Oscar nominations made Branagh far more famous in the United States than he had been hitherto. Along with that celebrity came the inevitable intrusions. 'I think he felt a lot of pressure at being recognised,' recalls Richard Briers. 'He had a table outside the stage door [for *Lear* and the *Dream*] for autographs. Queues of people came up. He began to get a touch of that frightening thing of movie-type fame where you can never go anywhere and have a quiet time. It was his first taste of surreal movie stardom. He rode it, but when he had a workload that heavy he felt like going away and having a quiet time. Well, that was not possible in America.'

The Dorothy Chandler Pavilion, next to the Mark Taper Forum where Branagh's *Lear* and *Dream* had been playing, was the setting for Oscar night on 26 March 1990. Rubbing shoulders with the likes of Jack Nicholson, Robert De Niro, Gregory Peck and Martin Scorsese, a weary Branagh, who had taken a flight from Tokyo the day before to attend the ceremony, must have thought he had arrived. Along with Elizabeth McGovern he presented the Oscar for Best Makeup, which went to *Driving Miss Daisy*. When Candice Bergen announced that the winner for Costume Design was *Henry V*'s Phyllis Dalton, Branagh's glee was unrestrained. He yelled his approval while Bergen was still reading Dalton's name. This award, however, proved to be *Henry V*'s only success that night. In the Best Acting category Branagh lost out to Daniel Day-Lewis, who had given a powerful performance in *My Left Foot* as Christy Brown, the Irish writer and painter who suffered from cerebral palsy. Day- Lewis had managed to edge out Tom Cruise and Morgan Freeman, whose respective performances in *Born on the Fourth of July* and *Driving Miss Daisy* had been much admired. The competition for Best Director was strong. Woody Allen for *Crimes and Misdemeanors*, Peter Weir for *Dead Poets Society*, Oliver Stone for *Born on the Fourth of July*, and Jim Sheridan for *My Left Foot* were nominated alongside Branagh. It was Robert De Niro and Martin Scorsese who announced Oliver Stone as the winner, proving that the Vietnam War remained fertile subject matter for the controversial director. Three years earlier he had been so honoured for *Platoon*.

Disappointing perhaps, but for Branagh Oscar night 1990 was an important milestone, capping a remarkable journey from the meaner streets of Belfast to suburban England, and then on to RADA, the West End, and the Royal Shakespeare Company, before becoming – in the spring of 1990 – an international star. Millions of people throughout the world had watched Branagh on Oscar night on their television sets. He was now a household name.

By this point he had succeeded in theatre, television, and film in Britain. There was only one thing left: to make it in Hollywood. With characteristic confidence, he resolved to do just that.

5

Hollywood

At the age of seven Kenneth Branagh saw *The Birdman of Alcatraz*, a film starring Burt Lancaster. It made a deep impression. 'I was struck by how real it seemed,' he recalled twenty years later. 'No one appeared to be "acting". Lancaster's own performance was tremendously powerful and affecting, and I was so engrossed that I studied the end-credits list so that I could check the names of the other actors and everyone else responsible for the movie.' Thus began a lifelong passion for the movies. The boy Branagh became a walking encyclopedia of film trivia. The names of not only the stars but also the character actors and the people responsible for lighting and make-up were stored away. Hollywood, as well as the stage, captured his imagination from an early age.

These formative experiences meant that Branagh's attitude towards the possibility of making a Hollywood movie was not that of the stereotypical British thespian; he did not view it condescendingly as a vulgar commercial enterprise that represented a distraction from his true calling and from real art, namely the theatre. On the contrary, to make a movie in Hollywood would be a childhood dream come true.

In 1990 he did get the opportunity to make a Hollywood film: *Dead Again*. When released in the summer of 1991 it rocketed to number one at the American box office, thereby sustaining his meteoric rise. At the same time *Dead Again* deepened the chasm that had developed around the time of *Henry V*'s release between the respect accorded Branagh in America and the criticism he received in England.

It was during the Renaissance company's run of *King Lear* and *A Midsummer Night's Dream* in the early months of 1990 that Branagh was asked to work in Hollywood. Based in Los Angeles, and with rave Stateside reviews for *Henry V* in the bag, Branagh found himself courted by America's movie moguls, eager to snap up the latest talent from Europe. As Hollywood weighed up Branagh, he reciprocated. 'He's got an instinctive understanding of the place,' said Emma Thompson. 'He just arrived there and started to work it out, because that's the kind of brain he has.'

Studios were soon sending him a slew of scripts, but he found himself unimpressed. They consisted of biographies of literary figures, including Shakespeare, Chekhov and Tolstoy, and all the Vietnam War films never made. Clearly Hollywood's perception of Branagh's range had been shaped by Shakespeare and Agincourt.

Branagh had his own views on the movie he would like to make next: an adaptation of Thomas Hardy's *The Return of the Native*. Aware of the success enjoyed by previous films of Hardy's work, such as John Schlesinger's *Far from the Madding Crowd* and Roman Polanski's *Tess*, he was convinced the novel had enormous potential as a film; but his enthusiasm for the project was not shared by the American studios. 'I know I'm being a bit of a sausage, but they really didn't understand it,' recalled a wistful Branagh. 'As far as they were concerned, Thomas Hardy was Shakespeare by another name.'

Just as his prospects for working in Hollywood appeared to be receding, Branagh received the script for *Dead Again*, written by Scott Frank. Back in 1986 Paramount production executive Lindsay Doran had produced a 'deal memo' with Frank to set up the project. Frank's screenplay wove together romance and Hitchcockian suspense in a tale of two pairs of lovers whose stories intersect. In contemporary Los Angeles private detective Mike Church is recruited to establish the identity of a silent amnesiac woman who suffers from nightmares. When put under hypnosis by antique dealer Franklyn Madson, she relives the past of Margaret Strauss, an English pianist whose tempestuous marriage to German composer Roman Strauss ended in her brutal stabbing with a pair of scissors, and the conviction and execution of Roman for the murder. As the story unfolds, Mike falls for the amnesiac, who is identified as Amanda Sharp, an artist whose work is dominated by scissor shapes. It appears that Mike and Amanda are reincarnations of Roman and Margaret, and that Amanda might suffer the same fate as Margaret at Mike's hands. It is revealed, however, that hypnotist Franklyn Madson is the son of Roman Strauss's housekeeper and was in fact responsible as a boy for Margaret's murder.

Having worked on *Ghost* and *Field of Dreams*, two popular films dealing with reincarnation, Doran was attracted to Frank's script. Despite Doran's enthusiasm, recruiting a director for the project proved difficult. 'We offered the script to all the usual suspects,' revealed Bill Horberg, a senior vice-president at Paramount. 'But the Larry Kasdans and Peter Weirs either weren't interested or weren't available.' Branagh would later speculate that it was the melodramatic aspects of *Dead Again* that had discouraged other directors.

Scott Frank, meanwhile, moved on to write another screenplay, *Little Man Tate*, which Jodie Foster decided to direct, while Doran kept an eye out for the right director. 'We wanted someone with a committed visual style who was also a humanist and would not sacrifice the characters for the visual,' Doran recalled, 'and that is a difficult commodity to find.' On seeing Branagh's *Henry V* she was convinced she had found the right director. Accordingly, the *Dead Again* script was dispatched to Branagh.

He did not think the title promising, but read the screenplay with Emma Thompson between matinee and evening theatre performances at the Mark Taper Forum in Los Angeles. They liked it. 'Three pages and we were utterly hooked,' Thompson remembered. For Branagh, the story was evocative of the films by Alfred Hitchcock and Orson Welles that he had watched as a child. 'I had a very powerful reaction,' he stated. 'My belief was utterly suspended while I was reading it. It reminded me of some of the movies I first saw on television: the woman with no memory, the private eye, the creepy house, the hypnotist. I thought of Hitchcock's *Spellbound* and its big dramatic score, the Salvador Dali designs, the dramatic lighting.' The thriller was the one American film genre, unlike westerns or science fiction, which Branagh adored.

He was drawn to *Dead Again* in part because he thought it a good story containing ingredients from masterpieces of yesteryear, but also because he found the characters appealing. Roman Strauss was 'clearly a man with a secret,' thought Branagh, and Mike Church 'a version of the wise-cracking detective of a thousand American films'. True to his populist instincts, he viewed *Dead Again* as a piece of entertainment that had strong commercial prospects. Branagh was also lured by the opportunity to demonstrate his versatility. 'I like the idea of surprises,' he acknowledged. 'That's in every actor's blood. Olivier described it once when he was talking about the night he played Mr Puff in

Sheridan's *The Critic*, and then played Oedipus the same evening, on the other side of the interval. One is a camp, foppish, post-Restoration funny guy; the other a Greek tragic hero. Somebody asked him why he had done this, and he said, very seriously, "I wanted to show off."' Proving himself as a purveyor of film noir as well as of Shakespeare would be eye-catching.

The crucial meeting with the Paramount top brass, in which Branagh would seek to convince them of the soundness of his vision for *Dead Again*, was set for the morning of the Oscar nominations. When it was announced that Branagh had bagged two nominations for *Henry V*, it was clear he would enter the discussions from a position of strength. At the meeting Branagh was bold, clear, and decisive: 'You have me in the white heat of enthusiasm, I'd love to make this movie, and here are my conditions ... I'd be delighted to direct if I could play those two [lead] male parts and my missus could play the other two [female lead roles]. Even if I don't do it, get two actors to play the four parts.' Branagh believed using two actors instead of four would add to the sense that the story was really about two souls. He felt Emma Thompson had the right period face to play Margaret Strauss, could do the American accent needed for the part of Amanda Sharp, and would bring flair to both roles.

But his demands did not end there. He insisted on retaining the same core creative team he had used on *Henry V*: production designer Tim Harvey, costume designer Phyllis Dalton and composer Patrick Doyle. Still regarding himself as an inexperienced movie director, Branagh felt that he needed this tried and trusted team to ensure that the look and sound of *Dead Again* would be just right. It was also reported that he insisted on final cut, so that the studio would be unable to add or remove any scenes without his approbation. Lindsay Doran recalled the executives' response to Branagh's demands: 'Everyone swallowed a lot.' Audacity has been one of the defining traits of Branagh's career; never was it more evident than on this occasion.

Although his demands were great, Paramount executives found reason to believe that Branagh's approach would work. Watching him and his wife in repertory with *King Lear* and *A Midsummer Night's Dream* helped convince them that the couple had the versatility to play dual roles. Studio executives were also able to evaluate Thompson's ability to act on film in *The Tall Guy*, a recently released comedy in which she starred with Jeff Goldblum. Also important to Paramount's calculations, according to Thompson, were her aesthetic qualities: 'I think once the executives at Paramount got a look at me and decided I wasn't a total dog, it made everyone rest a lot easier.'

Satisfied as to the feasibility of Branagh's demands, the executives gave *Dead Again* the green light. 'We all knew very well', stated Paramount's president David Kirkpatrick, 'that when you buy Ken Branagh you buy the whole package.' At the end of March 1990 it was reported to the press that Branagh would make his American film debut in a Mirage Productions' film for Paramount Pictures. He would direct, it was announced, and play 'multiple roles.'

The first priority was to assemble the production team, cast and crew. Charles H. Maguire, along with Lindsay Doran, came on board as producer. With a venerable track record that included work on *Reds* and *On the Waterfront*, Maguire was eminently qualified to guide *Dead Again* through filming. Sydney Pollack, the director of *Tootsie* and *Out of Africa*, served as executive producer. He would play a crucial role in helping to persuade Paramount that the 1940s scenes would work best in black and white.

In assembling the cast, Branagh steered clear of those he suspected of harbouring prima donna tendencies. Several people were rejected for precisely that reason. In the end a good group of actors was recruited. Andy Garcia, very much a hot property, with strong performances in *The Untouchables* and the then soon-to-be-released *The Godfather, Part III*, agreed to play a journalist whose attentions towards Emma Thompson's Margaret Strauss ignite Roman Strauss' jealous fury. Robin Williams signed up for a cameo as a seedy psychologist consulted by Branagh's private investigator for advice on reincarnation. Donald Sutherland was set to take the role of Franklyn Madson but ended up being replaced by Derek Jacobi. And Renaissance veteran Richard Easton came aboard the good ship *Branagh* once more, this time for a small role as the head of a convent.

As the initial planning for *Dead Again* got under way, Branagh returned to Britain with Renaissance in the summer of 1990. His *King Lear* and *A Midsummer Night's Dream*, watched by thousands around the world, were finally to be seen by British audiences. They played at the Edinburgh Festival before moving on to the West End for a brief run at the Dominion Theatre. The reviews were mixed. Charles

Osborne of the *Daily Telegraph* praised both productions, saying they had brought 'a much-needed air of excitement to Edinburgh'. Paul Taylor of the *Independent* also admired aspects of *Lear*, particularly Briers' central performance as the tragic king, but regarded the *Dream* as 'the flattest, emptiest production the Renaissance company has yet mounted'. Jeremy Kingston of *The Times* commended the *Lear*, finding much merit in Briers' monarch and Emma Thompson's Fool, but judged the *Dream* to be 'sorry and artificial'. Michael Billington was charitably disposed when writing in the *Guardian*. 'While it is fashionable to have a go at Mr Branagh,' he remarked, 'it strikes me as admirable that he is determined to keep the idea of touring Shakespeare alive at a time when the Bard is disappearing from the regional reps.' Billington was charmed by the *Dream*, arguing that it showed Branagh's forte to be comedy, but was more tepid about the *Lear*.

By this point Branagh was juggling so many balls – directing two plays, performing in two plays, preparing a Hollywood film, *inter alia* – that it was impossible for him to focus on his acting in *King Lear* and the *Dream* with the intensity that he had, for instance, in his earlier stage roles in *Another Country* and *Henry V*. This had particularly been the case in America, where he had initially shaped his interpretations of Edgar and Peter Quince. In addition to the acting (and directing) his time was taken up with a seemingly endless round of press interviews, workshops for actors, civic receptions, book signings, and after-show discussions for theatre audiences. Branagh was aware of the problem, telling one journalist:

> Sometimes it frustrates me enormously. Playing Edgar in *Lear*, my performance suffered from the work load I had around it. That doesn't mean I was particularly bad, just that I disappointed myself and was aware of paying a price. It was all such a whiz from the moment I left the RSC with the notion of forming a theatre company, a crazy race to keep things afloat, moneywise ... That's why I'm going to stop for a while and consider things more carefully.[1]

Though Branagh knew he had not been at his best, he was still sobered by the critical response to *Lear* and the *Dream*. After having left Britain for a lengthy world tour and received Oscar nominations, he thought or at least hoped that the harsh attacks on him would fade away. Returning home with two new productions, however, he encountered an enthusiastic public but frostiness from some of the critics. According to David Parfitt, it changed him: 'It made him much more cautious about who he spoke to and when ... He was always much more cautious in his way than I was. I have a tendency to probably say too much to press. But I think he was bruised by it.'

Despite the various pressures on Branagh during this Renaissance tour, he still found the time to offer encouragement to an actor, Alex Lowe, who was trying to find his way in the business. This was an example of one of Branagh's most commendable traits, namely his generosity towards young actors. Lowe had worked as a teenager with Branagh in *Another Country*, and when their paths crossed again at the Edinburgh Festival Branagh asked him what he needed most professionally. 'An agent,' Lowe replied. Branagh then proceeded to write down for him a list of suitable agents. He added that he was soon heading off to Los Angeles to film *Dead Again* but that if he wanted assistance in dealing with these agents Lowe should feel free to phone him and, knowing the impoverished state of most young actors, to reverse the charges. Branagh would cast Lowe frequently in later projects, including *Peter's Friends* and *Much Ado About Nothing*.

After the Renaissance theatre run was over, Branagh jetted off to America, where the shooting of *Dead Again* was due to commence on 1 October, while Emma Thompson headed for Grayshot Hall, where she recharged her batteries at a health farm. He set up base camp in an office at Paramount Studios. Sheets of paper with the outline of the plot adorned the walls, as did a poster from the previous year's blockbuster about the supernatural, *Ghost*. A gargantuan pair of scissors, which played a central role in the *Dead Again* story, hung on the wall too. Branagh kept reminders of the two great loves of his life: a portrait of Emma Thompson and the complete works of Shakespeare. On the domestic front he rented a house in the Hollywood Hills. With an agreeable garden and the obligatory swimming pool, it afforded spectacular views – but only, as Branagh remarked, 'if you could see through the smog'. Emma Thompson tried to make their new abode feel like home. She loaded up the refrigerator with fresh pasta and vegetables, and happily performed the cooking duties.

Branagh's preparations for the making of *Dead Again* had been assiduous. At an early stage he looked to the past masters for guidance, screening several Hitchcock classics in order to remind himself of 'just how far he [Hitchcock] went because with *Dead Again* you certainly need a lot of melodramatic Hitchcock approach to carry it off'. He also watched films involving Orson Welles, such as *Citizen*

Kane and *The Third Man*, and some modern thrillers. Having immersed himself in the noir genre, Branagh concluded that the key to success for *Dead Again* would be 'a breathless pace'.

In helping to scout locations in the Los Angeles area, where much of the film would be shot, Branagh was struck by the allure of the city. *Dead Again*, he resolved, must convey its glamour. 'The texture of that place was so wonderful. The city had to be used with love, as it was in the old films. I felt a very strong pull from Los Angeles.' Gifted director of photography Matthew Leonetti, who had worked on one of the outstanding thrillers of the 1980s, *Jagged Edge*, starring Glenn Close and Jeff Bridges, would prove to be an asset in helping Branagh to shoot a film of visual beauty.

Preparing his two roles required mastering a Germanic and an American accent. For the latter, he consulted a dialect coach, listened to tapes, and studied people in Los Angeles. If he noticed two men who somehow reminded him of Mike Church, he would walk behind them through the streets, eavesdropping, gleaning information about their speech and gestures. It proved to be a painstaking process. Initially his accent was too east-coast, and his gesticulations too extravagant. Once he thought he had got it right, he put it to the test, visiting a Hollywood bookshop. 'I was fuckin' terrified,' he recalled. 'I waited for someone to say, "Hey, you're not an Amerricun. How dare you come here with your fancy British ways!" But I got away with it – then went home and threw myself on the bed with the effort.' He worked hard at developing the appropriate body language as well as the right accent. Observing that people in Los Angeles walked in a loose, relaxed fashion, he sought to mimic that style.

The rehearsals for *Dead Again* gave Branagh his first extensive experience with American actors. He found himself fascinated by the differences between them and their British counterparts. The Americans cherished spontaneity and freshness, he noticed, but were reluctant to go all out in rehearsal, as though they feared that doing so would prevent them from reaching those emotional extremes when filming began. Branagh encouraged all his actors, American and British, to be bold, assuring them that any special moments in rehearsal could be recreated in front of the camera.

Branagh was grateful for the role played by Emma Thompson. By asking lots of questions in rehearsals, she lessened the sense of deference felt by the American actors towards Branagh because of his

Shakespearean background, an obsequiousness that could have eroded the collaborative spirit he wished to encourage. 'She was a very good influence on those Americans on the set who had me down as some kind of great white hope,' he said.

Branagh was now ready to start the film. But on the first day of shooting things did not go according to plan. Heading out from his house in the Hollywood Hills in a red Mustang convertible with the top down, sunglasses on, he felt uplifted by a sense of blissful ease. For the boy from Belfast, this was heady stuff. But then his eyes began to stream from the smog. By the time he passed through the pink gates of Paramount, he had a sneezing attack. When he reached the car park, he was unable to get the key out of the lock. 'It was a completely inglorious start,' he admitted. 'I was late for the first meeting. I was almost in tears.'

In directing his first Hollywood picture, Branagh was conscious of his inexperience: *Henry V* was the only other movie he had made. At times his greenness showed. When filming the scene with Amanda Sharp (Thompson) in her apartment full of scissor sculptures, producer Lindsay Doran recommended a close-up shot of Thompson and inserts of the sculptures in order to emphasise how scissors dominated her thinking and her art. A recalcitrant Branagh rejected the advice, thinking it would undermine the fluidity of the scene. He later regretted that decision. Reaction shots and inserts, he came to understand, provide more options in the editing.

As a result of his inexperience, self-doubt sometimes afflicted Branagh during the shoot, and he admitted:

> I was just so nervous. Real tummy-tickling nerves. All the time, and the same was true all the time I was doing Henry. Last weekend was a terrible black weekend: 'I don't know how to do films, I don't know how to direct films.' Black despair just tormented me. 'You're a fuckin' counterfeit, you can't do fuckin' anything.' I went and got some fish and chips on Santa Monica pier with a couple of friends and by the end of the evening, I'd turned it round. I'm thinking, Yeah! I've got this! Next day you're laughing at yourself: What a Drama Queen you are![2]

Those nerves did not prevent Branagh from directing *Dead Again* efficiently. A journalist invited to the set noticed his economy of effort, how everything had been carefully arranged so as to preserve his energy. All of the stage commands were given not by Branagh, who would just watch with arms folded, but by the assistant director. Any guidance for the actors would be given confidentially by

Branagh. Nobody knew what he had said unless the actor subsequently revealed it.

When problems emerged, Branagh solved them in decisive fashion. His first major difficulty was what he regarded as the elephantine pace at which the crew worked. 'He absolutely hated to wait,' Scott Frank said. 'And waiting is how you spend about 50 per cent of your time on a Hollywood set. He can get very impatient waiting for the lighting to be set up, say. The crew aren't used to working that fast, and he rubbed them the wrong way.' But for Branagh it was vital that everything moved along at a clip. As he was directing as well as acting, it would have been easy for him to lose focus on the two characters he was playing. The crew had to work quickly in part so that he could maintain the rhythm necessary to act and to direct together. Something had to be done. One option was to coax them into working faster during the shoot. Instead Branagh decided to cut the Gordian knot: he sacked the camera crew, and replaced them with another.

As the filming of *Dead Again* proceeded, the Paramount top brass were pleased with their young director. Producer Charles H. Maguire even compared him to the legends he had known in the past. 'All of the great directors I've worked with – Kazan, Lumet, Hitchcock, Logan, Robert Wise, Pakula – were prepared and focused,' he remarked. 'Basically the film was done, in their heads, before they started. Lumet averages thirty-five days a picture because he's focused and prepared and Kenneth reminds me very much of him.'

Playing a German composer and an American detective, Branagh's acting responsibilities matched his directorial obligations. *Dead Again* was not shot in chronological order, meaning that he would find himself playing Mike Church and then having to switch on the same day to the Roman Strauss character. 'It was like taking out one floppy disk and putting in another,' he said. His experience in the theatre, where he had often played multiple roles in repertory, was invaluable. He was also able to rely on the sage Hugh Cruttwell, who was again on hand to cast a watchful eye over his former pupil's acting.

Branagh relished the role of Mike Church. As a lover of American films from an early age, he was much taken with the idea of playing a variant of the archetypal detective around whom events swirl. He found playing an American liberating, as the character was more expressive, the emotions less concealed than was the case with the English characters he had previously portrayed. Feeling a desire to maintain control in conditions of great pressure was helpful, for that was precisely the state of mind he wished to suggest with the character of Mike Church.

Branagh would later say of his portrayal of the temperamental composer Roman Strauss, 'I eyebrow my way through the film.' In truth he brought great panache to the role, producing a more vibrant performance than he did as Mike Church. His Roman Strauss was passionate, and in equal measure charming and haughty. The most intimidating aspect of playing Roman was conducting an orchestra in concert, shot in the historic Orpheum Theatre in downtown Los Angeles – a key scene, as it is the moment when Emma Thompson's Margaret catches Roman's eye. Branagh admitted he was 'totally paralysed by fear of having to play the conductor. I was conducting real musicians; we had the first violinist of some hot-shit orchestra. I'm quite musical in the bathroom, but even having to pretend to be musical in front of anybody scares the hell out of me.' He appears to have found it more stressful playing Roman Strauss than Mike Church. The crew found him more irritable when he was performing as Roman.

A no-nonsense efficiency was the hallmark of Branagh's acting, as well as his directing. A journalist who visited the set of *Dead Again* for the *American Film* magazine was struck by the speed and confidence with which he tackled a challenging scene in which Mike Church goes under hypnosis. This writer's account provides a fascinating glimpse into Branagh's technique as a film actor:

> Getting there [on set] early is a good idea – but a lucky accident. I'm just curious to see how the crew members begin their day (mostly standing around half-asleep over a lavish array of doughnuts, bagels, bananas and cheeses). Branagh passes by at a clip, looking sharp in a 1990's suit: 'Hello-hello-hello!' And he promptly vanishes into the cloistered row of interlocking sets that dominate the stage. His camera and soundman drift in behind him for a quick strategy session. I remain standing with the rest of the crew members, who continue to gaze.
>
> Then by chance I glimpse a nearby monitor. Branagh is pictured there, eyes shut, head tilted back – mouthing soundless words. My God, is he doing a take already? I pick up the monitor's headphones – yes. A scene is in progress. I can make out the real Branagh through the alley of jumbled furniture, enthroned in a clearing almost too narrow for anybody to move in, much less wield a camera. The only people with him are the cameraman and his partner in the scene, Derek Jacobi. The sound-man is seated near another monitor 10 feet away.

Branagh grips both armrests of an antique chair. The scene is played at a whisper. Mike speaks his own name, describes what he sees in his trance and then – with a suddenness that makes me jump – cries out in agony.

As the take progresses, one can feel his performance building as he tackles the moment again and again. His timing – the beats and breath spaces – have been organized with exquisite care at some unseen rehearsal. He hits those inner marks each time – but in a telling way: What he's after is not the delivery, he's after the same momentary loss of control as his character. One can feel him getting it by take three – when his habitation of the moment, jumps from the 'exquisite' to the authentic. He starts surprising himself. He has it nailed by take six, but goes for seven, just for good luck – and there achieves a kind of 'dying-fall' timing that will probably cut well with the surrounding matter.

It is barely nine o'clock, most of the cast and crew have not even arrived yet, and the most excruciating work of the day is behind him. Branagh becomes lighthearted – he even seems light-headed – joshing with the crew, disappearing and reappearing with mercurial jest. His cheer infects everybody, and a rapid, enthusiastic tempo reigns as they do the next sequence.

Branagh's partner was finding the experience of acting in Hollywood equally invigorating. Playing two people from different countries and eras was 'an actor's dream', Thompson enthused. For the amnesiac American artist, she took pains to perfect the accent and to locate the emotional centre of the character. Sounding American, she discovered, required speaking in a higher register. Thompson decided to emphasise her character's profound sense of isolation. 'If you've lost your memory, you've lost your power to relate to anything at all,' she explained. 'You can't sit on a sofa and think, "This is a little like the material from my wedding dress." Memories are not available to you, and you find you have very little to say apart from "It's cold," "I am hungry." The principal thing you discover is it produces intense loneliness. That's the major emotion. Absolute aloneness. So I thought, "OK, I'll play that."'

Branagh was as grateful to have her around during the filming as he had been in rehearsals. He knew he could rely on her professionalism, that she would not demand changes to the script or shout at him on set or do anything to make his job more difficult. He also admired the quality of her acting. When later a critic suggested she lacked the beauty and sense of mystery that a Michelle Pfeiffer would have brought to the role of Amanda Sharp, Branagh bristled. He lauded her looks and praised her performance.

Branagh was happy, too, with the contributions made by the rest of the cast. Robin Williams was on set for only three days, but it was enough time for him to produce a performance striking for the way it undermined existing assumptions about his range as an actor. Heralded for his vast comedic talent, Williams was so sinister in *Dead Again* he even surprised himself. 'Christ! I didn't know I could be that seedy!' he declared on seeing the film for the first time. Andy Garcia was admirably unpretentious, despite his star status, and Derek Jacobi gave a professional performance on short notice. For his part, Jacobi must have relished the opportunity to play the final scenes in which his character reverts to a childhood stammer, reminiscent to his fans of his memorable performance as Claudius in the beloved 1970s BBC television series. Adding lustre to the whole project was German actress Hanna Schygulla, renowned for her work with Rainer Werner Fassbinder, in what was for her a rare outing in an American film. Branagh was delighted by her portrayal of Roman Strauss's housemaid, noting her ability 'to somehow confess to the camera, conveying suppressed grief or pain, occasionally a sense of the sinister'.

It would be reasonable to assume that the experience of working together on set for twelve hours and then going home together must have strained the relationship between Branagh and Thompson. This was not the case. These were their halcyon days, a time of genuine contentment. On the set Thompson aided Branagh's work by knowing when to play the resident comedienne and when to play supportive spouse. In a scene where a karate-kick from actor Campbell Scott caused Branagh to adjust his protective groin padding, his wife could not help but scoff. 'Ha! He wants more padding,' she mocked. 'His masculinity's at stake here.' She was in a similarly playful mood when her husband began to direct her a little too fastidiously. She told him what he could do with the camera, to the great amusement of the crew. But she was more sympathetic when his director's chair collapsed from under him, leaving him in a heap on the floor. An enraged but silent Branagh simply stared at the ground before heading off to another part of the set to be alone. He sat at the end of a chaise longue with fist on chin. Thompson removed her shoes, joined him on the chaise, and placed her feet under his sweatshirt so that they rested on his back. She remained with him for a considerable period of time, until his fury had abated.

In the interviews they gave to promote *Dead Again*, both Branagh and Thompson spoke affectionately about their relationship. For Thompson, it seemed the friendship was the most precious thing. 'We went through hell and high water, breaking up and getting together,' she admitted, 'but the very thing we enjoy most now is just being able to be at ease with each other. A lot of people get together and are not, in the most primal sense, at ease. I think the whole notion of romance is to blame for that. Romance is a bit of a con, really; it simply does not last, in that way. Friendship and humour, work and thought last. You have to find somebody whom you can sink into, as into a comfortable armchair.' For his part, Branagh spoke as touchingly about his marriage as he had at the time of their wedding. 'Em's and my relationship is and always has been much more than just a surface attraction,' he explained. 'It always felt like something strangely more ... something. I find it a totally, utterly mysterious and wonderful thing that I can barely talk about coherently.' From their fairly candid comments, the impression is of a passion that had diminished, not surprising for a relationship of several years' duration, but of a marriage suffused with mutual respect. At this point in time Branagh's marriage seemed as robust as his career.

Despite personal felicity and the professional achievement that a Hollywood film represented, there was for Branagh some Hamlet-like sense of isolation during the making of *Dead Again*. Directing and acting, the work was immense, and the rich feeling of collegiality that Branagh used to experience when only acting – the banter, the sense of being in the trenches together – had gone. He could never allow himself to relax entirely. His enormous responsibilities meant that he was different from everyone else on the set.

The celebrations for his thirtieth birthday, on 10 December 1990, were an example of the separateness he felt. Having arranged for a cake to be made in the likeness of Branagh's face, the cast and crew presented it to him at the end of the day's shooting. Branagh thanked them, before plunging a pair of scissors into his own throat as depicted on the cake. He then departed alone through a door, with a beer and a slice of cake, leaving his wife to cut cake for everyone else. While the others relaxed, he remained focused on the work to be done.

Branagh found not only his on-set experience with *Dead Again* a touch isolating, but also the general sensation of being in Hollywood. Moving there was a thrill, to be sure. He was impressed by its rich sense of cinematic history. A part of the set for *Dead Again* had apparently been used a half-century earlier in Hitchcock's *Rebecca*, starring Olivier. Branagh was also thrilled to learn that he was working on the lot where Welles had shot parts of *Citizen Kane*. But the move to

California was disorientating. Conscious of his inexperience in film compared with other Hollywood players, he kept his head down and concentrated on the work. 'I was ... really fucking scared shitless,' was how Branagh summed up his feelings. During his nine-month stay in Hollywood, the only social event he and Thompson attended was a tribute to Martin Scorsese. Branagh found an analogue to the way he felt in *Hamlet*:

> It's impossible to say you are unchanged by suddenly being at the helm of a Hollywood picture. Sometimes I felt very alone inside the system. Hamlet, textually, is 30, and he expresses so much of the indecision, neuroses, worry, anxiety and stress I see in this town, where one lives at a pace destructive to the human spirit: You get up too early, you work too long, you do not nourish your soul, you literally do not nourish your body because the air is so polluted. You grab leisure time, you grab space. Hamlet expresses the sea-change that occurs, that means a person like me is considering stopping for a while.[3]

Filming, however, continued to go well. The climactic scene where Branagh's Mike Church and Derek Jacobi's homicidal Franklyn Madson confronted Emma Thompson's Amanda was technically complex but expertly executed. It involved a moving wall, the creation of large shadows, and the positioning of special-effects technicians under beds so that they could flick blood onto curtains. Every member of the crew was needed for the scene. Once it was complete, a huge cheer went up.

The end result was that Branagh succeeded in completing *Dead Again* on schedule and for a budget of just under $15 million, which was exceedingly modest in Hollywood terms. 'It was probably the least expensive picture Paramount had made in the last year,' speculated Branagh. 'I was Mr Reasonable, Mr Efficient, so they liked me.' With filming over, he helped Peter Berger to edit the film. It turned out to be an arduous process. By May 1991 it was clear that there was still work to be done. 'You either like it or you go, "Fuck me, what is this?"' admitted Scott Frank.

The initial previews, designed to test the likely audience response, also indicated that all was not well. Emma Thompson's account of the first preview, for which a temporary score and sound effects were used, was chilling: 'One of the most unpleasant experiences in my life, like having your innards laid out in front of you. The movie wasn't finished and it wasn't right. You can feel the boredom and ridicule. And then they have a focus group where a spokesman stands up and says:

"I think that it's a piece of shit." You're standing at the back and the studio executives start looking at you as if suddenly you've grown an extra head.' The only good news for Branagh was that no one found his American accent unconvincing; in fact the audience tended to assume he was an unknown American actor. The second preview, though, was equally discouraging.

At this point Branagh benefited from a Robin Williams pep talk. He told Branagh about the excruciating preview for *Dead Poets Society*, his critically acclaimed Peter Weir film about an inspirational schoolteacher: apparently ninety people had walked out. By chiselling away with the editing (the final cut was forty-seven minutes shorter than the first), showing the 1940s scenes in black and white in order to differentiate the two storylines more clearly, introducing Patrick Doyle's stirring score, and by carrying out some reshoots to develop more strongly the romance between Mike Church and Amanda, Branagh ensured that the audience appreciation in later previews increased substantially. By the fourth preview *Dead Again* was reaching an audience rating as high as *Fatal Attraction*.

Branagh was ready in June to present the final cut of his new film to studio executives, cast and crew on the Paramount lot. As they all filed into the theatre, Branagh remained outside, composing a speech. He then entered the auditorium to enthusiastic applause. He asked for quiet, and then spoke: 'What you are about to see is the exciting combination of the film you read, the film you shot and the film we edited. I've been given lots of good ideas – all of which I will take credit for – and I've made the inevitable cuts, which I also take credit for. I stand by every frame. I'm very proud and hope you'll feel the same way.' Not exactly Churchillian, but it did the trick. At the end of the screening, a long line of well-wishers waited to show him their appreciation.

For Branagh, the work did not stop there. To maximise the chances of success, he set off on a breathless tour of America to promote *Dead Again*, taking in Dallas, Chicago, Seattle, New York and Los Angeles. Unlike many actors and directors, he did not begrudge having to play the role of salesman. 'It is not the hardest thing in the world to do,' he remarked, putting things in their proper perspective. 'I haven't spent the day lugging coal.' He even managed to consider the chore in romantic, historical terms. It was, he said, like 'going into villages and banging the drum', as actors had done in Shakespeare's time.

On 23 August 1991 – opening day for *Dead Again* in America – Branagh waited with bated breath. Could he conjure up another triumph in what had thus far seemed a charmed life? As it turned out, the news was rosy. Branagh would later convey a sense of the whirl of the film's release:

> You got into the opening weekend and there's such an obsession with numbers – and you're aware that you're opening with six other pictures, and there's incredible competition for ad space, for media time, even just for space in the public's imagination.
>
> In that opening weekend we did very well but four or five other pictures bit the dust, and you're bound to think there but for the grace of God go I.[4]

'Indeed I will go that way,' Branagh added prophetically, 'next time round or the time after that.'

That opening weekend *Dead Again* did indeed do good business. Opening at 450 theatres, it clocked up a very healthy $7,732 per screen. What no doubt helped the film's takings was the ecstatic response from the nation's scribes, as *Dead Again* notched up rave review after rave review. In the *New York Times* Vincent Canby took the film to be homage to, rather than a rip-off of, Hitchcock and Welles, a sentiment that would be shared by most American critics. *Dead Again* was evocative, opined Canby, 'of certain kinds of studio films of the 1940s and 50s and the manner in which we used to respond to them. Audiences took them not too seriously while thoroughly enjoying their grand passions and mad motivations, having little awareness of the great craft beneath the surface sheen.' Canby admired Branagh's directing, saying: 'For the most part, he demonstrates informed, easy control of the material and the medium.' The cinematography and the score were praised, as were the performances of Thompson, Garcia, Williams, Jacobi and Schygulla. As for Branagh's acting, Canby found the Olivier comparison irresistible. 'That he succeeds so well, and with such humor,' despite not being 'physically ideal' for the role of either Mike Church or Roman Strauss, 'would seem to be the result of sheer intelligence and, from time to time, a gesture that recalls those of the restless, ever-experimenting young Laurence Olivier.'

Canby was not alone in his admiration for *Dead Again*. Writing for the *Village Voice*, Manohla Dargis emphasised Branagh's audacity: 'Two years ago director Kenneth Branagh showed more than a little moxie by fearlessly taking on Laurence Olivier with his own grimy version of *Henry V*. Having scored with Shakespeare, Branagh has now taken on a different titan, Hitchcock, another British wonder who flourished upon crossing the Atlantic.' Not only taken on Hitchcock but not embarrassed himself, judged Dargis, whose overall assessment was glowing: 'He takes full cinematic advantage of Scott Frank's dynamite script, winding together its separate strands into a dazzling whole.'

Roger Ebert of the *Chicago Sun-Times* declared that *Dead Again* was for 'people who grew up on movies that were not afraid of grand gestures'. As had so often been the case throughout his career, Branagh was compared to the past masters. Unlike many British critics since 1989, however, Ebert did not do so in order to damn him:

> *Dead Again* is Kenneth Branagh once again demonstrating that he has a natural flair for bold theatrical gestures. If *Henry V*, the first film he directed and starred in, caused people to compare him to Olivier, *Dead Again* will inspire comparisons to Welles and Hitchcock – and the Olivier of Hitchcock's *Rebecca*. I do not suggest Branagh is already as great a director as Welles and Hitchcock, although he has a good start in that direction. What I mean is that his spirit, his daring, is in the same league. He is not interested in making timid movies.

Boosted by these rave reviews, *Dead Again* set the pace at the American box office in the late summer of 1991. After its strong opening weekend, Branagh's film hit the jackpot, reaching the number one position by early September, the second week of its release. In the process it nudged ahead of such formidable competition as *Terminator 2*. 'We are absolutely the definition of a sleeper hit,' explained Branagh. 'No one had heard of it the weekend before it came out. Then the promotion hit and from there it was word of mouth.' He attributed its success in part to timing. *Dead Again* was released just as the major summer films were losing momentum. Branagh's impression was that the film had been particularly popular with women, and that it had been a wonderful date movie. Ultimately *Dead Again* made more than $38 million at the American box office. Given that it had cost $15 million to make, Branagh reported, the Paramount top brass were 'cock-a-hoop'. 'I'm bloody pleased myself,' he added.

Showered with praise in America, Branagh continued to find such acclaim more elusive back home. *Dead Again* was due to open in late October, and with memories of the backlash against him in 1989 still fresh he must have been bracing himself for another onslaught from the critics. Before the film was released in Britain, however, his attentions were focused on the preparations for a stage production of Chekhov's *Uncle Vanya*, two-thirds of the budget for which came from the money he and Thompson had received for *Dead Again*.

Making a Hollywood film raised Branagh's profile, but the one negative consequence was its impact on the Renaissance company. For the previous three years it had been a hive of activity; but with Branagh working on *Dead Again* Renaissance inevitably took a back seat. The company diaries, replete hitherto, provide a sense of this. There were no entries for a month in September–October 1990 as the office closed down. When it reopened, the secretary's diary entries reflected Renaissance's new state of inactivity. 'LOOK AT OFFICE' she wrote on 16 October. 'LOOK AT OFFICE FURNITURE,' she added two days later. With *Uncle Vanya*, Renaissance regained some momentum.

Branagh has said that in casting the play he was determined to make clear that the company was not merely a showcase for his own acting talent. 'I didn't want Renaissance to be the Kenneth Branagh Gets All the Big Parts Company,' he said. 'It always makes me think of the conversation that goes, "Isn't it great about Ian McKellen and the Actors' Company? This week he's playing Hamlet, and last week he was in something where he just played the footman." "What was the play called?" "*The Footman*."' Given his involvement in the launching of *Dead Again* in America, it is difficult to see how Branagh could have given himself a big part in *Uncle Vanya*. In the end he decided against taking any acting role, confining himself to some directing at the start of rehearsals and periodically thereafter. It was Peter Egan, cast as the ecologically minded Doctor Astrov, who in fact did most of the directing. Having played Lear for Renaissance the year before, Richard Briers was given another opportunity to rid himself of his reputation as master of the television sitcom when Branagh cast him as Vanya. Sian Thomas took on the role of Yelena, for whom Vanya experiences unrequited love. Sonya, whose affection for Astrov is likewise unreciprocated, would be played by Annabel Arden of the much respected ensemble Théâtre de Complicité. Though Rachel Kempson started rehearsals, she pulled out, as it soon became clear that at eighty she was too frail to complete a long run.

As Branagh began the preparations for *Uncle Vanya*, he found himself influenced by his experience in the movies:

I was talking to the designer about it, and I was saying, 'We'll have a big gauze in front of the set, onto which we can project slides. We'll project a slide of a Russian plain to begin with, and then we see a little house, and then we dissolve', I said, 'into another slide closer to the house.' And I went on. I realised that what I was describing was the start of a movie. I find that that's the way I feel about the theatre – I want to make it as exciting visually as possible. I believe totally in the spoken word, but I feel there is a marriage to be made that cinema manages, and that the best theatre work manages as well.[5]

Opening in Belfast in June, the Renaissance *Uncle Vanya* embarked thereafter on an extensive nationwide tour, to which the public response was tepid. But it caught on after arriving in London at the Lyric Theatre, Hammersmith, where it played to packed houses. Accompanied by Emma Thompson, Branagh took time out from his promotional tour for *Dead Again* in the United States to attend *Uncle Vanya*'s opening night in London. Theatre-goers were treated to a foreword from Prince Charles in their programmes. Writing under the Kensington Palace letterhead, the heir to the throne stated: '[Chekhov] gives us a beautifully detailed, humorous yet harsh view of human nature,' and he wished everyone a pleasant evening at the theatre.

The critics responded in very different ways to the latest Renaissance production. Jeremy Kingston of *The Times* said this was 'a sensible, detailed, yet unfussy, interpretation', and praised the quality of the acting. In the *Daily Telegraph* Charles Spencer was also much taken with the performances. Renaissance, reported Spencer, 'presents the play dead straight, without editorial gloss. But after a couple of months on the road, the ensemble acting is excellent, and like all the best Chekhov productions, the performance creates the illusion that we are watching not a work of art, but the messy sprawl of life itself.'. Spencer found Briers' central performance as Vanya memorably poignant. In the *Guardian* Michael Billington felt more ambivalent. In Briers' Vanya and Thomas's Yelena there were two superb central performances, he acknowledged. But Billington berated Branagh and Egan for neither providing the production with a particular sense of place, nor plumbing the emotional depths of the play. 'I have rarely been so unmoved by *Uncle Vanya*,' he lamented. Writing in the *Independent*, Jeffrey Wainwright was likewise unimpressed. He said that the production lacked a social context, and that in general the humour of the play was conveyed more effectively than the characters' despair.

Any ideas Branagh might have had that the critics would greet his new film more charitably than his new theatre production must have been dashed by the English previews for *Dead Again*. A writer for *Time Out* reported that there were 'hoots of derision at the preview I attended', while an *Empire* magazine article linked this embarrassing episode to the whole phenomenon of Branagh-bashing:

> In a preview theatre in London ... much of the film – the mannered sweet nothing exchanges betwixt Kenny and his little woman in particular – is, sadly, greeted with hoots of derision. Kenneth Branagh, it seems, remains unloved in his home islands, as if we British will simply never forgive him for being so young, so keen, so damned, dashed *theatrical*. For being so successful and for being, as he readily refers to himself in self-mocking tones, 'so lovey'. For marrying fellow whizzkid Emma Thompson to become one half of a stage couple that seems, looking from the outside, to be oh so smug. For being an all-round whippersnapper with the accursed cheek to write a book about his life before he had even lived one.
>
> Forgive Kenneth Branagh? Not today. Maybe not tomorrow ... but some day, perhaps, for talent, as they say, will out.

Released in Britain on 25 October 1991, *Dead Again* made more than half a million pounds on its opening weekend. For the week of 1 November, it reached number one at the box office. The following week it was number two, overtaken by *City Slickers*, the new Billy Crystal movie. In the end Branagh's film made a little more than £3 million in the UK.

The degree of success that was achieved was in spite rather than because of the critical response to the film; for the reviewers excoriated Branagh. The *Guardian*, *Times*, *Daily Telegraph*, *Independent*, *Sunday Telegraph*, *Mail on Sunday*, *Independent on Sunday*, *Sunday Express*, and *Time Out* savaged the film. The general sentiment seems to have been that in making a thriller in the style of Hitchcock, Branagh was gilding the lily. Many reviewers expressed disbelief at *Dead Again*'s success in the United States. As with *Henry V*, some writers felt the film showed that Branagh was obsessed with Olivier, as *Dead Again* was reminiscent of Hitchcock's *Rebecca*, starring Olivier. In the *Independent* Adam Mars-Jones asserted that with *Dead Again* Branagh had been 'lucky enough to come across a script that takes his Olivier complex, this actor's version of the Oedipus complex, a stage further'. Christopher Tookey wrote sardonically in the *Sunday Telegraph* that, as Roman Strauss, Branagh looked 'like Olivier in a silly beard'.

The divide separating American and English critics in their appreciation of Branagh, discernible at the time of *Henry V*'s release, became a chasm with *Dead Again*. A raft of rave reviews in America had become an array of vicious attacks in England. The very things that excited America's leading critics – his audacity in combining acting and directing, and in tackling subject matter that invited comparisons with legends such as Olivier, Welles and Hitchcock, and the grand theatricality of his film-making – seemed to their English counterparts to be vexing signs of hubris.

With *Dead Again*, Branagh had in fact produced a solid piece of entertainment, as the American critics understood. The film was not without its shortcomings. Branagh's portrayal of Mike Church needed to be more menacing. To maximise the tension, the audience really needs to believe he is capable of killing Emma Thompson's Amanda Sharp. In addition, Thompson's Amanda was not sufficiently alluring or mysterious. She was already a fine actress, and with her subsequent performances, in such films as *Howards End*, she would show she was an outstanding one; but she was not ideal for the part of Amanda. Still, *Dead Again* is a beautiful-looking film. The cinematography and set design were excellent. Los Angeles was shot in a loving way. The story itself moved at a clip. Some of the cameos, especially those by Robin Williams and Hanna Schygulla, were impressive. In the role of Roman Strauss, Branagh himself was charming, charismatic, exotic, mysterious and dangerous. Unlike the Mike Church character, he does seem capable of murder. *Dead Again* was not a great film, but it did represent a bold undertaking. Certainly it did not merit the mauling it received on Fleet Street.

As he had two years earlier, Branagh was forced to reflect on Branagh-bashing in England, for the response to *Dead Again* in relation to the American reaction showed that the phenomenon was ongoing. Asked on one occasion for his view of the anti-Branagh bandwagon, he revealed:

> I do, and I don't understand it, to be perfectly honest. It's just an arbitrary thing that this country is very capable of: a resentment that just occurs against someone who is relatively young and relatively successful. It is always upsetting when you read abusive stuff about yourself. You feel bruised, you know. Christ knows, you make a film and it takes 18 months so that it is a great personal investment and when people don't like it, you have a bit of a blub. But swiftly you recover because, essentially, it's meaningless. It's just a fucking film. It is completely and utterly unimportant, isn't it? ... There's so many other fucking horrible things in the world that the fact that some people find you annoying is not the greatest revelation. So what the fuck? There's fucking nothing to complain about. You want

to be in fucking Bangladesh! If some people don't like your films, what a tragedy, what a great personal tragedy! You won't get rid of me that easily. I'm MUCH too fucking thick-skinned for that.[6]

The truth is that deep down it was impossible for him to be that philosophical and resilient. Such was the onslaught, reveals Richard Briers, that Branagh began to wonder not only whether there was merit in the criticism he received, but if he should even go on with his career:

The attacks hurt him. Undoubtedly hurt him. The chums around him, including me and the older friends, said, 'You must just keep on, just keep going, because it's an unattractive trait in this country to knock anyone who puts their head over the parapet.' ... It was disappointing for him, and he thought, 'Should I go on at all?' because when everyone says, 'You're no good, you're no good, who do you think you are?' eventually you get dispirited. But he didn't. He was tougher than that, and he bounced. But of course he was hurt ... He couldn't understand it. He thought perhaps they were right, because when so many people attack you, you think, 'Well maybe there's something in it.'[7]

What must have accentuated Branagh's sense of victimisation was the way he was treated as a hero when back in Belfast, as he was in the summer of 1991. On local television he was referred to as 'one of our own, now'. 'Good you're back, Kenny,' was the constant refrain he heard on the streets of his home-town. He could not walk into a pub without half a dozen drinks being sent his way. As an adolescent, Branagh had felt keenly the diminution of that feeling of community on his arrival in England. His homecomings brought back to him that sense of loss.

Dead Again marked the culmination of a relentless, decade-long thrust by Branagh towards the summit of the film and theatre world. RADA, RSC, Renaissance, Oscar nominations, and a number one hit at the American and British box offices, all by the age of thirty. He had fashioned a career that was quite simply the envy of any actor of his generation in the world. The journey had been one of ceaseless industry, and as *Dead Again* was released, Branagh spoke of his determination, finally, to take a break. His intention, he said, was to go with Emma Thompson to Scotland for a real holiday.

At the same time he began to plan the next phase of his career. He talked of tackling *Hamlet* once again, possibly on Broadway. He was intrigued by the idea of doing an *Othello* with himself as Iago and Gérard Depardieu in the lead role. Nor had he given up on the idea of filming Thomas Hardy's *The Return of the Native*. Two ideas in particular dominated his thinking: a new Renaissance theatre production of a Shakespeare play in the spring of 1992 to celebrate the company's fifth anniversary, and a film of *Much Ado About Nothing*, to be shot in Italy using American as well as British actors. After his spell in Hollywood, Branagh would turn again to the Bard.

6

Much Ado

To stay or not to stay in Hollywood – that was the question facing Kenneth Branagh in 1991. With the success of *Dead Again*, a future as a Hollywood player beckoned. But back in Britain were his family and friends, not to mention his reputation as a leading light in the theatre. Contributing to the dilemma was the fact that carrots were being dangled to keep him in the United States. He was offered more than £1 million to make another film. 'I slept on it for weeks,' he recalled. 'It couldn't possibly be rejected out of hand. After all, I can do lots of things with that sort of money. And it wasn't a question of "I'm not going to sell my soul".' But after much reflection Branagh turned his back on America. On the professional front he thought that making films on the other side of the Atlantic could help regenerate the moribund British film industry; but beyond that consideration, he simply wanted to go home.

This decision represented no dilution of Branagh's ambition. On the contrary, he worked at a feverish rate in 1992 and 1993, carrying out a multi-media assault on the works of Shakespeare. He would adapt the screenplay for, star in, and direct his second Shakespeare film, *Much Ado About Nothing*. To commemorate the fifth anniversary of his Renaissance company, he decided to play Coriolanus at the Chichester Festival. He agreed to return to the Royal Shakespeare Company to tackle the role that still obsessed him: Hamlet. He organised a radio programme of *Hamlet* with John Gielgud in the cast. He made a film of a Chekhov playlet, *Swan Song*, about an ageing actor, to be portrayed by Gielgud, who re-enacts some of the great Shakespearean roles he has played during his career.

Branagh's efforts during this period served to entrench his reputation as the premier Shakespearean artist in the world. A number of actors might have aspired to that position. Ian McKellen, Derek Jacobi and Antony Sher, for example, had each produced a formidable body of work on stage; but just as films such as *Henry V* and *Hamlet* ensured that Olivier eclipsed Gielgud as a Shakespearean artist in the public mind, so Branagh's Shakespeare films had the same salutary impact on his reputation as an interpreter of the Bard. To the public, Branagh's name was becoming virtually synonymous with Shakespeare's.

At the start of 1992 Branagh's cinematic plans for the year were announced: he would film *Much Ado About Nothing* in the summer, but before that a comedy, *Peter's Friends*, for which Branagh would once again put in overtime by directing as well as acting.

Emma Thompson's connections explain how Branagh came to make *Peter's Friends*. She had got to know Martin Bergman at school, a relationship that continued during their days at Cambridge, where both were active in the Footlights. Bergman would go on after Cambridge to become a sort of artistic entrepreneur, organising a Torvill and Dean world tour, *inter alia*, and to marry the American comedienne Rita Rudner. Both wanted Rudner to be in films, but in view of the lack of roles for female comics they started to write screenplays themselves. *Peter's Friends*, their fourth film script, had more than a hint of the autobiographical. It centred on six university friends who reunite for a New Year's celebration at the estate of one of their set, a young aristocrat called Peter, a decade after the farewell performance of their musical comedy revue. Comparing notes on their lives and loves over the course of the 1980s produces mirth and acrimony in equal measure. In some respects, the story was reminiscent of *The Big Chill*, the 1983 American hit about a reunion of youngsters from the 1960s whose ideals have been compromised by the practicalities of adulthood.

With Bergman close to Thompson, and Thompson married to Branagh, the screenplay ended up in Branagh's hands. He found himself attracted to the story for a variety of reasons. Its central theme – friendship – struck a chord with him. He found the uplifting quality of the story appealing. He was determined, he said later, 'to send out a positive message ... I just got offered a script about a serial killer. And while I don't want to put my head in the sand and pretend awful things don't happen in the world, I do not wish to make a movie about a serial killer.' As with *Dead Again*, Branagh must have liked the way *Peter's Friends* allowed him to demonstrate his versatility. By directing a light comedy, having done Shakespeare and film noir, he would show that he was a jack of all trades and hopefully a master of them all.

Branagh also felt that his working-class background was paradoxically ideal for a story about a privileged set. Determined that *Peter's Friends* should have more than just a preppy appeal, he was confident of being able to ensure that an atmosphere of smugness did not infect the film. 'I kept in mind that I wanted it to be seen by people whom I knew at comprehensive school,' said Branagh. The populist goals that had shaped Branagh's career hitherto thus continued to influence his thinking.

Another attraction of *Peter's Friends* was that it could be used to secure the finances needed for *Much Ado*, which Branagh was already planning when the script for *Peter's Friends* was sent to him. Getting the money for *Much Ado*, given that *Henry V* had not been a big hit in Britain, was proving difficult. But now *Much Ado* could be offered as part of a package with the more ostensibly commercial *Peter's Friends*, with any prospective backer told that if they wanted to finance one film, they would have to fund the other. In the end both movies were backed by the Samuel Goldwyn Company, and produced in collaboration with Renaissance Films, with Britain's Channel 4 Films providing additional support for *Peter's Friends* and BBC Films doing the same for *Much Ado*.

In casting the film, Branagh drew heavily on Emma Thompson's kith and kin. Of the six characters who had been at university together in *Peter's Friends*, three were played by actors who had actually been chums at Cambridge: Thompson herself, her former beau Hugh Laurie and Stephen Fry (who took the title role of Peter). The other three parts went to Thompson's husband, Thompson's friend Imelda Staunton, and Alphonsia Emmanuel. Another Cambridge friend, Tony Slattery, played the part of Emmanuel's latest lover. Thompson's mother, Phyllida Law, was cast as Peter's housekeeper; Rita Rudner took the role of Branagh's American wife. A couple of Renaissance stalwarts, Edward Jewesbury and Richard Briers, were given cameos.

According to Stephen Evans, surrounding himself with so many Oxbridge types exposed a degree of insecurity in Branagh. 'I think he was slightly chippy about the Oxbridge bunch,' he says, 'which of course was classically ironic because he was cleverer than they were, and also classically double-ironic to make *Peter's Friends*, which was so Oxbridge – Hugh Laurie, Stephen Fry.' He adds that Branagh had particular concerns about collaborating with Stephen Fry because 'this guy seemed to know everything and Ken didn't. I said, "Ken, look, you want to go to Oxford and Cambridge, that's tough. To get into RADA is much tougher. To get the Gold Medal at RADA is like a quadruple-starred First at Oxford."'

Branagh, nevertheless, believed that his approach to the casting of this film made sense. The fact that a good many of Peter's friends were to be played by actors who were themselves close would add to the authenticity of the piece. But casting in this way left Branagh open to criticism; and at the time of the film's release various journalists latched on to this as the most striking aspect of the *Peter's Friends* enterprise. The *Guardian*, for instance, suggested that it raised an important issue: 'Can Branagh get tough? Can he discriminate, do new and brave work with his mates forever in tow?' The implication of much of the press coverage was that Branagh, along with Thompson, was guilty of nepotism.

Branagh and his fellow actors reacted in no uncertain terms to these allegations. 'The idea of it being this kind of lovefest of chums enjoying themselves is utter rubbish,' asserted Stephen Fry. Branagh himself ridiculed the accusation:

> I'm sure that some will say it should be called 'Kenny's Friends', when in fact I have no past history with them at all. It's Em who goes way back with them. The other thing I'd like to say is should this company, the RSC, be known as [Artistic Director] Adrian [Noble]'s Friends because vast numbers of people work regularly in this organisation? And look at Martin Scorsese's films. Are people annoyed because Robert de Niro has worked with him six times? And, 'Apparently, he knows him!'[1]

The response to the casting of *Peter's Friends* indicated that the anti-Branagh sentiment that had surfaced in 1989 was still around.

When production of *Peter's Friends* began, on 24 February 1992, these concerns about the hostility that the film would provoke were already threatening to paralyse the cast. Huddled in a corner, Hugh Laurie and Stephen Fry speculated on the likely press response to the film. Overhearing their conversation, Branagh decided to confront the issue directly. Some eight years later Fry was able to recall the episode vividly:

Hugh and I [were] trying to imagine the kind of reviews that say a *Time Out* reviewer would give this film. And we were working ourselves up into a frenzy of self-hatred and horror at what we'd imagine that they would say. 'This incestuous wank.' 'This, this awful ghastly Oxbridge yick.' You know we were getting so upset about what we imagined. This is before we'd even turned over the camera for a single frame. We were already imagining how ghastly they were and uh, Ken had overheard us and he just said 'Dahling!' ... He said, 'People who read and listen to reviewers in *Time Out* constitute point nought nought one per cent of the population. If you're worried about what reviewers are thinking, you're allowing them to dictate to you. If you really have contempt for them have some memory that nobody else cares about what reviewers think. And if you are the only person who does, then what does that say about you?' And I thought about that for a bit and I thought he's absolutely right. It is nonsense. It is very easy in our profession to get terribly upset and to allow ourselves to be dictated to by others and one of the banes of being British, as we know, is a sort of self-consciousness of feeling that if I do this what will people think I am trying to do? How will they interpret what I am doing? How will I interpret what they interpret I'm doing? We drive ourselves in an appalling self-sodomitic kind of revolution. Like the dog running around in circles so fast that it injures itself twice. Ken is not like that. I don't know how he manages to avoid that. Perhaps because he wasn't born on the mainland. But simple and obvious as it sounds, he is not paralysed by self-consciousness and that allows him to be free as an artist and it gives him a terrible and splendid clarity about what he does and that is a remarkable and wonderfully valuable thing.[2]

Branagh's pep talk had done the trick. The shooting of *Peter's Friends*, which took place on location in London and at Wrotham Park in Hertfordshire, turned into an upbeat affair. Emma Thompson recalled that there was a lot of laughing on set. Branagh was struck by the relish with which the actors known primarily for their comedic gifts, such as Stephen Fry and Hugh Laurie, tackled the dramatic passages of the story. He was particularly impressed by Imelda Staunton's performance as the neurotic wife of the Hugh Laurie character, devastated by the death of her child.

Branagh himself played the part of Andrew Benson, best friend to Stephen Fry's Peter. Andrew has abandoned his writing partnership with Peter in order to move to Hollywood, where he has created a hit television sitcom, *Who's in the Kitchen?* Despite its popularity, the wealth he has acquired, his marriage to the show's star, played by Rita Rudner, and his success in giving up booze, Andrew is disturbed by the feeling that he has sacrificed his integrity on the altar of material success. The denouement of the story comes when Branagh's Andrew returns to the bottle and viciously berates Peter, before being sent into a state of profound contrition when Peter reveals his tragic secret to Andrew and the rest of his friends: he is HIV positive. The role of Andrew called for some adroit acting on the part of Branagh. He had to blend the character's self-loathing with his easy charm and humour. It was a brave piece of casting in that he did not give himself the plum, central role – that went to Stephen Fry – and his character was not particularly likeable.

Once the shooting of *Peter's Friends* was complete, Branagh turned to post-production. As had so often been the case during his career, he pushed himself through a gruelling schedule so that he could tackle multiple projects simultaneously. In this case he busied himself with the editing of the film whilst rehearsing the new Renaissance theatre production, *Coriolanus*. Not content to confine his involvement in *Peter's Friends* to acting, directing, producing and assisting with the editing, he also selected the music for the soundtrack! Wishing to convey the mood of the 1980s, he chose mainstream, melodic pop hits by the likes of Queen, Cyndi Lauper and Tina Turner.

Putting the film together caused Branagh to reflect on the decade that had just unfolded in terms of world events. The title sequence consisted of a montage of clips about the events and personalities – including Reagan, Thatcher, the Falklands War, the onset of AIDS, the Exxon Valdez episode and the Gulf War – that had dominated the 1980s and early 1990s. 'When we finally put together everything I asked for,' said Branagh, 'the montage was terrifying. I thought, "Christ, we've all lived through all that."'

Opening the London Film Festival at the Odeon, Marble Arch, on Bonfire Night 1992, a star-studded event that ended with a dinner for one thousand at the Café Royal, *Peter's Friends* was released in Britain eight days later. Despite the sage advice he had offered Messrs Fry and Laurie about the insignificance of reviews, Branagh must have feared, especially given his prior experiences with *Henry V* and *Dead Again*, that he would suffer another brutal assault.

As things turned out, a good many reviewers *were* acidulous. Geoff Brown of *The Times* castigated Branagh's acting. 'During his drunk scene towards the end,' he wrote, 'I felt like hiding under the seat.' He had a higher opinion of the performances of Emma Thompson, as the spinster put in touch with her own sexuality, and Phyllida Law, as Stephen Fry's grumpy housekeeper. Adam Mars-Jones of the *Independent* argued that too many of the acting personalities and the gags on offer in *Peter's Friends* were appropriate for television entertainment but not for the big screen. *Sight and Sound*, the official publication of the British Film Institute, was no more charitable: '*Peter's Friends* is in altogether too many ways a comedy of failures.'

Many other reviewers, however, were more enthusiastic. 'It's well written, beautifully performed and highly entertaining,' declared Derek Malcolm in the *Guardian*. Sheridan Morley, writing in the *Sunday Express*, liked it too, singling out Phyllida Law's performance for special mention. The London *Standard*'s Alexander Walker, who had admired Branagh's previous work, was again positive. *Peter's Friends*, he asserted, was 'one of the liveliest, most observant group portraits of class and generation our screen has seen in recent years'. The comedy, characterisation, pacing, social observation – Walker liked it all. At its best, he wrote, 'it is a dream'. Ironically, given the musings of Fry and Laurie at the start of the production, *Time Out* also praised *Peter's Friends*, describing it as an 'amiable enterprise'.

The critics who admired it proved to be more in tune with the public mood than its detractors. The film went to number one at the UK box office in late November, and remained in the top five for the next two months. It ended up making more than £3,350,000 – a tidy sum, given the film's miniscule budget of £1.6 million.

Peter's Friends was released in the United States on Christmas Day, showing in just a few cities before filtering out to cinemas across the country. The critical response was mixed, as it had been in Britain. In the *New York Times* Janet Maslin's praise was more gentle than gushing. She found the film pleasant but superficial. Emma Thompson and Rita Rudner took the acting plaudits, she felt, but the cast generally was effective. As for Branagh's direction, Maslin thought it 'blithe and serviceable without having any particular hallmarks, save perhaps an appreciation of the talent he has assembled'. Though it disliked the ending, the *Village Voice*'s overall view was that *Peter's Friends* was a 'sweet, intelligent, though small, movie'. The *New Yorker*, by contrast, was inimical. 'You cower in your seat,' wrote Terrence Rafferty, 'steeling yourself against the next grisly bit of repartee'.

The film barely made an impression on the American public, earning a paltry $4 million at the box office. The contrast with *Dead Again*, which had made close to ten times that sum in the US, was sharp – and to Branagh disappointing; but *Peter's Friends* had done so well in Britain and in other markets, especially France, that an overall profit was made.

Janet Maslin had got it about right: *Peter's Friends* was entertaining, often funny, but a touch superficial. There were some effective one-liners. Commenting on the mousiness of Emma Thompson's character, Rita Rudner claims she makes Mother Teresa 'look like a hooker'. Stephen Fry's bisexual Peter resists the advances of Thompson's Maggie by insisting he is 'not really in the vagina business'. But the quality of the quips should have been accompanied by deeper characterisation. As the initial badinage gives way to the realisation that not one of the characters is happy, the sympathy elicited (from the viewer) is slight. The moments of gravity prove less effective than the comedic exchanges. All in all, *Peter's Friends* was a decent effort, but far short of the quality shown by Branagh three years earlier in *Henry V*. Audiences would not have to wait long, however, before he scaled those dizzy heights again; for only six months after the opening of *Peter's Friends*, *Much Ado About Nothing* was released.

Before production began on *Much Ado* in August 1992, Branagh performed in another film, in a radio broadcast and in a theatre production. Pundits sometimes refer to the extra lung that political leaders seem to possess to enable them to undertake a daunting array of tasks. The point applies equally to Branagh.

Squeezed into his frenetic schedule in early 1992 was a cameo role in the Disney film *Swing Kids*. Filmed in Prague, directed by Thomas Carter, who had enjoyed considerable success in television with *Hill Street Blues*, *Swing Kids* told the story, grounded apparently in some degree of historical accuracy, of a group of German teenagers who articulated their opposition to the Nazis through their love of jazz. Starring a cluster of fine young acting talent, including Robert Sean Leonard of *Dead Poets Society* fame and Christian Bale, who had graced Branagh's *Henry V*, *Swing Kids* contained some magnificently choreographed dance scenes. Complementing the young actors on display were more seasoned hands, including Branagh and Barbara Hershey. Branagh played the small part of a charming but sinister Gestapo officer who pressures the Robert Sean Leonard character to throw in his lot with the Nazis. Branagh's chief motive for taking the role appears to have been to raise money for his Renaissance company.

Released in Britain and America in 1993, *Swing Kids* produced a wide spectrum of opinion from reviewers. The *Guardian* and London *Standard* castigated the film, as, in America, did the *New York Times* and the *Village Voice*. By contrast, the *Daily Telegraph* lauded the film as 'an original, well-acted, thought-provoking slant on history which should captivate any intelligent youngster', while the *Daily Mail* referred admiringly to the movie's 'gritty power and whiff of emotional truth'. On Branagh's contribution, opinion was likewise divided. The *Observer* praised Branagh's decision to play such an unsympathetic character, while the *Spectator* found his performance 'unexpectedly compelling'. But the *Daily Mail* judged his acting to be one-dimensional, and *Time Out* thought him miscast. Mixed reviews were followed by meagre business at the box office. In the United States *Swing Kids* made less than $6 million, while in Britain it opened on only twenty-four screens in the entire country and ended up with a paltry box-office total: less than £25,000.

What caused the most comment about Branagh's involvement in *Swing Kids* was his conspicuous absence from the credits. It was reported that his contract for the film stipulated that he could demand the removal of his name from the credits; and that is precisely what he proceeded to do. Speculation as to the reasons for this ploy ranged from dissatisfaction on Branagh's part with the film when finished to a calculation by his agents that to be billed for a minor part below Robert Sean Leonard and Christian Bale would not do justice to his elevated reputation. Branagh himself claimed that the issue was pecuniary. 'They didn't pay enough,' he told an American journalist. 'If they had paid better, they could have had me.'

Taking his name off the credits made a certain sort of sense; for clearly the nature of the part and of the film were never going to enlarge Branagh's reputation. The most valuable aspect of *Swing Kids* in retrospect was the practice it provided in playing a Nazi; a decade later he would give an award-winning performance as another Third Reich leader in *Conspiracy*, an altogether more distinguished piece of work.

Closer to Branagh's heart in the spring of 1992 than the diversion of *Swing Kids* was commemorating the fifth anniversary of his cherished Renaissance company in proper fashion. The celebration came in two parts: a stint at the Chichester Festival Theatre with *Coriolanus* preceded by a radio performance of *Hamlet* produced jointly by

Renaissance and the BBC. Branagh would take the title role in both. His decision to tackle Hamlet reflected his ongoing obsession with the Danish prince. He had already played Hamlet at RADA, Laertes with the RSC, and the lead role again in a Renaissance theatre production – and still he wanted more. Branagh explained to a journalist in April 1992 that over the years different aspects of *Hamlet* had sustained his interest:

> When you're 21 it's perhaps the adventure story, the romantic, noble Jacobean revenge hero who appeals. Ten years on, it's more a story of a man who works through his problems to find a sense of inner peace. Exactly the same words you spoke the first time strike a deeper chord. In your early thirties your parents or grandparents start to go and you start to think more about death.
>
> Hamlet's journey through the play is the journey of a man finally able to say: 'If it be now, 'tis not to come; if it be not to come, it will be now; if it be not now, yet it will come – the readiness is all.' Death truly is 'the undiscovered country from whose bourne no traveller returns'. Hamlet is a part which obsesses me, and I find death a subject of constant fascination and curiosity. The whole notion of mortality is what we are all obsessed with from the moment we arrive here. My intense enthusiasm for the play springs out of what light it sheds on all that.[3]

Branagh persuaded a formidable array of acting talent to join him for this radio *Hamlet*. John Gielgud, Derek Jacobi and Judi Dench would play the Ghost, Claudius and Gertrude respectively. Michael Hordern and Emma Thompson would tackle the roles of Player King and of Player Queen. Sophie, Emma's sister, would play Ophelia, as she had in the Renaissance theatre production of *Hamlet* four years earlier; and Michael Williams would portray Horatio. The *Sunday Times* described this as 'one of the most illustrious casts assembled in Britain in recent years'.

During the recording of the play, in January 1992, Branagh did his utmost to ensure that a mood of levity as well as a sense of purpose infused proceedings. He often liked to adopt a stereotypically effeminate, theatrical persona in dealing with other actors – a practice he would explain in his 1995 film *In the Bleak Midwinter*. When the recording of *Hamlet* was going less than perfectly, Branagh switched to his alter ego, declaring 'O-o-o-o-o-h! Dorothy Discipline needs to sprinkle some of her fairy dust in here!' The interjection had the desired effect: his colleagues laughed and then pressed on with the work.

At the end of the recording the principals were satisfied. Judi Dench felt that she had made more sense of Gertrude, a difficult part because of the paucity of lines despite the importance of the character, than when playing the same role opposite Daniel Day-Lewis in the National Theatre's 1989 production. For his part, Branagh found it liberating to be able to deliver the 'To be or not to be' soliloquy without worrying about the response of an audience, as he would in the theatre. The BBC broadcast this recording of the play on 26 April 1992, the sixtieth anniversary of John Gielgud's first Hamlet on radio.

With no pause for breath, Branagh moved on to one of Shakespeare's less sympathetic lead roles: Coriolanus, the haughty Roman warrior. The origins of this production lay in the invitation issued by Patrick Garland, director of the Chichester Festival, to Branagh's Renaissance company to stage the opening play in the theatre's thirtieth anniversary season. Branagh accepted the offer. Little-known director Tim Supple was recruited for the production, with Branagh explaining this decision simply: 'He's a very talented lad and it's our company's policy to encourage people to do the unexpected.'

In choosing the play, Branagh had considered tackling *Richard III*, a role that Olivier had made virtually his own with his memorable 1955 film version. Branagh remembered how, in 1989, his *Henry V* film had provoked the accusation that he was shamelessly trying to steal Olivier's thunder. Playing Richard, Branagh feared, would only resuscitate that suspicion. 'The idea of doing Richard III did seem like putting my head fully on the block to be severed in a brutal fashion,' he said. As things turned out, Branagh did not get to play Richard for another decade. This, then, was a notable occasion when Branagh's self-confidence failed him; he had allowed his concern over the critics to influence a major artistic decision.

So Branagh and Supple turned to *Coriolanus*, Shakespeare's play about the arrogant Roman general whose star waxes after a great military victory, but wanes when he refuses to show deference to the representatives of the people. Banished, he joins forces with Aufidius, who hitherto has been his greatest rival and Rome's greatest threat, and moves on Rome. When his friends fail to persuade him to spare Rome, his mother, Volumnia, who has previously cherished his martial endeavours, successfully pleads with him to withdraw his forces. Relenting in the face of this maternal pressure, Coriolanus utters the famous line in what is the emotional centre of the play: 'O mother, mother! What have you done?' Effectively, she has signed his death warrant: he dies at the hands of Aufidius and his supporters.

Coriolanus is the most political of Shakespeare's plays in the sense that he explores the relationship between leadership and the masses more vigorously than in any of his other works. But it also functions as a psychological drama, with the mother–son theme having a Hamletian ring to it. The love-hate relationship between Coriolanus and Aufidius also provides rich interpretative possibilities; in Robert Lepage's production in Quebec, also in 1992, it was portrayed as homoerotic.

In the twentieth century, the part of Coriolanus has attracted a number of outstanding actors. Henry Irving tackled the role in 1901, with Ellen Terry as Volumnia. Alan Howard portrayed Coriolanus in a 1983 BBC television production, and seven years later Michael Pennington played the part on stage for the English Shakespeare Company. But it was Olivier, more than anyone else, who made an impact in the role, in 1959, with his scintillating portrayal of the Roman. In playing Coriolanus, therefore, Branagh would not be able to escape altogether the Olivier comparison.

At first Branagh was reluctant to tackle Coriolanus. Not only was he attracted to the part of Richard III, he was also uncertain about exploring a character who seemed to have few redeeming qualities. In the end he consented, in part because, with its cast of twenty and the more than fifty locals who would be recruited for the crowd and battle scenes, *Coriolanus* was a true company piece and so ideal for Renaissance.

Iain Glen was recruited to play Aufidius, and Richard Briers was well cast as Menenius, friend to Coriolanus. Susannah Harker took the part of Coriolanus's gentle wife Virgilia. Judi Dench, who had always enjoyed working with Branagh and no doubt assumed this collaboration would be equally rewarding, was asked to play Volumnia. She had a clear concept of the character right from the outset, and wasted no time in explaining this to Branagh: 'She wanted a very sexy relationship with Coriolanus, more as a rival to his wife.'

At the first rehearsal Judi Dench confirmed her reputation as an inveterate giggler. During the read-through of the play, she burst out laughing on hearing the strange line, spoken when two characters meet: 'I know you well, sir; and you know me; your name, I think, is

Adrian.' Branagh's own mood was generally buoyant. Having saddled himself with so many onerous responsibilities on other projects, he relished the opportunity to be just another actor. 'I've had a renewal of the company experience as an actor,' he said. 'It's nice to be able to lark around and have a few jokes in the green room without worrying about the fact I'm wearing two hats.'

His good mood was amplified by reflection, prompted by the fifth anniversary of Renaissance, on the achievements of his beloved theatre company. A provincial audience loyal to Renaissance had been built up, a proud Branagh told a journalist. A signature style of lucid, naturalistic acting had been developed. Actors had been stretched and their careers regenerated. Richard Briers, for instance, had experienced a remarkable career shift from playing television sitcom characters to meeting some of the great challenges of the classical theatre repertoire, including Lear and Uncle Vanya.

The Renaissance diaries reveal the almost manic work levels that Branagh maintained in order to keep the company going. There was one day, in the summer of 1992, when he filmed *Swan Song* during the day, performed as Coriolanus in the evening, attended to post-production on *Peter's Friends*, and to pre-production on *Much Ado About Nothing*. Renaissance remained a collaborative enterprise, however. Branagh's diligence was nothing short of phenomenal, but the company diaries make clear that David Parfitt and Stephen Evans were also extremely busy.

Cheered by the camaraderie of his colleagues and proud of his company's accomplishments, Branagh nonetheless found himself all at sea with the role of Coriolanus. 'Quite frankly,' he confessed, 'it's the hardest thing I've ever done in Shakespeare. The language is tough and, to be honest, hard to understand. There is no lyricism, the rhythms are difficult. You just hope that by playing it with heart and passion you can make it clear.' Furthermore, the thrust of the character cut against Branagh's natural instincts, which, as he himself has acknowledged, tend to search for the hopeful, redeeming aspects of the human condition. 'Coriolanus might be called a fascist, or ruthless or thuggish,' said Branagh. 'Any attempt I've made to make him heroic the director, Tim Supple, is firmly squashing out of me.'

As well as fretting over the part, Branagh continued to ponder the question of why he had been on the receiving end of so many harsh attacks. With the fifth anniversary of Renaissance, there was some reflection in the press not only on the company, but on its leader in particular. Inevitably this coverage included a review of the assaults on Branagh's reputation, and he was obliged to field questions on the subject. In philosophical mode, he explored the issue with the press:

> In retrospect I can see there was a honeymoon period. After that there were equal and opposite reactions. Some people love you, others don't love you. But people's reactions are so subjective. Not everyone is going to like what you do. So you can get bashed about a bit as you go in and out of fashion. Yes, undoubtedly, sometimes people take very personal and perhaps unfair attitudes towards one, but I've always had my champions and supporters. There's a price to pay for every level of achievement. I have no complaints.[4]

Deep down, Branagh did not *feel* such equanimity, did not believe that he had no grounds for complaint. His very decision to plump for *Coriolanus* instead of *Richard III* showed that he was troubled by the media attacks, even if he seemed able to disregard them. Certainly his colleagues at Chichester remained vexed by the criticism heaped on their leader. 'It's the English disease,' groused Judi Dench. 'I know of no other country like it.' Richard Briers was no less disgruntled: 'It makes me so angry, it's all so unnecessary and I don't like it ... What does he do?' an exasperated Briers continued. 'He creates employment, he is dedicated to Shakespeare, he's a workaholic, he makes very little money because most of it goes back into the company. Unfortunately, it's not uncommon to knock someone who can do these things. In my book, he's heroic.'

When *Coriolanus* started its run at Chichester in the middle of May 1992, not everything went according to plan. In a sword fight with Iain Glen, Branagh's finger was fractured in the first act. He went on to complete the performance, despite the pain, but donned protective gloves thereafter. Judi Dench demonstrated the same belief that the show must go on when she sprained her ankle during a charity gala attended by the Prince of Wales. With a fifteen-minute break, assistance from two doctors who happened to be in the house, and the use of a stick, Dench completed the show to rapturous applause. As she turned with Branagh to leave the stage after the inevitable curtain call, Branagh offered her his own particular brand of appreciation: 'Get off stage, you limping bitch!'

With the likes of Branagh, Dench and Briers in the cast, and with the established reputation of the Renaissance company, *Coriolanus* was a hit with the public though not with the critics. In *The Times* Benedict

Nightingale said that Branagh was 'as formidable a Coriolanus as we have seen for some time'; but Paul Taylor of the *Independent* simply could not buy the idea of him as a great warrior. Nicholas de Jongh wrote in the London *Standard* that Iain Glen was better than Branagh who, he felt, 'lacks grand rage, that sense of danger, of arrogant self-assertion the role demands'. Whilst Michael Billington of the *Guardian* admired much about the way Branagh portrayed Coriolanus, he judged the performance to be lacking in psychological insight – and the production in general to be devoid of any directorial point of view. All in all it was a sobering set of reviews for what turned out to be, for Branagh, a show of historical importance. No one knew it at the time, but *Coriolanus* would be Renaissance's final theatre production.

With the year scarcely halfway through, and a number of projects already under his belt, Branagh turned to what for him was the main event of 1992: making a film of *Much Ado About Nothing*. His *Henry V* movie had sent his reputation skyrocketing. As his first Shakespeare film since then, *Much Ado* would serve either to confirm or to diminish his status as cinema's chief interpreter of the Bard.

Much Ado's intriguing cast of characters includes the group of soldiers – the gracious prince Don Pedro, his malcontent half-brother Don John, the witty Benedick, and the romantic Claudio – who return to Messina, Sicily, where Leonato rules as governor. As Claudio falls for Leonato's daughter, Hero, the famous feuding lovers Benedick and Leonato's niece Beatrice are tricked by their friends into acknowledging their affection for each other. A spanner is thrown in the works when Don John dupes Claudio into believing that Hero has been unfaithful; Claudio subsequently jilts Hero at the altar. All is put to rights and love prevails when the comically pompous constable Dogberry and his assistants reveal Don John's villainy.

Much Ado is one of Shakespeare's most effective comedies. The humour ranges from Dogberry's malapropisms to the impressively agile wit of Benedick and Beatrice. As with his other comedies, Shakespeare balances the humour with darker passages – in this case, the malevolent spirit of Don John, Claudio's brutal discarding of Hero, and Beatrice's injunction to Benedick, following the humiliation of her kinswoman, to kill Claudio. But for the most part *Much Ado* functions as a funny, uplifting, genuinely romantic piece of work.

The idea of converting this play into a film first occurred to Branagh back in 1988 during a Renaissance stage performance of

Much Ado, in which he was playing Benedick. 'I have to confess my concentration wandered,' Branagh recalled:

> One night ... the title sequence of this film played over and over in my mind: heat haze and dust, grapes and horseflesh, and a nod to *The Magnificent Seven*. The men's sexy arrival, the atmosphere of rural Messina, the vigour and sensuality of the women, possessed me in the weeks, months and years that followed. This long-term marination process was vital in convincing me that a film of *Much Ado* could work. Opening the story for the cinema, I thought, should not mean drowning the words and characters in endless vistas and 'production value'. Yet the play seemed to beg to live outside in a vivid, lush countryside. Making the right stylistic connection between word and picture took me four years and three more films to achieve.[5]

Formulating his ideas for a film of *Much Ado*, Branagh thought it important that Beatrice and Benedick not be allowed to dominate the story – something hard to prevent given their verbal brilliance. The other characters needed to be fleshed out so that a more well-rounded story could be presented. In line with his preliminary thoughts about the project, in 1988, Branagh decided that the setting would be of vital importance. A lush, sensuous country setting would be used to convey a sense of the sexual desires that drive the story. 'I felt it should be surrounded by nature and ripeness and grapes and sweat and horses and just that kind of lusty, bawdy thing,' he said. Branagh also aimed to emphasise what he regarded as *Much Ado*'s positive message about 'how important love is', believing that *Much Ado* was the ideal vehicle, as its darker side was less conspicuous than was the case with some other Shakespeare comedies. As he conceptualised his film version in these ways, Branagh's faith in the enterprise was sustained by his immense respect for the piece of work he was tackling. 'The play', he declared on one occasion, 'is one of the greatest romantic comedies ever written.'

Throughout this process of defining his ideas for a film of *Much Ado*, Branagh kept uppermost in his mind the populist aspirations that had long influenced his career. He was determined to make this *Much Ado* accessible. He wanted people who had not spent a lifetime going to productions by the Royal Shakespeare Company to see his movie. Furthermore, he felt the prospects for achieving this objective were promising. The success enjoyed by his film of *Henry V*, which he knew had a struck a chord from the correspondence he had received from all over the world, could be built upon. The signature acting style developed by Renaissance – clear, naturalistic, free of bombast – could be utilised to good effect on *Much Ado*, as it had been on *Henry V*. In addition, the nature of *Much Ado* as a play accentuated its accessibility. Three-quarters of it is in prose, making the language naturalistic, conversational.

If Branagh were to succeed in presenting his vision of *Much Ado* in a way that connected with more than just the art-house crowd, it was imperative that he produce an adaptation of the text that worked in film terms. As a lifetime devotee of movies, Branagh had the ability to visualise how the Shakespeare plays he had performed on stage could work cinematically. Nevertheless, adapting the text of *Much Ado* was no easy matter, as it does not have the same sort of linear plot, the same strong narrative drive, as *Henry V* or Shakespeare's other history plays. Branagh, therefore, had to impose himself on the text in order to realise his cinematic vision, without reference to the purists who would regard every word in the play as sacrosanct. Accordingly, lines were cut, scenes were sometimes deleted, sometimes fused, and, if judged necessary, their position in the sequence of the story was moved. For instance, the scenes in which Benedick and Beatrice are each tricked into believing they are loved ardently by the other, separate in Shakespeare's play, were integrated by Branagh into one continuous passage of the story.

Branagh's refashioning of Shakespeare's text for cinema was most in evidence at the start of the film. It opens with Beatrice (Thompson) reading the words of a song:

Sigh no more, ladies, sigh no more.
Men were deceivers ever,
One foot in sea and one on shore,
To one thing constant never.
Then sigh not so, but let them go,
And be you blithe and bonny,
Converting all your sounds of woe
Into hey nonny, nonny.[6]

Though the play does not start like this, it was a sensible change, as it allowed the audience to feel confident that they would be able to understand the language, and introduced the central theme of the story, namely the battle of the sexes. In the opening scene of the play, the annoucement that Don Pedro and the rest of the men are returning from the battlefield is immediately followed by Don Pedro's arrival and his greeting of Leonato. In Branagh's published screenplay there are almost four pages of elaborate descriptions of numerous interior and exterior shots between the announcement of the arrival of Denzel Washington's Don Pedro and his initial greeting. Those delightful moments in the early part of the film – Beatrice and the other women running down the hill, Don Pedro and the rest of the soldiers arriving on horseback as in *The Magnificent Seven*, the shots of the men bathing and the women showering, the formal meeting of Leonato's household and Don Pedro's soldiers, and the whole celebratory, sexual atmosphere that is generated – were the product of Branagh's fertile imagination. The success that Branagh's film of *Much Ado* ultimately represented was based to a significant extent on his adroit conversion of a theatrical text into a screenplay.

What made this even more commendable was the speed with which he did it. According to Stephen Evans, he wrote the screenplay during the course of a weekend in Scotland with Emma Thompson. 'What Ken did on that weekend was remarkable,' says Evans, adding, 'He's got this terrific brain. He probably understands Shakespeare in the true sense better than even the Peter Halls and Trevor Nunns because he can come at it from the directing side and also the acting side.'

He might have had a strong vision of the story as well as a screenplay in hand, but Branagh still needed the money. Securing financial backing for a film of *Much Ado* was not straightforward – not just because it was Shakespeare, but because it was a Shakespearean comedy. Surveying the history of Shakespeare on the big screen, it is clear that the great artistic or commercial successes have been, almost without exception, Shakespeare's histories or tragedies – films such as Olivier's *Henry V*, *Hamlet* and *Richard III*, and Orson Welles's *Othello*. The cinematic track record of the comedies has been far more uneven. Zeffirelli's *Taming of the Shrew* in 1966 was well cast with Richard Burton and Elizabeth Taylor, and Paul Czinner's 1936 version of *As You Like It* – starring a young Olivier – had its moments. But it was only Max Reinhardt's visually arresting *A Midsummer Night's Dream* (1935), with Jimmy Cagney as Bottom and Micky Rooney as Puck, that had been truly memorable. As for *Much Ado About Nothing*, only four versions had been attempted: an American silent film in 1926, and three from behind the Iron Curtain – two Russian, one East German.

Approaching the moneymen with *Much Ado*, therefore, was a hard sell for Branagh and for Renaissance's financial adviser Stephen

Evans, even though the budget of £5.6 million was relatively small and the carrot of *Peter's Friends* was dangled. But the kudos from *Henry V* proved an asset. 'It's always been a bit of a struggle [raising money for films],' admitted Evans, 'but *Henry V* provided the best kind of visiting card. These days I'm not wandering aimlessly up Wardour Street and around Los Angeles. The phone calls are returned almost before you made them!' Branagh's own approach to convincing the financiers of *Much Ado*'s commercial promise was to couch the enterprise shamelessly in terms that Hollywood would understand. 'You have to jump through the hoop,' he explained, 'saying, "It'll be sexy! Young! It'll have a beautiful location!"' In the end, the Samuel Goldwyn Company agreed to stump up most of the money required for *Much Ado*, as well as for *Peter's Friends*.

The cast assembled by Branagh was a mélange of Renaissance regulars and Hollywood hot-shots. The former included the trusty Richard Briers, who took the role of Leonato, along with Brian Blessed, Richard Clifford, Jimmy Yuill, and Gerard Horan. The plum parts of Benedick and Beatrice naturally went to Branagh and Thompson. Young, beautiful English actress Kate Beckinsale, daughter of the late 1970s sitcom actor Richard Beckinsale, was given the ingénue role of Hero. Still at Oxford University, where she was studying Russian and French, Beckinsale had caught the attention of a number of people whose views Branagh valued. One British actress who had worked with Branagh a good deal but missed out on this occasion was Judi Dench. During the Renaissance run of *Coriolanus*, she told a journalist of her efforts to secure a part in *Much Ado*. 'He hasn't said anything yet,' revealed Dench, 'but I'm spending a lot of time hanging round his dressing-room door.' A role she could have played, that of Ursula, went to Branagh's mother-in-law, Phyllida Law.

Branagh's motivation for recruiting American stars was twofold. Firstly, he believed that an international cast would further his cherished objective of taking Shakespeare to the masses. 'Choosing American actors', he said, 'was more to do with trying to allow Shakespeare to sound and look as though it belongs to the world – which is what I feel – and also to blow the cobwebs off any potentially smug English Shakespearean acting, from people like me.' Secondly, as he acknowledged to the press, there was some 'box-office pressure' on casting. An all-English cast, in other words, would have meant a smaller budget. There was talk at one point of Branagh enlisting the services of his friend Gérard Depardieu, and he was interested in some Italian actors as well. In the end, though, the international portion of the cast was confined to Americans.

In what would be his first film since taking on the Herculean challenge of the title role in Spike Lee's *Malcolm X*, Denzel Washington would bring dignity to the role of Don Pedro, as well as experience in doing Shakespeare on stage. Having been impressed by his performance in the 1982 film *Night Shift*, Branagh thought Michael Keaton, who had become a big star in the wake of the *Batman* movie, would be effective in the comic role of Dogberry. Robert Sean Leonard had bent Branagh's ear during the filming of *Swing Kids* in Prague to win the role of Claudio. Best known for his performance in *Dead Poets Society*, Leonard's fresh-faced good looks seemed appropriate for the passionate, romantic Claudio who would fall for Kate Beckinsale's Hero. Branagh cast Keanu Reeves as the contumacious villain of the piece, Don John. Generally regarded as little more than a teen-idol, in part because of his role in the 1989 hit *Bill and Ted's Excellent Adventure*, Reeves had in fact appeared in a number of worthy projects such as *Dangerous Liaisons*, *My Own Private Idaho*, and *Bram Stoker's Dracula*. In *Chasing the Light*, a documentary on the making of *Much Ado About Nothing*, the American actors emphasised, in explaining their interest in the project, both their desire for an artistic challenge and their respect for Branagh. That these Hollywood stars were willing to forsake the astronomical salaries they could usually command for the pittance they would receive for *Much Ado* speaks volumes not only about Shakespeare's enduring appeal to actors of any stripe but of the stature already acquired by Branagh among his peers.

For the production team, Branagh relied on the group that he had originally assembled for *Henry V*. With Tim Harvey as production designer, Phyllis Dalton as costume designer, Patrick Doyle as composer, and Hugh Cruttwell and Russell Jackson as special consultants, it was a case of the usual suspects coming on board. Cinematographer Roger Lanser was more of a newcomer, but even he had worked with Branagh a decade earlier in Australia on the television series *The Boy in the Bush*.

Team Branagh soon got to work. Tim Harvey discharged the vital task of identifying a suitable location, a setting that could conjure up an atmosphere of rustic sensuality. Though the play is set in Sicily, Branagh believed that a lusher, more verdant location was needed, and so instructed Harvey to look around Tuscany. Harvey ended up selecting the fourteenth-century Villa Vignamaggio, near the town of Greve, at the heart of the Chianti wine region and within striking distance of Florence and Siena. Once owned by the Gheradini family, whose daughter was portrayed by Leonardo Da Vinci in the Mona Lisa, it was reputed that he had painted her in the very villa where *Much Ado* was to be shot. Branagh was adept at seizing upon juicy bits of information that could promote his films. Just as he had stressed that part of *Citizen Kane* had been filmed by Orson Welles in the lot where *Dead Again* was made, so he would get mileage out of the Mona Lisa connection in doing the publicity for *Much Ado*. Despite his strained relationship with journalists, he had a good understanding of their needs, of the information they could use to enliven their stories – a reflection perhaps of the time he had spent as a teenage journalist for the *Reading Evening Post*.

Selecting the Villa Vignamaggio as the location for the shoot was important to the success of Branagh's *Much Ado*. He needed a visual metaphor for the passions that drive the story. Vignamaggio, which I visited in the spring of 2004, was a perfect location in this respect. It is surrounded by a sensually undulating landscape, fecund with olive groves and vineyards, one's idealised conception of rural Tuscany. What that corner of Italy evokes, as one actor in the film puts it, is 'a sense of sex. It really was sexy.' The choice of location thus ensured that this film would be visually seductive.

Tim Harvey, however, still needed to work on the Villa Vignamaggio so that it was ready for filming. Within a matter of weeks a chapel, open-air baths and a formal garden fashioned out of what had been a builders' rubbish heap adorned the villa. Along with costume designer Phyllis Dalton, Harvey evoked what Branagh wanted in terms of period for the film – a nebulous setting some time between 1700 and 1900.

Before the start of rehearsals, Branagh thought it best to provide special coaching for Keanu Reeves, who felt diffident about Shakespeare but was keen to give it a go. Branagh put Reeves through his paces, focusing on his vocal technique. 'He's a stickler for clarity, for diction,' observed Reeves. 'He wanted me to chew the words, to go higher, with more fire.'

In the initial read-through, the greater Shakespearean experience of the British actors was evident. Russell Jackson, who assisted Branagh during rehearsals, noticed: 'The British actors had a confidence and attack that sounded like a finished performance – the Americans were, well quieter, and I think some of them were a bit worried. They were reassured when they found out that, for the British, giving it a lot of "welly" at that stage was really like clearing the lungs, limbering up – not a finished characterisation ready for the first few feet of film.' In the end the rehearsals boosted the confidence of the American actors, with Branagh encouraging them to speak in their natural American rather than acquired English accents. With all the actors, he insisted that they consider the background to the story in order to establish their characters more effectively. Hence the cast found themselves mulling over a series of questions: 'How long had the soldiers [such as Benedick and Don Pedro] been away? What kind of war had it been? How violent? Which of our men had been killers? How often had they visited Leonato prior to this? How well did they all know one another? How old were they? How long did these soldiers expect to live?' Branagh also advised the cast to view *Much Ado* not as a distant, historical tale but as a story about a family in turmoil that everyone could relate to in some way. As an ice-breaker, and to show the play's contemporary resonances, he then asked each actor to reveal something of his or her relationship with a family member.

A key aspect of the preparation was how Branagh and Thompson would decide to portray Benedick and Beatrice, the famous feuding lovers. What was exceedingly useful to Mr and Mrs Branagh was the way they could use their own relationship in developing their interpretation. 'Of course there are similarities between Beatrice and Benedick and myself and Emma,' acknowledged Branagh. 'We danced around one another for years before we finally went for it. And a lot of our relationship came through humour. Still does. It can be very feisty.' What they decided to suggest about their characters was that it was not simply a case of two wits coming together to great comic effect, but that there was a poignant dimension to their relationship. Branagh and Thompson wanted to imply that in times past Benedick and Beatrice had been lovers who had been profoundly hurt by their parting; and they found the textual justification for such an interpretation. When she is told that she has lost Benedick's heart, Beatrice reflects:

> Indeed, my lord, he lent it me awhile; and I gave him use for it, a double heart for his single one: marry, once before he won it of me with false dice, therefore your grace may well say I have lost it.

Branagh and Thompson would attend not only to the rhetorical flourishes of wit and irony for which their characters were renowned, but to their imagined history of the painful earlier relationship between Benedick and Beatrice.

The shooting of *Much Ado* began on 3 August 1992. On a tight seven-week schedule, things initially did not go well. Shot one, take one, was the film's opening scene – a view of a painting of the villa followed by a view of the villa itself, on to a picnic scene, and ending up with Beatrice nestled in a tree and reading the words to the 'hey nonny, nonny' song. A tricky start, it took no less than twenty-nine takes.

After that Branagh pushed on through the shoot more speedily. The documentary *Chasing the Light* shows him to have been clear and forthright in explaining to cast and crew what he wanted – and, if necessary, strict and urgent. As Alex Lowe, who was cast in a cameo role, recalls, he was 'not afraid to crack the whip. I remember Brian Blessed of course arsing around a lot on *Much Ado*. I was living with Brian at the time, and ... we were late for something once, which caused a lot of aggro.'

Within the parameters he always set in terms of keeping to schedule and to budget, Branagh was keen to explore alternatives for shooting scenes. Michael Keaton's Dogberry was shot buffoonishly riding an imaginary horse in a fashion reminiscent of *Monty Python and the Holy Grail* – and this was what was included in the final cut. But to give himself options Branagh had also shot the segment with Keaton walking and running. In the end he plumped for the imaginary riding shot, as the comic effect was broader. His most elaborately conceived shot was the final one of the dance following the reconcilement of Robert Sean Leonard's Claudio and Kate Beckinsale's Hero, and the public pledge by Benedick and Beatrice to marry. Branagh envisaged the camera weaving between the dancers before mounting a crane in order to provide a closing aerial view of the dancers, villa and surrounding countryside. A two-and-a-half-minute segment with no cut, it took fifteen takes – in 106 degree heat – but was worth it. It provided a stirring, celebratory conclusion to the film.

Branagh's feelings during filming were mixed. On the one hand he found himself enchanted by the idyllic Italian setting. Every morning he got to walk to work through an olive grove and a vineyard. On the other hand, the picturesqueness did not reduce the stress caused by the tight schedule, extreme heat and numerous night scenes. At the start of each day he felt physically sick. The pressure became almost too much to bear at one point. 'You get to the moment when you think you're going to crack,' admitted Branagh. '[On one occasion] I sent everybody away and just sat in the garden – "Nobody ask me for anything or need anything." Denzel [Washington] came up and gave me a big hug and said, "What's up, boss?" He said, "Listen. You're allowed to have these feelings. If you send all the crew away, people won't take you for granted." He's good company, Denzel. I've got a lot of time for him.'

For the other actors the experience was more consistently pleasurable. With lots of old Renaissance hands involved and no less than eight actors from the *Peter's Friends* cast in *Much Ado*, a team spirit soon emerged. 'By the time we'd all fallen off horses together, learnt the song at the end, done all this stuff that you would do in the theatre,' recalled Branagh, 'within a day, we were a company.' The fact that a number of the actors shared villas during the shoot, and would travel on days off to Florence or Siena to play tourist, heightened the sense of conviviality.

Used to big-budget, perhaps more impersonal Hollywood film-making, the Americans found this experience charming. Denzel Washington spoke of the relief of not being the star with the responsibility for carrying the film. Initially Michael Keaton sensed his British counterparts were 'nervous about my coming there, because I was a big American movie star', and feared the Brits 'would be aloof'. As things turned out, it was, he said, 'the best job I ever had'.

What must have been particularly gratifying for Branagh was the mutual respect that developed between the American and the British actors. There was always the possibility that the Americans might have dismissed their British counterparts because of their lack of star status, big-screen experience and box-office clout, while the British actors might have been patronising, given their greater experience with Shakespeare. That scenario did not materialise. Richard Briers, for instance, admired the Americans' naturalism and presence in front of the camera. Likewise the Americans came to appreciate actors whose previous work was largely unknown to them. After sharing a scene with Richard Briers, Michael Keaton told Branagh, 'This guy knows about timing. This guy is funny. This is a funny guy.' 'He's been funny in our country for about the last thirty years, you know, he's a kind of national institution,' explained Branagh. The Americans were struck as much by the eccentricities as by the acting skill of the Brits. This was particularly the case with Brian Blessed. 'They take the piss out of each other all the time,' said Washington of the British contingent, 'just constantly swearing and, what's the guy's name, Brian Blessed? Oh man, he's *great*. He's a madman, but he's great.'

Despite the general Anglo-American accord that prevailed, the differences in acting styles inevitably caused some raised eyebrows. Alex Lowe recalls a scene in which Denzel Washington's character had to laugh: 'He had to have something funny to laugh at. He had to work up to the laughter. And I just remember Dickie Briers [asking], "What's the problem?"' Elaborating, Briers says,

> In those days we all smoked, and were always lighting fags and telling stories about other old actors and long-since-dead actors, and lots of jokes and giggles. And the Americans of course take it much more seriously and get in the mood. They concentrate before the scene whereas we stub the fag out and go straight on, mainly because most of the English actors were stage actors, so they were very experienced [and could] just ... turn it on. Rather than just working yourself into a rage, you just turn on rage. Press the rage button.[7]

By the time the shooting of the film had come to an end, the signs for artistic and box-office success looked good. Branagh was happy with the performances turned in by the cast. With no one was he more impressed than with his wife. Not only did she look more attractive than she ever had, she had shown what a fine actress she had become.

Branagh's confidence in his film remained undiminished during post-production. Patrick Doyle produced an appropriately joyous, high-spirited score. A preliminary screening of the film also boded well. To get a sense of how the public would respond to *Much Ado*, Branagh arranged for his London driver to see a cut of the film. 'Blimey! I loved it,' the driver remarked after watching it. 'I even understood everything.' For his part, Stephen Evans felt sufficiently inspired at this juncture to write Branagh a letter saying that what was special about their relationship was the reciprocity: he had changed Branagh's life, but Branagh had changed his too.

Shakespeare was the focus of not one but two Branagh films made during the summer of 1992. With the financial support of the Commission of European Communities, Branagh was able to direct a short film of *Swan Song*, an adaptation of a Chekhov playlet, on location at London's Criterion Theatre. *Swan Song* tells the story of Svetlovidov, who, after the end of his benefit show, reminisces in an emptied theatre with the prompter, Nikita, about his sixty-year career on the stage. Initially sullen, lamenting the financial security and the love of a cherished woman that he forfeited by becoming an actor, he is boosted not only by the praise of the idolising prompter but by re-enacting several great Shakespearean roles. He delivers speeches from *King Lear*, *Hamlet*, *Romeo and Juliet*, and *Othello* – and their poetry and philosophy raise his flagging spirits. The story explores the role of the theatre. Whilst Nikita argues that it can have a life-enhancing impact on the audience, the actor is more cynical. After acting the great Shakespearean parts again, however, he moves some way towards the prompter's positive view of theatre's importance. When Nikita asks, 'You still do believe, don't you sir, the theatre, it can inspire, it can lift up the spirit, it can remind us what a godlike thing it is to see the imagination soar and the words take wing?' the actor replies, 'Of course it can. We all know that. The bugger of it is, it hardly ever does. Still we have to keep on trying. Nothing else to keep us going.'

For Branagh, it was a wonderful story to film. 'It's a brief but brilliant dialogue about life, love and the theatre,' he observed. Branagh succeeded in recruiting the actors who could do justice to the piece. John Gielgud would play the ageing actor, with Richard Briers as his prompter. Gielgud looked forward to working with Branagh. 'I am doing *Swan Song* next week with young Branagh,' he wrote in a private letter in June 1992. 'He is a nice fellow with enormous energy and ambition with a most charming wife who is splendid in the Forster film *Howards End*.'

Knowing it would be inappropriate to lecture Gielgud, Branagh was sparing in the direction he gave. All that he asked of Gielgud was that he deliver the Shakespearean speeches in the grand manner rather than in a more understated, naturalistic way. Gielgud remained charmingly modest during filming. 'Oh, I've forgotten the words again,' he said at one point. 'I can't do it. I'm not good.' Branagh enjoyed the interaction with one of his heroes. 'He loved it,' recalls Richard Briers. 'He realised he was being rather cheeky asking this great man, very old man, then, to come and do this. He got a tremendous kick out of it.'

On 25 October 1992 *Swan Song* received its première at the Criterion Theatre, where Gielgud had first performed sixty years earlier. On what was a festive occasion, Ian McKellen introduced a cabaret involving the likes of John Sessions and Alec McCowen, and when the film was screened Gielgud was compelled to rise in order to acknowledge the unrestrained applause. Rounding off the evening was a party at the Criterion Brasserie, where Branagh and Emma Thompson helped with the cake-cutting duties.

As a short, *Swan Song* is perhaps the least widely known of Branagh's films. It was screened on British television in December 1993, but in order to see it now a visit to the British Film Institute, where a viewing copy is held, is necessary. So few have seen it. More's the pity, because it is a gem. Gielgud is deeply poignant; Briers effective in support. It is simply thrilling to see Gielgud – acknowledged by many as the greatest Hamlet of the century – delivering the 'Do you think I am easier to be played on than a pipe' speech, as well as other memorable lines from *Lear*, *Romeo and Juliet*, and *Othello*. The piece as a whole offers moments of uplift against an elegiac emotional backdrop. It would go on to receive an Oscar nomination for Best Short Film.

In autumn 1992 Branagh returned to the stage, to the role that still obsessed him, and to the company he had left rancorously seven years earlier. Determined to be regarded as a great Hamlet, he had resolved to play the part as often as possible in order to achieve that objective. Though he had already tackled the role at RADA and for his Renaissance Theatre Company, he thus agreed to play the Danish prince once again – this time with the Royal Shakespeare Company. Given that he had walked away from the RSC in 1985 believing the company to be excessively bureaucratic, and that he had established Renaissance as a clear alternative, returning to the RSC could have been construed as a conflict of interests on Branagh's part – and also as an error in judgement. If the RSC had become an impersonal bureaucratic behemoth, why return to it? As he had thrown his lot in with Renaissance, could not a stint with the RSC be viewed as some sort of betrayal? Branagh explained his decision this way: 'I'm doing *Hamlet* with the RSC, not the RTC, because I'm now going through a learning period again. I don't want to direct any more for the moment. I want to be directed. It's a very interesting period for me coming up. Putting myself in other hands. Discovering new things.'

Those 'other hands' would be Adrian Noble's. Having directed Branagh in *Henry V* in 1984–5, he had gone on to become the RSC's artistic director. Noble decided to use an uncut text, ensuring that audiences would be kept in their seats for over four hours, opted for an Edwardian setting, and complemented Branagh's acting talent with those of some experienced RSC actors. Jane Lapotaire, John Shrapnel and Clifford Rose would play Gertrude, Claudius and the Ghost of Hamlet's father respectively. Joanne Pearce, who had become Noble's wife, took on the challenge of Ophelia. The cast also had strength in depth. Guy Henry, for instance, who played the minor part of Osric, went on to become a major player with the RSC.

To his credit, Noble did not dwell on past tensions between Branagh and the RSC. Asked whether it was difficult to work with Branagh again, as rehearsals got under way, Noble said, 'It wasn't awkward at all. There's that great healer, time. I think Ken will be a great Hamlet and I wanted to direct him in it. He has the quality all great actors have, an astonishing inventiveness in front of your very eyes. Why do people go to the theatre? They go because there is a heat, an energy, generated on stage, and Branagh has that in spades.'

As opening night approached, the pressure mounted. Playing Hamlet for the RSC was in many ways the ultimate challenge for Branagh, the equivalent of a World Cup Final for David Beckham or Everest for a mountaineer. One critic was quoted in November 1992 as saying that for Branagh, 'Hamlet will be the great test.' Immense public expectations were manifest in advance bookings. Prior to opening night it was reported that takings had exceeded £1 million, the greatest box-office advance for a Shakespeare play in the history of the Royal Shakespeare Company. Every ticket was sold prior to the first performance.

Branagh felt more comfortable with the part of Hamlet than he ever had before. Taking on the challenge with more life experience behind him was enriching his performance in rehearsals. Reacquainting himself with this play, he found himself again entranced by its keen appreciation of the doubts afflicting everyone about the meaningfulness of life, and by its remarkable contemporary resonances. As Branagh told a journalist:

> I mean you've only got to say, 'Well, what about Somalia?' And that's fine because we do feel and Hamlet feels, indeed, the extraordinary pressure of world events. 'To be or not to be ...' is full of that. 'Who would bear the whips and scorns of time? Th'oppressor's wrong (Yugoslavia), the proud man's contumely (John Major), the pangs of despis'd love (everyone's had their heart broken), the law's delay (Guildford Four and the Birmingham Six) and the spurns that patient merit of th'unworthy takes (anyone who's had anything to do with the government or whatever).' I mean, who would do this, you know, if you could actually take a dagger and kill yourself?[8]

Despite his careful preparations and the fact that he had played the part before, he was tense when *Hamlet* opened. Michael Billington recalls Branagh telling him years later: 'You know that Hamlet I did at the Barbican, you have no idea how paralyzed with fright I was that first night.' But those nerves did not prevent Branagh from producing an exceptional performance. His was a Hamlet motivated to revenge his father's slaying at the hands of Claudius not so much by sexual jealousy at his mother's decision to share her bed with Claudius, an interpretation favoured by Olivier, but by an authentic filial devotion to his father. When his father's Ghost explained to Hamlet that he had not died accidentally but been killed by Claudius, Branagh was on his knees, indicating the deference felt by son for father. Nor was Branagh's Hamlet mad or by nature depressive. In his first scene with Polonius, Hamlet's 'madness' was clearly feigned. Though hurt by his father's death and his mother's marriage, he did not come across as an inveterate depressive, but as contemplative and philosophical whilst at times being dynamic and animated.

What was striking about Branagh's performance was its technical proficiency: his diction and phrasing, the clarity, power and suppleness of his voice. He showed the ability that he has demonstrated consistently on film, and which explains in part his following among the public – namely, to make Shakespearean verse more comprehensible than when most other actors are saying the lines. With the soliloquies, one had the impression that in preparing the part Branagh had put each under the microscope and come to a very precise view as to how it would be delivered in terms of technique and interpretation.

Also in evidence were his comedic gifts. He succeeded in getting big laughs at the right moments. When Hamlet says to Horatio, about the proximity of his father's death and his mother's nuptials, 'The funeral baked meats did coldly furnish forth the marriage tables,' when he chirps, 'O wonderful!' – having just seen his father's Ghost – in response to Horatio's query about the news, and when, in the 'mad' scene, he declares that Polonius is a fishmonger, Branagh would elicit uproarious laughter from the audience.

Separating this performance from his Hamlet with Renaissance a few years earlier was the sense of introspection, a quality lacking in his earlier portrayal; it seemed that his experiences since 1988, perhaps especially the buffeting that had accompanied his rise to fame in

Britain, had given him a keener sense of life's vicissitudes, and this had enabled him to offer a performance of greater subtlety and depth.

The quality of Branagh's individual performance was mirrored by the overall quality of the production. Using the full text had all sorts of advantages. A proper balance was established between Hamlet's personal journey and the political dynamics of the story. Because Hamlet's psychology is so fascinating it is easy for that theme to predominate; but the play is also a political thriller with a number of rivals – Claudius, Laertes, Fortinbras of Norway, as well as Hamlet – vying to secure the throne of Denmark. Indeed it is Fortinbras who ends up as king. But in many productions that theme is slighted, particularly the Fortinbras angle. In Adrian Noble's version, however, Hamlet's story was anchored in a properly established political setting.

Another benefit of the uncut text was that the characters other than Hamlet were fully realised. Polonius came across as a wily politician as well as a figure of mirth because of his periodic pedantry. Claudius cut an imposing figure, as an effective statesman rather than a two-dimensional malcontent. Gertrude was bright, vivacious, dignified in the early part of the play – it was easy to see why Claudius had fallen for her. Fleshed-out characters rather than adjuncts to Hamlet's story inhabited Noble's production.

When the reviews came out, it was clear that the pundits in the press were no less enthused than the public. All but the most severe critics praised Branagh's performance and the production in general, with many judging them to be of landmark significance. Michael Billington said in the *Guardian* that the show was 'highly original' and 'filled with a poignant Chekhovian melancholy', while Branagh's performance was 'deeply moving', conveying strongly – in a way that he had not four years earlier in his performance for Renaissance – Hamlet's internal pain. In *The Times* Benedict Nightingale argued that Branagh was 'the most impressively princely Hamlet I have seen in ages; and a good deal more than that, too ... I can imagine profounder Hamlets and more instinctively electric ones, but I do not expect to see a solider, more thorough version.' Charles Spencer of the *Daily Telegraph* declared that 'Kenneth Branagh gives the finest performance of his career as Hamlet,' while Jack Tinker of the *Daily Mail* was even more effusive: 'He is undoubtedly the great Hamlet of our time. I have seen none to match him in many a season.'

It was during *Hamlet*'s run in Stratford that the Academy Awards took place, on 29 March 1993. This was of interest to Branagh not only because of the nomination of *Swan Song* in the Best Live-action Short Film category, but because his wife was up for a Best Actress Oscar for her accomplished performance in *Howards End*, the Ismail Merchant/James Ivory version of E. M. Forster's novel. Tongues wagged when Emma Thompson turned up at the Dorothy Chandler Pavilion without Branagh, escorted instead by her mother. But the reason for Branagh's absence was simple: he had to stay in Stratford to play Hamlet. Whilst *Swan Song* lost out, Thompson did not. She saw off formidable competition from the likes of Catherine Deneuve, Michelle Pfeiffer, and Susan Sarandon to collect the Best Actress statuette from her good friend and *Howards End* co-star Anthony Hopkins. After fielding questions from the backstage press, she called Branagh, who had stayed up all night watching the ceremony with some pals at the house of a friend who had satellite. Branagh and Thompson had what he later described as 'a very excited and weepy conversation'. He celebrated with a champagne breakfast before finally retiring at 8.30 in the morning.

On her return to London, Thompson placed her Oscar on top of the tank in the downstairs toilet of her house in West Hampstead. Branagh noticed that guests would spend longer in the toilet than they used to, practising their imaginary Oscar-winning acceptance speeches. Thompson took the Academy Award in her stride. Joking with the press, however, Branagh said that the Oscar had transformed her into a tyrant: 'She's completely impossible. I have to make appointments to see her. She goes to bed with the Oscar.'

Juxtaposed with the subsequent breakdown in their marriage, Thompson's Oscar triumph in 1993 could be viewed as a contributory factor. It could be argued that the event marked a decisive shift in the balance of power – or, rather, the balance of artistic credibility – in their relationship. To be sure, the Academy Award did enable Thompson to establish herself as an independent artist. Many of her films had involved collaboration with Branagh, and it would not be uncharitable to say that she almost certainly would not have got those roles had she not been Branagh's partner. In other words, prior to *Howards End* her film career had seemed largely dependent on her husband's success. But with *Howards End*, a project with which Branagh had no connection, she became an actress of the first rank.

She would go on to cement her reputation with other fine performances, such as those in *The Remains of the Day* and *In the Name of the Father*, both of which resulted in more Oscar nominations the following year. Did all of this success change the dynamics of their relationship? Did Branagh become envious of his wife's success? Who could say? – but it is worth noting that, despite her achievements, he had a stronger track record as a stage actor, enjoyed a reputation as a film-maker that she of course did not, and had garnered three Oscar nominations himself – impressively in three separate categories. To say that her overall reputation as an artist now exceeded his is not convincing; and Branagh's comments that all he felt at the time of his wife's Oscar triumph was pride should be taken at face value.

A few weeks after the Oscars, late on the evening of Saturday, 1 May 1993, Branagh walked off the stage of the Royal Shakespeare Theatre in Stratford having completed his final performance as Hamlet for the RSC. Only a decade out of RADA, he had been an outstanding Henry V, a great Hamlet, and a memorable Touchstone in *As You Like It*; shone in the West End in *Another Country*; directed an acclaimed production of *Twelfth Night*; and had established a theatre company that had attracted major actors as well as an enthusiastic following among the public. As a man of the theatre, he had become his generation's most prominent artist. At that time it could only have been anticipated that his triumph as Hamlet for the RSC would pave the way for other stage successes. A number of the great Shakespearean parts still beckoned: Macbeth, Iago, Richard III. It could not have been predicted, therefore, that it would be the best part of a decade before Branagh next performed on stage.

In one sense, the career change from mixing stage and screen to working exclusively in the movies was understandable. Including his acting at school and at RADA, Branagh had spent much of the past two decades working in the theatre at a feverish rate. He remained a relatively inexperienced movie actor, having appeared in only six films (including *Much Ado*). To want to work more in film, to collaborate with the leading actors and directors of the big screen, was logical. To do so at the expense of any stage work was a mistake. Not a little of the credibility enjoyed by Branagh in the world of films flowed from his kudos as a major classical stage actor. Furthermore, his outstanding film work – *Henry V* and *Much Ado About Nothing* – had been inspired by his experience with these works in the theatre. In the spring of 1993, however, even Branagh himself could not have imagined that his absence from the stage would have spanned the rest of the 1990s and beyond.

With Hamlet behind him, for the time being at least, Branagh's attention switched in May 1993 to promotion of his film of *Much Ado*. This meant heading off to the United States, where a round of television and newspaper interviews and book signings (for his published screenplay) awaited, as the decision had been made to open in America first and Britain second. It was the belief that critics at home were more likely to be uncharitable than their American counterparts that governed the decision to open in the United States. Better to return to the UK with a raft of rave reviews for *Much Ado* than to go to the States having been bashed in Blighty.

Opening on 7 May, *Much Ado* did indeed attract the sort of ecstatic reviews that Branagh had thought would be less forthcoming at home. Describing the film as 'triumphantly romantic, comic and, most surprising of all, emotionally alive', Vincent Canby ran out of superlatives in the *New York Times*. He found Michael Keaton's performance as Dogberry 'fascinating', Denzel Washington's portrayal of Don Pedro 'amazingly good', and the confession by Branagh's Benedick of his love for Beatrice to have 'an emotional impact I've never before experienced in Shakespeare, on stage or screen'. Todd McCarthy sang from the same hymn sheet in *Variety*, applauding the movie's accessibility, the performances of its cast, and the sheer enjoyment it evoked. By contrast J. Hoberman of the *Village Voice* lambasted the acting, direction, production and score. Fortunately for Branagh, few American reviewers subscribed to such harsh views.

Critical acclaim was followed by public enthusiasm. *Much Ado* clocked up over $22.5 million, a great success for what could be regarded as a low-budget art movie. When one considers that in the same year *A Bronx Tale*, De Niro's debut as director, grossed $17 million, and Woody Allen's *Manhattan Murder Mystery* with Diane Keaton made a little more than $11 million, the appeal of Branagh's *Much Ado* to the American public is clear.

The UK première took place at the Empire, Leicester Square, on 26 August, almost four months after its opening in the United States. A crowd of three hundred, double the number present for the première six weeks earlier of Steven Spielberg's *Jurassic Park*, turned up to cheer Branagh, Thompson and a host of artists that included Richard

Attenborough, John Mills and Helena Bonham Carter. The mood was buoyant, as shouts of 'Up the British film industry' were heard from the assembled throng. Branagh said he was moved to hear those sentiments. He must have been equally pleased by the standing ovation he received at the end of the film's screening. The celebrity guests voiced their admiration for the film, but Lord Attenborough added a caveat for the critics to his praise of Branagh and Thompson. 'It was an evening of absolute joy,' he said. 'Complete ecstasy. Some of those critics need their backsides smacked. There's blood, sweat and tears, and some condescending bastard is ready to condemn it all. Ken and Emma are bitter about the attacks. Like hundreds of others, they'll go to Hollywood.'

As things turned out, some reviewers were unsympathetic. Philip French of the *Observer* thought *Much Ado* had a fake merriness, and that Branagh's performance was 'overly-theatrical'. In the *Independent* Adam Mars-Jones dubbed the movie 'lacklustre'. He said of Branagh's acting, 'His charm always has an edge of smugness,' and of Thompson's: 'There is something tired about her vitality and forced about her brightness.' Though admiring a number of individual performances, especially Denzel Washington's, Geoff Brown's overall assessment in *The Times* was that 'the film's pleasures prove shallow'.

These harsh views represented one side of a division of opinion rather than a consensus of condemnation; for a number of critics were charmed by *Much Ado*. In the *Guardian* Derek Malcolm found fault with the cinematography but described the film generally as 'fresh, unaffected and rumbustious'. 'As a crowd-pleaser,' he added with perhaps one eye on Branagh's detractors, 'Branagh's *Much Ado* is the genuine article and the usual British sneering would be out of place.' Nigel Andrews of the *Financial Times* stated: '*Much Ado About Nothing* is a travesty, but oh what a lovely one.' He particularly enjoyed the performances of Thompson, Washington and Branagh himself. In the *Daily Telegraph* Hugo Davenport said the film was 'full of pleasures', and lauded Branagh and Thompson for the 'wit and clarity' of their verbal sparring. As many had judged the 1989 *Henry V* to be a case of Branagh throwing down the gauntlet to Olivier, so Alexander Walker of the London *Standard* spoke of *Much Ado* as a contest between Branagh and Franco Zeffirelli, whose films included *The Taming of the Shrew* and who had 'hitherto had an armlock on the sun-kissed slapstick of the Bard's lighter bits of work'. In Walker's opinion, Branagh 'wins this round' over the Italian maestro.

The public also embraced the movie. Remarkably for a Shakespeare film, Branagh's *Much Ado* reached number two at the British box office in early September 1993, behind the Clint Eastwood vehicle *In the Line of Fire*. A month later it was still in the top five. *Much Ado* would go on to clock up over £5.5 million at the British box office, more than eight times the total for *Henry V*. This, combined with the success enjoyed in the United States, was a dream come true for Branagh. All those people in Britain and in America going to the cinema and paying around $30 million in total to see a work by an Elizabethan playwright. For some of them it would have been their first exposure to the Bard. The divide between elitist diversion and mass entertainment was actually being crossed.

Branagh's *Much Ado*, however, represented much more than sheer entertainment. It was a landmark achievement. In my view it was and still remains the finest film of a Shakespeare comedy. Richard Burton and Elizabeth Taylor provided Zeffirelli's *Taming of the Shrew* with real electricity; the 1935 *A Midsummer Night's Dream* conveys well a sense of the supernatural magic of the story; and Trevor Nunn's *Twelfth Night*, released three years after *Much Ado*, was a solid and exceedingly well-cast version of Shakespeare's greatest comedy. But none of them has that same uninhibited and authentic sense of exuberance as Branagh's *Much Ado*, and none of them was so expertly translated from a play intended for the stage to a story that worked in cinematic terms. Because many aspects of Shakespeare's comedies, such as the malapropisms and the dependency on instances of eavesdropping to advance the plot, seem wooden and simply unfunny to modern sensibilities, it is intrinsically far more difficult to make an effective film of one of the comedies than of a history or tragedy. With *Much Ado*, Branagh succeeded gloriously.

By the summer of 1993 Branagh had celebrated the fifth anniversary of his own theatre company. He had given a stage performance as Hamlet that was one of the finest of his generation. He had directed the best film of a Shakespeare comedy ever made. To be sure, he still had to contend with Branagh-bashing. Though its ferocity had abated since 1989, it remained a factor. Moreover, it influenced Branagh's thinking – the decision to play Coriolanus rather than Richard III; the decision to open with *Much Ado About Nothing* in the United States rather than in Britain. Nevertheless, the truth could not be denied: Kenneth Branagh was the biggest Shakespearean star in the world. He was only thirty-two. It seemed that nothing could go wrong.

7

Monster

It was on an evening in June 1816 that one of literature's great Gothic horror stories originated. Mary Shelley, the teenage daughter of celebrated writers Mary Wollstonecraft and William Godwin, was staying with her lover Percy Shelley at the Lake Geneva villa of another radical poet, the infamous Lord Byron. In attendance were Byron's doctor and lover John Polidori, and Mary Shelley's stepsister Claire Clairmont, who also had an affair with Byron. It proved to be one of the most remarkable and productive meetings of literary figures in history. As one wag put it, 'It vindicates the traditional Hollywood method of locking up a bunch of talented writers with a liberal supply of drugs, and letting them get on with it.' It was Polidori who provided the drugs.

The group entertained themselves by reading German ghost fables, and this, it appears, is what prompted Lord Byron's sudden proposition: 'We will each write a ghost story.' While Byron and Percy Shelley got going but never finished, Polidori pressed on, making an important contribution to Gothic literature by completing *The Vampyre*. For her part, Mary Shelley resolved to write a story that would 'speak to the mysterious fears of our nature and awaken thrilling horror – one to make the reader dread to look round, to curdle the blood, and quicken the beatings of the heart. If I did not accomplish these things, my ghost story would be unworthy of its name.'

Initially she struggled to come up with characters or plot. Then one night, as she tried to sleep, it came to her:

> My imagination, unbidden, possessed and guided me, gifting the successive images that arose in my mind with a vividness far beyond the usual bounds of reverie. I saw – with shut eyes, but acute mental vision – I saw the pale student of

1 First fame: after winning a place to study at RADA, the local press take his picture and write up the story.

2 Making his debut for the Royal Shakespeare Company as Henry V.
3 Becoming a star and a target: the film version of *Henry V* earned Branagh Oscar nominations but also contributed to a backlash against him.

4 Tying the knot with Emma Thompson.

5 Directing *Dead Again* in his Hollywood debut.

6 Mission accomplished: Branagh realizes his longstanding ambition to be regarded as an outstanding Hamlet with his 1992–3 stage interpretation of the Danish prince.

7 A tender scene with Emma Thompson in his movie version of *Much Ado About Nothing*.

8 Playing Iago to Laurence Fishburne's Othello in Oliver Parker's 1995 film.

9 With Derek Jacobi, whose work had inspired the teenage Branagh to become an actor, and Julie Christie in his epic film of *Hamlet*.

10 As Berowne in his musical version of *Love's Labour's Lost*, with Matthew Lillard, Alessandro Nivola and Adrian Lester.

11 With Helena Bonham Carter in *Mary Shelley's Frankenstein*. The film did not live up to expectations, but it brought him together with the actress who would become an important part of his life in the 1990s.

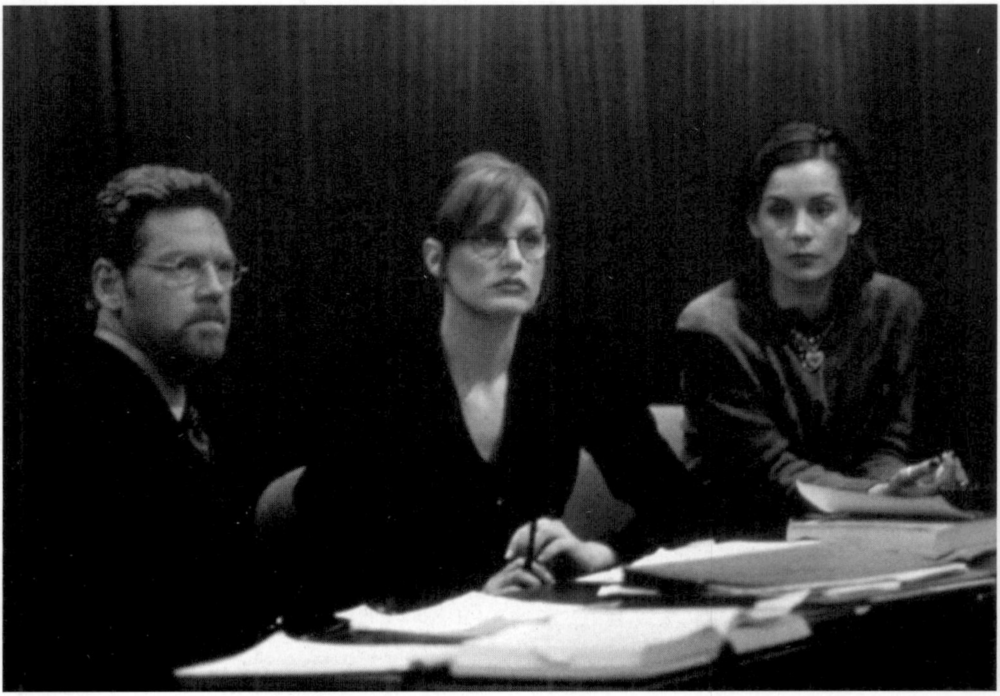

12 By the late 1990s Branagh was working with some of the great names of American cinema, including Robert Altman in whose film, *The Gingerbread Man*, he appeared with Daryl Hannah and Embeth Davidtz.

13 Rolling the dice with Leonardo DiCaprio in Woody Allen's *Celebrity*.
14 Comeback: in 2002 Branagh acts again on stage, after a nine-year absence, in Michael Grandage's production of *Richard III* at the Sheffield Crucible.

15 His mesmerizing, Emmy-winning portrayal of Nazi leader Reinhard Heydrich in *Conspiracy*.

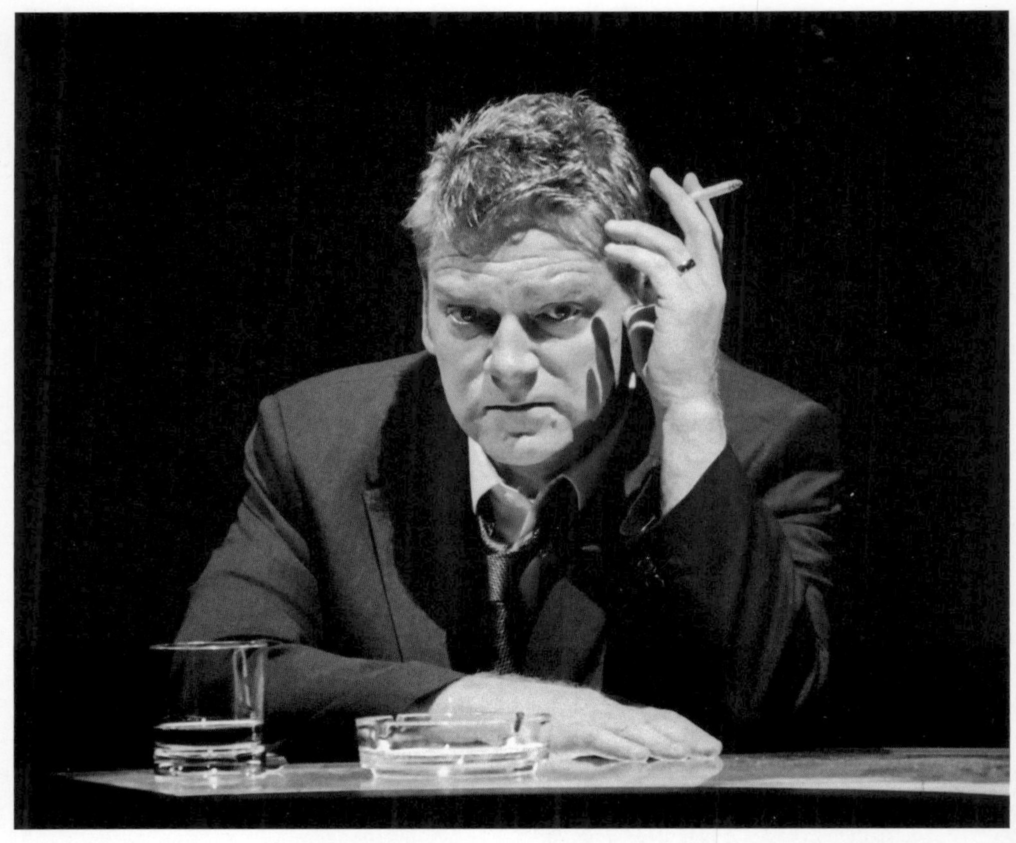

16 Playing the lead in David Mamet's *Edmond* at the National Theatre in 2003.

unhallowed arts kneeling beside the thing he had put together. I saw the hideous phantasm of a man stretched out, and then, on the working of some powerful engine, show signs of life, and stir with an uneasy, half-vital motion. Frightful must it be; for supremely frightful would be the effect of any human endeavour to mock the stupendous mechanism of the Creator of the world. His success would terrify the artist; he would rush away from his odious handiwork, horror-stricken.[1]

Thrilled and terrified by the power of her idea, encouraged by her husband, Mary Shelley produced a full-length novel by the spring of 1817. When *Frankenstein* was published a year later, it proved to be a resounding success. 'An extraordinary tale,' stated Sir Walter Scott, 'in which the author seems to us to disclose uncommon powers of poetic imagination.' A hit with the public, *Frankenstein* was released thirteen years later in a revised edition. Such was the appeal of Mary Shelley's story of the scientist who plays God by creating then abandoning a creature who exacts a bloody revenge that by 1823 a production of the story, entitled *Presumption: or the Fate of Frankenstein*, had been successfully mounted on the London stage.

Mary Shelley would go on to write other works, but none had the impact of *Frankenstein*. Its success can be ascribed in part to a richness and a powerful authenticity that derived from the author's own tragic life experiences. With her mother having died from giving birth to her, Percy Shelley having come a-courting at her mother's grave site, and her first baby by Shelley having died two weeks after birth, the twin subjects of birth and death were obsessions that informed her first novel.

Exactly 175 years after the publication of *Frankenstein*, Kenneth Branagh made a cinematic version of the story. A big-budget Hollywood picture, it should have confirmed his reputation as an emerging film-maker. Instead the enterprise proved to be a poisoned chalice, damaging his confidence, his professional standing, and his marriage.

Branagh was busy rehearsing *Hamlet* with the Royal Shakespeare Company in the autumn of 1992 when Francis Ford Coppola, director of the *Godfather* films and *Apocalypse Now*, asked him to make *Mary Shelley's Frankenstein*. A devotee of Gothic horror, Coppola had recently directed the box-office smash *Bram Stoker's Dracula*. He had considered tackling *Frankenstein* himself but, exhausted from making *Dracula*, he decided to delegate. For a time it was rumoured that Roman Polanski was in the running; but in the end Steph Lady's script for *Frankenstein*, backed by Coppola's American Zoetrope company and TriStar Pictures, was forwarded by Coppola to Branagh, who seemed an ideal choice as director. He had already demonstrated a marked ability to popularise pieces of classic literature for the big screen; and Coppola saw him as a kindred spirit. 'He's clearly an energetic young man,' the great American film-maker enthused. 'I recognised in him some of the same kind of energy and competence to do whatever it takes that I fancied I had myself, also coming out of the theatre.'

Branagh's initial reaction was wary. The screenplay did not strike him as being particularly fresh. On the other hand, he recognised the story had themes that would resonate with a modern movie audience. This fable 'makes so much more sense today', he said. 'People can almost create life now, can't they? We've got test-tube babies, we can choose the sex of our own children.' Branagh, moreover, connected with the story in a personal sense. With the screenplay arriving in October 1992 as he prepared *Hamlet* for the stage, he was already pondering the fundamental issues of life and death that Mary Shelley explored. For Branagh, the thematic link between *Hamlet* and *Frankenstein* seemed strong.

What dispelled Branagh's doubts about making *Frankenstein* was his decision to go back and read the original novel by Mary Shelley. Familiar with the old film versions, including *Frankenstein* and *The Bride of Frankenstein* – the classic 1930s James Whale movies starring Boris Karloff as the Monster – as well as the versions by the British company Hammer and Mel Brooks' superb spoof of the genre, *Young Frankenstein*, Branagh was struck by the differences between Shelley's story on the one hand and the way it had been told cinematically on the other. 'Right there on page one,' he explained, recalling his reaction to the novel, 'I said, "What the heck are we doing in the Arctic?" and the questions never stopped.' Why had Frankenstein invariably been portrayed in the movies as a mad doctor who is aided by a hunchback called Igor when in the novel he is a quite rational young medical student who has no such assistant? Why is 'the creature' described by Shelley as articulate and intelligent referred to as 'the Monster' in the movies and often mute? Why had the important themes in the novel, such as that of parental responsibility, been largely unexplored on the big screen? Like an academic searching for a fresh approach to a trite area of investigation, Branagh liked to have a clear rationale for the films he made. For *Mary Shelley's Frankenstein* he now had one: he would make a movie more faithful to Shelley's original vision than any previous film.

Branagh informed TriStar Pictures of his conditional interest in the project: 'If we can perhaps start again, get back to square one and really attempt to do the Mary Shelley book, then I'd be very interested.' TriStar obliged, bringing on board Frank Darabont, writer and director of *The Shawshank Redemption*, to make the screenplay conform more to Shelley's novel. Branagh's other demand was that the film be made not in Hollywood but in Britain. He did not want to be away from home for eighteen months, or to have every suit in the studio breathing down his neck. Once again it was decided to do things Branagh's way: the film would be shot at Shepperton Studios, where he had made *Henry V*.

In addition to directing the film, Branagh would play Victor Frankenstein, a part for which he seemed ideal, as he shared Frankenstein's obsessive drive. With a budget of $44 million, exceeding the total spent on all of his previous films, this was big news. When the story broke in Britain that Branagh was taking on the project, newspaper placards proclaimed: 'BRANAGH IN MONSTER MOVIE DEAL'.

Mary Shelley's Frankenstein was an exciting venture for Branagh. This was the first time he had made, or even been involved in, a big-budget film. The fact that it was at a time when a number of Gothic horror movies had been or would be made – Coppola's *Bram Stoker's Dracula*, Mike Nichols' *Wolf*, with Jack Nicholson, and Neil Jordan's *Interview with the Vampire*, starring Tom Cruise and Brad Pitt – meant that he would be going head to head as a film-maker and actor with some of the biggest names in the business. The money on offer was unlike anything received by Branagh in his career; $5 million, according to one estimate, was his payment for the project. For the first time in his life, he would be rich. In addition to these factors, it was the calibre of his collaborators that made it such a special opportunity. Not only did Coppola remain involved in the project as a producer, but the man regarded by many as the most powerful screen actor since the days when Marlon Brando was at the top of his game, Robert De Niro, agreed to play the Creature.

There had been rumours that Andy Garcia and Gérard Depardieu were in the running for the part made iconic by Boris Karloff; but

Coppola was determined to recruit De Niro, with whom he had worked on *The Godfather, Part II*. When Branagh signed up as director, he joined Coppola in that undertaking. As a relative newcomer to the world of film, Branagh was understandably intimidated by De Niro's credentials. From his Oscars for *The Godfather, Part II* and *Raging Bull* to his searing performances in *Mean Streets*, *Taxi Driver* and *The Deer Hunter*, De Niro had produced a body of work, much of it as part of a legendary collaboration with director Martin Scorsese, perhaps unequalled for the breathtaking intensity with which he infused his characters. Branagh wanted De Niro to take on the role of the Creature because of his truthfulness in front of the camera, and his ability to convey both the character's sweetness and its malevolence. De Niro turned out to be interested in a role which he thought would stretch him as an actor. But he was wary too; and the reason for his wariness was Branagh himself. Concerned that he would prove to be an overly intellectual, pretentious theatrical type who would insist on a quintessentially English accent for the Creature, De Niro would have to be courted.

Coppola and Branagh set out to do just that. Having played Hamlet for the RSC on the previous night, Branagh flew to New York on Concorde to meet both Coppola and De Niro for the first time. It was at De Niro's own Tribeca Centre restaurant that these three men convened. They enjoyed some wine brought by Coppola from his Napa Valley estate, as well as stories from the director's great fund of movie anecdotes, and literally broke the bread. 'I was careful not to put my hands on the fucking table in case a fucking steak knife came down on them!' Branagh later joked, feeling as though he had walked into a scene from *The Godfather*. Interestingly, De Niro was far more comfortable once he learned that Branagh was Irish, not English. 'I think he felt safe with that Italian-American-Irish-Celtic kind of singing, drinking, we're-all-a-bit-loyal-and-mad sort of thing,' observed Branagh.

Though this was a promising start to the De Niro–Branagh collaboration, the cautious American actor was not yet convinced. He wanted to make sure that his and Branagh's conception of the Creature were compatible – they were, with both determined to avoid the schlock horror square-head-and-bolts-through-the-neck approach, and get back to the original characterisation in Mary Shelley's novel – and he vetted Branagh with staggering thoroughness. The *sine qua non* of any artistic collaboration for De Niro was trust. Accordingly, he watched all of Branagh's films and television work. He spoke to people who knew Branagh. He acquired a general sense of his reputation for dealing with actors. Evidently Branagh passed muster. By April 1993 the press reported that De Niro had signed up.

As with his previous pictures, Branagh developed a clear conception of the film before shooting began. Fidelity to the novel was a priority. Hence Frankenstein would not be aided by a hunchbank, and Shelley's device of opening and closing the story in the Arctic with an encounter between Captain Walton, an explorer determined to reach the North Pole, and Frankenstein and the Creature, would be retained.

As for characterisation, Branagh resolved to steer clear of the simplistic idea that the story is about a mad scientist and a Neanderthal monster. Branagh's Frankenstein would be high-minded, driven by a genuine albeit misguided desire to help mankind. With an emphasis on the emotional impact of the untimely death of Frankenstein's beloved mother, his determination to recreate life would come across as the longing of a rational scientist, not a madman.

Rather than the grunting primitive associated with other Frankenstein films, De Niro's Creature would be intelligent and articulate. This would come across most clearly in the ice cave scene in which he peppered Frankenstein with pertinent, poignant questions: 'What of my soul? Do I have one? Or was that a part you left out? Who were these people of which I am comprised? Good people? Bad people?' And most tellingly: 'Did you ever consider the consequences of your actions?' The intention was for this Creature to come across as a sort of noble Japanese warrior with a philosophical bent. A richer, more nuanced portrait would thus be presented.

Important to Branagh's vision was the part played by Elizabeth, Frankenstein's adopted sister, who becomes the love of his life. It seemed appropriate for a film of a novel by an important woman writer who was the daughter of an eminent feminist that Elizabeth be more than just a minor, passive character. This would be a vibrant Elizabeth with a mind of her own. In Branagh's version, for instance, it is she who proposes marriage to Frankenstein. By emphasising Elizabeth's worthiness, the risk involved in Frankenstein's obsessive drive to create life – what he stands to lose – would be highlighted.

For the overall feel of the movie, Branagh wanted to convey the sense of an epic fairy tale, of small people playing out a drama against imposing landscapes and buildings. The construction of oversize sets at Shepperton Studios, combined with a week of shooting in the Swiss Alps, was arranged accordingly. Such was the work involved in building the sets that the British film industry received a palpable boost from *Mary Shelley's Frankenstein*. Supervised by production designer and old Branagh collaborator Tim Harvey, as many as two hundred people were put to work. The set for the grimy town of Ingolstadt, where Victor Frankenstein studies at university, was in fact the biggest ever built at a British studio, covering an area of 70,000 square feet and utilising more than 57 miles of scaffolding. For the Arctic scenes, a full-size hundred-foot whaling vessel was constructed. The work involved in designing and making the costumes, and preparing the prosthetic make-up for De Niro's Creature, was no less arduous. With *Mary Shelley's Frankenstein*, Branagh was responsible for an enterprise dauntingly vast even for someone of his self-belief.

As work continued apace during the summer of 1993 on sets, costumes and prosthetics, De Niro researched the role of the Creature. Famed for his meticulous, method-style preparations, he left nothing to chance. He spoke to stroke victims who had struggled to restore their power of speech – a useful analogue, De Niro thought, to the Creature's attempts to verbalise his thoughts. He mined doctors and plastic surgeons for the clinical information he needed for the role, asking about the movement of the joints and whether the arms could flex with a body that had been put together from miscellaneous parts.

Branagh's approach involved tending not only to issues of characterisation but to the physical requirements of the part of Victor Frankenstein, as he would be depicted as more youthful and vigorous than in previous films. Working with a trainer, Branagh followed a strict diet and worked out intensively, reportedly running five miles to the studio every morning. Such were his exertions that, as costume designer James Acheson recalls, 'The body we were putting clothes on at the start of rehearsals was completely different from the one we were dressing two months later.' For the scene where the Creature was brought to life, fans would get to see a toned, muscular Branagh stripped to the waist.

Branagh and De Niro were not the only stars to sign up. Most important, not only in terms of the film but – as things turned out – for Branagh's life, was the decision to cast Helena Bonham Carter as Elizabeth. After appearing in 1985 in Trevor Nunn's *Lady Jane* and the Merchant–Ivory production of *A Room with a View*, Bonham Carter had carved out a reputation as Britain's foremost actress in period films, her alabaster beauty, acting talent, and perhaps her distinguished lineage – she was the great-granddaughter of Prime Minister Herbert Henry Asquith, no less – making her ideal for such roles. E. M. Forster heroines were her particular bailiwick; she had appeared in not only *A Room with a View*, but also *Maurice*, *Where Angels Fear to Tread*, and *Howards End* alongside Emma Thompson.

Having starred in all of the previous films he had directed, Thompson was conspicuous by her absence from *Frankenstein*; and if she had played any part, it would have had to be that of Elizabeth. Christopher Hampton reveals that Branagh did want Thompson to appear in *Frankenstein*, until Hampton asked her to star in his own film, *Carrington*. Branagh supported that idea, telling Thompson she should do *Carrington*, as it was a better part for her.

Helena Bonham Carter agreed to take the role of Elizabeth not only as she was keen to play a feisty, dynamic character but because she was impressed by Branagh, whom she had met socially. It was one thing getting Bonham Carter to agree to participate, quite another to get TriStar Pictures to play ball. Their initial view was that a major Hollywood star should be cast. Among the names that were bandied about were those of Demi Moore, Jodie Foster, Geena Davis and Sharon Stone. 'They, the Hollywood backers, were not thrilled with having a Merchant–Ivory girl in the lead,' Bonham Carter revealed at the time of the film's release. 'I'm sure they would have preferred a Hollywood name. I'm sure they would have preferred Arnold Schwarzenegger as the Creature. But Ken wanted me to play Elizabeth.' On this matter Branagh prevailed.

Joining Bonham Carter in what was the most fascinating piece of casting was John Cleese as Dr Waldman, Frankenstein's university mentor, a role which Sean Connery was said to have declined. A comic genius whose triumphs had included *Fawlty Towers* and *A Fish Called Wanda*, the latter earning him an Oscar nomination for Best Screenplay, Cleese was given the opportunity by Branagh to immerse himself in a part with more gravitas than those to which he was accustomed. Branagh had deep respect for comedians, such as Morecambe and Wise, and this influenced his decision to recruit Cleese. 'I didn't want Waldman to be the clichéd old mad scientist,' said Branagh. 'I was looking for the terrific melancholy to which great comedians have access.' Cleese would transform his appearance for the role, using a dental prosthetic and a long, flowing wig based on the hair of a scientist in a Joseph Wright painting. With new hair, new teeth and a different demeanour, Cleese would be almost unrecognisable on screen.

The rest of the cast was of a high calibre. Tom Hulce, a polished actor on stage and screen whose career peaked with his Oscar-nominated performance as Mozart in Milos Forman's *Amadeus*, would play the part of Henry Clerval, Frankenstein's close friend at university. Another American actor, Aidan Quinn, best known for his performance opposite Madonna in *Desperately Seeking Susan*, took the role of Arctic explorer Captain Robert Walton. British thespians Ian Holm and Robert Hardy were cast as Branagh's father and university lecturer respectively. The other actors included many of Branagh's friends: Richard Briers, Mark Hadfield, Richard Clifford, Jimmy Yuill and Gerard Horan.

When this cast convened for rehearsals, Branagh emphasised the importance of avoiding the camp excesses of the schlock horror approach to the *Frankenstein* story. To that end he screened for the actors his favourite film in the genre, Mel Brooks' *Young Frankenstein*, which satirised the clichés of previous movie versions that Branagh wished to avoid. To highlight the complexities of the issues involved, Branagh proceeded to ask his cast: 'Do you believe we should interfere with nature to the extent Victor Frankenstein did?' Their unanimous response was that they did not. Putting a different slant on the dilemma, Branagh then said: 'What if someone you loved died and, because of technology, you could bring her back to life? Would you do it then?' This time all the actors said they would, as the issue becomes different once it is personalised. If that was the case, though, Victor Frankenstein's actions were fathomable; clearly he was no madman.

Beginning in October 1993, filming continued at Shepperton Studios throughout the winter, winding down in February 1994. Shooting at Shepperton was supplemented by a week's filming on location in the Swiss Alps. The weight of responsibility for the making of the film fell primarily on Branagh's shoulders. During this period he directed with more confidence than he had shown on his previous films. With the experience of directing four movies behind him he had become more comfortable with the technical side of film-making. He was developing his own style as a director, not so much English in an understated way, but passionate, romantic, feverish. The febrile camerawork on *Mary Shelley's Frankenstein* reflected those sensibilities. As for the acting, he found it a welcome relief from the directing. Once again he used his mentor Hugh Cruttwell as a candid critic to help hone his performance.

His fellow actors were struck by Branagh's versatility and stamina. 'He very instantly jumped from director to character,' noticed Helena Bonham Carter. 'He has amazing energy and ability to communicate. He's very articulate, very clear, and he makes sure everyone is treated fairly.' Simply working with Branagh was one of Cleese's chief reasons for doing the film; he was not disappointed. 'My God, he gives you a workout! You think you're going to get away with seven takes, but he gets you doing fifteen, sixteen – "Can you give me more of that? – just a little bit more – now play it a bit more angry," etc. I very much admired what he was doing and thought, "If I did that for three weeks, I'd be in a nursing home."'

Ian Holm took note of Branagh's physical preparations:

> I had worked with Branagh a few years before, on *Henry V*, and thought him an inspiring man, a powerhouse of ambition. However, I had not until that point appreciated quite how driven he was. He used to get up at five a.m., and his driver would drop him at Hanger Lane, from where he would run to Shepperton Studios. On arrival, he would work out furiously in the gym and then emerge glistening and toned on the set, ready to act, ready to direct, clad in not much more than a pair of tights. I believe that several pre-torso scenes had already been shot and rejected. Though the film then became a movie about Branagh's body, I liked him a great deal. He was funny and witty, but (a little like Pinter) carried with him a vague but certain air of threat. In addition, the technical team he had assembled were extremely loyal, and such allegiance would not have been granted unless it had been earned.[2]

Apart from Branagh, no one faced greater demands than De Niro. He had to display the patience of Job when having his make-up applied. It took nine hours when the full body prosthetics were put on him for the first time. Even as the process was accelerated, De Niro would still need to be picked up at 2.30 a.m., in the make-up chair by 3, and then remain there for another six and a half hours.

The most intriguing aspect of the shoot was the interaction between De Niro and the rest of the cast. Not a little forelock-tugging went on, with Richard Briers and John Cleese especially anxious about working with him. Such was the state of Cleese's nerves before doing his scene with De Niro that the American felt compelled to take him aside to boost his confidence, keeping a hundred members of the cast and crew waiting in the process. It did the trick. Cleese proceeded to do what Branagh regarded as a perfect take. This courtesy reflected De Niro's general *modus operandi*. Though he could cut up rough if something was not to his liking, as Branagh observed, he was more often than not affable, approachable, attuned to the needs of others and, most surprisingly, an inveterate giggler – a far cry from the image of the obsessive method actor who always stayed in character. He took direction well, with Ian Holm recalling: 'Branagh would say something like, "Lots of eye contact, Bob ... I'd like to see the soul inside that collection of cuts and bruises you're carrying around." And de Niro would just do it, quickly, efficiently, convincingly, and entirely without fuss ... De Niro trusted his director, and the two of them often disappeared into Branagh's mobile editing suite to watch the dailies, chatting and laughing like two old drinking pals.'

Branagh was delighted by De Niro's contribution, describing him as 'the most painstaking, thorough actor I have ever come across', though sometimes that thoroughness manifested itself in unusual ways. Richard Briers recounts the story of his scene with De Niro in which the blind man, played by Briers, hears the Creature outside and invites him in. When they did a take De Niro did not enter as the script indicated he would. Branagh approached Briers and whispered, 'You've got to make him come in, because he's a method actor.' In other words, De Niro would only come in when he felt that the blind man really wanted him to do so. Only when Briers implored him with particular earnestness did De Niro enter.

The bonding that took place between Branagh and De Niro was most in evidence during the shooting of the scene in which the Creature was brought to life. With Mary Shelley's novel offering no detailed account of the creation process, Branagh was able to give vent to his imagination. As he conceptualised it, the scene would conjure up the setting of a delivery room in which a child is born and then abandoned. The sexual imagery would be explicit. Branagh's interpretation would have Frankenstein struggling to help the naked Creature to its feet on a floor drenched with amniotic fluid. Shooting the scene in a ton of warm K-Y jelly, De Niro would spin around in circles for three minutes with his eyes closed before the take in order to lend authenticity to the Creature's attempts to stand up. As Branagh's

Frankenstein helped him to stand, De Niro's body prosthetic started to come apart at his posterior. Branagh had to put his hand on De Niro's backside to ensure that the split was not in the shot. 'Please, please take this in the spirit in which it's meant,' said Branagh, as an anxious De Niro shouted, 'Don't get the K-Y up my ass! Don't do that, for fuck's sake!' Playfulness and banter were part of the good rapport Branagh struck up with his leading actor.

It seems that only Helena Bonham Carter was less than enamoured of working alongside De Niro. She found doing scenes with him awkward, as his preferred practice was to say his line anywhere between three and ten times, with the best delivery of it selected later in editing; and only when he stopped repeating the line would Bonham Carter be able to deliver hers. 'I'm not sure I would want to work with him again,' she said, 'but I wanted this experience – once.'

Through all the trials and tribulations of making the film, a grateful Branagh received the support of Francis Ford Coppola. During rehearsals and the initial and final stages of the shoot, Coppola gave Branagh the benefit of his vast experience. When the studio became nervous about the film, Coppola protected his protégé.

Branagh's father, William, also kept an eye on him during filming. Visiting the set, Branagh senior could have felt only immense pride at the sight of his son directing some 150 people, including Robert De Niro; but, as a joiner by trade, what impressed him most was the immense construction work that had gone into the making of the sets. He ended up spending the day talking to the chief carpenter.

On a personal level a far more important development was afoot, one with immense ramifications certainly for his marriage and possibly for his career: he began a relationship with Helena Bonham Carter. This took place against the backdrop of what had appeared to be a stable, tranquil domestic life. He and Emma Thompson had settled into what was, when the demands of work allowed them to be together, a cosy, unpretentious lifestyle. Though at one point on the verge of moving into an upmarket Victorian town house in Hampstead, north London, they spent their marriage in Emma Thompson's far more modest semi-detached abode in West Hampstead. Eschewing glitzy celebrity parties and London nightclubs, their preferred mode of relaxation was more mundane: videos, take-aways or dinner at home with a few friends. 'Our house has a lovely study,' said Branagh, extolling the virtues of the quiet life. 'I like to sit there. The walls are full of ghosts. There's a little open fire and cup of tea. I can put my feet up and read a book or drink a glass of wine. That's my idea of heaven. I don't like going out and being pecked apart in one of those social situations where you're rent-a-celeb.'

Anchoring the marriage between Branagh and Thompson was the strong support they received from both sides of the family. With the Thompsons, that support was very close at hand. Thompson's mother lived on the opposite side of the same street, while her sister, gifted actress Sophie Thompson, lived just a few doors down. Branagh, likewise, had sustained a strong relationship with his parents, who still lived in Reading. 'We're a very close family,' his father once explained, 'and we know his every move.' What Branagh junior described as 'one of the most magical [days] in my life' was when he bought for his parents the three-bedroom, semi-detached house that they had rented since their arrival from Belfast.

During the making of *Frankenstein* there was speculation on set that a romance between Branagh and Bonham Carter had developed. 'I heard the rumours but I didn't see a thing,' revealed Richard Briers. A technician working on the film acknowledged more, saying there was a 'general awareness' that 'a serious relationship' was under way between Branagh and his leading lady.

> I think it was most apparent [this source added] when they were doing their love scenes. We all sensed a self-consciousness that you always get between actors and actresses when they are involved with each other off the set.
>
> I remember, too, that when Branagh was having his make-up put on, Helena would always be around, watching what was happening and joking with him. It was all very playful and quite touching. She really loved looking at him and he, naturally enough, seemed quite flattered.[3]

In a sense, the burgeoning amour between Branagh and Bonham Carter requires little explanation. For Branagh to have had the affair was no less commonplace, particularly in the world of film, where fictional love affairs can easily become real ones, than if he had not. If asked today to identify the reasons why they came together, the parties themselves probably could not do so with any degree of certainty. As the American novelist Philip Roth has put it, 'What underlies the anarchy of the train of events, the uncertainties, the mishaps, the disunity, the shocking irregularities that define human affairs? *Nobody* knows ... You *can't* know anything. The things you *know* you don't know. Intention? Motive? Consequence? Meaning? All that we don't know is astonishing. Even more astonishing is what passes for knowing.'

Speculatively, then, the factors behind the development of the relationship between Branagh and Bonham Carter probably included a strong mutual attraction. Bonham Carter was a beauty, and in a kind of quintessentially English-rose way that Branagh, when one thinks of his previous partners, tended to find appealing. While Branagh did not have a matinee-idol appearance, he was pleasant-looking, and his vitality, intelligence and confidence gave him a stronger sex appeal in person than he displayed on screen. A female journalist once said of him, he is 'one of those engaging young men who mysteriously become more handsome the longer you spend in their company'.

There may also have been a celebratory aspect to the Branagh–Bonham Carter relationship. These were thrilling times for them both. With *Mary Shelley's Frankenstein* Bonham Carter found herself being promoted for a role by the hottest young British director around, and finally making the transition from low-budget, costume dramas to what seemed to be Hollywood blockbuster territory. For Branagh *Frankenstein* fulfilled all of his loftiest dreams. Courted by Coppola, directing De Niro, heading up a big-budget Hollywood movie – these were heady days. Conceivably, a passionate love affair with Bonham Carter felt like another part of this exciting, intoxicating experience.

After his separation from Emma Thompson, Branagh gave the time-honoured explanation that the weeks and months spent apart as a result of their busy careers contributed to the collapse of their relationship. It is true that Branagh's obsession with *Frankenstein*, from being approached to take on the project to the film's release, spanned no less than two years. Emma Thompson was also working hard. In 1994 alone she could be seen in three films: *My Father, the Hero*, *Junior*, with Arnold Schwarzenegger, and *Carrington*. She also devoted considerable time to honing the screenplay for her pet project, a film version of Jane Austen's *Sense and Sensibility*. The extent of Branagh and Thompson's professional commitments, therefore, did not help matters.

Whatever the causes of the domestic strife that engulfed his life during this period, the result was that Branagh's marriage was in jeopardy at the same time as his professional reputation was more on the line than ever before because of his responsibility for the success of a $44 million Hollywood movie. Branagh's emotions must have been a mélange of excitement and painful, soul-searching introspection.

The wrap date for *Mary Shelley's Frankenstein* came at the end of February 1994. After that it was a case of a little reshooting so that more could be seen of Frankenstein's mother, played by Cherie Lunghi, incorporating Patrick Doyle's intense, dramatic score, and spending six gruelling months in the editing room. 'There were times when I thought it would never end,' confessed Branagh.

An intriguing diversion to the hard work on *Frankenstein* was the consideration given by Branagh to the rumours in the press in the summer of 1994 that he was in line for the role of Obi-Wan Kenobi, played by Alec Guinness in the original, in the planned prequel to the *Star Wars* films. Branagh did not rebuff these reports, saying he would be interested in the role. As things turned out, the part went to Ewan McGregor.

By the autumn, with the release of *Frankenstein* set for 4 November both in Britain and in the United States, the pressure was mounting. Branagh's track record with *Henry V*, *Dead Again* and *Much Ado About Nothing* created high expectations. Moreover, success was imperative in a business sense for Columbia TriStar. Having experienced a drop in box-office market share over the course of the year, studio executives were pinning their hopes on Branagh's film. It was reported that they were looking for the movie to do at least as well as *Bram Stoker's Dracula*, their 1992 film that had grossed $85 million in the American market alone.

It was in Los Angeles that *Mary Shelley's Frankenstein* received its American première at a star-studded event attended by such Hollywood royalty as Jack Nicholson and Tom Cruise. British royalty was present too as Prince Charles, grateful for the boost given to the UK film industry by the fact that *Frankenstein* was made in Britain, showed his continuing support for Branagh's career. 'I hope he likes it,' Branagh was heard to say to Emma Thompson as he moved towards the royal motorcade to greet Prince Charles. Introduced to the cast, Charles was especially delighted to meet Helena Bonham Carter. *A Room with a View*, in which she had starred, was his favourite film, he told her. Much was made of De Niro's absence from this event, with some interpreting it as a snub to Charles. The American actor had simply been busy filming in Las Vegas, royal aides explained.

Mary Shelley's Frankenstein was not Branagh's only work available to the American public in November 1994. Coinciding with the film's release was the US première of *Public Enemy*, the play written by Branagh back in the 1980s about a young Belfast man obsessed with James Cagney. The Irish Arts Centre, an off-Broadway group, decided to stage the work. Branagh was flattered and even revised parts of it for this New York production.

After embarking on a promotional tour for *Frankenstein*, attending the film's LA première and lending a helping hand to the *Public Enemy* production, Branagh jetted back across the Atlantic for the British opening of his new movie. An ominous portent came in the form of a conversation between politician Gerald Kaufman and a senior Columbia TriStar executive at a reception prior to the première. 'It's time to go and watch your movie,' remarked Kaufman. 'Kenneth Branagh's movie,' clarified the executive, rather pointedly, as if to distance himself from the work. Branagh left the Odeon on Leicester Square, as the lights went down, saying that he had seen the film often enough already. When at a post-première dinner a journalist told him, 'I think you've made a very durable film,' Branagh gave him a withering look as though the comment was designed to damn with faint praise. His sullenness was easily explained: the first reviews were already in, and they did not make pleasant reading.

Geoff Brown upbraided Branagh in *The Times* for his 'jerky directorial manner', which 'robs the story of that inner coherence and forward thrust that keeps audiences glued to their seats', and for his frenetic acting. While Adam Mars-Jones of the *Independent* liked the scene in which the Creature was brought to life, as well as the supporting performances by Tom Hulce and John Cleese, he thought that the large spaces used for such parts of the set as Frankenstein's laboratory undercut the sense of claustrophobia needed for an effective Gothic film. Even the London *Standard*'s Alexander Walker, who had been a fervent admirer of Branagh's previous work, mauled the movie. There were some powerful moments, he thought, but the tone was too strident and the dialogue facile.

Other reviewers were more positive. 'This is a minor epic of many virtues,' asserted Derek Malcolm in the *Guardian*, 'the chief of which is honesty of purpose, great technical proficiency and acting which never lets it down'. In the *Sunday Times* Julie Burchill was even more effusive. This was a passionate, sexy film, she declared, and in Branagh Britain at last had a big film star. 'You've never seen any actor look so permanently aroused, so constantly in a real state as Branagh does in this film, and it's very exciting,' she gushed. 'It remains one of the great mysteries of the cinema how gigantic, iconic beauties such as James Dean and Montgomery Clift now seem such uninspired, mannered mini-talents when you see their films – yet this potato-faced, bland-seeming bloke can invariably turn any odd bit of mouldy old dough into a flaming crêpe Suzette by the sheer force of his talent.' These tributes notwithstanding, most Fleet Street reviews of Branagh's film were hostile.

Better disposed towards Branagh's work in the past, American critics found themselves on this occasion in agreement with their underwhelmed counterparts on the other side of the Atlantic. 'Mr Branagh is in over his head,' lamented Janet Maslin in the *New York Times*. 'He displays neither the technical finesse to handle a big, visually ambitious film nor the insight to develop a stirring new version of this story.' The *Village Voice* criticised the decision to make Branagh's Frankenstein, rather than the Creature, the centre of the story, while *Variety* found fault with De Niro's performance, the sets, the music and the film's heightened, operatic sensibility.

Such was the scale of the onslaught from the critics that Branagh stopped reading the reviews when he realised what was happening, saying, 'I've had hostile reviews before, but these were very personal and hurtful. In a sense it was impossible for me to remain sane if I was to identify with any of that hostility.' The temptation to run away and hide must have been considerable. But that was not an option. Branagh was committed to a six-week world tour to promote the film. Invariably he found himself defending his movie from unimpressed interviewers. The experience must have been excruciating.

As Branagh has pointed out ever since, *Mary Shelley's Frankenstein* was not the commercial disaster usually assumed. Its performance in America was poor, making only $22 million at the box office; but it grossed over $80 million outside the United States, ensuring that worldwide it took more than $100 million. In the end the film did see a profit. It also enjoyed two weeks as the number one film in Britain. Certainly the movie had underperformed in relation to expectations, but its box-office performance had been disappointing rather than catastrophic.

Did *Mary Shelley's Frankenstein* deserve the reputation it acquired as an inferior piece of film-making? I recall feeling disappointed when watching it in 1994, having so much admired *Henry V* and *Much Ado*

About Nothing; but viewed again recently the film held up well. De Niro's portrayal of the Creature was moving, the actors in supporting roles, such as Tom Hulce, were effective, and the film was striking visually. The screenplay should have been revised, however. The critics were right in saying that some of the language was clichéd. Branagh's acting, though passionate, lacked the depth and subtlety of his Henry V five years earlier. Humanising the Creature did make De Niro's performance less frightening than it would otherwise have been; and that probably explains in large measure the disappointment felt by some cinema-goers.

There was also a sense in which Branagh paid a price for inverting the usual relationship between screenplay and original text. With *Henry V* and *Much Ado About Nothing* Branagh had taken Shakespeare's plays, adapted them and abbreviated them, so that they worked cinematically. With *Mary Shelley's Frankenstein*, by contrast, he had abandoned an approach, embodied in the classic James Whale versions of the 1930s, that had worked on the big screen in favour of a greater fidelity to the novel. Due deference may have been shown to Mary Shelley, but the emphasis needed on translating a piece of literature into something that worked as a movie had been reduced.

In a sense, Branagh's reworking of the Frankenstein story was reminiscent of Timothy Dalton's reinterpretation of James Bond in the 1980s. In the hands of Roger Moore, a tongue-in-cheek sensibility had infused the character. The classically trained Dalton resolved to suggest a greater seriousness of purpose on the part of Bond. Dalton was a fine actor, his approach was well conceived, and his performances as Bond were intense. It should have worked, but somehow it didn't. The same kind of dynamic was evident with Branagh's Frankenstein film. Perhaps playing characters such as Bond, Frankenstein or the Creature, which have become iconic, almost cartoonish in the popular imagination, works better with a more frivolous approach.

Branagh must have pondered these sorts of issues as he licked his wounds in the wake of the criticism that the film had provoked. Patricia Marmont recalls, 'He was in a terrible state.' 'It did shake my confidence,' Branagh admitted. 'It was a tough time for me.' Strangers would approach as he walked down the street, squeeze his arm and gaze at him sympathetically. 'I thought: "Have I got a strange disease? Yes, I've got failure disease."' He had not been accustomed to the affliction.

It was in this mindset of deflation and anguish that Branagh wrought major changes in his life. Essentially he decided to replace the team he had built around himself since the 1980s. Hence he dismissed his British agent Patricia Marmont and his American agent Clifford Stevens. Marmont recalls that 'he flipped his lid with the failure of *Frankenstein* and, I think, decided to change everything. I knew there was trouble afoot and I rang Clifford, who was very important in his life ... I said, "Clifford, get over here. I think we've got a problem." So he came over.' Marmont and Stevens then met with Branagh who, as Marmont puts it, 'just delivered the death blow to the two of us together, which had us fairly stunned'. The next morning Stevens told Marmont he was 'not going to accept this lying down. I've rung him and insisted on another meeting. And I think you should be there.' At this second meeting Branagh reiterated his earlier decision. He did not give a full explanation as to the reasons why he was dismissing Marmont and Stevens, but did say that he wished to go in another direction.

A few months earlier Branagh had also called time on his involvement with the Renaissance company. The final Renaissance production, it had been announced, would be the radio broadcast in April 1994 of *King Lear*, with John Gielgud in the lead role. The making of *Frankenstein* away from the auspices of Renaissance had carried clear implications for the future of the company, but the relationship between the leaders of Renaissance also had a bearing on this. Though sustaining a professional partnership until 1994, Branagh and Parfitt had become less close personally. This had been a gradual, long-term process, beginning with the Renaissance theatre tour in 1988, and accelerated by their respective marriages. Parfitt acknowledges that he behaved quite badly during the filming of *Much Ado About Nothing*. He had considerable responsibilities for producing the movie, his marriage was crumbling at the time, and the pressure got to him – he was not at his best. Branagh persuaded Columbia TriStar to hire Parfitt as a co-producer on *Frankenstein*, but during the shoot Parfitt felt marginalised. He did not have much to do, and a busy Branagh had little contact with him. Parfitt left during post-production, and, along with Stephen Evans, embarked on his own project: producing *The Madness of King George*, with Alan Bennett adapting his own play for the screen. By this point Branagh's partnership with Stephen Evans and David Parfitt was a thing of the past.

Branagh's departure from Renaissance made sense, reflects Evans, as the initial sense of enthusiasm and the colossal success of the company would have been difficult to maintain. Parfitt would have preferred a more definite sense of closure. 'It was a very sad moment for me,' he says, 'because there was never really a moment, I don't think, where we sat down and said, "This is what we're going to do, we're going to stop now." It just fizzled, and that was a great shame ... I wished it had ended in a different way. Even a row would have been good.' Still, Branagh tied up the loose ends graciously. He had intended to buy Renaissance Films. At the last moment he bailed out, but not before handing over shares in the company to Parfitt and making a payment to Evans, which he had not requested, that amounted to £250,000. Parfitt and Evans would proceed to run Renaissance Films together, then Evans did so by himself. Finally, after refinancing Renaissance, Evans struck out on his own with a new production company.

Committing himself to *Frankenstein* had weakened Branagh's ties to Renaissance, as did the perceived failure of the film, which strengthened his desire for a new beginning, to surround himself with new people. The disintegration of his marriage served only to fortify that feeling. As David Parfitt suggests, an impulse to start afresh seemed to underpin the ending of so many relationships that had been of importance to him:

> Obviously he was probably slightly bruised by *Frankenstein*. That didn't go as it should have done. There was that. His relationship with Emma was breaking up. And, if you look, all of these things happened at the same time. Pat Marmont – he let her go. He ended his time with Renaissance, and he got divorced. It seemed like – I don't know whether it was ever as calculated as this – a sort of drawing a line under a period in his life, and starting again, which you can understand.[4]

Over time, others would emerge to step into the shoes of Parfitt, Evans *et al.* David Barron would produce Branagh's subsequent films, including *In the Bleak Midwinter* and *Hamlet*. Tamar Thomas, wife of Branagh's good friend Gerard Horan, would play an increasingly important role as his vigilant personal assistant, an effective buffer between Branagh and the outside world, especially the media. The powerful American agency CAA would help Branagh to secure movie roles in the United States. Family and his inner circle of friends, such as Richard Briers and Jimmy Yuill, stayed close to him; nevertheless the period from 1993 to 1995 saw important changes in Branagh's life.

As the composition of Team Branagh changed, the man himself continued to deal with the ongoing media attacks. Finally he felt he had no choice but to respond in a very direct way to his detractors. The straw that broke the camel's back was an article in the London *Standard* entitled 'The breaking of Branagh?' in which journalist Neil Norman suggested that Branagh had become petulant since the *Frankenstein* disaster. His decision to dismiss Patricia Marmont as well as Clifford Stevens was cited as evidence that he had become grumpy and graceless. The claim was also made that Branagh had approached CAA in order to secure big-money movie roles in Hollywood. In addition, Norman alleged that *Mary Shelley's Frankenstein* had been a financial disaster, that Branagh had been blaming studio interference for the film's shortcomings, that prior to *Frankenstein* he had received little criticism – and that which had been directed at him had been 'in the spirit of affectionate envy.'

Branagh was clearly stunned by the attack. He fired off a vigorous rebuttal to the London *Standard*, published on 2 March 1995, only a day after Norman's article had appeared:

I write in response to your article in yesterday's *Evening Standard*. I wanted to clarify the following:

1) You list *Mary Shelley's Frankenstein* as 'commercially one of the all-time grand flops'. In fact the film was made on time and at a final budget of $44 million, not $55 million as you say. Its worldwide theatrical income currently stands at $77 million, not $35.5 as you say. Worldwide video and TV income are still to come.

2) You claim I have been 'passing the buck' and 'blaming studio interference' for the film's performance. I have blamed no one publicly or privately. My contract gave me final cut, a clause I have had on all of my films to date. TriStar were tremendously supportive of the work but the responsibility for the content of the final picture was solely mine. I happily accept this sole responsibility.

3) You discuss my change of representation and its manner, using the word 'cruel'. The changing of representation is a common matter in the business lives of actors, with some making changes many times, and almost every actor doing so at least once in his or her career.

The reasons for my decision remain entirely between myself, Patricia Marmont and Clifford Stevens but are in no way linked to the performance of *Frankenstein*. Both agents have given me excellent representation and have supported me fully throughout my career. I therefore informed them privately, in person, and before having spoken to any other possible representation. I was then approached by a number of agents, including CAA, who I am now represented by in the US. I did not, as you claim, 'go knocking on doors'.

4) You say I have had 'remarkably little criticism until Frankenstein'. A simple scan of your own paper's files over the last 10 years would disprove that. I have

had extremely savage criticism throughout my career that is attendant on those also lucky enough to earn significant praise from their audiences. I accept this perfectly normal state of affairs and am grateful that this has allowed me to continue working.

5) You claim my behaviour of late has been 'cruel', 'arrogant', 'churlish', 'mean', 'peevish' and that I have behaved like a 'spoilt child'. You substantiate none of these so-called reactions with your own first-hand experience, nor do you quote any instance or individual by name who can do so.

All of the above address the confusing hearsay of your article. Its facts are incorrect and the innuendo and surmise are unworthy of a journalist for whom I have respect (having, incidentally, been the recipient of both your praise and criticism).

So there you have the truth from the stoically unpeevish mouth of the horse with the thin lips.

This was a clear, cogent, point-by-point rebuttal of Norman's claims; but underlying the letter's lucid logic was a sense that Branagh was hurt and angry at yet another intemperate press attack. This exchange with Norman, as well as the array of hostile reviews accompanying *Frankenstein*'s release, showed that Branagh-bashing, born in 1989, was still thriving in the mid-1990s. Some of the criticism was no doubt an authentic response to his work. But the personal nature of it indicated there was more to it than that.

Throughout 1994 and 1995, actors, directors and journalists continued to mull over this issue. 'In England, if someone does well, it's a threat to anybody's potential success,' mused Michael Maloney, who had acted in Branagh's film of *Henry V*, while Garth Pearce made his feelings felt in no uncertain terms in the *Daily Mirror*: 'The critics are gloating, because Branagh is a working-class guy who dared to succeed in a business littered with sneering theatre snobs.' The *Independent* even published a table presenting a series of 'PRO KEN' and 'ANTI KEN' quotes from various people. For Branagh, an affable man whose artistic tastes – centring, as they did, on the classical repertoire – seemed essentially conservative, and whose work had had indisputably positive consequences in terms of popularising Shakespeare and providing employment to a good many actors and technicians, that he should have ended up as a focus for such abuse must have struck him as odd as well as painful.

Amplifying his anxiety over the fate of *Mary Shelley's Frankenstein* and his treatment by the media were the strains in his marriage. By the spring of 1995 he and Thompson were charting separate career paths.

While Branagh filmed *In the Bleak Midwinter*, Emma Thompson fulfilled her dream of making a movie of Jane Austen's *Sense and Sensibility*. Thompson had written what would turn out to be an Oscar-winning screenplay, Columbia Pictures had agreed to back the project, and a cast – including Alan Rickman, Hugh Grant, Kate Winslet and Thompson herself – had been assembled. As Branagh had rejected Thompson's offer to direct the film, that responsibility passed to Ang Lee from Taiwan.

The film was shot at Shepperton Studios and at various locations in England between April and July 1995. Emma Thompson's published diaries provide clues as to her state of mind during this period. 'I feel unattractive and talentless,' she wrote on 28 April. The next day her spirits remained unchanged: 'I feel the most appalling frump.' Twenty-four hours later her mood was buoyed by the arrival of Greg Wise, the actor cast as John Willoughby. He was 'full of beans and looking gorgeous. Ruffled all our feathers a bit.' Thompson's attraction to Wise was reciprocated. 'He was running after her like a puppy,' one source has revealed, 'getting her cheese and drinks. They were both smoking roll-up cigarettes and laughing ... At dinner, it was clear they were obsessed with each other. Emma was even copying the way he spoke.' Chris Nickson, Emma Thompson's biographer, says she sought to keep the affair secret during the shoot. There had been rumours about Thompson's relationship with Anthony Hopkins. This, however, was a more serious matter. Wise would become her long-term partner, the father of her child in 1999, and her husband four years later.

Branagh busied himself with his latest film project, *In the Bleak Midwinter*, as Thompson pressed ahead with *Sense and Sensibility*. Having disappointed with *Frankenstein*, Branagh wasted no time in trying to restore his reputation. In January 1995 he burned the midnight oil, completing a screenplay about a group of actors who stage a version of *Hamlet* in a country church at Christmas. *In the Bleak Midwinter* is a comedy but also a study of actors as a breed, their virtues and vices, with Branagh drawing on his own experience of theatrical life.

Working at a cracking pace, Branagh finished the screenplay in time for a February read-through by the actors cast in the film. Continuing at breakneck speed, a shoot of only four weeks began in March, with three of them on location at St Peter's Convent in Old Woking, and one week at Shepperton Studios.

As a piece of film-making, *In the Bleak Midwinter* was the antithesis of *Frankenstein*: a miniaturised tale as opposed to a sprawling epic, a personal story (with the main character Joe bearing some similarities to Branagh) rather than an adaptation of a classic novel, a twenty-one rather than an eighty-one day shoot, and a budget of £2 million not $44 million. Making *In the Bleak Midwinter* would also be quite different in terms of the autonomy that Branagh would feel as a director. It was an independent, privately financed film, with Branagh stumping up a good deal of the money himself; he was discouraged from pre-selling it to a studio when one potential backer tried to dissuade him from shooting the movie in black and white, which Branagh thought would provide a 'sense of heightened reality' appropriate for a story about the world of theatre. Free from studio pressure, Branagh felt liberated: 'I didn't have to explain anything to anyone. I didn't have to talk about casting, didn't have to send them rushes to America, didn't have to preview the movie. We made it, finished it and then we sold it. I was on the phone a fucking sight less, and you're not in front of that vast army of people representing the particular bureaucracy you're working for, stroking them.'

Branagh was not obliged, therefore, to cast stars with box-office clout. Many of those he recruited were long-time collaborators, a number of them close friends. Michael Maloney took the key role of depressed actor Joe who hatches the plan to direct a production of *Hamlet* with himself as the lead. John Sessions was given the part of Terry Du Bois, a theatrical queen who ends up playing Gertrude in drag. Nicholas Farrell would play Tom, an actor enamoured by all things New Age, Gerard Horan a diffident dipsomaniac whose career has not matched parental expectations. Celia Imrie, Julia Sawalha, and Mark Hadfield also joined the latest Branagh venture.

Art blended with life as Branagh wrote many of the parts with the actors in mind. Richard Briers, for instance, was cast as Henry, a caustic veteran of the stage whose irascibility conceals a genuine warmth. To Branagh, Briers was perfect for the part, for in addition to being affable Briers was an inveterate grumbler. Branagh remembered how Briers had ranted shortly before going on stage in Tokyo to play Lear: 'I fucking hate acting. I fucking hate actors. I fucking hate audiences. I fucking hate Shakespeare. I fucking hate King Lear.' All grist to Branagh's mill as a screenwriter.

The two most striking pieces of casting were comedienne Jennifer Saunders as a philistine American film producer, and Joan Collins as Joe's sharp agent. When Collins had met Branagh at a film première, she had told him of her eagerness to tackle some meatier roles. He liked her enthusiasm, and so decided to hire this actress who had become the biggest television star in the world in the 1980s with her portrayal of Alexis Carrington in the long-running soap *Dynasty*. So he could concentrate on directing, Branagh decided against casting himself on this occasion.

The team ethic that emerges among the characters of *In the Bleak Midwinter* was also evident among the cast and crew that made the film. A profit-share principle was established with everyone from Joan Collins to the electrician initially paid a flat rate. Each person also received an additional percentage that reflected their status; so in this case Joan Collins would command a higher percentage than the electrician.

An egalitarian spirit thus characterised the enterprise. There was much joking, bantering and gossiping on set; but there was a lot of focus and application too. Joan Collins, in Branagh's words, 'worked like a real trouper'. Such diligence was required. A shoestring budget meant it was necessary to shoot seven pages of dialogue a day.

Despite the crisis in their relationship, Emma Thompson continued to support Branagh professionally. One day she visited the set as she herself was ensconced at Shepperton Studios for pre-production on *Sense and Sensibility*. 'Here you are, you old tart,' she said playfully as she handed her husband a cup of tea.

Once the film was in the can Branagh sought an American distributor; he found one in Castle Rock. Despite liking the movie, they did not care for the title. Nobody in the United States knew the hymn, they told him, and including the world 'bleak' in the title would not be a good idea from a commercial point of view. They also informed him that some film people in Hollywood had responded to the title by asking: 'Is this his Bergman film?' in reference to the great Swedish director. 'Tell them it's my *Carry On* film,' Branagh replied, 'that's what it is!' Unaware of the English series of bawdy comedies, he had to explain: 'It's British and funny!' In the end, a new title for the American release of the film was agreed upon: the somewhat more inviting *A Midwinter's Tale*.

Though it garnered an award at the Venice Film Festival, the release of Branagh's film in Britain, in December 1995, and two months later in America, produced small cinema audiences – neither in Britain nor in the United States did the movie make half a million pounds – but some decent reviews. In *The Times* Geoff Brown argued that the film was ruined by an implausible plot and clichéd characters; but otherwise the British broadsheets were favourable. Derek Malcolm of the *Guardian* thought it well written and well acted; Nigel Andrew of the *Financial Times* found it charming, while the *Daily Telegraph*'s Hugo Davenport liked the film's pacing and exuberance. In the London *Standard* Alexander Walker also judged it to be 'a modest but successful entertainment'.

Along with *Love's Labour's Lost* (1999), *In the Bleak Midwinter* is the most underestimated film directed by Branagh. It is also his most personal movie. The dialogue, for instance when Michael Maloney's Joe reflects on the feasibility of making Shakespeare relevant and exciting to a young audience, articulates Branagh's own philosophy: 'I think if we can do it [*Hamlet*] with humour, passion and reality people will be interested in seeing it. I saw this play when I was fifteen, and it changed my life. You don't forget that. I don't think I was any different then to any of your hormonally confused kids now.' Branagh succeeded in drawing out some able performances, particularly from Michael Maloney. The overall sense is of Branagh shedding a personal light on the types of people who inhabit the world of theatre. It is a warts-and-all view, as the insecurities and vanities of actors are exposed, but an affectionate one all the same. Most importantly for a comedy, the film is funny. Though the ending, in which the actors' personal problems are neatly solved, is sentimental, *In the Bleak Midwinter* came across as a modest, sweet, charming picture.

After completing this movie in the spring of 1995, Branagh worked with Irish actor Stephen Rea on a BBC television production of *The Shadow of a Gunman*, and prepared another Shakespeare film role – as the treacherous Iago in Oliver Parker's *Othello*. A few months after that Branagh would be engaged in a project which for him represented the culmination of his journey as an artist: a film of *Hamlet* with himself in the lead role. This quest to produce a unique version of the greatest play by the greatest writer in the English language would be pursued as Branagh's marriage teetered on the brink of collapse. Throughout 1995 and beyond, personal calamity and professional opportunity would intermingle.

8

Sweet Prince

The idea of a modern film version of *Othello* was the brainchild of Oliver Parker, a jobbing actor and son of former British Rail chairman Sir Peter. Parker began to write a screenplay for *Othello* after playing Iago in repertory in Wales. In doing so, he was stepping on hallowed ground. Orson Welles had directed and starred in a 1952 film version, done characteristically in film noir style, and thirteen years later Stuart Burge directed Laurence Olivier's landmark performance as Othello for the National Theatre in a picture that earned him yet another Oscar nomination for Best Actor. But Parker was convinced that a fresh interpretation of the play was possible. In all the versions he had seen, the allure of Iago's malevolence had overshadowed the love story between Othello and Desdemona. To Parker's way of thinking that skewed the play, because only if the passionate love between Othello and Desdemona was brought into focus could the tragedy of Othello's murder of Desdemona and his suicide be maximised. A younger, sexier Othello than was usually cast would facilitate, Parker believed, his view of the story as more an erotic thriller than a study of Iago's psyche.

As Parker set to work on his screenplay, he was unencumbered by excessive reverence for the text of *Othello*. It was not so much cut as slashed, and flashback and fantasy scenes were introduced in order to fashion an exciting, fast-paced version of the story. As he began to seek financial backing, Parker found that his credentials did not help matters. He wanted to direct himself, even though the only experience he had at the helm of a film was limited to three shorts. Struck by Parker's boundless enthusiasm, however, independent British producer Luc Roeg, son of celebrated director Nic Roeg, agreed to help develop the project.

What made Parker's film viable was the recruitment of Branagh to the cause. It was Helena Bonham Carter, a friend of Parker, who suggested that he offer Branagh the part of Iago. Sent the script on a Friday in early 1995, Branagh was so enthused that by the Monday he had contacted Parker to discuss the project. What Parker picked up when meeting Branagh was a sense of how the media onslaught had bruised him: 'It must be terrifically exhausting having to sustain the body blows, and it changes you as a person ... In some senses you have to toughen yourself up ... and buckle on your armour, and you get your head down and you charge. In some senses that can be dangerous to yourself because it's a fight you're in rather than a creative process.'

Getting Branagh involved made it easier for Parker to secure the services of a major star for the part of Othello. Laurence Fishburne, the outstanding American actor who had won a Tony for his work on stage, an Emmy for a television performance, and an Oscar nomination for his portrayal of Ike Turner in *What's Love Got To Do With It?*, said his heart stopped beating when his agent told him he was being approached to play Othello opposite Branagh, an undertaking that would make him the first black actor to play the Moor of Venice in a major motion picture. Branagh's participation also facilitated the financing of the film; for only when he came on board did Castle Rock stump up £6 million for the budget. Parker later acknowledged that Branagh was 'instrumental in raising the money'.

The other key piece in the jigsaw was the actress who would play Desdemona. In the end the part went to the Swiss-born Irène Jacob, whose star was in the ascendancy following her acclaimed performances in Krysztof Kieslowski's *The Double Life of Veronique* and *Three Colours: Red*. The composition of the rest of the cast and crew of course reflected Parker's preferences. Keeping things close to home, he recruited his brother Nathaniel to play Cassio, and his sister-in-law Anna Patrick for the role of Emilia, Iago's wife; but Branagh's fingerprints were all over the movie too. Longstanding Branagh collaborators Michael Maloney and Nicholas Farrell took supporting roles. Tim Harvey, who had worked on all of Branagh's feature films, was installed as production designer. Caroline Harris would design the costumes, as she had for *In the Bleak Midwinter*. Russell Jackson once again served as text consultant. Branagh's sister

Joyce, who at the time of writing is carving out a reputation for herself as a theatre director, gained valuable experience as third assistant director. Branagh also brought on board David Barron, who would produce his forthcoming film of *Hamlet*, to assist Luc Roeg. Branagh himself was involved in scouting locations in Italy for the shoot. *Othello*, then, was not a Branagh project in the sense that he did not provide the bedrock vision of the film nor did he serve as director. But his influence was still considerable.

In agreeing to play Iago, Branagh needed to come to grips with perhaps the most enigmatic of all of Shakespeare's villains. The question of what prompts Iago to wreak havoc by conning Othello into thinking that his Desdemona has been unfaithful with Cassio had exercised the minds of actors through the years. Was it anger over Othello's promotion of Cassio ahead of Iago? Was there a racial dimension, as Iago had been treated this way by a black leader? Was it sexual jealousy, as Iago expressed concern over whether his wife had slept with Othello? Or was it simply pure malevolence on Iago's part?

What Branagh came to believe was that this was not a case of malice aforethought – that Iago did not set out with a plan to undo Othello. Rather he idolised the Moor, bonded to him by the battles they had fought together. It was the intense feeling of rejection triggered by Othello's decision to make not him but Cassio his right-hand man that corrupted Iago. 'I interpret his journey', said Branagh, 'as the turning of an honest man.' Once Iago discovers how easy it is to disturb Othello's equanimity, Branagh also felt, he experiences a gleeful thrill at his talent for deceit. 'There's now a moment-to-moment enjoyment of that manipulation which turns demonic,' he explained.

Branagh's performance would also highlight Iago's apparent honesty and affability with those he dupes – a shrewd decision, as this would safeguard the credibility of the other characters. Were his Iago to be dripping in malevolence, then the likes of Cassio and Roderigo would appear naïve for trusting a character so transparently nefarious. Branagh believed he would benefit from his own aura of decency, having played various solid characters in the past; that would make projecting the superficially trustworthy side of Iago's character easier. This dissection of Iago's character, as Branagh prepared for the film, was done with great relish. As he put it, 'Villains are always fun.'

The filming of *Othello*, which started in June 1995, allowed Branagh to return to Italy with all the happy memories it held for him from the making of *Much Ado* three years earlier, and to make use of his Italian – the one foreign language he had acquired during his schooldays. Six weeks of shooting at the fifteenth-century castle of Bracciano, just north of Rome, would be followed by five days in Venice for the filming of exteriors. Despite the sometimes oppressive heat and what he later acknowledged to be the unnerving experience of talking directly to the camera, as Iago was required to do in Parker's adaptation, Branagh felt relaxed, free from the rigours of directing. Bantering with extras and even with visiting journalists, he was in an amiable mood.

Making for a tension-free shoot were the solid working relationships Branagh forged with Oliver Parker and Laurence Fishburne. He reached an informal agreement with Parker whereby Branagh would resist any temptation to direct the film and Parker would not try to play Iago. Branagh was available to dispense advice, if solicited, but he did not throw his weight about, despite his special experience in directing Shakespearean works for the big screen. He did not want to interfere with Parker's attempt to realise his own vision of the story.

Branagh and Fishburne enjoyed a good rapport – right from the start. Wanting to reassure Fishburne that his lack of experience with Shakespeare was no bar to producing a performance of quality, he told the American at their first meeting, 'I'm a kid from Belfast. I'm not supposed to be able to do Shakespeare.' 'Hey, I'm a kid from Brooklyn,' replied Fishburne. 'I'm not supposed to be able to do Shakespeare either!' Branagh's liking for Fishburne was enlarged by his admiration for his portrayal of Othello. He felt 'inspired' by Fishburne's performance, judging him to be 'a Shakespearean natural'. Nor was Branagh's enthusiasm dampened by his co-star's penchant for improvisation. 'Hey, wouldn't it be good if I kind of held his head under water?' suggested Fishburne when shooting a scene with Branagh on the shoreline. 'That would be good, wouldn't it? I could try to drown him.' After being dunked under water, take after take, Branagh decided enough was enough. 'OK, we've done surprises now,' he said. 'Surprise is good, now I'd like to try planned.'

Observing Branagh's work during the shoot caused Oliver Parker to reflect on his attributes. 'He has an amazing facility as an actor,' says Parker. 'A lot of things he finds incredibly easy … technically he can do all sorts of things. He's a great mimic. He's got great range to his voice, and great understanding ... As much as people will say Orson Welles or Olivier, I would say Jimmy Cagney. What he has is a terrific toughness and streetwise quality coupled with enormous vulnerability.'

Along with his acting duties on *Othello* Branagh juggled what had become a complex personal life. Helena Bonham Carter visited him at Bracciano Castle; a journalist noticed her, 'a waif-like beauty, floating along in a floral sundress'. She would account for her presence to the press by claiming that the woman she needed to help with her hair was working on *Othello*. Emma Thompson, it was reported, also flew to Italy in order to discuss with her husband the state of their marriage. According to one source, she and Branagh agreed that their work-enforced separations had corroded their relationship. Accordingly, they spoke of the importance of spending more time together, and even broached the idea of starting a family.

Opening in the United States in December 1995 and in Britain two months later, *Othello*'s box office performance both sides of the Atlantic disappointed. The critical reaction left a lot to be desired too, but Branagh came up smelling of roses. In review after review, he was said to have stolen the show. 'Engrossing,' enthused *The Times* about Branagh's performance, while the *Daily Telegraph* argued that Oliver Parker's attempt to make the Othello–Desdemona love story the film's centrepiece had been undermined by his decision to cast such a consummate Shakespearean actor as Iago. Both *Time Out* and the *Sunday Telegraph* judged Branagh's Iago to be the finest performance of his film career. Accompanying this raft of rave reviews was some tabloid buzz that Branagh would be in the running for an Oscar nomination. Though that accolade did not come his way, he was nominated for a prestigious Screen Actors Guild award.

His portrayal of Iago was well conceived, assured and in places electrifying. The straightforwardness of Branagh's Iago when with the other characters contrasted so sharply with the intense viciousness he displayed when talking to the camera that the impact was spellbinding. For his part, Parker had succeeded in crafting a movie with a strong narrative drive, and the passion and eroticism that he saw at the heart of the story were to the fore. The sweeping cuts in the text perhaps diminished the philosophical weight of the play, and the sorts of arresting visual images that enriched Orson Welles' version were not in evidence. But it was a promising debut from a director who would go on to bolster his reputation with an excellent film adaptation of Oscar Wilde's *An Ideal Husband*. Parker would stay in touch with Branagh after *Othello*, and a few years later they came close to collaborating on a film in which Branagh would have portrayed one of his heroes, Orson Welles.

It was not only *Othello* that occupied Branagh in the middle of 1995. Celebrations in May for the fiftieth anniversary of VE Day saw him advising Prince Charles on the reading to be given by the heir to the throne for a special gala concert at London's Coliseum Theatre, and the transmission on BBC television of *Anne Frank Remembered*, a Branagh-narrated documentary about the remarkable Jewish girl who spent the war in Amsterdam hiding from the Nazis. The documentary would go on to win an Oscar. There was also speculation in the summer of 1995 that Branagh would be starring in a major new BBC television series about the bawdy life of seventeenth-century diarist Samuel Pepys. A television project that did materialise for Branagh was *The Shadow of a Gunman*, broadcast on the BBC in October 1995.

Putting the release of this IRA drama into the shade was the announcement, made a week earlier, that Branagh and Thompson had separated after more than six years of marriage. Issued jointly, the statement read:

> It is with great sadness that we have decided to separate. Our work has inevitably led to our spending long periods of time away from each other and, as a result, we have drifted apart.
>
> The separation is entirely amicable but, as with the breakdown of any relationship, it is painful for both of us and we ask the media to respect both our privacy and that of our friends and families.[1]

Hugh Grant, who had been dogged by the media ever since an encounter with a prostitute in Los Angeles around the time he was working on *Sense and Sensibility*, remembered the announcement of Thompson's separation wryly. 'I was delighted when all that happened to her,' he said. 'That day I could hear the sound of knuckles scraping against concrete as the British press left my flat and headed for [her] Hampstead [house].' An emotional, drained and rather brave Thompson emerged from her home to greet the assembled photographers. She said she could not add to the previous night's statement, and refused to be drawn on the subject of her relationship with Greg Wise. By this point, Branagh had moved out and was said to be staying at the house of his personal assistant, Tamar Thomas.

Over the following days a media frenzy ensued. Journalists conducted a post-mortem on the Branagh–Thompson marriage, speculating on the causes of its disintegration. Busy careers, Thompson's professional success and class differences were cited as possible factors, and the names of Greg Wise and Helena Bonham Carter were thrown into the mix as well.

Branagh, meanwhile, had identified a sanctuary where he could lick his wounds, escape intrusion from the press and relax. A ten-bedroom Surrey mansion, owned by a couple of menswear tycoons, afforded Branagh the privacy and convenience he required. It had an elaborate security system with no less than seventeen surveillance cameras, and its Cobham location was close to Shepperton Studios, where Branagh would soon be shooting his epic version of *Hamlet*. An indoor swimming pool, billiards room and fifty-inch television were among the many comforts at his disposal. He agreed to rent the estate at a reported £15,000 a month, and brought in all his own staff.

By the turn of the year press interest in the estranged couple had not subsided. Branagh was photographed walking hand in hand with Helena Bonham Carter across Esher Common in Surrey, close to his new home. Emma Thompson cut a more forlorn figure as she was spotted walking alone outside her Scottish retreat.

It was Thompson who first offered the public an extended insider's view of the marital breakdown. Chewing the cud with *Vanity Fair* in an interview published in February 1996, she spoke candidly about the heartache she felt:

> Ken will always be family. That's a given. There has been a metamorphosis, perhaps. I don't know yet ... I committed every molecule to my marriage, so relinquishing it has been very hard. It's been like breaking your fingers as you let go. But that's perhaps important in itself ... Certainly it was like sitting on a time bomb ... If you like, the pain sort of started such a long time ago. Three years. I know I'm steering into a calmer phase. Despite the pain, one comes through it.

She added that she had no regrets about not having children with Branagh, though it was later reported that she had suffered a miscarriage during the latter part of their relationship, and did not feel a sense of failure over the separation. Nor should she, Branagh was quoted as saying. 'Not even a grain of failure in any sense could be attributed to Emma in any of this,' he commented. 'She's been absolutely magnificent throughout. She is able to remind herself, and me, that what's happened to us has happened to a trillion people in much more difficult circumstances.'

For anyone, a separation would be an event of seismic importance; but with Branagh and Thompson the implications were broader. It brought to a close an artistic collaboration significant to the performing arts in Britain. It marked the end of a celebrity couple that had been grist to the media mill, as Richard and Liz had been before them and Posh and Becks have since. For Branagh, pain and sadness were the inevitable corollaries of separation. His marriage had been more than simply a romantic attachment. 'Soul mates' is a hackneyed term, but they were kindred spirits. Despite their disparate social origins, they shared the same prodigious talent, confidence and drive. Both had gained from the relationship when it had been thriving, not only in a personal sense but professionally too. It is inconceivable that her rise would have been as meteoric without the roles he had given her. To him, she had been a trusty support and sounding board – and something of a lucky charm. With her, he had enjoyed a largely unbroken sequence of success. Without her, he seemed to lose his bearings; for the rest of the 1990s his artistic choices were not as consistently sound as they once had been. Whatever the professional ramifications, the important thing was that this relationship that had been the cornerstone of his life for the best part of a decade was over.

As his marriage to Emma Thompson crumbled, Branagh's career received a major boost. In the late summer of 1995 it was announced that Castle Rock, owned by Ted Turner, had decided to back Branagh in a new movie version of *Hamlet*. His quest to make *Hamlet* dated back to 1987 – this was the play, not *Henry V*, that he had originally wanted to film. The stumbling block was that Franco Zeffirelli had been working on his own movie of *Hamlet*, starring Mel Gibson and Glenn Close, and the feeling was that it would be difficult to persuade the public to see another picture of the same play. Branagh would have to bide his time.

What made Branagh's mission to film *Hamlet* even more problematic over the following years was the conclusion he reached about the cuts to the play that he would make in his version: there wouldn't be any. Having used the full text for the Renaissance radio production in 1992 and then on stage for the RSC, he became convinced that this was how to present the play in a fresh way to a cinema audience. In arguing for use of the full text, Branagh was pushing the envelope with Shakespeare on the big screen. It had been a long-established axiom of Shakespeare film-making that the text had to be pruned in order to remove the most incomprehensible passages and to create a cinematic pacing. It was a view embodied in the films of the original master, Olivier. His Oscar-winning *Hamlet*, in 1948, had come in at two hours and thirty-five minutes. Branagh had adopted a similar approach with his *Henry V* and *Much Ado About Nothing*, cutting the text, though managing to retain to a commendable extent the substance and the poetry of those plays. A full-length version of *Hamlet* would keep audiences in their seats for four hours. It really was an astonishing notion. Convincing Hollywood's accountants to back such an idea would be challenging to say the least. It is difficult to imagine any other artist trying, never mind succeeding in such an endeavour.

He continued to be thwarted, however. For a time he was told he could have half of the $18 million he wanted, so that he could make a film of two hours not four; but an indomitable Branagh refused to compromise his vision. In order to persuade Hollywood executives that his idea of an uncut *Hamlet* was viable he produced a screenplay notable for its adornment of the text with contemporary references, such as 'He's into Norman Schwarzkopf mode' when describing Claudius as he delivers his opening speech. Evidently his screenplay did the trick. Castle Rock agreed to finance the film with the proviso that an additional, shorter version be produced for airlines and for countries unwilling to show it uncut. Though it was not until the summer of 1995 that he received the go-ahead from Castle Rock, preparations were already advanced in terms of set designs and location photographs.

Branagh was now in a position to realise his vision of the story. Influenced by the 1992–3 Adrian Noble production in which he himself had starred, Branagh wanted this to be a *Hamlet* with the politics as well as the personal relationships to the fore. For Branagh the point was that the personal stories did not exist in a vacuum; that the inability of Hamlet *et al.* to resolve their differences ends in the map of Europe being redrawn, with Fortinbras of Norway seizing the Danish crown. An uncut text would ensure that the Fortinbras angle was not slighted, which meant that the theme of international politics could be explored. The full text would also allow characters such as Gertrude and Polonius to be presented in a more well-rounded way.

As for Hamlet himself, this would be a prince quite unlike that portrayed by Olivier in his 1948 film as a man who could not make up his mind. Branagh's Hamlet would not by nature be depressive, vacillating, neurotic or wracked by incestuous designs on his mother. Rather he would be a vibrant, witty, multi-faceted prince with the potential to have been a great king. His initial melancholy was an understandable reaction to the death of his father and the hasty remarriage of his mother, not an inveterate character flaw. His hesitation over carrying out the Ghost's command to murder Claudius was due not to an incorrigible indecisiveness but to his highly developed moral sense, his qualms about killing a member of his own family. Central to the journey of Branagh's Hamlet would be a quest for self-enlightenment. He wanted to know what it took to be at peace with himself. Tragically he achieves this just before he is about to die, when he says to Horatio, 'there's a special providence in the fall of a sparrow. If it be now, 'tis not to come; if it be not to come, it will be now; if it be not now, yet it will come: the readiness is all.' The whole of his performance, said Branagh, would be directed towards that moment when Hamlet achieves the peace he craves by simply accepting whatever fate has in store for him.

The other characters would also undermine the expectations of cinema-goers. Claudius would be a leader of substance and potential, not a clichéd villain. Polonius would be portrayed as a wily, manipulative politician, not a figure of mirth. And Ophelia would be not ethereal but a vital, engaging woman, whose relationship with Hamlet has been physically consummated, until her father's death at the hands of her lover deranges her.

The efforts of production designer Tim Harvey reinforced Branagh's conception of the story. After considering the merits of filming in Russia, Sweden or Denmark, it was decided that Harvey would do his work in England. The set he built at Shepperton Studios was bright and vibrant, with the State Hall – in which much of the action would take place – particularly striking. Gone was the Gothic gloom associated with *Hamlet*. The deliberate implication was that this would not be a film inhabited by a series of depressive characters. Branagh insisted that alongside this regal glamour would be a sense of corruption and intrigue provided by a series of two-way mirrors and secret doors. In this Elsinore, it was easy to be spied upon, a reality that made it even more difficult for Branagh's Hamlet to find peace of mind. For the exterior shots, the Duke of Marlborough permitted Blenheim Palace to be not only used but transformed, as Branagh's predilection for a wintry setting resulted in colossal quantities of artificial snow being to used to cover the grounds.

Blenheim Palace and the set at Shepperton would give Branagh's film a sense of the epic. That was precisely what Branagh had in mind, as he dreamed of a movie to match the sort of spectacle provided by David Lean's *Lawrence of Arabia* and *Doctor Zhivago*. To the same end, he decided to shoot *Hamlet* in 70 mm format, rather than the usual 35 mm. No movie had been filmed in Britain in this way since David Lean's *Ryan's Daughter*, in 1970, and at the time that *Hamlet* was made it was estimated that there were only two studio cameras in existence that could use 70 mm. The advantage of 70 mm over 35 mm was that it showed the detail in each frame with four times the clarity; and so this *Hamlet* would be a visual feast. Branagh's determination to provide the epic sweep of a David Lean film was confirmed by his choice of cinematographer: Alex Thomson. Lean had selected Thomson to film *Nostromo* on 70 mm, but the great director had died before the movie could be made.

The casting was no less sumptuous than the sets and the cinematography. Most important to Branagh was persuading his mentor, Derek Jacobi, to take the role of Claudius. Jacobi was reluctant at first, feeling he did not possess the requisite lecherousness for the part, but Branagh worked his charm on him – as he did with Julie Christie, who would play Gertrude. With Jacobi and Christie signed up, Branagh's task in recruiting some American stars was eased, such was their interest in working with these two actors. Billy Crystal and Charlton Heston agreed to play the First Gravedigger and the Player King, respectively, while Jack Lemmon and Robin Williams accepted cameo roles. Rising star Kate Winslet, nervous about tackling Shakespeare as well as the prospect of doing a love scene with Branagh, would take the part of Ophelia. Longstanding Branagh associates Richard Briers, Brian Blessed, Michael Maloney and Nicholas Farrell would portray Polonius, the Ghost, Laertes and Horatio. Richard Attenborough consented to play the English Ambassador. Gérard Depardieu took the microscopic part of Reynaldo, an aide to Polonius. Even more remarkable was the recruitment of Judi Dench, John Gielgud and John Mills. In scenes not in the text but created by Branagh, not one of these greats would utter a single line; nor would

British comedy legend Ken Dodd, delighted to win the part of Yorick in a flashback scene devised again not by the Bard but by Branagh. The greatest Hamlet of the century (Gielgud), one of the most renowned British film actresses since Vivien Leigh (Christie), and probably the greatest Hamlet of his generation (Jacobi), along with a variety of other formidable talents, all together in one film. With the cast for *Hamlet*, Branagh had put together a winning hand.

During the autumn of 1995 he prepared intensively for this vast undertaking. In addition to the casting, he practised the elaborate sword fight with Michael Maloney (Laertes) that would round off the film, experimented with his hair to find the right shade of blond, and flew to the United States to provide one-on-one coaching sessions for Billy Crystal, Charlton Heston and Robin Williams. Having played the part of Hamlet so many times on stage, and having such a clear view on what sort of prince this would be, Branagh did not, as he told a French journalist, 'particularly prepare for the cinematic interpretation of this role'. He wanted to remain free and relaxed so that the subtleties of his performance flowed from his acting in the moment.

Two days after bringing in the New Year, Branagh joined his colleagues to start what would be a three-week rehearsal period at Shepperton Studios. He handed around a favourite herbal remedy before discussing various issues of theme and character, including the nature of royal families, politics, and the relationship between Gertrude and Claudius.

For Branagh and old hands like Jacobi and Briers, all of this could be taken in stride. To those with less experience, it was more daunting. Kate Winslet recalled:

> On the first day I walked into the rehearsal room and there was Ken Branagh, Julie Christie, Derek Jacobi, Michael Maloney, all these amazing actors that I have admired so much. I thought, Oh my God, they are all going to be completely sussed about this, they all know exactly what every word means, and they all know their lines. That was very hard to overcome. It was the toughest film in testing my strength and confidence. I just spent the whole of the rehearsal period ... with my hand clamped to my cheeks. I looked like a goddamn lobster.[2]

To alleviate those sorts of nerves and to create a sense of camaraderie, Branagh circulated a questionnaire, to be completed by the actors on behalf of their characters, that produced some interesting responses. Not all of his ideas for the rehearsals went down so well. Julie Christie queried his decision to schedule a run-through of the entire play, with the actors having committed all their lines to memory. 'Why do we have to do this?' she asked. 'Well, you know,' he replied, 'it'll tell you some things. It's not a performance, but you'll find that doing it all in order will answer some questions that you're asking me about but that I can't tell you because it has to do with the experience of playing the part.' When this run-through took place, it had an other-worldly feel. A square was demarcated in the middle of the State Hall, the lights lowered, and the performance given by candle-light.

In discussing interpretation of character with his cast, Branagh was willing to give his actors latitude. Julie Christie recalls that on the issue of whether Gertrude knew that Claudius had killed her first husband there was a difference of opinion. Branagh thought she did know, whereas Christie felt there was no textual evidence to support that idea. In the end he said to her, 'If that's how you feel, then that's where we'll go.'

Rehearsals were not all work. Robin Williams treated everyone to a lunch-time showing of his very own musical about the life of Gandhi. While Williams was rehearsing his part as Osric, a woman arrived in a bizarre art-deco ensemble. Russell Jackson, serving as text consultant, assumed it was a typically garish individual from the movie business. It was in fact Glenn Close in costume as Cruella de Vil. *101 Dalmations* was being filmed at Shepperton at the same time.

On 24 January 1996, the last day of rehearsals, Branagh convened a meeting of all his cast and crew. No less than two hundred people assembled in the State Hall to hear a speech from their director. He revealed that making this film represented the realisation of a dream he had cherished since childhood. He asked them to bring to bear all the commitment and focus they could muster. Drinks were then passed around, lightening the mood. The next day principal photography began. It was time to get the show on the road.

In directing *Hamlet*, Branagh knew when to be clear and decisive, when to adopt a nurturing tone, and when to jest. 'You drink in the morning, don't you?' he joked with a grip. 'I don't have a problem with it, except for the way it affects your judgement.' He also used humour to make a potentially awkward love scene relaxed. Lying naked with Winslet in bed after shooting that scene, he announced, 'I'll just check the monitor,' before declaring: 'Oh no! We'll have to do it again. You can see my todger!'

Julie Christie, who had worked with some of cinema's most distinguished directors, was struck by Branagh's stamina. 'Fantastic amount of energy,' she recalls. 'Absolutely fantastic ... He bounces in like a puppy every day ... yet you know there are things that are eating away there, probably emotional things and private things, domestic things, as well as the hugeness of what he's taken on. But I guess his nature needs all that.'

What Julie Christie also observed was how creating the sort of positive atmosphere on set that would enable actors and technicians to do their best work was as important to Branagh as the technical aspects of directing:

> One of his main priorities, it seemed to me, was ... that he was going to make everyone involved have an extremely uplifting and happy experience; and to that end he worked as hard as he worked at the other end of making a good film, which is quite unusual in a way ... So that was the thing that most struck me about Ken as a director was this absolute determination ... to make it an extremely happy experience for everyone. And he is so good at that. Boy, he's skilled at making people happy, making them laugh. As a director, he's put as much into making you laugh as any comic would.[3]

In this relaxed atmosphere, Branagh was able to draw from his cast some strong performances. With Brian Blessed, for example, he succeeded in nudging his old friend towards a more measured portrayal of the Ghost than his effusive personality would normally have allowed. Hugh Cruttwell, on hand yet again, helped Branagh to shape the actors' performances. In the scene where Polonius (Briers) orders Ophelia (Winslet) to keep away from Hamlet, Cruttwell felt Winslet was too robust. It was not plausible, he observed, that she would later jilt Hamlet, as her father insisted, and go mad. Whispering to Winslet, Branagh passed on Cruttwell's concerns. The scene was repeated again and again, with Branagh encouraging Winslet to find the right sense of having to submit to paternal pressure. 'Once again that last line,' said Branagh.

'I shall obey, my lord.'

'Slower.'

'I shall obey, my lord.'

'Slower.'

'I shall obey, my lord.'

'Once more, even though it's impossibly painful to say again.'

'I shall obey, my lord.'

'Just close your eyes.'

'I shall obey, my lord,' said Winslet with the requisite feeling of resignation.

'Cut,' instructed Branagh, who then asked Cruttwell to tell Winslet how impressive she had been. 'That was brilliant,' obliged the venerable teacher, putting his arm around her.

Branagh's direction of *Hamlet* showed the technical hallmarks that had come to characterise his films. One was his penchant for long tracking shots in the style of Martin Scorsese, aided on this film by the joining of two sound stages. These shots gave Branagh's version of the story a sense of majestic sweep. The second was the frenetic use of the camera, which usually moved with the aid of a dolly or sometimes a crane. This febrile camerawork was one of the features of *Mary Shelley's Frankenstein* that had vexed the critics, and on *Hamlet* director of photography Alex Thomson felt the need to pass on words of wisdom he had received from director John Huston: that the camera should remain still if the audience is to focus intently on the dialogue. Branagh rejected the advice. 'What are you going to do?' he said to Thomson. 'You can't have a static camera when you are shooting seven pages of dialogue. The audience [are] going to fall asleep if they aren't interested.'

Branagh found the acting on *Hamlet* to be a welcome relief from the pressures of directing. In the diary he kept during the making of the film, Russell Jackson wrote, on 31 January 1996: 'Ken [was] in good spirits, buoyant. Seems happy to be acting, able to release some energy.' He kept to his plan of acting in the moment, of not determining beforehand every nuance of his performance. Julie Christie picked up on this: 'You do it different every time, don't you?' 'If you say it [your line] different to me,' he replied, 'I'll say it different to you.' The anguish he had experienced with the collapse of his marriage and the media attacks enriched his performance, accentuating its emotional power. 'It has been a ghastly couple of years; ghastly on a personal level,' he acknowledged. 'In the process of playing this part I released into it absolutely everything one could be as a human being.' In the 'Get thee to a nunnery' scene, even Branagh was surprised by the intensity of the anger he was able to summon up.

Filming the 'To be, or not to be' speech, probably the most famous lines in all of literature, was a special experience. Russell Jackson noticed how the crew, hardened professionals and not reverential hitherto towards Shakespeare's words, became exceptionally quiet as Branagh spoke, as if affected by the reputation or perhaps the power of the speech. The first take seemed to be going well when, two lines before the end, someone on set waved a piece of paper that caught his eye. Branagh stuttered, then stopped, before saying, 'Would you mind not doing that. It puts me off.' By take eight he had delivered the great speech to his satisfaction.

Hugh Cruttwell proved to be a commendably candid on-set critic of the performances not only of Kate Winslet and her colleagues but of Branagh himself. 'Yes, yes, physically it's fine,' he remarked of Branagh's portrayal of Hamlet's death, 'but we still don't have the essential feeling of a man who's about to die.' 'Hugh, I've never died before,' pointed out Branagh. 'I don't know what the fuck the essential feeling is.' 'I can't tell you. I'm just saying it's not there.' It was not always good for his self-esteem, but such frankness helped to polish his performance.

Branagh attended to the physical requirements of playing Hamlet, as he saw them, as well as to issues of characterisation. Keeping a strict exercise regimen with the help of a personal trainer, his Hamlet was toned, muscular and tanned. He seemed to alter not only the contours of his body but of his face too, which appeared more sculptured and handsome than before. Dyeing his hair platinum-blond also ensured that this 'sweet prince' would be glamorous.

As the long weeks of the shoot passed by, Branagh found himself presiding over a goodly crew of actors. Despite the starry cast, there was a healthy dose of humbleness on display. Robin Williams, Billy Crystal, Jack Lemmon and Julie Christie were conscious of their lack of experience with Shakespeare, while the likes of Derek Jacobi and Simon Russell Beale (Second Gravedigger) had impressive CVs when it came to Shakespeare in the theatre but were hardly household names on the big screen. It was one of those cases where all the actors seemed to be in awe of each other. When Julie Christie came on the set, for example, Billy Crystal could barely speak.

With so many actors at close quarters for such a long shoot, it was a time for badinage and a little nostalgia. Charlton Heston reminisced about Orson Welles, while Ken Dodd recalled his comedic contemporaries Tommy Cooper and Frankie Howerd. Some of these history lessons were lost on Branagh. 'Did you ever work with Pappy Ford, kid?' Jack Lemmon asked him. 'Pappy Ford? Oh, you mean John

Ford. Of course I haven't. I wasn't even born.' 'Oh yeah,' said Lemmon, 'I forget you're so fucking young.'

By April 1996 the end of the shoot was nigh. Having completed his last day in front of the camera, Derek Jacobi staged a special ceremony. He held up an old copy of the play that had been passed from actor to actor over the course of the last century. Each recipient was charged with awarding it to the man who in their judgement was the best Hamlet of the next generation. In its time it had been in the possession of Johnston Forbes-Robertson, Henry Ainley, Michael Redgrave, Peter O'Toole and Jacobi himself. Jacobi now made clear his assessment of the quality of Branagh's performance as Hamlet: he gave his copy of the play to Branagh. Given his knowledge of theatrical history, the way Jacobi had inspired him to become an actor, and his dream of becoming a truly great Hamlet, the poignancy of this moment for Branagh was considerable.

Ten days after Jacobi's tribute, the filming of *Hamlet* came to an end. All that remained was post-production, hours in the editing room and the incorporation of Patrick Doyle's score. 'Well, we have a go, don't we?' remarked Branagh as he walked off the set for the last time.

As *Hamlet* was honed in the editing room and then released in the winter of 1996–7, Branagh continued to keep his personal life under wraps. As far as he was concerned, the way the media had scrutinised and criticised his partnership with Emma Thompson was a lesson he must not forget. He was determined that his relationship with Bonham Carter would not become fodder for the gossip columnists, as his marriage to Emma Thompson had. When asked by journalists about Bonham Carter, he would remain coy, conceding only that they were good friends. But press photographs of Branagh and Bonham Carter kissing in Holland Park, London, in June 1996, confirmed publicly that they were an item.

It was not until a year later that either partner would talk to the press in any meaningful way about their romance. Speaking to a London *Standard* journalist, Bonham Carter stated:

> Yes, OK, of course we are together and it's very nice, thank you very much. We have never actually sat down and decided not to say anything or tried to make some sort of policy about it. God knows, relationships are difficult enough and we are both aware of the pressures that are created in this business. We don't feel the need to talk about details of our private life. If you concede anything then journalists always want a bit more.

Bonham Carter's mother gave Branagh her blessing in public a few months later, saying: 'I think he is a marvellous man, very nice.'

As it had for the latter part of his marriage, work intruded on Branagh's private life. He devoted 1996 to *Hamlet*, and starred in a number of other films the following year. This was also an exciting and hectic phase in Bonham Carter's career. The second half of 1995 saw her working on two movies, *Portraits Chinois* and *Twelfth Night*, and by the summer of 1996 she was pouring her energies into a film adaptation of Henry James' *The Wings of a Dove*. Filmed in Venice as well as in Britain, her dark, sexually candid performance as the unscrupulous Kate Croy would win her an Oscar nomination for Best Actress.

These career demands meant that Branagh and Bonham Carter spent long spells apart. This issue – balancing work and his personal life – was one of many that Branagh grappled with in a period in which he was afflicted with a sort of identity crisis. He had been portrayed as a nice, solid chap by the media, but at the same time raked over the coals for his work and for his relationship with Emma Thompson. He was coming to terms with the collapse of his marriage, while trying to construct a new life with Bonham Carter. All of these concerns were grafted on to more long-standing issues such as the tension between his Irishness and his acquired Englishness, and the excessive concern he felt about being liked. 'Over the past three or four years', he said in early 1997, 'I was really losing a sense of who I was. The media construction of my personality was changed according to whim and I was never sure whether to second-guess it, to be it or not to be it, or just get very paranoid about it.'

Friends encouraged him to see a psychiatrist to sort out his problems, but Branagh balked at the proposition. 'I have a basic suspicion of handing over a hundred quid at the end of an hour talking about myself,' he said, 'during which someone has apparently plucked out the heart of my mystery. That's a ridiculous attitude, I have to add, because it's worked wonderfully with friends, but we actors have endless chances to talk about ourselves whether or not we like. I don't think it's healthy. It blows everything out of perspective.' With his Basil Fawlty-type attitude towards modern psychiatry, Branagh would try to sort out his problems on his own. In doing so, he concluded that it was important for him to show the same sort of acceptance of the hand life had dealt him that Hamlet displays by the end of his journey.

'Now I just say to myself,' he said, '"Well, you are who you are. You have done these things and there is no point worrying about it or trying to analyse it."'

One decision Branagh did make in the summer of 1996 was to build his own house. Owning a flat in Covent Garden, but not a good-sized home, he bought Keepers, a Victorian mansion, in Sunninghill, Berkshire, for £1.3 million. 'Mr Branagh always had the idea that he wanted to create a dream home,' revealed the estate agency arranging the sale, 'and just wanted to find the right location. He viewed it and fell in love with the place.' By January 1997 he had received planning permission to knock the house down and then rebuild it according to a design that would provide a gym, swimming pool, cinema, computerised lighting, a master bedroom with its own sitting room and three other en suite bedrooms. Adding to its convenience was the location, as it was secluded but within striking distance of London, Heathrow airport, and his parents' home in Reading. Whatever vicissitudes would befall him in the years ahead, he would have this home base to fall back on.

Augmenting his sense of rootedness and, indeed, fun was the close network of friends he sustained. Avoiding the standard celebrity restaurants or clubs, he preferred to socialise privately. He enjoyed eating, drinking and smoking with his mates. He even set up his own rock 'n' roll band, the Fishmongers, with the film editors from *Hamlet*. Contributing vocals and guitar, he described the band as 'one of the worst combinations of musical non-talent ever put together. But very enjoyable for us.'

By the winter of 1996–7, however, it was Branagh's career that absorbed his attentions; it was time to unveil his epic version of *Hamlet* to critics and public alike. Released in the United States on Christmas Day, it received generally enthusiastic notices. Branagh's film, the *New York Times* asserted, had 'keen instincts for the essence of the play'. It also lauded the acting, particularly Branagh's performance. *Variety* judged that the use of the complete text made for 'increased meaning and richness', and that as both actor and director Branagh displayed 'an energy and forcefulness that is contagious to the huge and varied cast'. Not all the reviews were as positive, but overall they showed that the love affair between Branagh and America's critics, having survived the experience of *Frankenstein*, was ongoing. At the US box office *Hamlet* performed well in the major cities and made close to $5 million *in toto*, disappointing in relation to the success enjoyed by *Much Ado About Nothing* but more impressive when compared to the sum earned by Ethan Hawke's *Hamlet* in 2000.

Opening in Britain seven weeks later, Branagh's *Hamlet* divided his own critics. Philip French gave it a rave in the *Observer*. The *Daily Telegraph*, *Guardian* and London *Standard* were complimentary. But *The Times* was ambivalent, the *Independent*, *Financial Times* and *Sunday Times* frosty, while the headline of the *Sunday Telegraph* said it all: 'Blond bombshell can't keep his mouth shut'. The length of the film probably deterred some people; it made only £605,000 at the British box office.

The response to *Hamlet* suggested that the divide separating Fleet Street and American critics in their appreciation of Branagh's work had not narrowed, seven years after it first emerged with *Henry V*. In the same period as Branagh was described by the *Houston Chronicle* as 'the most accomplished Shakespearean of our time', and as *Hamlet* received a number of Oscar nominations including one for Branagh for Best Adapted Screenplay, two articles were published, indicating the extent to which Branagh remained a polarising figure at home. On 19 January 1997 Christopher Goodwin offered up a robust defence of the man in the *Sunday Times*. Surveying his achievements, he declared that Branagh, 'by any objective criteria, and certainly from the perspective of Hollywood, is the great British cultural success story of the past decade':

> People in Hollywood are astonished to learn that in his own land, Branagh is a prophet without honour.
>
> 'My God,' said one studio executive when I read him some of the more fetid quotes about Branagh from the British papers. 'Not even O. J. Simpson gets that bad a press.'
>
> From the moment when, in 1988, the 28-year-old Branagh, against specific advice of such a luminary of British cinema as David Puttnam, undertook his film version of *Henry V*, every step he has taken, professional and personal, has been dogged by vicious and insistent attacks in Britain. You would have thought that the working-class Ulster boy had been despatched to England from the slums of Belfast ... as a sleeper by a group of fanatical barbarians bent on tearing out the heart of all that was best and true within British culture. Branagh's terrible mission? Sneak into RADA. Infiltrate British theatre. Find Shakespeare and destroy his proud legacy.

Goodwin rounded off his article with a striking quote on Branagh from a Hollywood studio executive: 'He has a lot of qualities that the British hate in Americans – his naked ambition, his relentless chirpiness, his optimism. And people in Britain loathe him even more because he found commercial and critical success in Hollywood with Shakespeare; critical success on its own would have been OK.' 'Still,' opined the executive, 'the fact they hate him says more about Britain than it does about Branagh, doesn't it?'

A month after the publication of this piece, Tom Hutchinson wrote an article for the *Guardian* entitled 'Once more unto the snore, dear friends', exhibiting all the excesses identified by Goodwin among Branagh's detractors. 'Why does my heart sink at the thought of Kenneth Branagh?' began Hutchinson. 'Because his art is so sunk in the conventional.' Baz Luhrmann, in his recently made film version of *Romeo and Juliet*, took risks with Shakespeare; Branagh did not. Olivier and Welles had been blessed with genius; Branagh was not. In addition, his film performances were theatrical, and their emotional range narrow. Branagh's cautious, conservative work, concluded Hutchinson, was 'as soothing as a child's pacifier: a cosy comfort'. 'And I do not go to the cinema to sleep,' he added tartly.

Speaking to the Irish press at the start of 1997, Branagh gave his understanding of the animus against him:

> There is this sort of cycle – in my experience anyway – when you're young and achieve some sort of success people are delighted to discover you. Then there just comes this point where you've been given too much too soon. When the very facts of it reveal themselves. Like if you've only done a few parts but people are calling you the greatest actor since whoever ... it just doesn't hold up, it simply doesn't hold up. There's no way you can justify such a remark and having it said about you imbues you with the idea that you might believe that – I mean, that's what they think you think.

Relating this phenomenon to his movie of *Henry V*, he added:

> I now see and didn't at the time – that it was such an astonishing success as a first film and, although I was very aware that I could not remotely call myself a film-maker, the over-praise, the disproportionate amount of attention given to me and my so-called talent meant I would be carrying various difficulties. One would be the internal pressure of succumbing to the expectations, that you had to be a genius or something when you knew yourself to be inexperienced and ignorant about so many things.

Plaintively, he considered the factors that could have prevented the backlash: 'Maybe if I looked incredibly handsome – maybe if I wasn't Irish working-class – I don't know whether there's a class thing to it.'

That critics in England remained sharply divided about Branagh's work as *Hamlet* opened, and in general far less appreciative than their

American counterparts, should not obscure what Branagh had achieved with this movie. As the only feature film to use the full text of this great play, it is an important cinematic document. Fuller, more satisfying portraits of characters such as Claudius and Polonius were drawn than in other movie versions of *Hamlet*. The political as well as the psychological theme of the story was well developed. The film was visually gorgeous. If not all the casting of the minor roles worked out ideally, Branagh elicited some fine performances. Derek Jacobi and Julie Christie were exceptional as Claudius and Gertrude, as was Charlton Heston as the Player King. At the centre of the film, moreover, was a Hamlet that was clear and technically proficient, but at the same time vibrant, dynamic and passionate. In the 'Get thee to a nunnery' confrontation with Ophelia (Winslet), Branagh's acting was blisteringly powerful. It is no doubt the case that he would have enjoyed greater commercial success with his *Hamlet* had he pruned the text, but on this project – which to Branagh was artistically sacred – he was prepared to brook no compromise.

What was clear by the time of *Hamlet*'s release was that Branagh had not only produced yet another striking Shakespeare film, he had succeeded in breathing life into what had become a moribund genre of film-making, the Shakespeare movie. With the films of Olivier, Welles, Zeffirelli and others, major films of Shakespeare's plays had been produced with pleasing regularity from the 1940s until the start of the 1970s. But after Roman Polanski's vivid, violent *Macbeth* in 1971, cinema became less enamoured of Shakespeare. That all changed with Branagh. Around the time that he was making *Hamlet* a multiplicity of other Shakespeare films were in the works: Trevor Nunn's *Twelfth Night*, Baz Luhrmann's *Romeo and Juliet*, Richard Loncraine's *Richard III*, with Ian McKellen, and Al Pacino's *Looking for Richard* (which included excerpts of an interview with Branagh). More generally, in the period from 1989 to 2001 fifteen movies of Shakespeare's plays were made – in other words, it was the most productive period in the history of Shakespeare on film, surpassing even the decade after World War II.

It is clear that the success of Branagh's *Henry V* and *Much Ado About Nothing* has inspired other artists and demonstrated the commercial feasibility of the Shakespeare movie to the money-men. This is a major accomplishment, and even if he has not always received the credit he deserves, it is worth noting that the weight of opinion in the academic community which works on Shakespeare and film is clearly in his favour. Kenneth Rothwell, who has described the post-1989 period as 'The Age of Kenneth Branagh', has written: 'By a shrewd merger of art and commerce, Kenneth Branagh magically resuscitated the Shakespeare movie just when everyone was announcing its death at the hands of television.' Samuel Crowl, in *At the Shakespeare Cineplex: the Kenneth Branagh era*, states: 'We can clearly see that Branagh's *Henry V* did introduce the most prolific and dynamic decade in the hundred-year history of Shakespeare on film.' Sarah Hatchuel is no less effusive. 'Branagh's Shakespearean body of work', she says, 'has unexpectedly changed the way people all over the world feel about and react to Shakespeare.'

9

Only an Actor

Exhausted by the Herculean labour that was the making of *Hamlet*, Branagh concentrated over the next two years on acting in other people's pictures, rather than directing his own. His absence from the stage, where he had not appeared since 1993, continued. On paper, 1997 and 1998 should have been the high point of his career. Working with directors of the calibre of Robert Altman and Woody Allen, stars as prominent as Leonardo DiCaprio and Will Smith, and some of the most adroit actors in film, including Robert Duvall, Judy Davis and William Hurt, Branagh had the opportunity to broaden his public appeal, hone his skills as a movie actor, and add a dimension to his film career beyond Shakespeare productions and low-budget British pictures. Instead the late 1990s turned out to be the nadir of Branagh's professional life. Weak scripts, the politics of the film world, and some unsound artistic choices resulted in a dip in his fortunes. It was a far cry from the days when everything he touched seemed to turn to gold.

Branagh's first post-*Hamlet* project was *The Proposition*, an American film based on a screenplay by Rick Ramage and directed by former dance choreographer Lesli Linka Glatter. Set in the 1930s, Ramage's story centres on an affluent Boston couple whose plan to recruit a Harvard graduate to impregnate the wife (the husband is sterile) goes awry when he ends up madly in love. Michael McKinnon, a young Catholic priest, becomes drawn into their world, as he too falls for the wife. Amongst other things, the story seeks to highlight the way in which people delude themselves over the extent to which they can control their own lives.

In retrospect it should have been a warning sign, but the screenplay had been lying around for four years. When sent his way, however,

Branagh reacted with enthusiasm. 'I found it to be a terrific page-turner,' he said. 'It immediately involves the audience with strong issues about love, death and life, but it's very lightly done so it never feels pretentious.' Branagh's evaluation of the script was simply a misjudgement on his part. In truth the plot was implausible, the dialogue mannered and the treatment of social issues, such as the rise of feminism, decidedly facile. Neither a solid performance from Branagh nor the recruitment of a strong cast would be able to overcome these shortcomings.

What *The Proposition* did demonstrate was the clout Branagh continued to wield in the movie business, for it was his interest that breathed life into a project that had seemed moribund. 'After Kenneth signed on,' the director acknowledged, 'it was easy [to attract other good actors].' Madeleine Stowe and Oscar-winner William Hurt agreed to play the couple at the centre of the story, while Blythe Danner, Gwyneth Paltrow's mother, took a supporting role. Branagh himself agreed to portray Father McKinnon, who narrates the story.

Starting in October 1996, the production was based in and around Boston. As was usually the case, Branagh impressed his director and fellow actors. 'He was a dream to work with,' gushed Glatter, while Madeleine Stowe commented: 'Work is everything to Kenneth. I really liked him a lot. He's tremendously focused, but he made me laugh every single day.'

When released, in 1998, *The Proposition* made barely a dent at the box office in either the United States or Britain. Nor were the critics any more enamoured than the public, as reviewer after reviewer expressed disbelief that so many fine actors had associated themselves with such an unworthy project. In addition, the movie elicited the most embarrassing form of praise – namely that it was so bad it was almost good.

If Branagh sensed during the shoot that *The Proposition* would flop, he must have been buoyed by the prospect that awaited him at the start of 1997: collaborating with one of modern cinema's true giants, Robert Altman, on *The Gingerbread Man*, a film based not on a novel but on an original screenplay by the most famous purveyor of the legal thriller, John Grisham. On receiving the script, Branagh was interested but made his participation conditional on the recruitment of an exceptional director who would invest the material with a distinctive sensibility. Julie Christie had urged him to select his film projects on the basis of the calibre of the director; he was now putting that advice into practice. As it happened, Altman, whose credits included *M*A*S*H*, *The Long Goodbye*, *Nashville* and *Short Cuts*, was a fervent admirer of Branagh's work, remarking later: 'The main reason, the only reason really, I did the project was because of Branagh.' In particular, he admired the sheer audacity shown by Branagh during his career. Altman's respect for Branagh's work was reciprocated, and once Altman came on board Branagh confirmed his interest, signing on – one report claimed – for $5.5 million.

An initial impression would be that a Grisham story, linear and somewhat formulaic, and Altman's improvisational and quirky style were as compatible as oil and water. Altman, however, had no intention of adhering to Grisham's screenplay. Following on from discussions with Branagh, he reworked it in order to create a darker sensibility and to make the central character played by Branagh more flawed. It was widely supposed that the Al Hayes to whom the screenplay was ultimately credited was a pseudonym for Altman. Branagh was fascinated to observe how Altman re-imagined Grisham's script. 'When Altman signed on,' he recalled, 'he immediately made it clear he wanted the film to have a different look and emphasis. Bob wasn't interested in the intricacies of the legal system, and wanted it instead to be a film of moods, moments and atmospheres. Hearing him discuss the film was like listening to a painter – he talked about wind, the colour red, close-ups of rain.' Altman did send Grisham the revised script, but received no reply; he pressed ahead regardless.

As reworked by Altman, *The Gingerbread Man* was very much in the film noir genre. Rick Magruder (Branagh), a vain Savannah lawyer whose success in the courtroom contrasts with a less-than-smooth personal life that includes fractious relations with his ex-wife, has a one-night stand with *femme fatale* Mallory Doss. She tells Magruder that her deranged father, who is part of a back-country cult, is stalking her. Magruder takes legal action to put her father behind bars, but when he escapes it seems that the safety of Magruder's children has been jeopardised. As the story unfolds, Magruder uncovers a plan hatched by Mallory Doss and her husband to separate her father from the valuable land he owns. The elements, as much as the characters, would shape the mood of Altman's film. A hurricane approaches Savannah as the tension of the story mounts, providing an ominous ambience and a metaphor for the disruption afflicting the lives of Magruder and the other characters.

Altman had as much difficulty attracting actors of quality as Branagh had with his own films: practically none. Accordingly a coterie of talent was hired to complement Branagh's. Embeth Davidtz, who had caught the eye in *Schindler's List*, would play Mallory Doss. Robert Duvall took the part of her father, and Tom Berenger her husband. Daryl Hannah, Famke Janssen and Robert Downey, Jr, rounded off the cast.

Branagh prepared assiduously. He took on board advice from Altman to emphasise his character's flaws. He mined local lawyers for information on a range of issues from their average working day to what it took to make partner. Hiring a voice coach, he decided to base his accent on one of the lawyers he had met. His attempts to test his Savannah dialect on the locals were not always successful. When Branagh declared in a bar, 'I'd just love a glass of wine here,' in his newly acquired accent, a bemused barman asked, 'What are you speaking like that for? You're that Shakespearean guy.'

Commencing work on *The Gingerbread Man* on location in Savannah, Branagh was immediately struck by Altman's unique approach as a director. As he began to read through a scene with Embeth Davidtz, to whom he had just been introduced, Altman stood up suddenly. 'You should do this by yourselves for a while,' he told the two anxious actors, as he headed for the door.

Once principal photography began, Branagh was able to further his film education by observing one of the great directors at work. Within the parameters set by his overall vision of the story, Altman loved to improvise; and, as a result, Branagh had to be on his mettle. Turning up on set one day to shoot a scheduled scene at a pet shop with the two young actors playing his children, he saw, much to his amazement, a carnival organised with hundreds of extras. 'I thought we were going to do the pet shop,' he said to Altman. 'What's all this?' 'Nah, boring, all that,' replied Altman. 'So listen, what I want you to do is go all the way up, about two hundred yards, down there. Just take the kids with you, walk towards the camera through the carnival and make stuff up.' 'What do you mean, make stuff up?' 'Just do something, stuff. It's a carnival. Lots of things to do along the way.' Branagh did as he was told, but sometimes Anglo-American language differences undermined his attempts at improvisation. In a scene where his character is running after a car in the belief that his children are inside, Branagh exclaimed, 'They're in the boot. They're in the boot!' 'Cut,' shouted Altman. 'Ken, what the hell is a boot?' The scene was reshot with the word 'trunk' used instead.

Branagh studied, too, the director's innovative use of the camera. In a scene of a party at a law firm to celebrate Magruder's latest triumph in court, Altman asked Branagh and the other actors to extemporise while a couple of cameras weaved through them. They were not entirely sure whether any particular snippet of conversation was being filmed. Altman's approach challenged the actors and endowed the scene with an exceptionally naturalistic feel.

Stimulated by the collaboration with Altman, Branagh also found the cast congenial. The actor with whom Branagh had the most in common was Robert Duvall. Spending time with each other, they discovered a shared passion for soccer. They discussed the great Brazil team of 1970, and Duvall revealed that his all-time favourite player was George Best. On hearing of the American's plan to film a story about a Scottish football team, Branagh said he had to have a part. Ultimately, however, the movie was made in the summer of 1999 without his participation.

As the film wrapped, Branagh had reason to be happy about the performance he had delivered. His portrayal of a slick Southern lawyer undone by his own vanity had the stamp of authenticity. Accused in the past by some critics of being too expansive and theatrical, he gave a performance unadorned by any flashy excesses. It would have been all too easy for an actor with that role to have offered up a caricatured Southerner; but Branagh's portrayal was subtly crafted, blending arrogance with affability, professional assuredness with personal immaturity. Embeth Davidtz, as the enigmatic *femme fatale*, was compelling. Altman, too, was in good form. Working alongside gifted Chinese cinematographer Changwei Gu, whose track record included *Farewell, My Concubine*, he used colour with a painter's facility to conjure up the appropriate ambience. Sombre browns, the dominant hue, supplied the ominous feel of an old black-and-white Hitchcock, while the lurid splashes of red provided by cars, umbrellas and items of clothing alluded to the seedy world inhabited by Mallory Doss (Davidtz) and her husband (Berenger) as well as the sexual appetites that drove the story. Indeed a metaphorical cleverness enriched the film. Branagh's character's choice of automobile, for instance, says much about his selfishness: Magruder drives a swanky two-seater sports car – hardly practical, given that he has two children. In short, *The Gingerbread Man* was an intelligent piece of work. Branagh could look forward with high hopes to a success at the box office.

Those hopes were dashed because, in the period between the movie's wrap and its release, Polygram, the film's backer, and Robert Altman went to war. Unhappy with the audience response to *The Gingerbread Man* at test screenings, Polygram acted decisively: they replaced the director's editor with their own. Famed for his willingness to lock horns with Hollywood executives, Altman countered by petitioning the Directors Guild of America to remove his name from the credits. In the end the controversy resolved itself. The version provided by Polygram's own editor fared no better with preview audiences, and so Altman was allowed to finish the film using his own cut.

When *The Gingerbread Man* was finally released in the United States, in January 1998, its prospects appeared rosy because of the rave reviews accorded the film by some of the nation's leading critics. Janet Maslin of the *New York Times* applauded Altman's 'brooding, richly atmospheric style', as well as Branagh's success in meeting the 'cultural challenge' of portraying a character from the American South so far removed from his Shakespearean roots. In the *Chicago Sun-Times* Roger Ebert commended Altman and his cast for the way they 'invest the material with a kind of lurid sincerity', and Branagh for his 'quickness as an actor', a quality Altman was able to use 'to make scenes seem fresh'. The *Wall Street Journal* went so far as to suggest that Hitchcock himself 'would have been intrigued, and maybe envious.' Branagh's performance, it added, was 'so solid, specific and self-effacing that he can sustain our unswerving interest'.

The Gingerbread Man's initial success at the box office boded as well as the reviews. Polygram decided to use a platform release, opening in just New York and Los Angeles, and relying on media coverage and word of mouth to build momentum for the film as it was shown in other parts of the country. It made more than $14,000 per screen on its opening weekend, an excellent performance, given that $10,000 was considered to be a healthy figure for a platform release. Even so, Polygram waited a fortnight before taking the film to another city, Toronto, and even there it showed on only one screen. At no point did *The Gingerbread Man* play on more than thirty screens. In stark contrast, a film such as *Lost in Space*, which was released in April 1998, opened on more than 3,300 screens. *The Gingerbread Man*'s final box-office total was a meagre $1.68 million.

Polygram maintained that audiences in Los Angeles and New York had not responded enthusiastically, and had it been otherwise Altman's movie would have been screened more extensively elsewhere. Altman and his supporters, however, believed that Polygram's tepid backing of the film was a thinly disguised act of revenge for the trouble Altman had caused them earlier, particularly his threat to remove his name from the credits. Much more could have been done, they were convinced, to invest in advertising, to build publicity around Robert Duvall's Oscar nomination that year for *The Apostle*, and to use the excellent reviews to promote the film. 'We'll never know how the picture would have performed,' argued the film's associate producer David Levy, 'because the mechanisms that you rely upon to market a film and get the word out were never utilised.' 'Their [Polygram's] actions and behavior would be more consistent with having to teach Robert Altman a lesson or win some imaginary war,' he added.

The actors were powerless to effect the outcome of that war; but that did not prevent Embeth Davidtz from railing against Polygram. 'How could they?' she thundered. 'Robert delivered something really interesting and the studio blew it.' In public Branagh adopted a diplomatic approach. 'The strange thing about this power struggle', he commented, 'is that it sprang from a strong belief in the movie on both sides.' In private he assured Altman it would all work out, and even bet him $100 that this would be the case.

Before *The Gingerbread Man* opened in Britain, Branagh arranged a special screening for a dozen of his most devoted fans, namely the family. They put money in a pot to bet on who could predict the outcome of the story; only his mother got it right. Even though Branagh no doubt expected Fleet Street journalists to be a less sympathetic audience, he must have been dismayed by the reviews. An eminent American critic such as Janet Maslin of the *New York Times* might evaluate a picture directed by an outstanding American auteur in film noir style, essentially an American genre, by lavishing praise on it, but curiously her British counterparts were dismissive. Geoff Brown of *The Times* was in a distinct minority when he judged *The Gingerbread Man* to be 'superbly visualised, broodingly atmospheric'. The *Independent* said that with this work Altman was treading water, the *Guardian* asserted that only Davidtz emerged with any credit, while the *Daily Mail*'s assessment of the film as 'half-hearted hackwork' was brutal. Evaluations of Branagh's acting were mixed. The *Daily Telegraph* hailed it as his finest screen performance outside his Shakespearean work, and Alexander Walker of the London *Standard* also gave it his seal of approval. The *Independent*, however, cited the film as another example of how 'this incandescent stage actor dies on screen in non-Shakespearean roles,' and joined the *Sunday Telegraph* in even expressing distaste for how Branagh looked in the film.

Ultimately *The Gingerbread Man* was a disappointment for Branagh in two respects. First, it showed that, as of 1998, he was still held in less critical esteem at home than in the United States. Second, the politics of the film world resulted in fewer people seeing what was not only a worthy and original picture but one of Branagh's most consummate performances in a non-Shakespearean role on the big screen.

In a personal sense, though, Branagh had gained. He had developed with Altman a close friendship that has continued. Altman would later ask him to take the part of the detective (played in the end by Stephen Fry) in *Gosford Park*, but Branagh had to decline because of a schedule clash. Reciprocally, Branagh invited Altman in 2001 to see his theatre production *The Play What I Wrote*. Altman attended and had a hugely enjoyable evening.

Branagh followed up his collaboration with Altman by co-starring in a low-budget British movie, *The Theory of Flight*, with Helena Bonham Carter, the first time they had worked together since *Mary Shelley's Frankenstein*. The film's origins were humble. On completing his first screenplay, Richard Hawkins dispatched it to the BBC, where it ended up in a pile with numerous other scripts. BBC staff were so impressed when they finally read it that they decided to sponsor its development.

The script was wry and original. It told the story of two damaged people drawn together initially by circumstance. Sentenced to community service for trying to fly from the roof of a London building, depressed, aviation-obsessed artist Richard finds himself providing care for motor neurone disease sufferer Jane. She enlists Richard's help in her quest to lose her virginity before she dies. The escapades which ensue result in a botched bank robbery and the recruitment of a gigolo whose services Jane ultimately declines. A resolution is achieved when the couple fly his plane and consummate their relationship physically.

Before dying, Jane serves as 'best man' at Richard's wedding with Julie, the girlfriend he has been shunning. An irreverent, bitter-sweet story, *The Theory of Flight* explores how two characters dealt with disability, one physical, the other emotional.

The script was sent to Helena Bonham Carter, who found it 'startlingly original'. Struck by his partner's enthusiasm for the project, Branagh became intrigued. He read the screenplay himself and took a fancy to the idea of playing the character of Richard opposite Bonham Carter's Jane. Branagh was at pains to point out it was the merit of the piece, not the convenient opportunity to mix business with pleasure, that motivated his interest. The couple worried that working together would give the press a reason to spotlight their personal relationship rather than the film; but in the end they decided their passion for the project outweighed those concerns.

Having already cast Bonham Carter, director Paul Greengrass was wary about Branagh's involvement. Theoretically they could outnumber him in any discussion during the shoot on how to approach the making of the film, but it was a reservation he soon discarded. Branagh won Greengrass over, not least by his willingness to audition for the part. As Greengrass thought that a good idea, Branagh did indeed do a reading.

With much of the shoot taking place on location in Wales, Branagh and Bonham Carter were gratified that the paparazzi left them alone that summer of 1997. 'The British press has finally realised,' Branagh later told a Canadian newspaper, 'that people around the world don't wake up every morning wondering what I'm doing in my private life.' Left in peace, the filming of *The Theory of Flight* proved to be a harmonious affair. Branagh and Bonham Carter were professional, but the politically incorrect sense of humour they shared provided moments of light relief. 'Oh come on, would you speak up, otherwise this is going to be a three-hour film,' he berated her as she spoke in character with a speech impediment. Bonham Carter loved the teasing but got her revenge by laughing at her boyfriend as he was doing his close-ups. At one point he ordered her to leave the room. 'Don't you need me to react off?' she asked. No, he replied, as she was hindering rather than helping his performance. A not very contrite Bonham Carter thus departed, still laughing.

Of great satisfaction not only to Bonham Carter but to Branagh as well was her convincing portrayal of the plight of those afflicted by motor neurone disease. Her extensive research, including meetings with a Surrey housewife diagnosed with MND and reflections on her own experience with her wheelchair-bound father, was paying off. On its completion *The Theory of Flight* was screened before a group of MND sufferers, who confirmed the accuracy of Bonham Carter's portrayal. Additional validation came in 1999 when the British Motor Neurone Disease Association decided to show the film at its national conference.

Originally *The Theory of Flight* was scheduled for BBC television, but Branagh believed the film deserved a chance on the big screen. Accordingly he met with BBC2 controller Mark Thompson to urge that its airing on the television be delayed so that the film could enjoy a theatrical release. Taking on board the success achieved by such BBC films as *Mrs Brown*, Thompson consented. *The Theory of Flight* opened in the United States in December 1998, generating mixed reviews, weak box office, and for Helena Bonham Carter's performance an Oscar buzz that came to naught. When released on the other side of the Atlantic the following year, the critical and popular response was much the same.

While *The Theory of Flight* hardly made the sort of splash produced by some of his other films, it held a special place in Branagh's heart. He loved the story and the part he played. As a personal memento, he kept the aircraft that his character had built, relocating it to his garden. 'I'm so damned attached to it because it represented my character's freedom,' he said. 'It's practically made of canvas and oddly beautiful.' Even though it could not fly and did not impress the neighbours, it proved a big hit with the children of visiting friends.

Branagh's fondness for *The Theory of Flight* was understandable: the film was charming, funny and poignant, and it did not fall into the obvious trap of being overly sentimental. The character of Jane, who is feisty, swears like a trooper, watches porn on the internet, and steals food from the supermarket, ensured that this pitfall was avoided. The story also sustains the viewer's interest by inverting the anticipated relationship between Richard and Jane. In the end she becomes his carer, making clear to him how lucky he is. She will die soon, she points out, while he has a life in front of him; and he must gratefully accept this gift. Through her, he grasps that some responsibilities, such as his relationship with the girlfriend he has been mistreating, are potentially life-enhancing opportunities. In this way,

Branagh's character makes a satisfying journey from immaturity to enlightenment, while Jane's brief life is given a stronger sense of purpose and achievement. To be sure, *The Theory of Flight*'s production values were of the low-budget, television-movie sort and the soundtrack came across as incongruously boisterous, but those shortcomings were more than offset by the freshness of the story, the sharpness of the dialogue, and the calibre of the performances given by Branagh and Bonham Carter.

On a personal level Branagh and Bonham Carter had relished the experience of working together again, a sign that their relationship remained robust. Bonham Carter gave the impression, as she always had, of being infatuated with her partner. 'I am definitely happy and definitely in love,' she said in an interview in the summer of 1998. 'I have had other loves in the past, but this is the most long-lasting, grown-up one.' Branagh felt a genuine affection too. But on the question of becoming man and wife, it was a case of once bitten, twice shy. 'Oh, I have no idea about marriage,' he said around the same time that Bonham Carter was publicly declaring her love. 'I've no fixed views on that, children, you name it.' While certainly an item, Branagh and Bonham Carter maintained their independence. Not only did they pursue hectic and generally separate career paths, they kept their own home bases. At the start of their relationship Bonham Carter lived with her parents in north London. When she did finally leave home, she moved into her own place nearby.

As a couple, they continued to be coy with the press. Not until the spring of 1998, at a party given by the Queen at Windsor Castle to celebrate the arts in Britain, did they make a public appearance together. The second such outing did not occur until the end of 1998 at the New York première for *The Theory of Flight*. By making their joint appearances in public few and far between, they effectively limited the media scrutiny of their relationship.

Throughout his romance with Bonham Carter, Branagh remained on civil terms with his ex-wife. 'Not only do we talk,' he revealed in 1999, 'but we have stayed friends, and I hope we always will be.' Despite his break-up with her daughter, Phyllida Law thought fondly of her former son-in-law. 'I owe young Kenneth Branagh a very great deal for [casting me in] *Peter's Friends*,' she said. 'I shall never forget that.'

The ferocity with which he pressed ahead with his career continued to dog Branagh's attempts to achieve a well-balanced life. In an interview given in the summer of 1999, his brother Bill reported that Kenneth had resided in the new home he had built in Berkshire for only six weeks of the previous year. 'I wish he could spend more time there, rather than hotel rooms,' he lamented. 'He needs to be able to relax, and smell the flowers. It would help his peace of mind.'

When he was at home, Branagh led a normal life. He watched television, went occasionally to a football match, attended the theatre more than in the recent past, and called his mother once a week. He stayed close to old friends such as Gerard Horan, Jimmy Yuill and John Sessions. He continued to play in his band, the Fishmongers, teaching himself the piano as well as the guitar. He enjoyed going to the cinema, and not just to see art-house fare. *There's Something About Mary*, the 1998 hit starring Cameron Diaz, had him in stitches.

For Branagh, an ideal day of relaxation consisted of waking around 5 a.m., going for an early run, then reading a book outdoors for the rest of the day, weather permitting. The mid-point of the decade had been traumatic, with the breakdown of his marriage to Emma Thompson. By the autumn of 1998, however, he felt able to say: 'I'm a much happier guy these days.'

Away from the camera Branagh became increasingly active on behalf of a wide range of charities. He undertook this philanthropic work with a minimum of publicity, and it was something to which he would remain devoted in the coming years. The National Autistic Society, Multiple Sclerosis Society, Cancer Research Campaign, National Missing Persons Helpline, Friends of the Earth, and Battersea Dogs Home were but a few of the many organisations to which he gave his support.

Branagh continued to enjoy exciting challenges on the professional front in this period. Woody Allen had long been one of his idols. He had watched all of the New Yorker's films, rating *Manhattan* among his all-time favourites, and had acknowledged the influence of Allen's work on *Peter's Friends* and *In the Bleak Midwinter*. Hence it was a thrill for Branagh when, at the 1997 Cannes Film Festival, he learned that Allen wanted him for the lead in his upcoming film, *Celebrity*. In a faxed letter to Branagh, the doyen of American film comedy explained that he wished to cast an actor who did not have matinee-idol looks but was sufficiently attractive to make his relationships with a string of beautiful women plausible. Branagh was bemused by Allen's comments about the character's appearance: 'This man is somewhat attractive to women, therefore no facial hair.' It might have seemed unusual for a director whose films had a quintessential New York flavour to cast someone whose reputation was chiefly as a classical actor, but Allen had done his homework. As an avid movie-goer, he was familiar with Branagh's films – and had admired them. In addition, he arranged for Robert Altman to dispatch rushes from *The Gingerbread Man* so that he could verify Branagh's ability to manage an American accent.

Allen's respect for Branagh was evident in the courtesy he showed in sending him the entire script, thereby breaking with his usual practice of providing actors with only the scenes in which their characters have dialogue. Reading Allen's screenplay, Branagh was struck by the bleakness of the piece. *Celebrity* examined the lives of Lee Simon (Branagh) and his wife Robin (to be played by Australian actress Judy Davis, veteran of several Allen films) in the aftermath of their divorce. One issue explored was what it takes to achieve happiness in one's personal life, with Allen's conclusion being that it is mainly a matter of luck. While Robin finds bliss with an amiable television producer, the restless Lee becomes ever more disillusioned, stumbling from one relationship to another.

The second major theme was, as the title of the film suggests, the nature of modern celebrity culture. 'There's a ridiculousness and superficiality to so much of it,' said Allen on one occasion, accounting for the phenomenon by the expansion of the media, with the advent of cable television converting a few channels into hundreds, all with airtime to fill. 'Every clergyman seems to have his own show on Sunday,' he stated, 'every chef and plastic surgeon, every lawyer in the O. J. Simpson trial now has his or her own television show.' By making Branagh's Lee Simon a celebrity journalist who encounters actors (played in the film by the likes of Melanie Griffith, Leonardo DiCaprio and Winona Ryder) and models (such as the one portrayed by Charlize Theron), Allen exposed the vacuousness at the heart of contemporary celebrity culture. That Allen regarded this phenomenon as a serious social malaise was evident not only in his casting of a major classical actor in the lead role, but in the manner in which he intended to open and close the film, with the word 'help' written in the sky.

This collaboration between Branagh and Allen promised much. A gifted comic writer, an outstanding actor and a meaty subject – the prospects were dazzling. The potential richness of the work was enhanced by their first-hand knowledge of an intrusive, celebrity-obsessed modern media: Branagh, ever since he had decided to film *Henry V*, and Allen when it became known that his break-up with Mia Farrow had been triggered by his affair with her adopted daughter Soon-Yi. This was an opportunity for both men to reverse the normal state of affairs: rather than the media spotlighting them, they would be spotlighting the media.

In preparation for his part, Branagh spoke to magazine and travel writers. He probably consulted Helena Bonham Carter about Allen's approach as a director, as she had worked with him on *Mighty Aphrodite*; but his performance would not be aided by the fine-tuning that rehearsals provide. Cherishing spontaneity above preparation, Allen did not schedule any. When filming began in late August 1997, therefore, Branagh was thrown in at the deep end, with the rest of the cast.

Branagh's initial objective during the shoot was a modest one: not to be sent packing. Aware that Allen was not averse to dismissing actors whose performances underwhelmed him, such as when he replaced Michael Keaton with Jeff Daniels on *The Purple Rose of Cairo*, Branagh was tense when filming began. His nerves multiplied when Allen assessed his acting in the first scene of his to be shot. Only a few lines into the first take, Allen said, 'Cut.' Looking dejected, as Branagh recounts the story, he approached and articulated his concerns: 'So I think, erm, I think, I think you should do it again. Erm, it's too broad. It's like Jerry Lewis and er, it's not funny. You shouldn't, you know you shouldn't do it like that.'

As filming continued, Branagh was intrigued to observe Allen at work. He noted the differences between Allen's screen persona and his true personality. There was nothing neurotic or nervous about him. He was clear, decisive and serious-minded. In general he enforced a surprising degree of fidelity to the script; Branagh had expected there to be a greater emphasis on improvisation.

He managed to strike up a decent rapport with Allen. They chatted amiably about sports, politics and contemporary cinema. Allen was generous with his time whenever Branagh, furthering his film education, asked him to explain a particular decision he had made in terms of the directing of the movie. Not once did he scratch his ear, which Branagh noticed was his method for terminating a conversation he was not enjoying by having an assistant announce that there was a telephone call for him. Branagh even reached the stage where he felt able to tease him. 'What do you know about funny, anyway?' he said to Allen at one point. 'What have you ever done? I never even fucking heard of you until this movie.'

On the all-important issue of how Allen responded to Branagh's acting, however, their relationship was more strained. Melanie Griffith has testified to Allen's frustration, recalling his admonition that Branagh just didn't get it. Branagh himself has acknowledged receiving notes from Allen during the shoot saying, 'What you are doing is not funny.' Allen's chief concern was the issue that the critics would seize upon, namely that Branagh's performance seemed to be an uncannily accurate impersonation of Allen's own acting style, including his intonation, stuttering and gesticulations. A gifted mimic, Branagh had clearly drawn on this talent and his affection for Allen's work in fashioning his portrayal of Lee Simon.

Allen and Branagh would later differ in their recollection of the extent to which Branagh's interpretation of his character had received the director's blessing. Allen insisted he had not endorsed Branagh's approach, explaining to the New York press:

> Kenneth is a great actor and I thought it would be a breeze for him. And then as he was doing it, I would go over to him and say, 'You know, it seems to me that you're doing me. A lot.' And he'd say, 'I hear what you're saying, don't worry.' And then guys on the crew would tell me that he was doing me. And I just sort of threw in the towel and felt, that's how he sees this character. This is how he sees him, and this is a great Shakespearean actor. What's the smartest thing to do here? Do I try to force him into a different mold, or do I go with his take on the character?
>
> In the end I had so much respect for him as an actor that I felt, look, I don't wanna sit down and say we gotta reshoot everything and you gotta do it my way.[1]

From Branagh's perspective, his hands were tied. He said later the comic energy, pacing and even such specifics as the stuttering of the neurotic character portrayed over the years by Allen were there in the writing of the part of Lee Simon. (There may be some truth in this: a friend of a journalist once came across the shooting script of an Allen movie in the gutter of a street where he had been filming. She was struck by how the multiple hesitations in the dialogue were actually scripted.) Branagh also recalled Allen's dissatisfaction when he insisted his character wear jeans instead of corduroys. According to

Branagh, Allen commented that he would never wear jeans, implying that Lee Simon was indeed a version of the character he usually played. Branagh, moreover, claimed that the direction he received nudged him towards an Allenesque performance:

It's a very particular kind of comedy, and the character of Lee is a particular kind of Woody Allen comic engine for the piece. And early on where Woody didn't like it, it was almost always where I would try and somehow adjust or adapt or play a different kind of writing. A lot of times it's the necessity to score a nervous energy that adds a kind of pace to the scene, against which other people react – that you can puncture or react to, and to not do that would make the scene go very flat. So he was very keen that that be maintained and inevitably because of the voice in the script, it sounds like him.[2]

Alongside his interaction with Allen, the most intriguing collaboration for Branagh on *Celebrity* was with Leonardo DiCaprio, already a heart-throb following his performance in *Romeo and Juliet*, and soon to become one of the biggest stars in the world with the release of *Titanic*. DiCaprio plays a bratty actor who takes drugs, trashes hotel rooms, and physically abuses his girlfriend. In one of the film's most memorable scenes, the attempt by Branagh's character to interest DiCaprio's in his screenplay is thwarted by DiCaprio's suggestion that they share a bed with two groupies. Lee Simon demurs, saying, 'The woman thing is not a [problem] ... the guy thing I feel a little uncomfortable with,' before reluctantly going along with the idea.

Away from work Branagh and DiCaprio hit it off. There was even a report that they had indulged in a spot of gambling together at a casino when the shoot took them to Atlantic City. Branagh came away from *Celebrity* with a good deal of respect for the young American star: 'For a man so thrust into the limelight, I find nothing of the craft of acting diminished with him ... He has wisdom about his situation, a very old head on his shoulders. He had a significant career before this, and that's kept him sane. There's no sign [the fuss] has swelled his head in the wrong way, and he retains a sense of humour about it.'

Celebrity's release in the United States in 1998 and in Britain the following year met with tepid public interest and a generally hostile set of reviews. The consensus was that this was weaker fare than usually served up by Allen, and that the film suffered by comparison with its obvious cinematic analogue, Federico Fellini's *La Dolce Vita*. Many critics identified Branagh's performance as the film's Achilles' heel. It was a case, they said, of exceptional mimicry but weak characterisation; by aping Allen he had introduced a distracting element into the picture, and had rendered his own performance superficial.

Sven Nykvist, the cinematographer on many of Ingmar Bergman's films, did shoot *Celebrity* beautifully in black and white. Judy Davis gave a fine performance, and DiCaprio a mesmerising one. There were moments of real comic vibrancy – Branagh's character fainting at a chic party on meeting the reviewer who had savaged his book, a rabbi worrying that the skinheads with whom he was sharing a television programme's green room had eaten all the bagels.

Celebrity, however, failed to measure up not only to Allen's earlier classics but also to his more recent work such as *Bullets Over Broadway* or *Deconstructing Harry*. It was simply less funny and charming than most Allen films. That being the case, it would be unfair to ascribe all of the film's shortcomings to Branagh's performance. Still, he would have been better off adopting a neutral American accent. Though he succeeded in presenting the veneer of the neurotic New York persona associated with Allen, a more generic accent would have allowed him to explore more freely (and the audience to observe more easily) the nuances of his character. It was a disappointing outcome – the film, the performance and the response from the public and the critics – to a collaboration between Branagh and Allen that had promised so much.

The year 1997 had been a typically frenetic one for Branagh, with no less than three pictures in the can; 1998 would see no let-up. He acted in the opening scene of *The Dance of Shiva*, a short film directed by Jamie Payne about the experiences of Indian troops in World War I, with a formidable array of talent behind the camera. Cinematographer Jack Cardiff, who had won an Oscar for *Black Narcissus*, production designer John Box, whose four Oscars included one for *Lawrence of Arabia*, and sound recordist for Hitchcock's *The 39 Steps* John Mitchell were among those who lent their services to this project. As *The Dance of Shiva* was being made, the behind-the-scenes work of these old masters was filmed for a documentary, which, it was hoped, would help train the next generation of British film-makers. Unfortunately, lack of financing prevented the completion of the documentary.

Jamie Payne recalls the strong feeling of mutual respect between Branagh and the legends working behind the camera. One other luminary who had been a fan of Branagh, it emerged, was David Lean.

John Box told Payne that when Lean had been labouring on *Nostromo*, the film he had been unable to complete before his death, he had had to name, for insurance purposes, other directors who he felt could step into the breach if he became too ill. Having admired *Henry V*, Lean had identified Branagh early on as someone he would like to complete *Nostromo* if it became necessary. A document on *Nostromo* which raises the issue of insurance and the need for a standby director is to be found in the David Lean papers at the British Film Institute, but does not refer to Branagh or any other director. Still, there is no reason for thinking that Box's account would be inaccurate.

Continuing his efforts to work with the finest directors, following his collaborations with Altman and Allen, Branagh signed on for *Alien Love Triangle*, a sci-fi short film directed by Danny Boyle, who had enjoyed a huge hit in 1996 with *Trainspotting*. Branagh played a scientist whose wife turns out to be a male alien. Starring alongside Heather Graham and Courteney Cox, and backed by the redoubtable team of Bob and Harvey Weinstein, the prospects seemed rosy. Ultimately, however, *Alien Love Triangle* never made it to the big screen. It had been filmed as part of a trilogy of sci-fi shorts, but when Miramax's Dimension Films decided it would be best to turn all three shorts into full-length movies, Boyle refused to alter his twenty-eight minute film. As a result, *Alien Love Triangle* was not released.

Branagh's main undertaking in 1998 was Warner Brothers' *Wild Wild West*. A Hollywood movie with a gargantuan budget, overtly commercial ambitions and special effects galore, it seemed the antithesis of the sort of picture associated with Branagh. But there was a logic to his participation. A demonstration of his box-office clout would not have gone amiss at this point in his career, and *Wild Wild West* seemed to have smash hit written all over it – not least because it reunited director Barry Sonnenfeld and charismatic actor Will Smith, the team that had triumphed in 1997 with *Men in Black*. By playing the psychotic Dr Arliss Loveless, Branagh would also be continuing a rich tradition of British actors, including Anthony Hopkins, Alan Rickman and Jeremy Irons, playing the villain of the piece in American movies. Branagh said another consideration was that *Wild Wild West* gave him the chance to work with his good friend Kevin Kline, who was cast as Smith's partner.

Inspired by the hit 1960s television series of the same name, *Wild Wild West* was a western-comedy-sci-fi-buddy movie hybrid. It told the story of trigger-happy James West (Will Smith) and fussy inventor Artemus Gordon (Kevin Kline) who, at the behest of President Ulysses S. Grant, track Branagh's character. Having been crippled fighting for the South during the Civil War, Loveless has been kidnapping scientists with a view to acquiring the military wherewithal that will enable him to overthrow the US government. Naturally West and Gordon succeed in thwarting his ambitions. Gadgetry and special effects, including a huge mechanical spider, light and often politically incorrect banter, and a large number of sexy, scantily clad female sidekicks – including one played by Salma Hayek – were among the diversions offered by *Wild Wild West*.

In preparing his role as the literally legless Loveless, Branagh heeded advice from his director to highlight the anger Loveless feels about the loss of his legs as well as the South's defeat in the Civil War. He also dissuaded Branagh from watching the *Wild Wild West* television series, as his Loveless was to be very different from the original incarnation of the character – and from shaving his head bald, as Branagh had initially intended, as it would be too reminiscent of the villain in *Austin Powers*.

Branagh turned to his girlfriend, as well as his director, in pondering his role: the knowledge acquired by Bonham Carter about how to play a disabled person for *The Theory of Flight* was invaluable. As for the style of his character, Branagh drew on the frenzied oratorical technique of Hitler, and the operatic delivery of television evangelists.

Branagh's preparations made for what from an early stage was an eye-catching performance. Sofia Eng, who played one of Branagh's beautiful sidekicks, said: 'When I first heard that he was cast in the role [of Loveless], I thought, "There must be a mistake here. Kenneth Branagh for this part?" because I couldn't picture him as this character. And then, at the table reading – the first time we all met and read the script together – I was laughing so hard that when I came home, I had the worst headache!'

Away from the camera, Branagh was able to relax during the filming of *Wild Wild West*. For one thing, Helena Bonham Carter was also based in Los Angeles at the time, for the making of *Fight Club* with Brad Pitt. For another, he was able to indulge his passion for soccer by watching the 1998 World Cup, having insisted that a clause be inserted in his contract stipulating that the television in his trailer must have the channel carrying the competition.

Those distractions were welcome because the making of *Wild Wild West* turned out to be a gruelling affair, stretching through the summer of 1998, well into the autumn. Not only was the shoot long, it made severe physical demands on Branagh. In order to simulate a character who had lost the lower half of his body, his legs were strapped together and a metal plate screwed down to conceal his thighs. Two weeks into filming, he began to suffer from a variety of aches and pains. Branagh found he could only endure the ordeal if every twenty or thirty minutes he was unstrapped and massaged. In addition to the contortionism involved, he had to display patience for the sorts of visual spectaculars that had hardly been part of his movie-making experience on *Hamlet* or *Henry V*. A journalist visiting the set watched Branagh shot out of the hat of a massive papier mâché model of Abraham Lincoln, take after take. 'The only thing I didn't ask Kenneth to do', Barry Sonnenfeld said to an assistant, 'was drop his drawers and wear a witness mark on his privates.'

Despite the stresses and strains involved in making *Wild Wild West*, Branagh refrained from playing the prima donna. One of the scriptwriters on the film noticed how he remained a dutiful team player. 'Once they [some of the actors] found their characters,' he observed, 'they're saying stuff like, "I wouldn't shoot that guy in this scene, would I?" But the person who had the least to say about his role was Ken Branagh; he does a writer's heart good. He got his part, he knew exactly the ins and outs of it, he was fantastic. People are going to be blown away by him.'

Wild Wild West's opening in the United States would demonstrate whether that would in fact be the case. Boding ill was the negative publicity that preceded the film's release. The audience response at the first preview screening left a lot to be desired, though Sonnenfeld insisted that it was no worse than with his previous hit movies, *Addams Family*, *Get Shorty* and *Men in Black*. The press picked up on not only the unsuccessful preview, but the additional days of photography (with all the concomitant costs) that were required. A bit-part actor in the movie, moreover, posted on the internet a diary which portrayed the making of the film in a harsh light. Sonnenfeld began to suspect that the negative buzz might have come from rival studios or from someone with a political agenda at Warner Brothers. *Titanic*, however, had initially been dogged by hostile publicity. So none of these unfortunate pre-release developments was necessarily fatal to *Wild Wild West*'s prospects.

Branagh did some promotional work in support of the film but far less than was his norm. By the summer of 1999 he had moved on to the editing of his next picture, *Love's Labour's Lost*. But this decision – to keep a lower profile with the press – was a sign of things to come. In future Branagh would position himself far from the madding crowd, thereby diluting the media focus that had accompanied his career since 1989.

For *Wild Wild West*, the response of both the paying public and reviewers left a lot to be desired. It did make $50 million in the first six days of its American release, ending up with a box-office total of nearly $114 million. But given the film's colossal budget, it would probably have needed to make in the $150–200 million range to have been deemed a success. In Britain *Wild Wild West* earned £7 million, disappointing for a film of its blockbuster aspirations. (The new *Star Wars* film grossed more than £50 million the same year.) At the hands of critics on both sides of the Atlantic Branagh fared better than the film itself, but even so his notices were mixed. What to his admirers was exuberant acting was to his detractors a case of overacting.

Branagh did bring an admirable gusto to his portrayal of Loveless; and his decision to be bold made sense for a story that had an almost cartoonish feel to it. His performance was the most striking feature of the movie. Nevertheless, *Wild Wild West* had little to recommend it. The lack of chemistry between Smith and Kline, due to a wooden script as much as anything, prevented it from working as a buddy movie. As Salma Hayek's part was underwritten, she was largely superfluous to the story. The politically incorrect banter proved to be more embarrassing than amusing. The attempt by Will Smith's West to placate a baying white crowd was a case in point: 'The whole slavery thing, I don't understand what the big deal was anyway. I mean, come on, who wouldn't want folks running around doing things for them, doing chores.' All in all, *Wild Wild West* could hardly be considered one of Branagh's more impressive undertakings.

Film acting was not the only feature of Branagh's work in the late 1990s. He developed a penchant for television narration, for which there were distinguished precedents – Olivier had served in that capacity on the excellent 1970s series *The World at War*. Branagh provided narration for *The Great Composers*, *The Cold War* and the *Walking with Dinosaurs* series. He also supplied the voice of Miguel on the animated DreamWorks film *The Road to El Dorado*, which made $50 million at the US box office.

Ever since he had decided to film *Henry V*, Branagh's career had moved along diverging tracks: one was forged by the work he had actually undertaken, the other existed at the perceptual level – the discussion in his own country over who he was and what he had done, with savage criticism a salient feature of that debate. This state of affairs continued during the late 1990s. Certainly he had his defenders. In March 1998 William Hickey described him in the *Daily Express* as a 'national treasure', adding: 'The British hate a winner. Thus the past few years have witnessed a peculiar backlash against this Renaissance-flavoured actor, director, film-maker and writer. But if ever a man was destined since birth to overcome the slings and arrows of outrageous criticism, it is the brilliant Branagh.' The following spring tribute was paid to Branagh's career when the National Film Theatre in London scheduled a month-long retrospective of his work. Michael Billington chose this occasion to write for the *Guardian* an article in which he argued that Branagh's ability to provide visual metaphors that illuminate the text's meaning had made him an exceptional director of Shakespeare on the big screen: 'Branagh has set new standards in Shakespearian film-making, which makes it all the more puzzling that Branagh-bashing is a popular British media sport. But I suspect his achievement in Shakespearian cinema, which, in directorial terms, outdistances Olivier's, will survive attempts to put this passionate Belfast puritan down.' Branagh's *Henry V*, Billington also declared, was 'better, in almost every respect, than Olivier's'.

A better maker of Shakespeare films than Olivier: how difficult to square that view of Branagh with the one propagated by his detractors, who remained vocal. Around the time that Billington was singing Branagh's praises, David Thomson was asserting in the *Independent on Sunday* that Branagh had suffered a fate worse than death for an actor: he had gone cold. A profile in the *Sunday Telegraph* the following month was equally disparaging: 'These days the Great White Hope seems to be on cruise control – content to motor along on automatic pilot: a bit of undemanding Hollywood pap, fine, but no more stage company, no more playwriting, no big four-and-a-half-hour uncut Shakespeares.'

Once again his critics were excessive. Still, it would be true to say that the late 1990s represented the nadir of his career. That this should be so was curious. He had worked with Robert Altman, Woody Allen and Danny Boyle, directors of the highest calibre. But the performances had not matched the promise. Of the five films released after his epic *Hamlet* only one made more than a million pounds at the UK box office, and only one earned more than $6 million in the United States. With *The Theory of Flight* and *The Gingerbread Man*, Branagh had done himself justice; but the truth was that, in general, the quality and the commercial success of the work he was producing needed a boost. During the next few years Branagh would provide one, by returning to Shakespeare, to the stage and to television, as well as by sustaining his high-profile film career.

10

The Comeback Kid

But love, first learnèd in a lady's eyes,
Lives not alone immurèd in the brain,
But with the motion of all elements
Courses as swift as thought in every power,
And gives to every power a double power,
Above their functions and their offices.
It adds a precious seeing to the eye.
A lover's eyes will gaze an eagle blind.
A lover's ear will hear the lowest sound ...
Love's feeling is more soft and sensible
Than are the tender horns of cockled snails.
Love's tongue proves dainty Bacchus gross in taste.
For valor, is not Love a Hercules,
Still climbing trees in the Hesperides?
Subtle as Sphinx, as sweet and musical
As bright Apollo's lute, strung with his hair.
And when Love speaks, the voice of all the gods
Make heaven drowsy with the harmony.

It seems just conceivable that the desire of Kenneth Branagh, fulfilled in 1999, to make a film of *Love's Labour's Lost* was due in part to a simple wish to be able to say those lines, uttered by Berowne, in what is surely one of the most beautiful speeches ever written by Shakespeare.

Love's Labour's Lost, Shakespeare's comedy about the failure of the King of Navarre and his three friends to keep their vow to study and to avoid the company of women when they fall in love with the visiting Princess of France and her companions, is one of Shakespeare's most obscure plays. In fact it was not performed in Britain for more than two centuries after Shakespeare's death; and it was not until a landmark Peter Brook production just after World War II, in which a young Paul Scofield appeared, that the play became a more accepted part of the regularly performed Shakespearean canon. Not surprisingly, no feature film of the play had ever been attempted.

The limited appeal of *Love's Labour's Lost* to actors, theatre directors and film-makers is not hard to fathom. The density of the language means that it is not one of Shakespeare's more accessible offerings, and its gossamer plot would seem to make it unworkable on film. Furthermore, the melancholy of the play's ending, with the death of the Princess's father, and the women asking their suitors to wait a year rather than marrying immediately, can sound a jarring note to an audience, coming as it does after the mood of silliness that pervades the earlier part of the play.

There were still sound reasons for Branagh to be attracted to *Love's Labour's Lost* as his next Shakespeare film. Never was Shakespeare's linguistic exuberance more in evidence than in this play. Distinguished scholar Harold Bloom has written: 'I take more unmixed pleasure from *Love's Labour's Lost* than from any other Shakespearean play ... I entertain the illusion that Shakespeare may have enjoyed a particular and unique zest in composing it. *Love's Labour's Lost* is a festival of language, an exuberant fireworks display in which Shakespeare seems to seek the limits of his verbal resources, and discovers that there are none.' Despite cutting the text liberally, Branagh would be able to convey a sense of the beautiful ornateness of the play's language. From his experience as the King of Navarre in the Royal Shakespeare Company's 1984–5 production, he also thought that the play was deceptively entertaining. 'It played much more winningly than it reads,' he said. 'It's very tough to read. It's very dense. But in the theatre it's an audience-pleaser.' This boded well for a film of the play.

As always, Branagh had from the outset a clear conception of how he would convert a Shakespearean text into a feature film. In this case, he planned to turn the play into a musical set in an Oxbridge-style college in the late 1930s. Branagh's own experience with musicals was limited: he had performed in a RADA production of *Lady Be Good*, and none thereafter. But the notion of filming *Love's Labour's Lost* as a musical made sense to Branagh for a number of reasons. First, it was a logical extension of Shakespeare's own practice of often incorporating song and dance into his plays. Second, it reflected the various references to music and dance in the text of *Love's Labour's Lost*. When, for instance, Berowne meets the woman with whom he is to fall in love – Rosaline – he asks: 'Did not I dance with you in Brabant once?' Third, the songs could serve as helpful substitutes for portions of the text that were particularly dense and abstruse. Finally, in Branagh's view the theme central to *Love's Labour's Lost* of the transforming power of love – it is their ardour for the women rather than their commitment to study that turns the men into poets – would blend well with the sensibilities of musical comedy.

As for the chronological setting, Branagh pinpointed the 1930s as this would provide an appropriate feeling of uncertainty, of the imminence of change. The onset of World War II, which he would touch on in his movie, would heighten the sense of the men having to part from the women (though in Branagh's film they would be reunited after the war), and magnify the sadness that takes a grip in the latter part of the story.

It is easy to think of Branagh as a traditionalist, given his penchant for Shakespeare. That is true in terms of the subject matter with which he worked, but not in terms of his *approach* to that subject matter. Making a movie of *Hamlet* with an uncut text, and then attempting a musical of *Love's Labour's Lost* – these were the ambitions of a film-maker guided by an innovative, daring spirit.

In order to make *Love's Labour's Lost*, Branagh teamed up again with David Barron, who had produced *In the Bleak Midwinter* and *Hamlet*. The Branagh–Barron partnership approached the London-based company Intermedia Films, who agreed to back the project. Soon Pathé Pictures, the Arts Council of England and Miramax Films did likewise, ensuring that a budget of £8.5 million was in place.

The way Branagh envisioned it, *Love's Labour's Lost* would be but the first in a series of new Shakespeare films. To that end he established the Shakespeare Film Company, which in 1998 announced plans to film not only a musical version of *Love's Labour's Lost*, but a *Macbeth* set contemporaneously on Wall Street, and *As You Like It* with the story transported to Japan's Kyoto at cherry-blossom time.

Before the filming of *Love's Labour's Lost* began, at Shepperton Studios in February 1999, Branagh hacked away at the text to guarantee a picture of a more audience-friendly length than his *Hamlet* and to ensure there were moments when a transition from speaking to singing and dancing would seem natural. Coming up with songs which evoked the appropriate emotion, and with lyrics which were thematically consistent with the preceding portion of the text, was tricky. At first the intention was to write new songs, but, as Branagh commented, 'You can imagine how long it took for me to realise that my lyrics would not be sitting nicely next to Shakespeare's. It took about ten minutes to get myself out of that job.' Then Branagh turned to relatively obscure songs by some of the great popular composers of the twentieth century. Finally, he concluded it would be best to use the famous pieces that these composers had written. 'It seemed as though we needed classic songs to match this classic text,' he explained, 'songs that in themselves were very complete, that had the beauty of memorable and instantly affecting melodies.' So standards by George Gershwin, Jerome Kern, Irving Berlin and Cole Porter were selected, with Branagh integrating them seamlessly into the screenplay. Berowne, for instance, would begin to sing 'Heaven, I'm in heaven' from the Irving Berlin classic *Cheek to Cheek* having just spoken Shakespeare's lines, 'And when love speaks, the voice of all the gods / Make heaven drowsy with the harmony.'

In working out his ideas for the music for *Love's Labour's Lost*, Branagh collaborated once again with Patrick Doyle. The approach they adopted was not always of the high-tech variety. 'I spent a day with him in my house,' recalled Branagh, 'with both of us dancing around the house, in order to explain to the other what we wanted for the music. We were using pots and pans from the kitchen to tap rhythm ... There's a song "Let's face the music and dance" ... that's in the film. It has this very dirty drum beat ... at the beginning ... So, that song, that arrangement of that song, began with two saucepans in my house.' In addition to the classic songs, arranged in the style of the old MGM musicals with lavish orchestrations, Doyle provided an elegant underscore with a very English sensibility to complement the Oxbridge setting.

Branagh's influence was to be seen not only in the music, but in the set as well. He has spoken of the long-term marination process that has taken place with his Shakespeare films, whereby he visualises the movie's look over a number of years. *Love's Labour's Lost* was no different. 'I've got several scenes ... where I can see the film and hear it,' he stated in an interview back in 1996. 'I can see the dance routine in *Love's Labour's Lost*: I can see a fantastic library, a fantastic circular library.' When the picture was made, in 1999, that impressive circular library was indeed the main part of the set designed by Tim Harvey – an obvious representation of the bookish aspirations of the King of Navarre that will go unrealised as love rather than scholarly endeavour brings self-enlightenment. As with his films of *Much Ado About Nothing* and *Hamlet*, *Love's Labour's Lost* would be a visual feast. After toying with the idea of shooting in black and white, he opted for the Technicolor look of a 1950s Stanley Donen musical, with bright, vivid primary colours.

In casting the film, Branagh wanted actors who could sing and dance passably rather than singers and dancers who were less proven on the acting front. As always, he wanted to be surrounded by some familiar faces. Accordingly, Geraldine McEwan, Richard Briers, Timothy Spall, Richard Clifford and Jimmy Yuill were given roles. For the most part, however, Branagh cast young actors, generally inexperienced in Shakespeare, who would supply a feeling of freshness and exuberance. Alicia Silverstone, who had become a star following her performance in the 1995 film *Clueless*, would play the Princess of France, while Natascha McElhone, Emily Mortimer and Carmen Ejogo would portray her three ladies-in-waiting. Alessandro Nivola won the part of the King of Navarre; his friends would be played by Matthew Lillard, Adrian Lester and, as Berowne, Branagh himself. Nathan Lane, the revered Broadway star, was cast in the comic role of Costard. Along with Adrian Lester, he was the only actor who could lay claim to a track record in musicals.

As Branagh prepared for the shoot, he picked the brains of illustrious talents who could give him the benefit of their own experience with musicals. Martin Scorsese, in particular, was a great help. Though renowned for such gritty, violent pictures as *Raging Bull*, Scorsese had made a musical, *New York, New York*, and was knowledgeable about old Hollywood. Having known Scorsese for a number of years, Branagh felt able to put to him a series of questions: 'How do you schedule dance numbers? What about fatigue and injury? How many rehearsals are necessary? What are the risks and benefits of shooting dancers in full-body shots, rather than in shots of isolated body parts?' During the making of *Celebrity*, Branagh drew from Woody Allen an explanation of how he had approached his recent movie musical *Everyone Says I Love You*. Allen said he had encouraged his actors *not* to rehearse their singing and dancing so as not to appear too polished. Branagh did not adapt the same practice but did want the musical numbers in *Love's Labour's Lost* to be performed with a certain freshness.

With filming set to begin in February 1999, Branagh worked with the choreographer during the final months of 1998 in order to learn the dance steps; with his responsibilities as director, he would be unable to do so during rehearsals, as the rest of the cast could. Branagh had always been willing to take on different roles at the same time, but even by his standards his obligations on *Love's Labour's Lost* were wide-ranging: selecting the songs, acting, singing, dancing, producing, directing, adapting Shakespeare's text for the screen, as well as his involvement in casting and editing. As one observer put it, with this project Branagh took multitasking to new heights.

A three-and-a-half-week period was scheduled for rehearsals. On the first day Branagh gave his charges a stern lecture on the importance of professionalism and punctuality, and showed them the 1935 classic *Top Hat* starring Fred Astaire and Ginger Rogers. When the lights came up, Branagh saw a group of actors whose faces expressed both admiration and fear. Clearly it would be impossible to match the technical brilliance of these legends. 'Look, here's what we can't do,' Branagh told them candidly. 'We just can't do this.' But, he added, they could aim to capture the same spirit of joyous, romantic silliness. The rehearsals that followed were rigorous. Arriving at eight each morning, the actors would do two hours of singing and dancing as a group before following their own, specifically tailored routines comprising singing, dancing, and speaking the verse. After a fortnight Branagh called for a complete run-through of the film, with singing and dancing included. It proved to be a salutary exercise. It was during this run-through, recalled Branagh, that Alicia Silverstone came on leaps and bounds, and that the actors in general became convinced that this challenging venture would work well.

The start of principal photography signified a milestone in Branagh's career. With it, he had exceeded the extent of the achievements of the other major directors of Shakespeare on the big screen. Olivier, Welles and Zeffirelli had each made three feature films of Shakespeare's plays but no more. With the lack of obvious commercial appeal of Shakespeare to a cinema audience and the accompanying problem in raising money, it had always been difficult to get these projects up and running. Note the struggles of Welles to film *Othello*; and the failure of Olivier to make *Macbeth*, as he so fervently desired.

Love's Labour's Lost was Branagh's fourth Shakespeare film as director. He had gone past them all – and had done so while still in his thirties.

In directing *Love's Labour's Lost*, Branagh adopted a camp manner that was rooted in his experiences in theatre. 'It's very disarming,' commented Nathan Lane, 'he pretends to be this very camp director, and he talks to you in this certain way, he calls all the men by women's names. "Oh, Mrs Lane is a little cranky this morning, we'll have to squeeze the performance out of her!"' 'The important thing', said Branagh in response to this recollection, 'is to create an atmosphere of fun ... Especially with this play, because we wanted to give people the sense which I think does transmit itself through the celluloid, of the company itself having had fun.' The company did have fun – despite the demands of a shoot which meant the musical numbers often required as many as fifteen takes – with Nathan Lane playing the role of court jester. One out-take showed the actors laughing at what appeared to be flatulence on the part of their director.

Branagh was particularly pleased with the contributions of his experienced song-and-dance men, Adrian Lester and Nathan Lane. As Dumaine, Lester had few lines but the chance to shine in an extended solo dance segment in which his declaration of love is overheard by his friends. 'Please be absolutely brilliant and would you do the thing with the chairs that Fred Astaire did on *Shall We Dance?*' asked Branagh when inviting Lester to take part in *Love's Labour's Lost*. Lester obliged so impressively that the rest of the cast broke out into a round of applause after watching his slick footwork. As Nathan Lane sang 'There's No Business Like Show Business' Branagh found himself transfixed, thinking, 'You really believe in this, don't you? You really believe in this show business being the cure of all ills.'

Throughout his work on *Love's Labour's Lost*, Branagh enjoyed not only support but constructive input from Helena Bonham Carter. It was she who suggested the segment in which Branagh and his fellow actors tap to the words with their feet in the rhythm of iambic pentameter; and it was she who came up with the idea of Timothy Spall (as Don Armado) concluding his musical number 'I Get a Kick Out of You' by kicking the moon. It turned out to be the last such collaboration. Within the year, their relationship would be over.

On 24 April 1999, precisely two months after the shoot began, *Love's Labour's Lost* wrapped. Post-production proved problematic.

Once it had been edited to his satisfaction Branagh arranged a preview in Wimbledon for an audience that included Miramax's Harvey Weinstein and the film's other backers. It turned out to be a painful experience, with the audience's response tepid at best. A chastened Branagh went with Weinstein and the other money-men to a Wimbledon restaurant to conduct the necessary post-mortem. They all agreed that the audience had been uncertain how to respond, that somehow the idea had to be conveyed that the film was not bizarre but simply a light comedy which should be taken in that spirit. The problem was how to achieve that objective. The answer came to Branagh a few days later, as he lay in bed at 3 a.m.: newsreel segments, inserted periodically to signpost the story. Branagh himself provided the newsreader's comically plummy voice. It was a good idea, as the newsreel inserts helped to structure the story, and to anchor it in a strong sense of period. The audience responded far more approvingly at the next preview. Martin Scorsese and Stanley Donen also reacted appreciatively at a pre-release screening in New York. They gave Branagh some useful feedback, and accepted Harvey Weinstein's request that they endorse *Love's Labour's Lost* by becoming 'presenters' of the film, with their names to be listed in the credits.

There were signs prior to the film's release in 2000 that it would do well. Shown to the faculty of Branagh's alma mater, RADA, the response was favourable. Alicia Silverstone conducted her own research by slipping into six separate screenings of the film, and was delighted to observe audience members, enchanted by what they had seen, leaving the cinema singing and dancing. On the whole, however, the public reaction to *Love's Labour's Lost* was indifferent. The combined box office in Britain and America was about $1 million. It was a far cry from the days of *Much Ado About Nothing*, which had clocked up no less than $30 million in Britain and America. When *Much Ado* had opened there had been a frenzied atmosphere in London's Leicester Square. With the *Love's Labour's Lost* première, by contrast, the smaller number of fans who congregated showed polite interest rather than the fervour evident eight years earlier. The reviews also left a lot to be desired. A. O. Scott conceded in the *New York Times* that the film was fun, but Roger Ebert of the *Chicago Sun-Times* found it an insubstantial entertainment, and Kenneth Turan told his *Los Angeles Times* readers that the dancing and singing were unimpressive, the text had been cut excessively, and that there was too much unfunny farce. Reviewers back home had similar reservations. Philip French's description of the film in the *Observer* as 'utterly charming' was untypical of the reaction of his fellow critics.

Love's Labour's Lost was a brave attempt by Branagh to offer the public a joyously romantic entertainment. To select one of Shakespeare's more obscure plays, and to interpret it in a genre – the musical – that had for decades spelled box-office disaster, was a risk. In many ways he succeeded, despite the intrinsic difficulty of the venture. The movie was a lot of fun to watch. His integration of the songs into the text was adroit. His touching respect for the history of the movies – seen previously in the doffing of his hat to Alfred Hitchcock in *Dead Again*, and to Woody Allen in *A Midwinter's Tale* – was evident in the swimming routine filmed as homage to Esther Williams, and in a scene lifted from *Casablanca* with the women departing by aeroplane as the men say farewell.

The film could have been more effective, though. One problem is that the audience does not develop enough emotional investment in the characters and their relationships. As a result, the parting of the men and women does not have the impact it should. In the scene where we first meet the ladies of France, when the Princess asks the other women what they know of the King of Navarre's pals, Shakespeare's play and Branagh's October 1998 screenplay provide much fuller responses from the women, in which the men's personalities are described, than were included in Branagh's final cut. Establishing the characters more fully at the outset would have paid greater dividends at the end. Another ten or fifteen minutes of screen time would not have gone amiss, especially as the ninety-three-minute movie was short compared to previous Shakespeare films. Indeed Branagh shot a good deal that ended up on the cutting-room floor.

Another issue was the technical proficiency of the singing and especially the dancing. Branagh and his choreographer Stuart Hopps did a good job in eliciting competent performances from largely inexperienced dancers; but as it was a movie musical, the old classics of that genre would inevitably be used as a yardstick to measure the worth of *Love's Labour's Lost*. In the film shown by Branagh to the cast during rehearsals, *Top Hat*, it is not only its joyous spirit that is striking, it is the breathtaking virtuosity of Fred Astaire and Ginger Rogers. It is no coincidence that the most memorable moments of *Love's Labour's Lost* were provided by the two cast members with an established pedigree in musicals – Nathan Lane in his consummate rendition of 'There's No Business Like Show Business' and Adrian Lester with his scintillating solo dance routine. Casting more extensively from the ranks of musical theatre would have created more of those exhilarating moments.

Despite these shortcomings, *Love's Labour's Lost* was a charming movie. Its lack of success can be attributed chiefly to the moribund status of the musical. Changes in sensibility over the course of time meant that to many people a movie musical such as this, for which the public appetite would have been considerable decades earlier, would seem saccharine and trivial. *Chicago*, a musical which did enjoy box-office and Oscar success a few years later, had a much darker, harsher feel, one which modern movie audiences evidently found more to their liking.

Branagh ended up paying a price for his film's commercial failure; securing the financing for the next two Shakespeare films he had scheduled, *Macbeth* and *As You Like It*, depended on a strong performance by *Love's Labour's Lost* at the box office. Hence in the wake of its poor showing it was announced that Branagh had been compelled to put on ice his plans to film the Scottish play and Shakespeare's pastoral comedy. His assistant Tamar Thomas was quoted as saying his next Shakespeare film 'could end up being made in fifteen years'.

In the autumn of 1999, between the shooting and the release of *Love's Labour's Lost* and following a stay at an Arizona health farm, Branagh slotted in a starring role in *How to Kill Your Neighbor's Dog*. Before he began work on this independent American production, he made a painful personal decision: he ended his relationship with Helena Bonham Carter. Their parting was reported in the British press and then confirmed by Bonham Carter in a statement which said it had been a mutual decision, although the general assumption was that it was Branagh who had instigated the break. He has never elaborated in public on the reasons for his separation from Bonham Carter. Given the intense media interest in his break-up with Emma Thompson, it was fortuitous that Branagh would be in Vancouver, where the shooting of his new film took place as his parting from Bonham Carter was mulled over.

How to Kill Your Neighbor's Dog was the handiwork of Michael Kalesniko, whose chief claim to fame was as the screenwriter for *Private Parts*, the hit biopic of controversial disc jockey Howard

Stern. Kalesniko wrote the script for *Neighbor's Dog*, a black comedy about an acerbic, LA-based British playwright who has lost his touch, is reluctantly going along with his wife's plans to try for a baby, and who develops a rapport with the neighbour's young daughter to help create authentic dialogue for the part of a child he is writing for his new play. Robert Redford's company was so taken with the script that Redford came on board as executive producer. At one point the film's financiers offered Harvey Keitel the lead role, but Kalesniko himself always had Branagh in mind, and once he and Robin Wright Penn had signed up, assembling the rest of the cast, which included Lynn Redgrave, was straightforward.

It is not difficult to see what attracted Branagh to the project. Kalesniko had penned a sharp script and, with the part of playwright Peter McGowen, had created for Branagh a character for whom the actor felt an affinity: 'It's a black comedy about an English playwright ... who's going through a mid-life crisis, creative and personal. His wife wants to have kids and he doesn't ... The character is terrifyingly like me.' The role also enabled Branagh to display his verbal agility and his gift for comedy: his character's stock-in-trade was the quick, sardonic retort. He was well cast, as he knew first-hand what it was like to be a playwright, having written *Public Enemy* in the 1980s.

The filming of *Neighbor's Dog* was due to get under way in the late spring of 1999, but the shoot had to be postponed until the autumn because of a freak accident to Branagh: he sneezed while shaving, damaging his neck so badly that his limbs felt numb. He saw a couple of doctors who, alarmingly, suggested that titanium bolts or something of that sort would have to be inserted in his neck. Other doctors recommended a more holistic approach, which turned out to be effective. On the personal front, then, 1999 was an *annus horribilis* for Branagh.

The anguish he felt over the break-up with Bonham Carter was clear for all to see when shooting began on *Neighbor's Dog*. Director of photography Hubert Taczanowski recalls the general awareness on set of his state of mind: 'There was a sense he was bumbed out about it. Also he talked ... a few times about [how] he was putting some finishing touches to this house [that he had built] ... He was down ... He would party with everyone else, you know going out, but ... there's always some women approaching [actors on movie sets] but I think he wasn't really interested in anything ... He would not really even consider it.'

Despite the heartbreak, Branagh remained the consummate professional, making sure he had done his homework. 'He always came in [and] he knew the dialogue perfectly,' says Taczanowski. 'Everybody else always stumbled and had to [reread their lines]. He never checked anything ... I never saw him reading ... he was absolutely superbly prepared.' He enjoyed a good rapport with Lynn Redgrave, who was playing Branagh's mother-in-law. She liked to tease him as to why he was not yet Sir Kenneth Branagh.

Michael Kalesniko, who directed as well as wrote *Neighbor's Dog*, was intrigued by the differences in technique between Branagh and his co-star Robin Wright Penn. 'It's really interesting to see these different acting styles,' he says, 'because Ken, I guess coming from the theatre and the British acting style, it's not really the method, and he gagged between takes with everybody. He'll have a cigarette and he's joking around and everyone's crying laughing, and you'll look to the side and there'll be Robin; but because the scene is a very sad scene, the next scene, [in which] she has to be crying, she'll be sitting in the corner crying.'

Away from the camera, Kalesniko noticed Branagh's charm and his wariness:

> I think because of what has happened in the press ... and some of these absolutely inexplicable attacks on his character, I find he can be quite private – and so he should be ... So it's funny that you warm up to him very, very quickly, but for me personally I found that the friendship didn't necessarily go to the next step. Not that it does with actors as a rule, and I mean name actors. They are naturally defensive. And also they are naturally charming. That's their job, to charm you. And Ken almost has charm-swagger. When he walks into a room he knows you're going to like him; and dammit if you don't like him, you just do.[1]

How to Kill Your Neighbor's Dog had an intelligent script, strong cast and a darkly engaging performance by Branagh. Despite winning film festival awards in New York, Philadelphia, Newport and Avignon, however, Kalesniko's movie struggled to secure distribution. It was aired on a US cable network in the autumn of 2001 before finally being released in American cinemas the following February. Few people saw the movie despite some good reviews. 'It is a tribute to Mr Branagh's considerable comic skills', wrote Stephen Holden in the *New York Times*, 'that he succeeds in making a potentially insufferable character likable by infusing him with the same sly charm that Michael Caine musters to seduce us into cozying up to his sleazier alter egos.' The millions earned rapidly by *How to Kill Your*

Neighbor's Dog when released on video indicated that the film did have commercial potential in the United States. Unfortunately it was not released in British cinemas.

Although the film did not have the impact for which Branagh would have hoped, the important thing was that he was doing good work again. He would continue, in the new millenium, to identify projects that did justice to his talents. In addition, he would soon enjoy the widespread critical acclaim and sustained commercial success that had eluded him for a number of years. This renewed success was coupled with an increasingly low public profile. Previously he had promoted his projects energetically. Now he let the work speak for itself. Rarely did he grant interviews. In Britain at least there may have been a connection between these two developments – the decrease in press coverage of Branagh as a personality and the greater praise for his work. If achieving celebrity status had been a reason for the backlash against Branagh a decade earlier, then the diminution of his celebrity effectively removed one of the factors that had incited his detractors. Also contributing to his resurgence was the less frenetic approach adopted by Branagh to his career. He remained busy over the next few years, but the sense one has is of an actor intent on showing more discretion in the work he accepted.

The next undertaking that would help restore Branagh's reputation was *Rabbit-Proof Fence*, an Australian film based on Doris Pilkington's book, which told the true story of three mixed-race Aboriginal girls, one of them Pilkington's mother, who in 1931 had been taken from their families in Jigalong, Western Australia, as part of government policy and relocated more than a thousand miles away to a settlement near Perth used to train servants for white society. The girls escaped and headed for home by following a fence which bisected Western Australia from north to south.

Phillip Noyce, an Australian who had spent the past decade in Hollywood making, with varying degrees of success, such action-adventure films as *Patriot Games*, *Clear and Present Danger* and *The Saint*, seemed at first glance a curious choice to direct this low-budget human-interest story. But his name helped secure financing for the picture, and his early work suggested that he would be able to handle the subject matter well. A nationwide search was conducted to find three Aboriginal girls to play the main parts. For the small but crucial role of A. O. Neville, the English bureaucrat who was responsible as Chief

Protector of Aborigines for the policy of removing mixed-race Aboriginal children from their families, Noyce wanted a household name who could 'add commercial weight to a cast of unknowns'. The part ended up being offered to Branagh, who, drawn to a character so replete with contradictions, accepted. Neville regarded himself as altruistic, as imbuing the abducted Aboriginal children with the benefits of white cultural values. In the film he declares that 'the native must be helped'; but driven by a belief in eugenics, his objectives were fundamentally racist. By integrating fair-skinned, mixed-race Aborigines into white society, he intended to breed out the Aboriginal stock within a few generations. It was 'interesting', Branagh said, to try 'to make a man, who ... many people in this country [Australia] may regard as a monster, also a human being'.

Branagh did not have a reputation for taking on controversial roles, but with A. O. Neville he would be portraying a character with considerable contemporary political significance. *Rabbit-Proof Fence* was filmed against a backdrop of intense debate in Australia over the history of white–Aboriginal relations, and in particular the plight of those who have become known as the Stolen Generations. In 1997 an official report, entitled *Bringing Them Home*, highlighted the immense psychological damage inflicted on generations of Aboriginal children who, as a result of government policy between 1910 and 1970, had been separated from their families. While some staunch conservatives challenged the accuracy of the report, and Prime Minister John Howard refused to issue an official apology to Aborigines, other Australians joined the 'reconciliation' movement aimed at repairing the damage done by white settlers to the indigenous people. Branagh's depiction of A. O. Neville, a key architect of the very policy that had created the Stolen Generations, would inevitably trigger, as a British newspaper put it, 'a flurry of soul-searching in Australia'.

Though the actual events in *Rabbit-Proof Fence* unfolded in Western Australia, filming took place in South Australia, chosen for the greater variety of locations it offered in a reasonably small area. When Branagh arrived on set, he made clear that he would not be offering up a caricatured villain. 'Look, I can't judge this man,' he told Noyce, 'I'm not here to do that by my performance. I'm only here to reveal him.' Rather than portraying a frenzied madman, Branagh evoked the stolidness of the meticulous bureaucrat. A distorted sense of idealism rather than malevolence, he suggested, was the engine driving Neville's policies. Inevitably, though, there was a sinister dimension to Branagh's depiction of him. Particularly disturbing was the scene in which he inspects the backs of some Aboriginal children to see if they are sufficiently light-skinned to merit special education. Cinematographer Christopher Doyle enhanced the ominousness of Branagh's character by using a Kodak stock that deepened the shadows when shooting the scenes in Neville's office.

Branagh, who felt certain that the performances of the young Aboriginal actresses would elicit strong feelings of sympathy from cinema audiences, was amused to encounter their healthy disregard for his reputation. A documentary on the making of *Rabbit-Proof Fence* showed the precocious Everlyn Sampi telling Branagh in no uncertain terms, as they were waiting for the camera to roll, to remove his glasses.

As with all the directors who had worked with Branagh after he had established his own reputation behind the camera, Phillip Noyce wondered whether he would prove difficult; and as with his predecessors Noyce discovered that there was nothing to worry about. 'Probably because his own experiences had allowed Ken to have an acute understanding of the unique problems that face any film director,' reflected Noyce, 'he could not have been more supportive.'

Rabbit-Proof Fence enjoyed considerable success following its release in Australia, in February 2002. It earned enthusiastic notices, played at cinemas for six months, and received ten nominations for the Australian equivalent of the Oscars, the Film Institute Awards, winning for Best Picture. Released with the backing of Miramax in the United States and in Britain later that same year, the movie met with approval from many though not all reviewers. A number wrote favourably of Branagh, with Philip French in the *Observer* describing his portrayal of Neville as 'chilling', and Stephen Holden of the *New York Times* lauding his 'understated performance'.

Rabbit-Proof Fence brought credit on Branagh not only for his performance but for the calibre of the film as a whole. It was moving, but not overly sentimental. Noyce drew out able performances from the three Aboriginal children, especially Everlyn Sampi, none of whom had prior acting experience. Christopher Doyle's cinematography emphasised both the beauty and the harshness of the Australian landscape, while Peter Gabriel's soundtrack made for a richly atmospheric film. It was a fine piece of work, and for Branagh a sign of things to come.

In his next undertaking, *Conspiracy*, Branagh again played a nefarious historical figure. General Reinhard Heydrich of the SS was the man who chaired the top-secret meeting in January 1942 at Wannsee, an idyllic Berlin suburb, in which he and other Third Reich officials planned the extermination of Europe's Jews. This television drama, funded by HBO and the BBC, was to be directed by Frank Pierson, who had won an Oscar in 1976 for his screenplay for *Dog Day Afternoon*. Loring Mandel wrote the script, basing it on the one surviving record of the Wannsee conference, found in 1947 by American officials in German Foreign Office files.

On reading Mandel's screenplay Branagh was horrified by the casual manner in which Heydrich (and his colleagues) discussed the slaughter of millions of people. Uncertain that he should accept the role, he met with the director. Frank Pierson recalls their discussion:

> Ken was a bit in doubt at first at playing what he saw as a villain with no corner of weakness or redeeming feature to ferret out. It was a lonely time in his life, and I think he was looking for something to occupy his mind and time, and that went into deciding to play this monster ... Ken asked me what I thought about how to play Heydrich. I said he was only interested in getting his own way with bureaucrats who had in mind only their own benefit or harm from putting the holocaust into high gear. That the morality never came into play. Ken nodded, then said this was a part he only wanted to play. He didn't want to direct. I'm sure he was reassuring me that he wouldn't be invading my authority, and I appreciated it.[2]

In preparation for the part, Branagh visited Holocaust museums, read extensively on Heydrich and absorbed a profile of the man written for him by Loring Mandel. Psychologically, however, Heydrich did not seem to make sense. Branagh searched in vain for clues that would explain Heydrich's willingness to engineer the murder of millions. 'He had a loving, supportive family,' ascertained Branagh. 'There seemed to be no traumatic incidents in childhood, no sibling rivalry.' In addition, there appeared to be no strong ideological motivation behind Heydrich's actions. 'Hitler had a sort of Aryan mysticism that somehow at least explained in the twisted, perverse, terrible way how he was motivated,' noted Branagh. 'But with Heydrich there wasn't that.' In the end, Branagh concluded that what made Heydrich tick was simply power, both the acquisition and the exercise of it.

The filming of *Conspiracy* began in November 2000 at Shepperton Studios, where a room virtually identical to the one in which the Wannsee meeting had taken place was designed, and was supplemented by the shooting of exteriors in Wannsee itself. The shoot was preceded by what was for the director and cast a helpfully long rehearsal period. At the initial read-through Frank Pierson stuck to his preferred practice of saying little so that he could see how the actors were approaching their parts before giving his input. But Branagh asked Pierson directly if he had any suggestions to make. He replied that what he wanted them to conjure up was 'an ordinary business meeting of executives but instead of discussing accounting measures, how to advertise and such they're talking about [how] to kill. But as though killing were accounting.' Branagh nodded his agreement and proceeded to read his lines at great speed. 'Too fast?' he asked Pierson at the end of the read-through. The director assured him that his pacing was perfect. 'I hate what I say,' declared Branagh, 'I hate it. I only tried to get through it as quickly as I could.'

The first week of rehearsals was taken up with tortuous discussions on the sort of German accent that the cast should adopt. Returning from lunch six days into rehearsal, Pierson was greeted by a plea from Branagh on behalf of his fellow actors. 'Please, let us act,' he implored. Thereafter the dialogue coach was sent packing, Pierson instructed his actors to employ subtle German accents in order to avoid the trite vocal traits of Nazis portrayed in World War II films, and Branagh became the spokesman for a cast that included Stanley Tucci, Colin Firth and David Threlfall.

Once filming began, Branagh was inevitably struck by the horror of knowing the hideous sentiments he was expressing had actually been articulated and had resulted in the deaths of millions. 'In twenty years of acting', he stated, 'I've never been involved with a character so disturbing to my own peace of mind.' He struggled to sleep during the making of *Conspiracy*, and at one point found the revulsion he felt for Heydrich almost too much to bear. When his character says to his colleagues in reference to the gas chambers, 'The machinery is waiting; feed it,' Branagh had to leave the set to compose himself.

At times he found it necessary to encourage the blackest sort of humour so as to defuse the tension he and the other actors felt. After making sure there were no journalists present, he asked Pierson's permission to allow the cast to do a Monty Python version of the scene they were working on. The result, Pierson recalls, was 'an uproarious parody of the script ... It was the only way to go on.'

These brief comic interludes notwithstanding, Branagh brought great focus to bear. Between scenes he sat quietly by himself. He was, judged Stephen Goldblatt, the director of photography on the film, 'very disciplined'. That discipline paid off. The release of *Conspiracy* on American and British television was met with acclaim. In the *Observer* Kathryn Flett asserted that Branagh 'has never been better than this', while in the *Independent* James Rampton described his performance as 'chilling'. Branagh would go on to win an Emmy, as well as to receive Golden Globe and BAFTA nominations for Best Actor.

Those accolades were richly deserved: Branagh's portrayal of Heydrich was mesmerising. It was precisely the matter-of-fact manner in which Branagh delivered his lines – such as: 'We will not sterilise the Jew and then exterminate the race. That's farcical. Dead men don't hump, dead women don't get pregnant. Death is the most reliable form of sterilisation, put it that way' – that was shocking. Even when Heydrich was being affable, Branagh was able to convey to the audience the inner core of cold calculation and the deficit of compassion that influenced his every move. Branagh was also convincing in his illumination of Heydrich's tactical flexibility. Heydrich's charm comes easily, but when that fails, he is prepared to adopt a sterner approach. Identifying Kritzinger (David Threlfall) and Stuckart (Colin Firth) as his chief adversaries, Branagh's Heydrich threatens them both privately in a genuinely intimidating fashion. His finest performance on television or film since Henry V in 1989, *Conspiracy* represented another milestone on the road to Branagh's artistic resurgence.

That resurgence would be sustained by a two-part television drama, *Shackleton*, in which he starred as the explorer whose 1914 expedition to the South Pole made him a legend. In what became one of the most remarkable feats of endurance in history, Shackleton's attempt to become the first man to cross the Atlantic failed when ice floes immobilised his ship. What followed was a remarkable and ultimately successful effort by Shackleton to return every man under his command to safety. In recent years there had been a renewed interest in Shackleton's endeavours. Best-selling books were penned, corporate executives studied his exemplary leadership techniques, and there was talk of a Hollywood movie in the pipeline.

Charles Sturridge, who had directed *Brideshead Revisited* and *Longitude*, conceived the idea for a television dramatisation of Shackleton's heroics. For Sturridge, the viability of the project depended on Branagh's willingness to play Shackleton; he did not want to proceed with any other actor in the role. 'At every key moment of Shackleton's struggle', he said, 'it was the way he talked to the men that changed their mood and made them go on. The one actor with the voice to make people believe what he said and the physical presence to override their hardships and inner terrors was Branagh.' It did seem to be a case of ideal casting. Branagh shared Shackleton's Anglo-Irish background, and – although in a totally different context – had exhibited marked leadership skills. He even bore an uncanny physical resemblance to the explorer. In fact when Branagh dyed his hair and gave it a centre parting, as the shoot was about to commence, *Shackleton*'s producer did a double-take, saying it looked like 'Shackleton in the flesh'.

Having identified his man, Sturridge set out to recruit him. He adopted a direct approach, firing off an e-mail to Branagh: 'Would you do a physically tough and dangerous job for not much money' – to play the greatest leader of men there had ever been? Meeting at a Chinese restaurant in London to discuss matters further, Sturridge told Branagh, 'I can't give you a script. Unless you agree to it, there's no point in my writing one.' Understanding that the success of the venture would depend in large measure on the authenticity with which Shackleton's expedition was depicted, Branagh asked: 'We're going to shoot on the ice of course?' 'Definitely,' Sturridge assured him, 'the real thing.'

As Sturridge secured a budget the like of which Britain's Channel 4 (working in tandem with America's A & E cable channel) had never before provided for a television drama, one that would ensure *Shackleton*'s production values were akin to those of a major motion picture, and the services of a supporting cast that included Mark McGann, Matt Day, Embeth Davidtz and Corin Redgrave, Branagh researched his role. He consulted diaries and archival materials, and spoke to present-day explorers. In January 2001, shortly before filming began, he visited Shackleton's alma mater Dulwich College, taking a look at its Shackleton exhibition, which included the *James Caird*, the boat in which Shackleton and his companions had made the 800-mile journey to South Georgia.

The shoot – long and hard – was a story in itself. Filming in the studio and on location in Britain was followed by a brief stint in Iceland, and then five difficult weeks in which cast and crew lived on a Russian ice-breaking ship in the frozen waters off east Greenland. On one occasion the ice floe on which they were filming began to crack and numerous pieces of equipment had to be hurriedly retrieved; and the unpredictable nature of the environment meant that the production schedule had to be constantly revised. 'When it was windy it was a nightmare,' said Branagh, 'when you were wet it was a nightmare. And even after you had just seen the most amazing biblical sky, you knew you were still in this incredibly threatening, unearthly place in which you were never likely to find yourself as a tourist.' The discomfort Branagh experienced, albeit a fraction of that which he was portraying, deepened his understanding of what Shackleton had been through emotionally. It magnified his appreciation of Shackleton's spirit, fortitude, generosity and resourcefulness – what it took Shackleton to maintain his men's self-belief. Those insights enriched his performance.

Jamie Payne, who had been hired to film a documentary on the making of *Shackleton*, noticed how Branagh maintained the morale of cast and crew during such a difficult shoot:

> What he did, which I think was absolutely essential to *Shackleton* working, was that as far as the cast were concerned he was Shackleton – not because Ken asked for it but because he's such a great leader naturally, which is one of the reasons he's perfect to play that part, that those actors really looked up to him, for reassurance as well because they were in situations where sometimes you'd step off the ice and the ice would crack and swallow a set literally five minutes after they'd stepped off the ice. There was one time when the ice was literally melting and cracking up, that it made it very dangerous to film on the ice. And it was Ken Branagh who reassured all the actors – he was out there first stepping off the boat – that it was going to be fine ... Ken's leadership skills, in a really quiet way, not wanting to tread on Charles [Sturridge]'s toes, really made a huge difference.[3]

Though it is not widely known, Branagh's role included some directing. 'There was one day ... in particular,' reveals Payne, 'where they were filming ... one of the Antarctic landings on the islands. They were really up against it, and I think Charles was exhausted and Ken took over ... Charles was very lucky to have that kind of support.'

Living with around one hundred cast and crew on an ice-breaker for over a month generated a sense of companionship, evident in the way everyone mucked in with cooking and cleaning chores when the kitchen staff were on their day off. 'There was intense emotional bonding, great generosity and a fantastic amount of banter,' recalled

Branagh, 'with everyone being ribbed senseless all the time and some filthy nicknames.' It was in this atmosphere that Branagh began what turned out to be a long-term romance with Lindsay Brunnock, who was working as an art director on the production. As he had with Helena Bonham Carter, Branagh did all he could to keep the relationship private, easier to achieve in this case as, unlike Bonham Carter, Brunnock was not a famous actress. A documentary on the making of *Shackleton*, which included a brief excerpt of an interview with Brunnock, showed her to be attractive and cheerful. Two years later, Branagh and Brunnock would marry.

Shackleton, aired on British and American television in 2002, found favour with most critics. Praise for Branagh's performance was nearly universal. He ended up receiving two BAFTA nominations for Best Actor, for Shackleton as well as for his portrayal of Heydrich in *Conspiracy*. He would lose out to Albert Finney, but compensation came with *Shackleton* and *Conspiracy* triumphing in the Best Drama Serial and Best Single Drama categories, respectively. *Shackleton* would also be nominated for a Golden Globe.

All in all, *Shackleton* and the central performance in it had succeeded. Filming on the ice was a gamble that paid off. As planned, it endowed the production with an exceptional authenticity, made for breathtaking cinematography and conveyed the sense that this was a special event in television. With both his screenplay and his direction, Charles Sturridge confirmed what was evident from his earlier work, namely that he was a lucid and fluent story-teller. Furthermore, Sturridge was accurate in his assessment that Branagh as Shackleton was a case of perfect casting. As an inspirational leader of men, Shackleton brings to mind Shakespeare's Henry V, not least when the explorer tries to rally his men by quoting Robert Browning: 'For sudden worst turns the best to the brave'; and Branagh knew just how to portray that sort of heroic leadership.

As David Hare argues, Branagh's work in *Shackleton* (and in *Conspiracy*) played to one of his strengths in that he excels with characters who can't let go: 'what do his latest, best performances as Heydrich and Shackleton have in common? Both men with a psychological need to be in control. Even his heroes – like Shackleton – have something a little repellent about them because you feel they can't ever be off-duty or spontaneous. They know the effect they have. They *calculate*. It's what he does best.'

A significant aspect of Branagh's resurgence during this period was his decision to accept a wider range of roles. Earlier in his career he had tended to avoid playing nefarious characters. Despite the variety of Shakespearean parts he had taken, for instance, there had been no Macbeth and no Richard III. But as shown by *Rabbit-Proof Fence* and *Conspiracy*, Branagh became more willing to play the villain of the piece. What was perhaps surprising to those who had Branagh down as a nice chap was that he proved effective in such roles. In playing parts that allowed him to explore the most malevolent human impulses, he was extending his range as an actor. His career, once again, was on an upward trend.

11

A Return to the Stage

Whereas Branagh's work in the second half of the 1990s had been confined to the big screen, his projects in the next decade were more broadly based. *Shackleton* had marked his television comeback, and now he planned his return to the theatre. In early 2000 he dipped his toes in the water by participating in a private reading of Yasmina Reza's *Life x 3* for financial backers of the play in New York. But then, in the autumn of 2001, after an absence that stretched back more than eight years to his Hamlet with the Royal Shakespeare Company, he came back to the theatre with *The Play What I Wrote*, a tribute to Morecambe and Wise. Like a financier who diversifies his portfolio after investing in one area, Branagh was now exploiting the best opportunities that became available in television, on stage and in film. That change explains in part the improvement in Branagh's fortunes since 2000.

It was producer David Pugh, who had enjoyed spectacular success with Yasmina Reza's *Art*, who hatched the plan to stage a tribute to Eric Morecambe and Ernie Wise, the most celebrated double act in the history of British comedy. At the peak of their popularity, in 1977, they were able to command a television audience for their Christmas special of almost 29 million, more than half the entire British population. Pugh invited the critically acclaimed double act The Right Size, comprising Sean Foley and Hamish McColl, to take on the challenge of portraying them. Initially they resisted the idea. Such was the public affection for Morecambe and Wise, they reasoned, any pale imitation of their genius would be met with derision. Once Foley and McColl came up with a solid premise for the play – they would neither impersonate Morecambe and Wise nor tell their story biographically, but put across how a double act like themselves viewed the venerable duo – they overcame their concerns.

As he mulled over the director to be recruited for the production, David Pugh cast his mind back to 1982 when, as an assistant to Robert Fox, the producer of *Another Country*, he had observed backstage a young Kenneth Branagh doing impersonations of Eric Morecambe. A conversation nineteen years later confirmed Branagh's affection for the double act. 'Do you like Morecambe and Wise?' asked Pugh. 'No,' replied Branagh. 'I adore them.' Indeed he did. As a child, he had written to them to ask for tickets for their television show, and had gratefully received the signed photo that they had sent instead. The passage of time had not lessened his admiration. In 1997 he had contacted Ernie Wise's literary agent to ask him to invite his client to the première of his film of *Hamlet*, but Wise had been too frail to attend.

Despite his long-standing affection for Morecambe and Wise, Branagh was reluctant to direct *The Play What I Wrote*. 'He was clearly having a bad time,' recalled Pugh. 'One of the reasons he said he didn't want to get involved with us at first was that he believed the production could get unfairly lampooned by the media simply because he was part of it. I said "bollocks". I told him to roll his sleeves up and get down to it.' Fear of another wave of Branagh-bashing was still influencing his thinking, but in the end he accepted Pugh's challenge. Branagh's one stipulation – in keeping with his recent drive to maintain a lower profile – was that he would not promote the play. 'Right from the beginning he said he didn't want to do any press,' said Pugh. 'He didn't want to do questions about his private life. He didn't want the focus to be on him. He wanted it to be clear it is the boys' [actors'] work.' Yet Branagh would do publicity in the United States when the play went to Broadway, consenting to an interview with *Time Out New York* and actually writing an article himself for the *New York Times*. This said a good deal about his distrust of English journalists vis-à-vis their American counterparts.

As Hamish McColl and Sean Foley pushed on with the writing of the play, they were aided by Eddie Braben, who had spent fourteen years writing for Morecambe and Wise. Contributing fresh material to *The Play What I Wrote*, Braben said he could hear Eric Morecambe's voice in his ear as he wrote, assuring him, 'Now that's funny.' Serving as a consultant on the production was Gary Morecambe, Eric's son, to whom Branagh revealed his ambitions for the project: 'I want this play not just to work but to be huge.'

The play fashioned by McColl and Foley tells the story of two characters, Hamish and Sean, who make up a struggling double act. In response to a threat from Hamish, the straight man, to quit so that he can become a serious playwright – risible, given his command of the English language – Sean tries to save the act by telling Hamish that he has managed to get a West End booking and a major star for Hamish's dreadful play *A Tight Squeeze for the Scarlet Pimple*. In fact Sean has promised the producer a more commercially viable show, a tribute to Morecambe and Wise, and hopes he can cajole Hamish into going along with the idea at the last moment. Certain that no stars will be willing to perform in Hamish's play, Sean recruits his mate Arthur (played by Toby Jones) to impersonate them. The play has a rich comic variety to it. Song and dance, slapstick, impersonation, ventriloquism, malapropisms and drag are all part of the mix.

This was the material with which Branagh would be working as director. Initially McColl and Foley were bemused to be collaborating with a noted Shakespearean on a play about two stand-up comedians. 'Kenneth Branagh walks around his house in Elizabethan tights,' said Foley, recalling their attitude. 'What does he have to do with us?' But once the four-week rehearsal period was under way, they found themselves pleasantly surprised by their director, who gave the impression of enjoying the simplicity of his surroundings – just himself and the three actors working away in a room in Highbury, north London. As he had with John Sessions' one-man shows in the 1980s, he ensured that a discipline was imposed on the actors' comic exuberance. 'We are a couple of professional idiots, who can improvise until the building falls down,' said Foley, 'but Ken imposes a sharpness on the overall performance.' Toby Jones recalls the emphasis Branagh placed on pacing – 'he was very rigorous about the show pinging along' – and the identification and removal of material that would work with a fringe audience but not necessarily in the West End. During its pre-West End run at Liverpool's Everyman Playhouse, however, the production's rough edges remained evident. Branagh worked hard to smooth them out. He was relentless, for instance, in making sure the choreography was precise and well practised.

As well as directing the play, Branagh also needed to recruit a series of surprise celebrity guests who would agree to appear in Hamish's

A Tight Squeeze for the Scarlet Pimple, and in so doing suffer the sort of humiliation inflicted by Morecambe and Wise on the luminaries who came on their show. For this, the contacts established by Branagh during his career were helpful. Most important was enlisting the services of a major star for the opening night at Wyndham's Theatre. Ralph Fiennes was the actor he wanted. Taking him to lunch to court him, Branagh gave Fiennes a taste of the dialogue that had been devised, including a reference to the pronunciation of his name:

HAMISH: Good evening, Ralph.
RALPH: It's Rafe!
SEAN: Well, put some cream on it.

As Branagh continued to explain the show, including the impersonation of Fiennes in *The English Patient* by Toby Jones, who would appear on stage with a bandage on his head mumbling, 'There's a posh bird out in the desert, rolling rags in a cave,' Fiennes began to laugh uncontrollably. Branagh assured him the audience would be laughing not at him but with him. 'I prefer to think', interjected Fiennes, 'that they'll be laughing near me.' Branagh's powers of persuasion had worked: Fiennes agreed to be the guest star on opening night.

Fiennes and the other guest stars needed to be rehearsed, and Simon Callow, who appeared early in the run, gives an account of how Branagh influenced those preparations. Along with the actors and the assistant director, the guest star would work on his or her portion of the play. Then Branagh would give his input. Callow recalls receiving 'half a dozen terribly astute notes. They were absolutely spot on and very useful.' Branagh was crucial in tightening up the performance, feels Callow, who was left with a favourable impression of his director: 'He is a brilliant mechanic of the theatre.'

On opening night the audience included not only the widows of Eric Morecambe and Ernie Wise but also many household names from the ranks of British comedy, including Rowan Atkinson, Ronnie Corbett, Frank Skinner, Ben Elton and Bruce Forsyth. By the interval, the actors knew they had a hit on their hands. Toby Jones has a vivid memory of Hamish McColl and Sean Foley cheering and jumping off the tables in their dressing room, so thrilled had they been by the audience response. No one seemed to enjoy the show more than Ralph Fiennes' partner Francesca Annis, who was spotted roaring with laughter. A crop of rave reviews followed the next day. 'The funniest and most inventive new comedy of the year,' enthused Michael Coveney, while Michael Billington wrote in the *Guardian* of his admiration for the 'genuine pace and invention' with which Branagh had directed the show. In the *Financial Times* Alastair Macaulay explained well the production's appeal:

> This isn't imitation, this isn't homage, it's something deeper. It's spiritual affinity. You don't feel you've seen Morecambe and Wise all over again. You feel you've been taken back into that state of blithe, daft, transporting bliss into which, for decades, Morecambe and Wise used to take their British audience. It's been months since I laughed quite so much as I did here, and yet that's not the most important thing. *The Play What I Wrote* is cathartic, and it is clever enough to let you see that. I left feeling that I'd come through laughter into some rare condition of childlike rapture.

Once these reviews were out, box-office takings soared. Within three days the advance went from $31,460 to $730,730 (as reported in an American source), breaking a record held by Alan Bennett's *The Lady in the Van*. Critical acclaim and commercial success were followed by prestigious honours. *The Play What I Wrote* won the Olivier Award for best new comedy of the year, and Toby Jones received an Olivier for Best Actor in a Supporting Role. After more than three hundred West End performances, the production moved to Broadway in the spring of 2003, attracting such guest stars as Liam Neeson, Kevin Kline and Glenn Close, running for 116 performances (including previews) and earning a Tony Award nomination for Best Special Theatrical Event. The play was changed so as to avoid any references to Morecambe and Wise, whose fame had not crossed the Atlantic, but in the process the sense of nostalgia enjoyed by London audiences was lessened. The one troubling moment of the New York run came when Roger Moore collapsed on stage with respiratory problems, bringing the show to a halt. Pluckily he completed the performance before being rushed to a Manhattan hospital, where he made a swift recovery.

Through it all, Branagh relished the collaboration with the procession of guest stars, marvelling at the extent to which they willingly contributed to their own humiliation. When Foley and McColl were searching for a misnomer for Liam Neeson, it was the actor himself who revealed that fans sometimes referred to him as 'Leslie Nielsen'. Likewise it was Sting who came up with the idea of having a communication brought to him on stage in the form of a message in a bottle.

Branagh did not endorse all of the guest stars' suggestions. In rehearsals Dawn French handed him a list of her ideas for the show. After reading them, he whispered to her: 'No!' The guest star with whom Branagh seemed least satisfied was himself. As he recalls it, he forgot his name, fell over during the dance and contrived to walk into a piece of scenery.

By the summer of 2004, some three years after its opening, *The Play What I Wrote* was continuing to entertain audiences across Britain. Part of its success can be attributed to the mood of glorious silliness it evokes, and part to the hypnotically high energy level it sustains as the jokes and comic action come thick and fast. By appearing to deflate the egos of its guest stars, it also provides a refreshing alternative to the mindless celebrity-worship that has become such a prominent feature of contemporary popular culture. One suspects that some of the actors who agreed to appear in *The Play What I Wrote* did so in part because of their own understanding of the absurdity of modern celebrity culture. The eyebrow it raises at celebrity, though, is not the only reason for the surprising depth of *The Play What I Wrote*. It serves too as a meditation on the psychology of the double act. Hamish, the straight man, is dogged by fears he is unfunny and thus superfluous, despite assurances from Arthur that the silences he hears when performing are in fact delayed laughs, anticipated laughs and inaudible laughs. Hamish needs to hear from Sean, the funny man, as he does by the play's end, that it is not a case of him, Sean, getting the laughs, but rather it is the vital interaction between the two of them that generates the humour.

The timing of the show was also significant. In the wake of the tragedy of 11 September 2001, one might have thought the opening of a joyously silly production such as *The Play What I Wrote* could not have been less opportune, given the public mood. Indeed this was an issue that had concerned Branagh and the cast during rehearsals. The success of the show was doubtful, they thought, as it would be years before anyone would want to laugh again. As things turned out, it was perfectly timed: an escape from all that pain and horror, just like those comedies and musicals that provided relief to movie audiences in 1930s America during the Great Depression.

As *The Play What I Wrote* opened in the West End, some journalists began to speak of a Branagh revival. In the *Daily Express* on 6 November 2001 Anna Pukas wrote:

> As comebacks go, it is very Kenneth Branagh. After several years in the wilderness of mediocrity, making a couple of indifferent films and a few truly ghastly ones, the Golden Boy of British acting is back in the sun again, his sheen more burnished than ever.
>
> It has been an extraordinary 48 hours for Branagh. It began on Sunday when he won a best actor Emmy (the Oscar of the television world) for his powerful performance in the made-for-TV movie *Conspiracy*. He had not travelled to Los Angeles for the ceremony, only because last night saw the opening of his new West End venture as director of *The Play What I Wrote*.

Five days later Jay Rayner's theme in an *Observer* profile of Branagh was the same: 'Is Nothing Beyond Our Ken? Apparently not. Just as our greatest living Shakespearian actor seems to have lost his way, he comes back with an Emmy, a West End hit and a stage return with *Richard III*.' His Richard III would materialise a few months later.

His next project held the promise of success on a global scale. The first Harry Potter film, based on the opening book in J. K. Rowling's monumentally popular series about the young wizard's exploits at his school, Hogwarts, had been a box-office phenomenon, raking in almost $1 billion for Warner Brothers. For the next movie, *Harry Potter and the Chamber of Secrets*, again directed by Chris Columbus, a Steven Spielberg protégé whose previous hits included *Home Alone* and *Mrs Doubtfire*, a new actor had to be cast for a character who had not appeared in the first novel, Gilderoy Lockhart, the vain Defence Against the Dark Arts teacher. Lockhart proves inept as Harry and his chums try to cope with the opening of the iniquitous chamber created by a malcontent founder of Hogwarts. It was reported that Hugh Grant had been in the running for the part, but Columbus happened to be an admirer of Branagh's film work, especially *Much Ado About Nothing*, *The Gingerbread Man*, and *Henry V*, which he rated 'one of the few flawless [cinematic] adaptations of Shakespeare'. He believed that Branagh's ability 'to disappear in any role' would serve the second Harry Potter film well, and so offered him the part. At their first meeting, Columbus recalls, Branagh 'wanted to assure me that just because he was a director didn't mean he would interfere with the directorial side of making the film ... He made it absolutely clear to me ... that he was working for me as an actor and he would give me whatever I wanted.'

The shoot, which took place just outside London at Leavesden Studios, was initially hectic, as Branagh had to divide his time between acting on *Harry Potter* and guiding the early West End run of *The Play What I Wrote*. That did not dilute his enthusiasm for the film. 'I'm delighted to be involved in the high adventures of young Harry,' he declared, particularly because of his admiration for Rowling's books. 'Her construction, the moral tone, the gallery of characters,' he said, reminded him of Dickens.

The movie allowed him to work with a veritable *Who's Who* of British stars of stage and screen, including Maggie Smith, Alan Rickman and Richard Harris. He especially enjoyed bantering with Rickman. 'I'm a huge fan of his,' Branagh revealed. 'Just the sitting and chewing the cud stuff was really exciting. He's so smart and he has a million stories. We had great fun.' Much of Branagh's screen time, though, was spent with the three young leads, Daniel Radcliffe (Harry Potter), Emma Watson (Hermione) and Rupert Grint (Ron). Branagh struck up a rapport with them too. He found success had not gone to their heads, and they spoke afterwards of his affability and humour.

With Gilderoy Lockhart, Branagh had the opportunity to play a comically narcissistic peacock of a man, a sort of cross between Malvolio and Marc Bolan. The flamboyance of his appearance – he dresses like a dandy, has curly golden hair and a smile as beaming as Tony Blair's – matches the exuberance of his personality. Hired to teach at Hogwarts, this publicity-seeking charlatan is intent on filching Harry Potter's fame. The girls fancy him, and he likes to show off to them. As a character, Lockhart brings colour and comedy to the story. Much of the humour derives from the discrepancy between Lockhart's claims to excellence in wizardry and the incompetence he shows on a regular basis. In a magic duel with Professor Snape (Rickman), for instance, Lockhart ends up on his backside.

Branagh played this larger-than-life character with gusto. 'The character on the page struck me as someone who must come across as just having a great time,' he explained; 'there was no point in approaching Gilderoy in any way other than a full-blooded spirit of complete daftness.' On the other hand Branagh, encouraged by his director, was keen to suggest a thinly concealed insecurity on the part of Lockhart, to show the diffidence he feels when challenged to display the virtuosity in wizardry he knows he lacks. That vulnerability would ensure that the audience retained a soft spot for a character they would otherwise find unappealing.

As filming progressed, Chris Columbus was more than satisfied with the work done by Branagh, noting the ease with which he could vary his performance from take to take, to make his character more comic or more theatrical or more insecure. As a result, says Columbus, 'he gave me a lot of different choices in the editing room'. His overall evaluation of Branagh's acting is equally positive:

> In a Harry Potter film or a fantasy-oriented film ... you don't tend to lean toward the comedic side of things ... [But] he provided us with an amazing amount of comic relief every day we watched the rushes because 90 per cent of it didn't end up in the film and we saw all of those choices every day at lunch; and it was staggering ... he is completely driven, and gives you 150 per cent all the time ... Truly one of the best I've ever worked with.[1]

Branagh's eye-catching performance contributed to the film's impact when it was released in November 2002. Not only did it enjoy blockbuster success at the box office, not only did critics concur that it was superior to the previous Harry Potter film, but many of them felt that Branagh had stolen the show. For Branagh, the most meaningful validation came from J. K. Rowling herself, who told him at the première, 'You were loathsome. It was brilliant.' Branagh would go on to win the London Film Critics' award for Best British Actor in a Supporting Role for his performance in *Harry Potter*. His purple patch had been sustained.

Once again Branagh let his work speak for itself. He did very little press for *Harry Potter*, and what he did do was confined to overseas journalists – from the United States, Canada and the Philippines. Talk in the English press of Branagh having become a recluse had started by this point, but when asked by the Canadian media whether it was an appropriate label he simply said, 'I've just been getting on with what I've been doing, basically.' Besides, he added, the Harry Potter movie hardly needed his help to guarantee its success.

For a time it seemed Branagh's involvement with the Harry Potter films would continue. With Chris Columbus deciding against directing the third movie in the series, Branagh emerged as a candidate to succeed him when he made it on to a short list of film-makers. In the end, though, the producers gave the job to Alfonso Cuaron, whose 2001 film *Y Tu Mamá También* had been much admired.

A few months after starting work on *Harry Potter*, in the spring of 2002, a landmark event occurred: Branagh returned to the stage as an actor, taking on the challenge of Richard III. It was a role that had long intrigued him. He had considered playing it a decade earlier, and in 1999 he had stated that, were he to act again in the theatre, the part he wished to play was Shakespeare's crookback.

Then, in 2001, Michael Grandage, who had been running the Sheffield Crucible with great success, luring stars such as Joseph Fiennes up to Yorkshire, contacted Branagh to ask him to consider a part in a production he was directing at London's Donmar Warehouse. With his customary promptness in responding to such offers, Branagh got back to Grandage within twenty-four hours, saying that, while the part did not appeal to him, he would like to meet to discuss other projects. Accordingly, they lunched at a West London restaurant. Branagh told Grandage that he had decided to return to the stage, and to do so in a Shakespearean role. His preference was for Richard III. Grandage recalls thinking that Branagh was too young for the part, but that as the meal went on it dawned on him he was talking not to the trailblazing artist of the 1980s but to someone who was in early middle age and at exactly the right point at which to tackle Richard. That very evening Grandage read the play with Branagh in mind as Richard. He was excited by the prospect, informing Branagh that he would like to direct him at the Sheffield Crucible. Aware of the work being done at Sheffield to reach out to younger audiences and the local community in general, Branagh was happy to make his comeback in Yorkshire.

Why had Branagh chosen this avenue – Michael Grandage and the Sheffield Crucible – to make his return as an actor on the stage? For one thing, he had taken in some of Grandage's productions, including his flawless *As You Like It*, and liked what he had seen. For another, Grandage's approach – a preference for minimalist sets, and productions that were not concept- and design-led but actor-centred, with an emphasis on clarity and accessibility in classical work – meshed with his own, as expressed in the work of his Renaissance company a decade or so earlier.

As with his tackling of Henry V back in the 1980s, Branagh's consideration of the part of Richard could not have failed to include an awareness of the distinguished portrayals of yesteryear. Most famously, Olivier's gleefully malevolent performance in his own film of the play had left an indelible impression. But there had also been notable stage interpretations in recent years, particularly those by Antony Sher on crutches and by Ian McKellen as a fascist dictator. If Branagh was aiming for a Richard III that stayed in the memory, as he surely was, these actors had set the bar high.

Shortly before commencing work on *Richard III* at the Crucible, Branagh prepared for the role by making for Naxos AudioBooks what would turn out to be an award-winning recording of the play, with himself in the lead. (Enjoying the medium, he would go on to record *King Lear* for Naxos, playing the Fool to Paul Scofield's Lear.) Doing *Richard III* as an audiobook played to one of Branagh's strengths – his exceptional vocal technique. The recording was spellbinding, the opening soliloquy sending shivers down the spine.

In readying himself for his stage performance in Sheffield, Branagh read biographies of Richard III, and visited the places associated with his life, including the Tower of London and Bosworth battlefield; but he did not wish to pre-determine his interpretation to an inordinate extent, feeling the rehearsal process should exert its due influence. Both the research undertaken by Branagh and his ability to remain open to fresh ideas were apparent to Michael Grandage as rehearsals got under way. 'He works ... very hard in advance of a rehearsal process,' notes Grandage:

> That's not unique in actors but it's unusual the amount of prep he does. There's one significant factor about him that I have not come across in anyone else, which is that he does a significant amount of preparation and yet remains very fluid in the rehearsal process. So the performance isn't entirely worked out ... [he had] the ability to change with a good note or getting something off another actor that he hadn't anticipated ... It's like he can hold 150 different things at any one time in his head, and act on any one of them within a second.[2]

Grandage was also struck by the importance Branagh attached to maintaining a congenial working atmosphere:

> He's not interested in conflict, and I think some actors' process is helped by conflict, whether it's internally in the rehearsal room with other actors or with their director or with themselves. I think he probably has a lot of conflict within himself sometimes in order to get to a place. If he does, he doesn't share that. But when he's in a process that involves other people he's clear and adamant that a conflict-free environment produces the best work; and I have to say I am in total agreement with that ... I believe that the best work comes out of a relaxed atmosphere, and that is absolutely Ken's philosophy. He brings it to everything he does. So conflict, where it even raises its head, is deflected. And from that point of view I have never worked with a more skilful actor ever about dealing with so many elements of the process that aren't to do with the building of their own character.[3]

It was in this supportive environment that Branagh developed his interpretation of Richard. He decided that it is anger that drives Richard rather than any depressive tendencies. He wanted to show Richard's frustration at being unable to become king naturally by consent despite being smarter and wittier than anyone else. It was also

Branagh who introduced the notion of traction. Early on in his discussions with Grandage, he said: 'Can we talk about what this man wants? I think he wants to be a perfect man. If he is as disabled as this character is, I think his entire life is about wanting to be like everybody else – straight-backed and upright ... Maybe we can even go as far as thinking about this man in traction.' This led to the design of the rack-like contraption to which Branagh's Richard would be strapped at the start of the play.

The biggest problem facing Branagh as opening night approached was his nervousness. When learning the lines for Richard back in the autumn of 2001, Branagh had told Toby Jones how tense he felt about returning to the stage. If anything, those nerves had multiplied by the time he got to Sheffield. 'He was fantastically nervous,' confirms Michael Grandage, 'and I think probably went through moments of great self-doubt about his ability to get on stage. But what happened was in the end an innate professionalism kept taking over ... I think there were some real demons to be faced about having to go back on stage after ten years away, and somewhere there was an internal battle going on about his need to get over it and get on stage and go, "Yes, here I am."' Helping to calm the nerves that Branagh felt were two of his closest friends, Gerard Horan, cast as Clarence, and Jimmy Yuill, who would play Hastings.

What the public got to see when *Richard III* opened was a production that in many ways could have been expected from the Renaissance Theatre Company had it still been up and running. Unencumbered by an overarching concept or an over-elaborate design, the emphasis was on lucid speaking of the verse and on the narrative drive of the play. Cuts to the text, making for a relatively pacey production at two hours forty minutes, had not been resisted. Branagh's portrayal of Richard included an emphasis on the performative aspect of his character. In that sense Branagh was an actor playing an actor. The opening of the play saw Branagh's Richard semi-naked, strapped to the rack-like contraption, putting on the clothes and calipers needed to conceal, at least in part, his physical deformity. His appearance of relative normality was thus an act. Likewise his manipulation of other characters required him to affect whatever personality facet was needed to achieve his objectives, be it charm or affability or wit or indignation. Branagh was particularly effective at maximising the comedic impact of the lines, and at establishing a strong rapport with the audience.

The critics were almost unanimous in their assessment of Branagh's Richard. This, they asserted, was a very good performance, though not a great one. In *The Times* Benedict Nightingale said: '[Branagh] fares better on his return to the stage than I had dared hope,' while Charles Spencer of the *Daily Telegraph* wrote that he had 'swept away almost all my reservations during his compelling performance in Michael Grandage's fine new production'.

Alastair Macaulay of the *Financial Times* also sang Branagh's praises. Listening to him speak the verse, it occurred to Macaulay that the hackneyed comparison made between Olivier and Branagh was ill-judged, and that a more useful parallel could be drawn with Gielgud:

> Nothing prepared me in his Shakespeare films for seeing *Richard III* live. That was the real revelation of what he's like as a Shakespearean actor. And it was the voice that was the revelation ... What hit me straightaway with *Richard III* is [his] ... speaking the speech trippingly on the tongue. His voice in the theatre is perfectly focused. It comes from support in the diaphragm and the chest, and the voice is right there in front of the face so he can speak very fast and without any artifice. I don't know that I've ever heard an actor who can project fast Shakespearean diction without it seeming at all period or mannered. I was amazed at how modern a lot of the lines seemed ... all the words, as I remember, were completely audible and natural ... Once I heard Branagh do that Richard III in the theatre I thought that was much like that effortless, vast connection to the verse and the ability to get the pulse of the verse and the diction of the words naturally ... [that] Gielgud always had and what Olivier always had to work at, against the grain ... Branagh, without having anything of the same kind of voice [as Gielgud], just has that [same] gift ... With him [Branagh] it's something more colloquial. I think it must be something he gets from his Northern Irish background. I don't pretend to know what that is. But it's just doing it for our generation naturally.[4]

The one shortcoming identified by the critics was Branagh's inability to weave into his performance a strong enough sense of disturbing malevolence. 'One yearns for a touch of genuine diabolism,' Michael Billington's observation in the *Guardian*, was a shared sentiment. That Branagh had the capability to convey that sort of malignancy has been demonstrated. Consider his shocking portrayal of Heydrich in *Conspiracy*, the audio recording of *Richard III* he had produced a year earlier, and the stage performance he would soon deliver in *Edmond*. One has the sense that for Branagh, Richard III could be akin to his Hamlet. It might take a second attempt to produce something truly exceptional – in this case by accentuating the villainy of the character. Still, Branagh's comeback had been marked by a very able performance, approval from the critics – and an ecstatic public response. With bookings taken not only from all over Britain but from Japan, France, Germany, Italy, Holland and the United States, *Richard III* became the fastest-selling show in the Crucible's history. Not surprisingly, numerous producers offered to take it to the West End or to Broadway. Branagh decided against the idea. Feeling that he had explored the character of Richard quite fully, he wanted to move on to other projects.

What became clear by 2003 was that *The Play What I Wrote* and *Richard III* were part of a renewed commitment to the stage that would be maintained. It was announced early in the year that he would make his debut at the National Theatre in the title role of David Mamet's *Edmond*. But before *Edmond* opened it was revealed, in May 2003, very much out of the blue, that Branagh had married Lindsay Brunnock, the art director to whom he had become attached during the making of *Shackleton*. This development came as something of a surprise because only five months earlier their break-up, due allegedly to his unwillingness at that time to marry her, had been made public. But in a small, clandestine ceremony in the New York apartment of the actors from *The Play What I Wrote* during its run in the Big Apple, Branagh and Brunnock had tied the knot. 'He rang us a week before,' recalls Toby Jones, 'and said "I want to get married in New York"; and I remember [thinking] why does he want to come here. He got a disguise together ... and went down to City Hall ... and we came back and had this beautiful, very private ceremony. We read at his wedding ... and it was just this really happy day.' Only seven people attended, and many of his friends did not find out about it until afterwards. The occasion was so different from his wedding with Emma Thompson.

Asked later to explain why he had suddenly been prepared to make this commitment, Branagh answered simply, 'I love my wife.' As to whether he would have taken this step at an earlier point in time, he reflected: 'I don't know ... and I think I think about it less ... and a journey in my life now is to be less analytical, and more helpfully for me, following one's instinct ... and in this case my heart ... and feeling happy to do so ... privileged to do so ... and being aware that there's something more powerful at work than my ability to understand it intellectually.'

Shortly after his appointment as successor to Trevor Nunn as the artistic director of the National Theatre, Nicholas Hytner asked

Branagh whether he would be interested in directing or acting on the South Bank. 'He has always been a major energy in British theatre and film,' Hytner told the press. 'His energy, intelligence and invention, as well as his experience and authority in a big theatre, is something I felt we really needed here. He is absolutely the kind of major, charismatic actor we want at the National. He is a stage animal.' Following on from that initial discussion, and as part of the consultative culture fostered by Hytner, playwrights Patrick Marber and Mark Ravenhill encouraged outstanding young director Edward Hall, whose recent successes had included *Rose Rage* and *The Constant Wife*, to revive *Edmond*, David Mamet's blistering 1980s morality tale about the journey of one seemingly ordinary man towards self-destruction. Taken with the idea, Hall asked Branagh if he was interested in the lead role. Branagh said he would read the play and let him know within four days. Struck by the power of Mamet's writing, Branagh felt 'compelled' to accept the challenge, 'which is not quite the same as wanting to do it'.

Edmond is a shocking play, in the best sense of the word. Hearing from a fortune-teller that in his life he is not where he belongs, Edmond leaves his wife and seeks adventure in the fleshpots of New York City. Polite, even nerdy at the start, he is coarsened by his encounters with the seedy side of the Big Apple. Assaulted by a card-sharp, treated unsympathetically by a hotel desk clerk, ignored by a woman when trying to strike up a conversation, Edmond explodes with rage. He stabs a pimp, murders a waitress, and spews forth a torrent of racist and homophobic abuse. Apprehended and incarcerated, Edmond achieves a strange piece of mind, and the play ends intriguingly when he kisses tenderly the gargantuan black prisoner who has earlier raped him.

Edmond operates on many levels. One is the almost Hamletian search of one man for meaning from his life. Linked to that is a spiritual dimension. Inspired by an evangelical preacher he encounters but unimpressed by a prison chaplain's observations, Edmond considers whether he can reasonably hope for solace beyond the dehumanising, unforgiving world he has thus far experienced. In the final scene, alone with his cell mate, he ponders that question:

EDMOND: Maybe we're here to be punished. (*Pause.*) Do you think there's a Hell?
PRISONER: I don't know. (*Pause.*)

EDMOND: Do you think that we are there?
PRISONER: I don't know, man. (*Pause.*)
EDMOND: Do you think that we go somewhere when we die?
PRISONER: I don't know, man. I *like* to think so.
EDMOND: I would, too.[5]

These themes are explored in a play which, because of its twenty-three brief scenes, has the feel of a film or television entertainment. The dialogue is likewise fast-paced, with the rapid and rhythmical language that is Mamet's hallmark very much in evidence.

With only three and a half weeks scheduled for rehearsals, Branagh and the rest of the cast had to be on their mettle. It was helpful that Branagh arrived knowing his lines word perfect. He worked with Hall on individual scenes, then on clusters of consecutive scenes, and finally on the play as a whole. Hall would later wax lyrical about his collaboration with Branagh, saying, 'He's faster than anyone I've ever worked with – a genius.' He particularly admired the way Branagh was concerned with locating the truths of the play in a general sense rather than focusing exclusively on his own part.

As opening night approached, Branagh established the routine he would maintain throughout the run. He would take breakfast, along with various vitamin supplements, but then eat nothing else prior to performance. Arriving at the National Theatre at 6 p.m., he would devote thirty minutes to meditation in order to clear his mind before the show started. At the end of the performance he would be on an adrenalin-induced high.

It may have struck Branagh that there was something auspicious about his debut at the National in the summer of 2003. *Edmond* would be staged in the Olivier Theatre, *Henry V* was playing at the National at the same time, and as part of a special discounted season most of the tickets in the Olivier were only £10 – during his absence from the theatre Branagh had said working in film had made him conscious of how expensive and hence relatively inaccessible theatre was, and that ideally he would like to return to the stage only when that state of affairs had changed.

Opening on 17 July 2003, *Edmond* proved to be an absolute triumph for Branagh. Michael Billington described his performance in the *Guardian* as 'mesmerising', Charles Spencer of the *Daily Telegraph* thought him in 'superb form', while Alastair Macaulay argued in the *Financial Times* that Branagh's technical gifts, particularly his vocal dexterity, had made for an outstanding piece of work. 'That was another revelation for me for the same reasons really as Richard III,' recalls Macaulay, 'just hearing how he could use that voice, because *Edmond* is, I would call it, brilliantly metric prose, that like Beckett, like Pinter, you play Mamet for the rhythm; and learning what he could do with the rhythm of Mamet was maybe the greatest revelation of all ... I just can't have enough of him doing either verse or metric prose.' The public reaction was equally rapturous. Soon every ticket was sold. On the two occasions I saw *Edmond* the audience response was ecstatic. It was a tonic for Branagh. Richard Briers, who took him and Lindsay Brunnock to the Garrick Club after seeing the show, recalls noticing that it had done 'a lot for his confidence, to get back to the theatre ... that and Richard III'.

Branagh's Edmond was a *tour de force*, a performance of blistering power that ranks along with his Henry V, Hamlet and Heydrich as the finest he has delivered. What he demonstrated, as he had consistently of late, was that the darkest roles, those that called upon him to portray feelings of fury, hatred and prejudice, were within his range as an actor. When he verbally and physically assaulted a pimp, there were audible gasps of astonishment in the audience. The observation had been made periodically that his niceness, his solidness, his apparent lack of angst and emotional complexity suggested that he would not be able to excel in sinister roles. *Edmond* proved otherwise.

What his portrayal of Edmond also suggested, however, was the paradoxically beneficial impact on his acting of the blows he had received since 1989, both in terms of the rather brutal attacks on his professional reputation and the vicissitudes of his personal life. Despite the technique and imagination they can bring to bear, actors, fundamentally, present facets of themselves. The difference between Branagh in 2003 and Branagh in the 1980s was that, owing to his experiences in the intervening period, there was more hurt, and probably more anger too. The trials and tribulations that had so vexed him had ended up plugging the one gap in his emotional repertoire as an actor. His performance in *Conspiracy* on television, as Richard III on audiotape, and then as Edmond on stage demonstrated this was the case. He was now a more complete actor than he had ever been.

His performance as Edmond was striking not only for the anger he conveyed, but for the kaleidoscope of character facets he was able to present. Edmond's politeness, his concern with social proprieties – the veneer which thinly disguised the more powerful emotions that would come crashing through – was made clear, as were his sense of curiosity and his concern with philosophical issues about life and death. Edmond's unintentionally comic dimension was also portrayed effectively – haggling with prostitutes to get the best deal possible; the deadpan manner in which he tells his wife he is leaving her because she does not interest him 'spiritually or sexually', and his matter-of-fact explanation for the mayhem he has caused and the murder he has perpetrated: 'I think I'd just had too much coffee.'

Edmond, in short, was one of the performances of his life. In the Whatsonstage.com Theatregoers' Choice Awards, the only major stage prizes voted for by the public, audiences selected Branagh as Best Actor of the Year for Edmond. He also received Best Actor nominations from the Olivier and *Evening Standard* theatre awards. Not surprisingly, Branagh spoke of his interest in working again with Edward Hall and Nicholas Hytner.

Edmond completed what had been for Branagh a smooth and successful return to the stage over the course of the previous two years – 2001: *The Play What I Wrote*, a hit; 2002: *Richard III*, a hit; 2003: *Edmond*, a hit. He had planned his comeback with no small degree of shrewdness. Not only had he chosen challenging material, but he had identified individuals who could help him produce his best work. Michael Grandage and Edward Hall were among the most exciting young directors in Britain, and Branagh's decision to put himself at their disposal showed that he had kept a close eye on what had been happening in the theatre during his absence. That this renewed commitment to the stage will be maintained seems likely. He was due to direct Sean Foley and Hamish McColl in the summer of 2005 in *Ducktastic*, which would open at the Theatre Royal Newcastle before transferring to the West End. No doubt Branagh, Foley and McColl hoped for the same sort of success that they had enjoyed when working together on *The Play What I Wrote*. In addition, Michael Grandage reports that he has spoken with Branagh about tackling Macbeth at London's Donmar Warehouse by 2006.

Branagh's stage comeback during this period could have been even more dramatic. One of my interviewees revealed that when the Royal Shakespeare Company was looking to appoint a successor as artistic director to Adrian Noble, Branagh – along with Sam Mendes – was approached before Noble's successor, Michael Boyd, had been installed. I was told that Branagh or Mendes would have been appointed on their own terms had either of them been interested. Branagh certainly had the leadership and organisational skills for such an undertaking. He had a proven ability to attract major talent, as his previous work with Gielgud, Scofield, Jacobi and Dench demonstrated. It would have been an appropriate and eye-catching appointment too: the world's most famous Shakespearean running the Royal Shakespeare Company. Branagh may have decided that such an onerous job would have had a deleterious impact on his ability to sustain his film career. Running a major company would perhaps make more sense a decade down the road.

Edmond was not Branagh's only undertaking in the summer of 2003. He also acted in *Five Children and It*, a film version of E. C. Nesbit's story, as the mad uncle visited by a group of children who are granted one wish a day by a sand fairy they dig up. Directed by John Stephenson at Shepperton Studios and on location on the Isle of Man, *Five Children and It* combined live action, animatronics, and special computer effects. This was something fans of Branagh's performance in *Harry Potter* could enjoy, as the film opened in Britain in the autumn of 2004.

Also during *Edmond*'s run at the National Theatre Branagh unveiled *Listening*, a short film he had written and directed. Starring Paul McGann and Frances Barber, shot in a week in Branagh's house and grounds, *Listening* tells the story of an encounter between a man and a woman at a rural retreat where people come to escape and recover from the pressures of modern life. Abiding by the retreat's rule that there should be no talking, the two central characters communicate through mime. It soon becomes apparent that a romantic connection has been established, but the story ends poignantly with Frances Barber's character departing without learning the man's secret: he is deaf. 'For me,' explained Branagh, 'it was a marvellous way to explore a compressed narrative where very little was said (a real challenge for me!), and where picture, sound and silence try to work in a different relationship than in my other work.' Beautifully shot by director of photography Alex Thomson, *Listening* is enigmatic and moving. It was screened at various film festivals across Europe and the United States, earning Branagh a Best Director award at the Rhode Island Film Festival. The short film is evidently something for which he has a particular flair. His other such venture, *Swan Song*, received an Oscar nomination a decade earlier.

The second half of 2003 had been hectic for Branagh. Accordingly, he slowed down during the early months of 2004. But by the summer he was gearing up for new work. First, he was set to appear alongside Tom Cruise in *Mission Impossible 3*. Cruise looked forward to their collaboration: 'Kenneth Branagh is one of the finest actors out there, and, to this day, I envy his portrayal of Henry V. I've seen just about everything Ken's done, including his TV role as Nazi henchman Reinhard Heydrich – and that was just so scary.' *Mission Impossible 3* had all the makings of a hit, but as production was postponed until the following summer Branagh had to pull out because of a schedule clash. Second, HBO cast him as Franklin Roosevelt in *Warm Springs*, a television movie about his pre-presidential years. Centring on the time FDR spent in Georgia attempting to recover from polio, and co-starring Cynthia Nixon of *Sex and the City* fame as Eleanor Roosevelt, filming took place in the autumn. Branagh was also busy planning future projects. He worked away on various screenplays, including a romantic comedy and an adaptation of *The Play What I Wrote*, and spoke of his interest in making a series of short films, following on from *Listening*, about the other four senses.

Overshadowing these developments was the news, reported in the British press, that Branagh was set to return to film directing. Having decided to finance a movie of Mozart's *The Magic Flute*, the arts philanthropist Sir Peter Moores identified Branagh as the man who – with his track record in popularising Shakespeare – could do the same for opera. By early 2005 Branagh was casting the film, and the possibility that he would act in as well as direct *The Magic Flute* was also reported. Filming was set for 2006.

Then, in March 2005, *Variety* announced that the following month Branagh would return to directing Shakespeare films with *As You Like It*. He had persuaded HBO Films to back the project, and had cast Kevin Kline, Bryce Dallas Howard and Adrian Lester along with old friends Jimmy Yuill and Brian Blessed. The news that he was to resume his work as a maker of Shakespeare movies was significant. It showed that his film of *Love's Labour's Lost* had not marked the end of his crusade to popularise Shakespeare. That important work would continue.

On the personal front things seemed tranquil. When an interviewer for a student newspaper phoned Branagh on a Friday evening in early 2004, he was surprised to hear that this Shakespearean actor was eating a Chinese take-away with Lindsay Brunnock whilst settling down to a night in front of the television to watch *Top of the Pops* and some soaps. 'He seems to be very content at the moment,' Richard Briers told me around the same time, 'and genuinely happy.'

By the autumn of 2004, Branagh could reflect upon a four-year period of renewal. *Love's Labour's Lost* and *How to Kill Your Neighbor's Dog* had been intriguing, but had not made much of a splash; but beginning with *Rabbit-Proof Fence* Branagh had produced a body of work that returned his career to where it had been in the 1980s and early 1990s, when almost everything he touched had turned to gold. By taking on the best theatre and television projects that were on offer, as well as maintaining his film career, and by being more selective – he did much less work in 2000 and 2002 than in years past – he enjoyed commercial success, critical acclaim and countless awards. The media attacks he had endured since the late 1980s finally seemed to be on the wane, and he had the stability and contentment that accompanied his marriage. From the perspective of where his life and career had been at the end of the 1990s, he had turned the corner.

Conclusion

Kenneth Branagh has been one of the success stories in the performing arts in Britain over the past quarter-century. He ranks alongside the likes of Simon Rattle and Bryn Terfel as one of those artists who has made an impression that one suspects will be lasting. As an actor, director, writer, producer and manager of a theatre company, there are few who can match his versatility.

In an age of celebrity-obsession and an ever-expanding media, there has unsurprisingly been a prurient interest in Branagh's personal life. Of course that is often an interesting dimension, especially so in Branagh's case, as two of his major relationships were with notable actresses, Emma Thompson and Helena Bonham Carter. Ultimately, however, this is not the most significant thing about the man. The essential contours of his personal life – playing the field as a young man, a marriage in his late twenties that broke down six years later, another lengthy relationship, then remarriage in his early forties – are hardly uncommon. There must be hundreds of thousands of people in Britain whose personal stories are similar. Some stars have lived out private lives that are extraordinary, such as Elizabeth Taylor or Vivien Leigh; but this has not really been the case with Branagh.

It is his career that demands attention, and in that he has enjoyed remarkable success. A great Henry V and a great Hamlet, he has delivered a number of other memorable performances in the theatre, including his debut in *Another Country* and his Edmond. His absence from the stage in the 1990s was too long, and it is to be hoped that his recent work in the theatre is not an anomaly but a sign of things to come. With his marked leadership skills – in another life he would have made a good football coach – running either the National

Theatre or the Royal Shakespeare Company would seem to be a possibility. His manifest talent for management, his track record in recruiting major actors to his projects, and his ability to inspire loyalty among those with whom he works, suggest he would do either job rather well.

His work in television, as well as in theatre, has been strong. The only area where there has been an unevenness has been in non-Shakespearean roles on the big screen, but even there the argument can be made that he has given a number of compelling performances – such as those in *A Month in the Country*, *The Gingerbread Man* and *The Theory of Flight* – that have been underestimated or largely ignored. By being more careful in his choices, moreover, he has achieved a greater consistency in his film work in recent years.

Branagh's most significant accomplishments, however, are his Shakespeare films. I would argue that his *Henry V* and his performance in it have not been matched; that his *Much Ado About Nothing* is the outstanding film of a Shakespeare comedy, and that his *Hamlet* also ranks as one of the finest examples of the genre. But this is a subjective matter, and others would hold a different view. What cannot be credibly contested, though, is his influence. *Henry V* brought about the most productive period in the history of the Shakespeare film. He paid a price for the fact that his films of *Hamlet* and *Love's Labour's Lost* (and also *Frankenstein*) did not prosper at the box office. The financial backing required for the films of Shakespeare plays that he wanted to make was not forthcoming for five years. But the announcement in 2005 that he would film *As You Like It* showed that his mission, to enlarge the audience receptive to Shakespeare by interpreting his plays on the big screen, was ongoing. It will be interesting to see what follows, but this author would be intrigued to see, in particular, how he would interpret *Macbeth*, *Richard III* and *King Lear* – all plays with enough narrative drive to work cinematically, and all plays with which Branagh feels a strong connection. If he continues to make more Shakespeare films, his legacy in this area will clearly be greater than any of his predecessors. Whatever happens in the future, there is an irrefutable bottom line to Branagh's career: he has done more than anyone on the face of the planet to popularise Shakespeare.

These achievements have been the product as much as anything of Branagh's drive and sheer audacity. Those attributes have enabled him to stand out from his contemporaries. A good many exceptional actors have emerged in Britain in the 1980s and in the 1990s, but how many of them have penned a play and started their own theatre company by the age of twenty-six, directed their first film – let alone a film of a Shakespeare play – at twenty-seven, and made their first Hollywood picture by the age of thirty?

What is also commendable is the resilience displayed by Branagh in achieving these things despite being subject to a severe backlash in England. It is true that he was not slow to seek coverage in the press, especially with the launch of Renaissance, as he tried to raise the profile of his new company. He was also adroit at handling the media, at understanding the sorts of information journalists needed to write a lively story. Furthermore, he has always had his supporters in the media, including Michael Billington, Alexander Walker and Barry Norman. That said, much of the coverage of Branagh has been intemperate, petty and unjustifiably harsh. As I have sought to demonstrate, a comparison of the critical response to his work in England and in the United States sheds light on this issue. With *Henry V*, *Much Ado About Nothing*, *Hamlet*, *Dead Again* and *The Gingerbread Man*, there was a marked and consistent difference of opinion, with America's critics far more favourable than their Fleet Street counterparts. This backlash at home was a media-driven phenomenon – not something generated at the grassroots. As Billington says, it wasn't as though people throughout the country were going to pubs muttering about Branagh.

One of the salient accusations made against Branagh was that he was obsessed with Olivier while being inferior to him as an artist. There is no doubt that he was influenced by Olivier; but it was also true that Olivier was but one of a diverse group of heroes, including John Gielgud, Orson Welles, Jimmy Cagney and Eric Morecambe, who inspired him. As has been argued earlier, it was Welles more than Olivier who shaped Branagh's direction of *Henry V*. And the fascination with the likes of Cagney and Morecambe was not trivial. It helps account for his populist leanings, as well as some of the specific work he has undertaken, namely *Public Enemy* and *The Play What I Wrote*.

The other point is that even if Branagh were strongly influenced by Olivier, which he was, this hardly represents any sort of shortcoming. On the contrary, this pattern, of one artist inspiring another, is an indispensable and historically identifiable part of the creative process. Does it change Titian's status as a painter that he was so influenced by

Giorgione? In turn, does the fact that Turner admired Titian so much alter his position as the greatest British painter who ever drew breath? Likewise, should one's view of Olivier be modified by the fact that he was so conscious of Henry Irving's legacy that he admitted to basing his voice for his stage interpretation of Richard III on impersonations of Irving he had heard from other people? The argument, therefore, that an unhealthy obsession with Olivier casts an unfavourable light on Branagh's career is without merit.

The overriding impression given by Branagh is of a man with a relentless drive. Achievement has often left him unsatisfied, and he has moved on to other challenges. From the Royal Shakespeare Company he went on to set up his own theatre company. From that he moved on to film directing, then on to Hollywood. That drive was not merely the product of the vanity that is probably a factor behind the rise of any prominent artist. More fundamentally, what has propelled Branagh is a search for identity, that perennial issue that affected him ever since he first arrived in England: a desire for distinctiveness, a specialness that would set him apart. Part Irish, part English, his early years did not provide him with a coherent sense of identity. Instead he sought to achieve that through professional success on a colossal scale. His work, not his background, would define him. If some time in the future he does become the first actor since Olivier to run one of the two great theatre companies in Britain, and if he continues his work as a maker of Shakespeare films, a secure sense of who he is may finally come to one of the most intriguing artists to emerge in the last few decades.

Notes

CHAPTER 1: Driven Youth
1 Antony Sher (2002), *Beside Myself*, Arrow paperback edn, p. 174.
2 *GQ* magazine, October/November 1989.
3 *Sunday Times*, 1 August 1999.
4 Interview with the author.
5 Kenneth Branagh (1989), *Beginning*, St Martin's Press, p. 57.
6 Ibid., p. 78.
7 Interview with the author.
8 Interview with the author.

CHAPTER 2: Renaissance
1 Interview with the author.
2 Interview with the author.
3 Interview with the author.

CHAPTER 3: King
1 Correspondence with the author.

CHAPTER 4: Backlash
1 Interview with the author.
2 Interview with the author.
3 *Daily Mail*, 11 April 2000.

CHAPTER 5: Hollywood
1 *GQ* magazine, September 1991.
2 *American Film*, September 1991.
3 *GQ*, September 1991.
4 *Western Mail Weekender*, 28 September 1991.
5 *American Cinematographer*, November 1991.
6 *Empire*, December 1991.

7 Interview with the author.

CHAPTER 6: Much Ado

1 *The Times*, 21 November 1992.
2 Transcript of the Gielgud Award ceremony, 16 January 2000, article archive, Kenneth Branagh web compendium.
3 *Sunday Times*, 19 April 1992.
4 *Plays and Players*, May 1992.
5 Kenneth Branagh (1993), *Much Ado About Nothing*, screenplay, Norton, p. viii.
6 Ibid., p. 5.
7 Interview with the author.
8 *The Times*, 21 November 1992.

CHAPTER 7: Monster

1 Mary Shelley, 'Author's Introduction' to *Frankenstein*.
2 Ian Holm (2004), *Acting My Life*, Bantam Press, p. 266.
3 *Daily Mail*, 4 January 1996.
4 Interview with the author.

CHAPTER 8: Sweet Prince

1 Quoted in the *Sunday Telegraph*, 1 October 1995.
2 *Empire*, January 1997.
3 Interview with the author.

CHAPTER 9: Only an Actor

1 *New York Daily News*, 16 November 1998.
2 National Film Theatre/*Guardian* interview with Branagh, 23 May 1999.

CHAPTER 10: The Comeback Kid

1 Interview with the author.
2 Correspondence with the author.
3 Interview with the author.

CHAPTER 11: A Return to the Stage

1 Interview with the author.
2 Interview with the author.
3 Interview with the author.
4 Interview with the author.
5 David Mamet (2003), *Edmond*, Methuen, p. 64.

Select Bibliography

ARCHIVES AND MANUSCRIPT COLLECTIONS

Berkshire Record Office, Reading:
Meadway School Logbook
Records of the Progress Theatre, 1947–1994

British Film Institute, London:
The Boy in the Bush pressbook
Coming Through pressbook
EDI box office reports for the United Kingdom and the United States
Hamlet brochure, Special Collections
Henry V Papers (including first draft of the screenplay, pre-production progress report, and call sheets), Special Collections
Interview with Branagh at the National Film Theatre, 8 August 1994
David Lean Papers
Mary Shelley's Frankenstein information folder
Microjackets (with press clippings and production notes) for *Anne Frank Remembered, Celebrity, Coming Through, Dead Again, Ghosts, The Gingerbread Man, Hamlet, Henry V, High Season, How to Kill Your Neighbor's Dog, In the Bleak Midwinter, Love's Labour's Lost, Mary Shelley's Frankenstein, A Month in the Country, Much Ado About Nothing, Othello, Peter's Friends, The Proposition, Swan Song, Swing Kids, The Theory of Flight, Wild Wild West.*
Microjackets (with press clippings) for Kenneth Branagh, Michael Caine, and Laurence Olivier
SIFT material on Branagh's film and television work

British Library, Department of Manuscripts, London:
John Gielgud Papers
Laurence Olivier Papers

Fortunes of War: personal scrapbooks of James Cellan Jones

Alan Plater Papers. Brynmoor Jones Library, University of Hull

Renaissance Theatre Company Papers (including the Renaissance Company diaries), Victoria & Albert Museum Archive, Blythe House, London

Richard III notes, taken by Alastair Macaulay

Shakespeare Centre Library, Stratford-upon-Avon:
- Theatre Records (press cuttings)
- Newscuttings file on Branagh
- Theatre programmes
- Video recordings of Branagh's performances with the RSC
- Brochure for the May 1999 National Film Theatre retrospective on Branagh's film and television work

Shakespeare Institute Library, University of Birmingham, Stratford-upon-Avon:
- Newspaper Clippings Collection
- Pre-rehearsal director's cut of *Richard III*
- Renaissance Films Collection
- Renaissance Theatre Company Collection
- Unpublished Screenplay Collection

Theatre Museum Library, Covent Garden, London:
- Kenneth Branagh personal box
- 'Renaissance Theatre Co.' folder

Miscellaneous material from Jude Tessel – including RADA programmes and information on Branagh's charity work – some or all of which will go towards the Kenneth Branagh collection being developed at Queen's University Belfast

Theatre programmes (personal collection) for *Edmond*, *The Play What I Wrote*, and *Richard III*

INTERVIEWS

Robert Altman
Michael Billington
Richard Briers
Simon Callow
Julie Christie
Chris Columbus
Michael Coveney
Stephen Evans
Stephen Goldblatt
Michael Grandage
Christopher Hampton
James Cellan Jones
Toby Jones
Michael Kalesniko
Alex Lowe

Alastair Macaulay
Patricia Marmont
David Parfitt
Oliver Parker
Jamie Payne
Clare Peploe
Al Senter
Hubert Taczanowski
Simon Woodham

CORRESPONDENCE

Alan Ayckbourn
Brian Friel
David Hare
Charlotte Jones
Janet Macklam (for Joan Plowright)
Frank Pierson
Paul Scofield

VIDEOS/DVDS/SCREENINGS

Another Country. The DVD of the film version in which Branagh did not appear includes an excerpt of an interview with him and Rupert Everett at the time of the opening of the original stage production
Celebrity
Chasing the Light (documentary on the making of the film of *Much Ado About Nothing*). Viewing copy held by the British Film Institute (BFI)
Coming Through (BFI)
Conspiracy. The DVD includes featurettes with excerpts of interviews with Branagh
The Dance of Shiva (courtesy of Jamie Payne)
Dead Again. The DVD includes Branagh's commentary on the film
Discovering Hamlet
Easter 2016 (BFI)
Fortunes of War
Ghosts. National Film Theatre screening
The Gingerbread Man
Hamlet
Harry Potter and the Chamber of Secrets
Henry V
High Season
How to Kill Your Neighbor's Dog
The Lady's Not for Burning (BFI)
Listening (courtesy of Kenneth Branagh)
Look Back in Anger

Love's Labour's Lost. DVD includes various scenes not included in the final cut
Mary Shelley's Frankenstein
Maybury: New Gods for Old (BFI)
A Midwinter's Tale (*In the Bleak Midwinter*)
A Month in the Country
Much Ado About Nothing
Othello
Peter's Friends
The Proposition
Rabbit-Proof Fence. The DVD includes a feature commentary with Phillip Noyce, Branagh *et al.*
Shackleton. The DVD includes a documentary on the making of *Shackleton*
Strange Interlude (part 3) (BFI)
Swan Song (BFI)
The Theory of Flight (BFI)
To the Lighthouse
Too Late to Talk to Billy (BFI)
Twelfth Night
Wild Wild West

BOOKS AND PERIODICAL, NEWSPAPER AND MAGAZINE ARTICLES

Abel, Robert. 'Othello', *Première*, March 1996.
Adamson, Colin. 'No looking back for triumphant stars', London *Standard*, 17 August 1989.
—. 'Wedding? Surely they're husband and wife already', London *Standard*, 5 August 1989.
Alberge, Dalya. 'Arctic shoot for Shackleton film', *The Times*, 12 May 2001.
—. 'Debutant director to make "erotic" Othello', *The Times*, 29 May 1995.
Alexander, Geraldine. 'I was at the Royal Academy of Dramatic Art with Ken', *Observer*, 26 November 1995.
Allen, Carol. 'Let's play down my brilliant career', *The Times*, 17 June 1999.
Alleyne, Richard. 'Branagh back in play what he directed', *Daily Telegraph*, 22 December 2001.
Andrew, Geoff. 'Celebrity squared', *Time Out*, 2–9 June 1999.
—. 'French kissing', *Time Out*, 7–14 February 1996.
Andrews, David. 'Hamlet', *Plays & Players*, February 1993.
Appleyard, Brian. 'Enter the outsider', *The Times*, 8 August 1987.
—. 'Renaissance Man', *GQ*, October/November 1989.
Appleyard, Christina. 'Why ET was the obvious choice', *Daily Mirror* ('Mirror Woman'), 24 August 1989.
Arar, Yardena. 'Director Gives All to Frankenstein', *Los Angeles Daily News*, 12 November 1994.
Arditti, Michael. 'Renaissance Man Ends Feud with the RSC', London *Standard*, 3 December 1992.
Atkinson, Dan. 'Branagh company aims at rebirth', *Guardian*, 30 August 1995.

Baker, Barry. 'His "wedding day" but Branagh can't stop acting', *Daily Mail*, 21 August 1989.

Bamigboye, Baz. 'Branagh's search for innocence', *Daily Mail*, 6 August 1993.

—. 'Charles is fighting for Agincourt!' *Daily Mail*, 24 September 1988.

—. 'Henry banned from the Cannes Festival.' *Daily Mail*, 8 April 1989.

—. 'Branagh's first Hollywood fracas', *Daily Mail*, 7 December 1990.

—. 'Leave my name off this film storms Branagh', *Daily Mail*, 26 February 1993.

—. 'Once more unto the breach', *Daily Mail*, 18 November 1988.

—. 'They were the new Oliviers. And just like the Oliviers', their love was doomed', *Daily Mail*, 2 October 1995.

Bamigboye, Baz, and Bill Mouland. 'Helena and Ken, the kiss that clinches it'. *Daily Mail*, 15 June 1996.

Bardsley, Barney. 'Waiting for the Renaissance of the Actor,' *Drama*, Winter 1984.

Barnes, Harper. 'Much to Do,' *St Louis Post-Dispatch*, 18 June 1993.

Basco, Sharon. 'Not a Quiet Actor's Life for Kenneth Branagh', *Christian Science Monitor*, 28 February 1996.

Bate, Jonathan, and Russell Jackson (eds.). *Shakespeare: An Illustrated Stage History*, Oxford: Oxford University Press, 1996.

Bates, Stephen. 'Me, Ken and the Moor', *Guardian* (section 2), 1 August 1995.

Beckerman, Jim. 'A Real "Labour" of Love', *Bergen Record*, 10 June 2000.

Benedict, David. 'Much ado about nothing', *Independent* (review), 18 January 2000.

Bennett, Catherine. 'Hyperbole's Favourite Son', *Sunday Correspondent*, 17 September 1989.

Bennett, Ray. 'The Bard meets Broadway in Branagh's Ambitious New Musical,' *Hollywood Reporter*, 21 March 2000.

Bennetts, Leslie. 'Catching Fishburne', *Vanity Fair*, December 1995.

Billen, Andrew. 'Citizen Ken', *Observer* (magazine), 6 October 1991.

Billington, Michael. 'First lord of the stage', *Guardian*, 12 July 1989.

—. 'The legacy of Larry', *Guardian* ('Weekend'), 15 July 1989.

—. 'Method in his Movies', *Guardian*, 19 January 2000.

—. 'A New Olivier is Taking on Henry V', *New York Times*, 8 January 1989.

—. 'Shakespearian Hero', *Guardian* (section 2), 21 May 1999.

Black, Kent. 'Married ... with Chutzpah', *Los Angeles Times*, 18 August 1991.

Bloom, Harold. *Shakespeare: The Invention of the Human*, New York: Riverhead Books, 1998.

Blume, Mary. 'Is Renaissance Theatre's Branagh the New Olivier?' *Los Angeles Times*, 16 October 1989.

Booe, Martin. 'Ken Again', *Première*, September 1991.

Boshoff, Alison. 'Branagh Alone Again', *Daily Mail*, 26 December 2002.

—. 'Is Ken Turning Over a New Leaf?' *Daily Mail*, 2 June 2003.

—. 'Ken Saddles up to be Hollywood Baddie', *Daily Telegraph*, 21 February 1998.

—. 'What *is* the matter with Michael Caine?' *Daily Mail*, 11 April 2000.

Bradley, Lloyd. 'Peter's Friends', *Empire*, December 1992.

Branagh, Kenneth. *Beginning*, New York: St Martin's Press, 1989.
—. 'A Life in the Day of Kenneth Branagh', *Sunday Times*, 10 July 1988.
—. *Hamlet: Screenplay, Introduction and Film Diary*, New York: Norton, 1996.
—. *Henry V* (screenplay), London: Chatto & Windus, 1989.
—. *In the Bleak Midwinter*, London: Nick Hern Books, 1995.
—. 'Kenneth Branagh's London', *American Airlines Magazine*, July 1999.
—. Letter to Neil Norman, printed in the London *Standard*, 2 March 1995.
—. *Mary Shelley's Frankenstein*, London: Pan Books, 1994.
—. *Much Ado About Nothing: the Making of the Movie*, New York: Norton, 1993.
—. 'My Perfect Yorick', London *Standard*, 7 July 1997.
—. *Public Enemy*, London: Faber and Faber, 1988.
—. 'The Stars What I Lured', *New York Times*, 30 March 2003.
Branagh, Kenneth, and Bill Branagh. 'Relative Values', *Sunday Times* (magazine), 1 August 1999.
Brando, Marlon. *Brando: Songs My Mother Taught Me*, New York: Random House, 1994.
Braund, Simon. 'Celebrity', *Empire*, July 1999.
Brett, Anwar. 'Creature comforts', *What's On In London*, 2 November 1994.
—. 'Dead Meet', *What's On In London*, 23 October 1991.
—. 'Just how famous can one man be?' *Film Review*, July 1999.
British Film Institute. *BFI Film and Television Handbook 1996*, London: BFI, 1995.
—. *BFI Film and Television Handbook 1997*, London: BFI, 1996.
—. *BFI Film and Television Handbook 1999*, London: BFI, 1998.
—. *BFI Film and Television Handbook 2001*, London: BFI, 2000.
Broadcast.
Brooks, Richard. 'To Cut or Not to Cut Ken's Film', *Observer*, 13 October 1996.
Brown, Geoff. 'Henry V', *Monthly Film Bulletin*, October 1989.
Brown, Georgina. 'Malvolio and The Good Life', *Independent*, 20 December 1987.
Broxton, Jonathan. 'Patrick Doyle – Lost and Found', *Soundtrack*, Winter 1999/2000.
Buhler, Stephen M. 'Double Takes: Branagh gets to Hamlet', *Post Script*, Autumn 1997.
—. *Shakespeare in the Cinema: Ocular Proof*. Albany: State University of New York, 2002.
Bush, Lyall. 'Fighting the Good Fight with Kenneth Branagh', *Moviemaker*, February 1997.
Butler, Robert. 'Kenneth Branagh's Bard Belies Bombast', *Kansas City Star*, 13 June 1993.
—. 'Screen Notes: Promising Film Shows in KC – But Maybe Not Elsewhere', *Kansas City Star*, 2 December 2000.
Callow, Simon. *Being an Actor*, London: Penguin Books, 1985.
—. '"The National should do what it uniquely can do, offering the whole range of world theatre"', *Observer* (review), 29 April 2001.

Carr, Jay. 'Branagh will play the indecisive Hamlet', *Asian Age*, 20 February 1996.
—. 'Shakespeare is Serious Stuff for Kenneth Branagh', *Boston Globe*, 11 February 1996.
Case, Brian. 'Fraught in the act', *Time Out*, 12–19 February 1997.
—. 'The Once and Future Ken', *Time Out*, 4 November 1992.
Champlin, Charles. 'The Wellesian Success of Citizen Branagh', *Los Angeles Times*, 9 November 1989.
Chrisafis, Angelique. 'West End Awaits Branagh's Return', *Guardian*, 20 February 2003.
Church, Michael. 'A particular talent', *Independent*, 25 September 1989.
Clapp, Susan. 'No more Madge', *Observer* (review), 29 December 2002.
—. 'Time for a Radical Shake-up', *Observer* (review), 28 April 2002.
Clark, John. 'Sweet "nothing"', *Première*, April 1993.
Clark, Steve. 'Branagh bounces back to Britain for two new films', *Mail on Sunday*, 19 January 1992.
—. 'The Shakespeare Superstar Returns', *Mail on Sunday*, 19 January 1992.
Clarke, Roger. 'Curse of the man who never was', London *Standard*, 20 August 1997.
Clarke, Steve. 'Branagh is lured back to TV screen', *Daily Telegraph*, 26 June 1995.
Cohen, Rachel. 'Branagh takes arms against sea of critics', *Today*, 23 October 1989.
Coles, Joanna. 'Branagh from heaven, cry tuned-in hacks', *Guardian*, 22 May 1993.
Collins, Andrew. 'Wild Wild West', *Empire*, September 1999.
Cordaiy, Hunter. 'The Truth of the Matter: An Interview with Phillip Noyce', *Metro*, 2002.
Corliss, Richard. 'Branagh the Conqueror', *Time*, 13 November 1989.
Coulbourn, John. 'O, Thou Empty Villain!' *Toronto Sun*, 28 December 1995.
Court, Louise. 'I do! (But not quite)', *Daily Express*, 22 August 1989.
Coveney, Michael. 'Alas, poor Charles. I know him', *Observer*, 20 December 1992.
—. 'Branagh, A Star by Stealth', *Financial Times*, 5 August 1989.
Cowley, Deborah. 'Kenneth Branagh, Theatre's New Young King', *Reader's Digest*, February 1990.
Cramer, Barbara. 'Peter's Friends', *Films in Review*, May/June 1993.
Crewe, Candida. 'Hometown', *The Times*, 24 May 1997.
Crowdus, Gary. 'Sharing an Enthusiasm for Shakespeare', *Cineaste*, December 1998.
Crowl, Samuel. *At the Shakespeare Cineplex: The Kenneth Branagh Era*, Athens: Ohio University Press, 2003.
Cunningham, Valentine. 'The monster in Mary's mind', *Observer* (review), 30 October 1994.
Cushman, Robert. 'My brilliant career', *Sunday Times*, 1 October 1989.
—. 'Reaching for the king's crown', *Daily Telegraph*, 6 April 1994.

Davenport, Hugo. 'Branagh: a talent eclipsed', *Daily Telegraph*, 2 October 1995.
—. 'Don't get mad, play Hamlet', *Daily Telegraph*, 13 February 1997.
Davis, Sally Ogle. 'Branagh thrills America with a touch of Hitchcock', *Daily Mail*, 5 September 1991.
Davison, John. 'Directing a regional renaissance', *Sunday Times*, 5 July 1987.
Dawson, Jeff. 'Healthy, Wealthy and Wise', *Empire*, September 1993.
Day, Carol. 'Not So Melancholy, Baby', *Madison*, December 1998/January 1999.
DeCurtis, Anthony. 'Hail the New King on the Block', *Rolling Stone*, 8 February 1990.
Dempster, Nigel. 'They're married: that IS official!' *Daily Mail*, 31 August 1989.
Diamond, Jamie. 'There is (Sexy) Life after Shakespeare', *Cosmopolitan*, September 1991.
Donovan, Paul. 'Baby grand old man', *Sunday Times* (section 6), 19 April 1992.
Dougary, Ginny. 'Oh, what a roguish and pleasant slave', *The Times* (Saturday Review), 21 November 1992.
Dougherty, Margot. 'Shear Talent', *Entertainment Weekly*, 20 September 1991.
Doyle, Abi. 'Being Branagh', *Edinburgh Student Newspaper*, March 2004.
Duncan, Andrew. 'The Andrew Duncan Interview', *Radio Times*, 15 February 1997.
Dyson, John. 'Hell on Ice', *Reader's Digest*, January 2002.
Earle, Laurence. 'More matter, less art', *Independent*, 28 April 1992.
Ebert, Roger. 'Perchance to Dream', *Chicago Sun-Times*, 19 January 1997.
Eimer, David. 'How the West was Lost', *Time Out*, 4–11 August 1999.
Ellen, Barbara. 'Weary of Harry', *The Times*, 14 November 2002.
Elliott, David. 'Branagh A Rising Maestro of Film and Theater', *San Diego Union-Tribune*, 18 August 1991.
Ellison, Mike. 'Branagh's home comfort in Belfast', *Guardian*, 7 November 1995.
Elrick, Ted. 'What's a Muggle to do?' *Director's Guild of America Magazine*, January 2003.
Entertainment Weekly.
Errigo, Angie. 'Dead Again', *Empire*, November 1991.
—. 'Mary Shelley's Frankenstein', *Empire*, December 1994.
—. 'Much Ado About Nothing', *Empire*, September 1993.
—. 'Othello', *Empire*, March 1996.
—. 'Phew, Acting!' *Empire*, November 1989.
—. 'The Proposition', *Empire*, November 1998.
—. 'The Theory of Flight', *Empire*, October 1999.
Exposure.
Eyepiece.
Eyre, Richard, and Nicholas Wright. *Changing Stages: A View of British Theatre in the Twentieth Century*, paperback edn, London: Bloomsbury Publishing, 2001.
Ezard, John. 'Stars become directors in new stage company', *Guardian*, 29 April 1987.

Falk, Quentin. 'The Iceman Kenneth', *Observer* (review), 9 December 2001.
Fanshawe, Simon. 'Zen Branagh', *Sunday Telegraph* (magazine), 6 July 2003.
Farndale, Nigel. 'This too too solid flesh', *Sunday Telegraph* (magazine), 2 February 1997.
Feay, Suzi. 'Mother to the Monster', *Independent on Sunday*, 6 November 1994.
Feeney, F. X. 'Vaulting Ambition', *American Film*, September 1991.
Fisher, Bob. 'Tragedy of Epic Proportions', *American Cinematographer*, January 1997.
Fitzgerald, Charles. 'Pride of place on Granny's wall!' *Belfast Newsletter*, 13 June 1989.
Flett, Kathryn. 'The art of darkness', *Observer* (review), 27 January 2002.
—. 'Truly, this was an Endurance test', *Observer* (review), 6 January 2002.
Fong, Lake. 'If You Knew Suzi', *Pittsburgh Post-Gazette*, 9 June 2000.
Foot, Paul. 'The monster spawned by misanthropy', *Guardian*, 7 November 1994.
Foreman, Jonathan. '"Labour" of Love for Ken Branagh', *New York Post*, 4 June 2000.
Fowler, Rebecca, and Tim Rayment. 'Star-crossed marriage of Ken and Em breaks up', *Sunday Times*, 1 October 1995.
Frampton, Diane. 'Lawrence film hit by Central dispute', *Broadcast*, 30 August 1985.
Francke, Lizzie. 'Creatures great and tall', *Guardian* (section 2), 27 October 1994.
French, Philip. 'Doom and broom', *Observer* (review), 17 November 2002.
—. 'Follow the rabbit-proof fence', *Observer* (review), 10 November 2002.
Froelich, Janis. '"Fortunes of War" Strikes Gold with Branagh', *St Petersburg Times*, 17 January 1988.
Fuller, Graham. 'It's a Monster!' *Interview*, November 1994.
Garrett, Stephen. 'Hit it, Bard! Kenneth Branagh Finds Easy Romance in Love's Labour's Lost', *Time Out New York*, 8–15 June 2000.
Gerstel, Judy. 'Acting As Fast As He Can', *Toronto Star*, 30 January 1998.
—. 'Extreme Hamlet, Branagh Style', *Ottawa Citizen*, 3 January 1997.
Gielgud, John. *Early Stages, 1921–36*, London: Hodder & Stoughton reprint, 1987.
Goodman, Joan. 'Why Rita will still stand up', London *Standard*, 8 October 1992.
Goodwin, Christopher. 'Love Him, Loathe Him: Ken Divides Us All', *Sunday Times*, 19 January 1997.
Graham, Alison. 'Today's Choices: Conspiracy', *Radio Times*, 19–25 January 2002.
Grant, Olly. 'In Pole position for new drama', *TV Times* 8 December 2001.
Grant, Steve. 'A Bit of Ado', *Time Out*, 18–25 August 1993.
—. 'Look Back in Anger', *Time Out*, 9 August 1989.
—. 'Luvvied up', *Time Out*, 25 October–1 November 1995.
—. 'Moor to the point', *Time Out*, 20 December 1995–3 January 1996.
Grimley, Terry. 'Festival is launched with tribute to CBSO', *Birmingham Post*, 6 September 1989.

—. 'New theatre company's royal patron', *Birmingham Post*, 29 April 1987.
Gristwood, Sarah. 'Glorious reign of King Ken', *Wales on Sunday*, 1 October 1989.
—. 'What is this thing called Love's Labour's Lost?' *Guardian* (section 2), 27 March 2000.
Gritten, David. 'Branagh's annus horribilis', *Daily Telegraph*, 29 November 1995.
—. 'Kenneth Branagh, On the Rebound', *Los Angeles Times*, 3 June 1995.
—. 'And the motion before us is genocide', *Radio Times*, 19–25 January 2002.
—. 'Why Branagh believes in friends', *Daily Telegraph*., 4 November 1992.
Guinness, Alec. 'There is no second Olivier', London *Standard*, 20 October 1989.
Guthmann, Edward. 'A Surprise Hollywood Thriller from Branagh', *San Francisco Chronicle*, 18 August 1991.
—. 'Why Branagh Keeps Braving the Bard', *San Francisco Chronicle*, 14 May 1993.
Hagen, Bill. 'Branagh Undaunted as the Latest "New Olivier,"' *San Diego Union-Tribune*, 10 November 1989.
Hall, Roger. 'Love's Labour's Lost: Patrick Doyle', *Soundtrack*, Summer 2000.
Halliburton, Rachel. 'To the theatre born', London *Standard* (magazine), 27 June–3 July 2003.
Hamer-Jones Brinley. 'Wonder "boy" Branagh', *Western Mail* ('Weekender'), 28 September 1991.
Hamilton, Alan. 'Olivier, actor supreme, dies at 82', *The Times*, 12 July 1989.
Hardy, Phil. 'Adapting the "beautiful little knitter"', *Listener*, 17 March 1983.
Harper, Elizabeth. 'Boy Wonder', *Girl About Town*, 13 February 1984.
Hassell, Graham. 'Star-spangled Branagh', *Plays and Players*, May 1992.
Hastings, Chris. 'Branagh Braves the Pole for Shackleton Epic', *Sunday Telegraph*, 17 September 2000.
Hatchuel, Sarah. *A Companion to the Shakespearean Films of Kenneth Branagh*, Winnipeg: Blizzard Publishing, 2000.
Hattenstone, Simon. 'Enter Branagh, the working-class hero', *Guardian* (section 2), 20 November 1998.
Hattersley, Roy. 'Heavy is the head that wears the media crown', *Guardian*, 23 September 1989.
Herbert, Susannah. 'Branagh in lead role with film institute', *Daily Telegraph*, 1 September 1993.
—. 'The end of the Renaissance', *Daily Telegraph*, 1 April 1994.
—. 'Final act for Branagh's Renaissance project', *Daily Telegraph*, 31 March 1994.
—. 'Branagh's big gamble with monster movie', *Daily Telegraph*, 24 October 1994.
Heron, Liz. 'Colonial boy', *Listener*, 2 February 1984.
Heuring, David. 'Déjà Vu Fuels Dread in *Dead Again*', *American Cinematographer*, September 1991.
—. 'The Director-Cinematographer Connection', *American Cinematographer*, November 1991.

Hewett, Rick. 'After Emma and Helena, has Ken found a soulmate at last?' London *Standard*, 29 May 2003.
Hewitt, Charles. 'Shackleton', *Eyepiece*, November/December 2001.
—. 'Hamlet in the Round', *Eyepiece*, August/September 1996.
Hewitt, Chris. 'Problem Child', *Empire*, October 2002.
Hibbert, Tom. 'What Makes Kenny Run?' *Empire*, November 1991.
Hickey, William. 'National Treasure No. 74', *Daily Express*, 7 March 1998.
Higginbotham, Adam. 'Sauce up your Shakespeare', *Empire*, December 1995.
Hillerstrom, Oscar. 'Rabbit-Proof Fence', *Empire* (Australia), August 2001.
Hindle, Maurice. 'Man of many parts', *Time Out*, 26 October–2 November 1994.
Hiscock, John. 'Branagh ready for the next stage', *Daily Telegraph*, 24 September 2001.
Hobson, Louis. 'Kenneth Branagh's Learned to be True', *Calgary Sun*, 9 February 1997.
—. 'Living Privately in Public', *Calgary Sun*, 3 January 1999.
Hochman, David. 'The US Interview: Kenneth Branagh', *US magazine*, November 1994.
Hodges, Adrian. 'Woolf adaptation from busy Gregg', *Screen International*, 19 March 1983.
Hoffman, Barbara. 'Harry Potter's Chamber of Hormones', *New York Post*, 2 November 2002.
Holden, Anthony. *Laurence Olivier*, New York: Collier Books, 1988.
Holden, Stephen. 'A Tale of 2 Neighbors, Both Pains in the Neck', *New York Times*, 22 February 2002.
Holland, Mary. 'Home is where Ken's art is', *Observer* (review), 5 November 1995.
Hollywood Reporter.
Holm, Ian, with Steven Jacobi. *Acting My Life*, London: Bantam Press, 2004.
Honeycutt, Kirk. 'How Many Festivals Does a Film have to Win to Land Distribution?' *Hollywood Reporter*, 4 September 2001.
Hope, Darrell L. 'Into the West with Barry Sonnenfeld', *Directors' Guild of America Magazine*, July 1999.
Horton, Marc. 'Branagh Slips into Something Small', *Ottawa Citizen*, 13 September 1995.
Howard, Mike. 'Royal festival opening', *Brighton & Hove Leader*, 6 July 1989.
Howell, Georgina. 'Renaissance Man', *Vogue*, September 1991.
Hruska, Bronwen. 'It's Alive Again!' *San Francisco Chronicle*, 30 October 1994.
Hubbard, Kim. 'The Man who would be King: Rising Star Kenneth Branagh', *People*, 26 May 1991.
Hutchinson, Tom. 'Once more unto the snore, dear friends', *Guardian*, 28 February 1997.
Isaacs, David. 'Out of the pigeonholes', *Bradford Telegraph & Argus*, 8 February 1985.
—. 'Season's measured success', *Newcastle-upon-Tyne Journal*, 29 March 1985.
—. 'Youth and maturity in concert', *Newcastle-upon-Tyne Journal*, 13 February 1985.

Isherwood, Charles. 'Broadway Brits', *The Times*, 7 April 2003.
Jackson, Russell. 'Branagh and the Bard', *Sunday Times*, 29 August 1993.
—. (ed.). *The Cambridge Companion to Shakespeare on Film*, Cambridge: Cambridge University Press, 2000.
Janusonis, Michael. 'Kenneth Branagh Loves Freedom of Short Films', *Providence Journal*, 5 August 2003.
Jays, David. 'Wherefore art thou?' *New Statesman*, 17 April 2000.
Jeffries, Stuart. 'Branagh waives fee for film on Aborigines', *Guardian*, 18 May 2001.
Jilla, Shireen. 'Oliver Parker', *Première* (UK), March 1996.
Joffee, Linda. 'Branagh Earns the Spotlight', *Christian Science Monitor*, 13 October 1988.
—. 'Britons Watching New Comet in the Theater', *Christian Science Monitor*, 16 December 1985.
Johnson, Reed. 'Releasing the Prince', *Los Angeles Daily News*, 19 January 1997.
Johnston, Helen. 'Branagh and Emma Thompson split up', *Sunday Telegraph*, 1 October 1995.
Johnstone, Iain. 'Banking on Branagh', *Sunday Times* (section 9), 15 August 1993.
—. 'Film set and match', *Sunday Times* (section 6), 22 September 1991.
—. 'Group dynamic', *Sunday Times*, 15 November 1992.
—. 'Will Hamlet cheer him up?' *Sunday Times*, 19 November 1995.
Jones, Alan. 'When will I be famous?' *Film Review*, Summer Preview 1999.
Jones, Alison. 'Branagh the Ginger-Brit Goes Down South', *Independent*, 9 August 1998.
Jongh, Nicholas de. 'Everything to play for', London *Standard*, 30 April 2002.
——. 'Playing to the camera', London *Standard*, 15 January 2003.
—. 'Pretender to the Crown', *Mail on Sunday*, 6 May 1984.
Joseph, Joe. 'Branagh Film Keeps the Luvvies Happy', *The Times*, 27 August 1993.
—. 'Why don't we like Ken?' *The Times*, 22 March 2002.
Judge, Elizabeth. 'Caine wins support on film snobbery', *The Times*, 13 April 2000.
Katelan, Jean-Yves. 'To Be or Not Mister B?' *Première* (France), May 1997.
Kaufman, Gerald. 'The monster waiting for Branagh's fall', London *Standard*, 7 November 1994.
Keeling, Judith, and Martin Delgado. 'Lonely Emma and my confused friend Greg', London *Standard*, 2 October 1995.
Kellaway, Kate. 'Branagh in the works', *Observer*, 21 September 2003.
Kempley, Rita. 'Besotted with the Bard Director-Actor Kenneth Branagh Has a Way With Will', *Washington Post*, 22 June 2000.
Kenny, Glenn. 'Love's Labour's Lost', *Première* (USA), July 2000.
Kent, Rolfe. 'The Theory of Flight', *Film Score Monthly*, June 1999.
Keogh, Tom. 'Cinemania Interview: Kenneth Branagh', *Cinemania*, December 1996.

King, Randall. 'Kenneth Branagh "Wild" About Evil Role', *Winnipeg Sun*, 28 June 1999.
King, Susan. 'To Wow-Wow the Audience', *Los Angeles Times*, 21 February 2002.
Kingston, Peter. 'Richard III, by William Shakespeare', *Guardian* (review), 28 April 2001.
Kirkland, Bruce. 'Branagh Brightens up Bleak Affair', *Toronto Sun*, 12 September 1995.
—. 'Couple under Siege: Kenneth Branagh and Helena Bonham Carter', *Toronto Sun*, 20 December 1998.
—. 'The Shakespeare Guy', *Toronto Sun*, 23 December 1996.
Kornbluth, Jesse. 'Grisham, Yes, but a Far Cry from "The Firm,"' *New York Times*, 1 June 1997.
Lamar, Jake. 'Out of Brooklyn', *Première* (USA), January 1996.
Landesman, Cosmo. 'Incredible journey', *Sunday Times* ('Culture' section), 10 November 2002.
—. 'Mild about Harry', *Sunday Times* ('Culture' section), 10 November 2002.
Lane, Anthony. 'Insubstantial pageants', *Independent*, 30 September 1989.
Lane, Harriet. 'Read my lips', *Observer* (review), 6 June 1999.
Langan, Sean. 'Star-spangled-Branagh', *Mail on Sunday* ('You' magazine), 15 August 1993.
LaSalle, Mick. 'The Reigning Prince of Shakespeare', *San Francisco Chronicle*, 19 January 1997.
Lavender, Andy. 'Darling!' *Blitz*, October 1989.
Lawson, Mark. 'More than an actor', *Independent*, 9 May 1987.
Leaming, Barbara. *Orson Welles*, New York: Penguin, 1985.
Lee-Potter, Emma. 'Our Phoney Wedding, by Emma', *Today*, 22 August 1989.
Lee-Potter, Emma, and Phil Tusler. 'Bride Emma goes Dutch for £30,000 Scandal Wedding', *Today*, 21 August 1989.
Leitch, Luke. 'Branagh returns to London stage after 11 year absence', London *Standard*, 19 February 2003.
Leith, William. 'Acts of a nervous conqueror', *The Times*, 16 September 1989.
Lennon, Peter. 'Breaking away', *Listener*, 19–26 December 1985.
Leonard, Tom. 'Stars make Much Ado about Branagh', London *Standard*, 27 August 1993.
Levin, Bernard. 'Silent falls the blazing trumpet', *The Times*, 12 July 1989.
Levy, Geoffrey. 'The blooding of Branagh', *Daily Mail*, 20 October 1989.
Lewin, Alex, and Matt Mueller. 'Making 'Love's', *Première* (USA), November 1999.
Lewin, David. 'In the court of King Ken', *Sunday Mirror* (magazine), 24 September 1989.
Lewis, Peter. 'Henry V,' *Sunday Times*, 10 September 1989.
—. 'Hal and High Water', *Sunday Telegraph* (magazine), 24 September 1989.
Linehan, Hugh. 'From Shakespeare to Shelley', *Irish Times*, 29 October 1994.
Lipson, Karin. 'Busy Branagh', *Newsday*, 2 November 1994.

Lisle, Tim de. 'A Case of Less is Moor', *Independent on Sunday*, 21 January 1996.

Lister, David. 'Abbey the fitting stage for theatre's tribute to Olivier', *Independent*, 21 October 1989.

—. 'Is this a slump we see before us? Ken calls off new Shakespeare film', *Independent*, 31 January 2001.

—. 'Shakespeare Meets Busby Berkeley', *Independent*, 17 April 1999.

Lockyer, Daphne. 'Passion, Poetry and a Touch of Therapy', *The Times*, 12 February 2003.

London Theatre Record.

Lovell, Glenn. 'As He Likes It', *San Jose Mercury News*, 22 May 1993.

Lybarger, Dan. 'Killing a Misconception', *Lawrence Journal-World*, 7 December 2000.

Macdonald, Andrew and Gina. 'Rewriting Shakespeare for film: Devore/Zeffirelli's *Hamlet* vs. Branagh's *Hamlet*', *Creative Screenwriting* 5:2 (1998).

Macdonald, Marianne. 'Alas, poor Shakespeare: Branagh rewrites Hamlet', *Independent*, 22 November 1996.

Mackie, Lindsay. 'A Big Hooray for Branagh's Henry', *Scotsman*, 14 October 1989.

Magid, Ron. 'New Look for Classic Creature', *American Cinematographer*, December 1994.

Malcolm, Derek. 'Darling, they are wonderful', *Guardian* (section 2), 18 September 1995.

—. 'Henry begins to clean up', *Guardian*, 12 October 1989.

Malkin, Marc S. 'Othello', *Première* (USA), November 1995.

Mamet, David. *Edmond*, London: Methuen, 2003.

Manelis, Michele. 'Ken Goes Hollywood', *Sunday Telegraph*, 7 June 1998.

Mangan, Richard (ed.). *Gielgud's Letters: John Gielgud in His Own Words*, London: Weidenfeld & Nicolson, 2004.

Mann, William J. *Edge of Midnight: The Life of John Schlesinger*, London: Hutchinson, 2004.

Marks, Kathy. 'Film portrays regime that betrayed generations', *Independent*, 3 February 2001.

Marshall, Lee. 'The Independent Interview: Kenneth Branagh', *Independent on Sunday*, 13 June 1999.

—. 'Squirming in the spotlight', *Sunday Telegraph Review*, 30 May 1999.

Martin, Adrian. 'Adrian Martin measures the distance of Australia's rootlessness, in search of a native cinema', *Film Comment*, July/August 2002.

—. 'Bouquet of barbed wire', *Sight and Sound*, November 2002.

Martin, Kevin H. 'A Walk on the Wild Side', *Cinefex*, October 1999.

Martland, Lisa. 'Theatre too pricey, says Branagh', *Stage*, 27 May 1999.

Maxford, Howard. 'Swing Nazis', *What's On In London*, 9 June 1993.

McAlpin, Colin. 'On the Throne', *Irish News*, 28 July 1997.

McFarlane, Brian. 'Peter's Friends', *Cinema Papers*, October 1993.

McIlheney, Barry. 'Mission Accomplished?' *Empire*, December 1994.

McIlwaine, Eddie. 'Is this a Winner I See Before Me?' *Belfast Telegraph*, 21 May 1999.

—. 'Ken Takes Potter Sequel in Stride', *Belfast Telegraph*, 7 November 2001.

McKee, Victoria. 'Kenneth Branagh: "Hamlet is the hub of his work. It's where plays go to and come from"', *Independent* ('Weekend'), 20 April 1996.

McKellen, Ian. 'Why actors do need collective control', *Guardian*, 4 May 1984.

Meier, Paul. 'With Utter Clarity', *Drama Review*, Summer 1997.

Middlehurst, Lester. 'Rich and famous with Branagh', *Daily Mail*, 13 October 1992.

Midgley, Carol. 'Bonham Carter split "amicable"', *The Times*, 18 September 1999.

—. 'Stage is set for Branagh demolition job', *The Times*, 15 January 1997.

Millar, Jeff. 'Shaking up Shakespeare', *Houston Chronicle*, 10 December 1989.

Miller, Carl. 'Beyond our Ken', *City Limits*, 28 September 1989.

Miller, John. *Judi Dench: With a Crack in Her Voice*, paperback edn, London: Orion, 1999.

Millner, Denene. 'Branagh Puts a New Spin on Old Will', *New York Daily News*, 9 June 2000.

Mills, Nancy. 'Introducing the "New Olivier,"' *Los Angeles Times*, 6 January 1988.

Mitchell, Sean. 'A Not-So-Proper Kenneth Branagh Has Some Fun', *New York Times*, 15 November 1998.

Mollard, Angela. 'Kenneth, quilt thou take this woman to be your live-in love?' *Daily Mail*, 1 January 1996.

Moore, Oscar. 'A good deal depends on talent', *The Times*, 5 January 1992.

Morecambe, Gary. *Eric Morecambe: Life's not Hollywood, it's Cricklewood*, paperback edn, London: BBC Books, 2004.

Morgan, Hilary. 'Made in Belfast', *Sunday Mirror*, 1 August 1999.

Morley, Sheridan. 'The company directors', *The Times*, 12 March 1988.

—. 'Renaissance Romeo', *Radio Times*, 24–30 April 1993.

Mottram, James. 'Pride & Prejudice', *Film Review*, December 2002.

Mouland, Bill. 'Laugh at your peril', *Daily Mail*, 28 October 1994.

Moult, Julie, and Justin Penrose. '007 Star Moore's On-Stage Collapse', *Sun*, 8 May 2003.

Muir, Hugh. 'Thompson fluffs her lines in last act of marriage', *Daily Telegraph*, 2 October 1995.

Murdin, Lynda. 'Lost for Words on Richard III', *Yorkshire Post*, 7 March 2002.

Music from the Movies.

Nathan, Ian. 'As Happy as Larry', *Empire*, March 1997.

—. 'The Gingerbread Man', *Empire*, August 1998.

—. 'Hamlet', *Empire*, March 1997.

—. 'Katy', *Empire*, January 1997.

—. 'No Holds Bard', *Empire*, June 1996.

Nathanson, Paul. 'Branagh and Emma split up', *Mail on Sunday*, 1 October 1995.

—. 'Entering stage right, a saviour of the Globe', *Mail on Sunday*, 16 January 1994.
Nathanson, Paul, and Sarah Oliver. 'The £15,000 a month, ten-bedroom Surrey mansion where Ken is nursing a broken heart', *Mail on Sunday*, 5 November 1995.
Naughton, John. 'Charity in Dallas', *Listener*, 2 January 1986.
—. 'Fuck This', *Première* (UK), December 1995.
—. 'What will everyone do?' *Listener*, 30 June 1983.
Nechak, Paula. 'Alas, Poor Branagh, We Know Him Well', *Seattle Post-Intelligencer*, 31 January 1997.
New York Times Film Reviews.
Nickson, Chris. *Emma: The Many Faces of Emma Thompson*, Dallas: Taylor Publishing, 1997.
Nolan, Abby McGanney. 'A Midwinter's Tale', *Village Voice*, 13 February 1996.
Norman, Barry. 'Much Ado About Branagh', *Radio Times*, 4–10 January 2003.
Norman, Neil. 'The breaking of Branagh?' London *Standard*, 1 March 1995.
—. 'Englishness from the outside', London *Standard*, 19 November 1987.
—. 'Will Branagh direct the new Harry Potter?' London *Standard*, 30 May 2002.
O'Carroll, Lisa. 'Bed and bawd as Branagh plays TV Pepys', London *Standard*, 13 July 1995.
O'Connell, Diog. 'Finding the Cinematic Story in History', *Film Ireland*, May/June 2003.
Ojumu, Akin. 'Expect frocks, not facts', *Observer* ('Screen'), 11 July 1999.
—. 'Love's Labour's Lost', *Empire*, March 2000.
Oliver, Sarah. 'How Helena Bonham Carter took to a wheelchair to tackle one of our great taboos ... sex and disability', *Mail on Sunday*, 3 January 1999.
Olivier, Laurence. *On Acting*, New York: Simon and Schuster, 1986.
Olliver, Paul. 'Stop knocking best in British cinema', letter to editor, *Sunday Telegraph*, 15 October 1989.
O'Neill, Brenda. 'Crowning Moment for Wacky Comic – Eddie Joins Up with Our Ken', *Belfast Telegraph*, 22 June 2003.
Orme, Terry. 'Branagh Keeps Perspective through First Hollywood Adventure', *Salt Lake Tribune*, 1 September 1991.
O'Toole, Fintan. 'Branagh: The man who would be king', *Irish Times*, 30 September 1989.
O'Toole, Lesley. 'Staking a Claim in the Wild West', *The Times*, 17 July 1998.
Owen, Michael. 'Birth of a monster', London *Standard*, 21 October 1994.
—. 'Branagh signs up De Niro as Frankenstein monster', London *Standard*, 5 April 1993.
—. 'Kate is riding the Oscar roller coaster', London *Standard*, 16 February 1996.
—. 'Ken and Helena (It's Official)', London *Standard*, 18 July 1997.
—. 'Loneliness of the Long-Distance Director', London *Standard*, 27 January 1997.
—. 'Perfect timing for Frankenstein', London *Standard*, 19 August 1994.
—. 'Stop Bashing Branagh', London *Standard*, 8 May 1992.

Palmer, Martyn. 'Moor sex and violence', *The Times*, 14 February 1996.
—. 'Smith and Western', *Total Film*, September 1999.
Parks, Louis. 'Mad About Hamlet', *Houston Chronicle*, 12 January 1997.
Parsons, Keith, and Pamela Mason (consultant editors). *Shakespeare in Performance*, London: Salamander Books, 1995.
Paskin, Barbra. 'A Cockney with intelligence and a million dollars', *The Times*, 16 February 2000.
Patterson John. 'Applied Will power', *Guardian* (section 2), 9 July 1999.
Payne, Vicky. 'I felt so at home', *Radio Times*, 19 March 1983.
Pearce, Garth. 'Better watch out, Gwyneth', *Sunday Times*, 11 April 1999.
—. 'The Funny Side of Kenneth Branagh', *Now*, Autumn 1999.
Pearlman, Cindy. 'Theory of Flight Q & A', *Chicago Sun-Times*, 21 January 1999.
Pearson, Harry. 'Much Ado About Nothing', *Films in Review*, July/August 1993.
Pendreigh, Brian. 'Common man outshines the star', *Scotsman*, 7 October 1991.
Peregrine, Chris. 'City director films £6.5m extravaganza', *South Wales Evening Post*, 24 September 1987.
Peter, John. 'Acting in a new-found spirit of enterprise', *Sunday Times*, 13 December 1987.
Peters, Pauline. 'The men behind Branagh', London *Standard*, 16 September 1994.
Petty, Moira. 'Kenneth Branagh's Burning question', *Daily Express* ('This Week' section), 25 November 1995.
Pevere, Geoff. 'Labour of Love for Branagh: Take Shakespeare, Add Music', *Toronto Star*, 9 June 2000.
Portman, Jamie. 'Branagh does Woody, by Woody, for Woody', *Ottawa Citizen*, 18 November 1998.
—. 'Branagh's at Home in LA', *Ottawa Citizen*, 23 August 1991.
—. 'He's Created A Monster', *Montreal Gazette*, 6 November 1994.
—. '"Love's Labour's Lost" A Labor of Love for Star', *Ottawa Citizen*, 13 March 1999.
—. 'What Makes Iago Tick?' *Montreal Gazette*, 23 December 1995.
Powell, Dilys. 'Fighting talk', *Punch*, 13 October 1989.
—. 'Wartime Olivier embraced by a beleaguered nation', *Sunday Times*, 8 October 1989.
Pratt, Desmond. 'The RSC sets out its stall', *Yorkshire Post*, 14 February 1984.
Pratt, Steve. 'When nothing is beyond our Ken', *Northern Echo* ('Event!' guide), 18 August 1989.
—. 'Where There's a Will', *Northern Echo*, 22 January 2000.
Press, Susan. 'Midas touch dubs actor "next Olivier"', *Manchester Metro News*, 22 September 1989.
Pukas, Anna. 'King Ken the Comeback Kid', *Daily Express*, 6 November 2001.
Purves, Libby. 'The King and I', *Radio Times*, 25 April–1 May 1992.
Quinlan, David. 'Henry V', *Films and Filming*, October 1989.
Quinn, Anthony. 'The Young Pretender', *Empire*, October 1989.

Raymond, Ilene. 'Adapting the Bard', *Creative Screenwriting*, Spring 1998.
Rayner, Jay. 'Is Nothing Beyond Our Ken?' *Observer*, 11 November 2001.
—. 'What a song and dance', *Observer* (review), 26 March 2000.
Rees, Jasper. 'The Importance of Playing Earnest', *Sunday Times*, 9 December 2001.
—. 'Shakespeare: The New Democratic Pact', *Harpers & Queen*, October 1989.
Renton, Alex. 'Renaissance Man', *Plays and Players*, July 1987.
Reynolds, Nigel. 'Branagh to bring a ray of sunshine to the West End', *Daily Telegraph*, 8 September 2001.
—. 'Branagh edition of Hamlet features Stormin' Norman', *Daily Telegraph*, 23 November 1996.
—. 'Theatre lights dim in memory of Olivier', *Daily Telegraph*, 12 July 1989.
Rhodes, Russell. 'Ken Goes Way Down South', *Birmingham Evening Mail*, 24 July 1998.
Richards, Terry, *et al*. 'Way Out West', *Film Review*, September 1999.
Rieschick, Anne. 'Kenneth Branagh: He's Cute, He's Smart, He's Sexy, and He's Frankenstein', *A & E Monthly*, November 1994.
Riley, Wendy. 'Branagh's Daring Challenge', *Film Monthly*, October 1989.
Roberts, Alison. 'Branagh is back – but where has he been?' London *Standard*, 20 March 2002.
Robinson, Anne. 'Oh no – it's Bran...aargh!' *Daily Mirror*, 4 October 1989.
Rosenthal, Daniel. 'Making a crisis out of a drama', *The Times*, 24 December 2001.
Rothwell, Kenneth S. *A History of Shakespeare on Screen: A Century of Film and Television*, Cambridge: Cambridge University Press, 1999.
Rowan, Ivan. 'Tribute to founder as show goes on at the National', *Daily Telegraph*, 12 July 1989.
Rozenberg, Gabriel. 'How hero Shackleton nearly went mad', *The Times*, 12 September 2002.
Ruebens, Michael. 'Branagh's dilemma', London *Standard*, 9 February 1990.
Rumbold, Judy. 'Kenny, Prince of Lightness', *Guardian*, 9 November 1992.
Salm, Arthur. 'Branagh to go back to the Bard', *San Diego Union-Tribune*, 23 August 1991.
Samson, Polly. 'The actor factor', *Sunday Times*, 11 August 1991.
Samuelson, Sydney. 'Much ado about Frankenstein', *Framework*, Spring 1994.
Sapsted, David. 'Branagh's epic Hamlet is given cool reception', *Daily Telegraph*, 28 December 1996.
Schaefer, Stephen. 'Branagh Touts "Hamlet" as More Bard for the Buck', *Boston Herald*, 19 January 1997.
Schneller, Johanna. 'Stratford on Sunset', *GQ*, September 1991.
Scott, Adam. 'BBC go independent', *A.I.P. & Co.* , March 1983.
Screen International.
Scroop, Catherine. 'Where There's a Will', *Empire*, September 1999.
Segal, Victoria. 'No more Mr Nice Guy: Kenneth Branagh's debut at the National is chilling and triumphant', *Sunday Times* ('Culture' section), 27 July 2003.
Selby, John. 'Kenneth Branagh: Crown Prince of our Theatre', *Woman's Weekly*, 3 October 1989.

Sessums, Kevin. 'Never Look Back', *Vanity Fair*, February 1996.
Shelley, Mary. *Frankenstein*, London: Penguin, 1994.
Sher, Antony. *Beside Myself*, paperback edn, London: Arrow, 2002.
—. *Year of the King*, paperback edn, London: Methuen, 1986.
Sherman, Betsy. 'Kenneth Branagh's First Love', *Boston Globe*, 18 June 2000.
Sherrin, Ned. 'First nights and last gulps', *The Times*, 30 September 1989.
Sherwin, Adam. 'Branagh pins hopes on love for the Bard', *The Times*, 23 March 1999.
Shone, Tom. 'Reeling from a Charm Offensive', *Sunday Times*, 3 December 1995.
Shorter, Eric. 'He that play'd the King', *Daily Telegraph*, 12 July 1989.
—. 'Who's for magniloquence?' *Daily Telegraph*, 25 June 1988.
Shuttleworth, Ian. *Ken & Em: A Biography of Kenneth Branagh and Emma Thompson*, London: Headline, 1994.
—. 'Sacrifice of the star-crossed lovers', London *Standard*, 2 October 1995.
—. 'They did the monster bash', *Independent*, 7 November 1994.
Sight and Sound.
Simon, Jeff. 'Making the Riches of the Bard Accessible', *Buffalo News*, 13 June 1993.
Simpson, David. 'A word or two about Ulster', *Belfast Telegraph*, 19 November 1984.
Simpson, Richard. 'Friar Kylie has Charles in stitches', London *Standard*, 22 November 2002.
Sinden, Peter. 'Do the Bard man!' *Film Review*, March 1997.
Smith, David James. 'In the Company of Ken', *Sunday Times* (magazine), 20 February 2000.
Smith, Dinitia. 'Much Ado About Branagh', *New York*, 24 May 1993.
Smith, Geraint. 'Branagh and the Ad for a Girlfriend', London *Standard*, 3 August 1992.
Smith, Sid. 'Branagh's Epic "Hamlet": Triumph or Folly?' *Chicago Tribune*, 5 January 1997.
Smurthwaite, Nick. 'Only the Beginning', *London Portrait Magazine*, October 1989.
Souster, Mark. 'Actors bid farewell to their leading man', *The Times*, 15 July 1989.
Spencer, Charles. 'How to make the best of a bad job', *Daily Telegraph*, 14 December 1992.
Spencer, Kathryn. 'Circles come to a halt', *Lancashire Evening Post*, 9 September 1989.
Starburst.
Starks, Lisa S. 'An Interview with Michael Maloney', *Post Script*, Autumn 1997.
Stearns, David. 'Branagh's Risky Business', *USA Today*, 24 December 1996.
Steyn, Mark. 'Playing Woody', *Daily Telegraph*, 17 June 1999.
Stimpson, Mansel. 'Henry V', *What's On In London*, 4 October 1989.
Stoddart, Patrick. 'A clean breast would have boosted ratings', *Broadcast*, 25 July 1983.

Stone, Judy. 'On the Path of Kings', *San Francisco Chronicle*, 10 December 1989.
Stoner, Patrick. 'Kenneth Branagh Q & A', *Flicks*, December 1996.
Stringer, Robin. 'Branagh, movies, sex and me by Helena', London *Standard*, 2 September 1999.
—. 'Creature comfort as fans cheer up Branagh', London *Standard*, 4 November 1994.
—. 'End of Branagh's movie version', London *Standard*, 30 March 1994.
—. 'Film institute gets a "yes" from Branagh', London *Standard*, 31 August 1993.
—. 'Laughter is first on the bill as Film Festival opens', London *Standard*, 6 November 1992.
——. 'Swansong for the grand old knight of theatre', London *Standard*, 26 October 1992.
—. 'Luvvie's Labour's Lost (and found?) for Ken', London *Standard*, 16 March 2000.
Stuart, Otis. 'Mold of Fashion', *Village Voice*, 25 May 1993.
Sutcliffe, Thomas. 'The Branagh-Bardic Express', *Independent tabloid*, 12 December 1996.
Swern, Phil. *Box Office Hits*, Enfield: Guinness Publishing, 1995.
Tanenhaus, Sam. 'Return to Hogwarts', *Vanity Fair*, October 2002.
Taylor, Noreen. '"I try not to let the depression torture me"', *The Times*, 15 March 2000.
Taylor, Vicki. 'Success of a man born to be king', *Evesham Journal & Four Shires Advertiser*, 26 October 1984.
Television Today.
Tench, Matt. 'Three Lions On His Shirt', *Guardian*, 23 July 1999.
Theatre Record.
Thomas, David. 'Spare us the parts', *Sunday Times* (section 9), 4 December 1994.
—. 'With Friends Like These', *Mail on Sunday* ('You' magazine), 8 November 1992.
Thompson, Bob. 'Branagh Ad-dresses Celebrity', *Toronto Sun*, 19 November 1998.
—. 'Taming the Beast', *Toronto Sun*, 6 November 1994.
Thompson, Emma. *The Sense and Sensibility Screenplay & Diaries*, New York: Newmarket Press, 1995.
Thomson, David. 'Not much ado about anything Branagh does now', *Independent on Sunday*, 9 May 1999.
Thornber, Robin. 'Fringe benefit', *Guardian*, 19 February 1985.
Thorpe, Vanessa. 'Polar hero inspires explorers and stars', *Observer*, 2 September 2001.
Thynne, Jane. 'Branagh and company plan film of Henry V', *Daily Telegraph*, 7 October 1988.
Torrens, Pip. 'Shiver me timbers', *Guardian*, 2 January 2002.
Tory, Peter. 'Bring down the curtain on calling Ken the next Olivier', *Daily Express*, 19 August 1989.

Tyler, Dana. 'Harry's War', *Film Review*, December 2002.
Updike, John. *Gertrude and Claudius*, paperback edn, London: Penguin, 2001.
Usher, Shaun. 'Sex, Lies and Henry V', *Daily Mail*, 16 September 1989.
Variety.
Vatirani, Shoba. 'Aisle be late to wed Emma', *Sun*, 21 August 1989.
Verdiani, Gilles. 'Woody Allen, C'est Moi', *Première* (France), February 1999.
Verniere, James. 'From Classics to Gothic: Branagh Turns to Frankenstein', *Boston Herald*, 30 October 1994.
Victor, Peter. 'Ken and Em split up', *Independent on Sunday*, 1 October 1995.
Vincent, Mal. 'Branagh Puts Bard on Hold to Go West', *Philadelphia Daily News*, 2 July 1999.
—. 'Out on a Limb', *The Virginian-Pilot*, 5 November 1994.
Viner, Brian. 'Luvvie in a cold climate', *Independent*, 31 December 2001.
Wagner, Erica. 'Cold comfort', *The Times*, 29 December 2001.
Walker, Alexander. 'Golden Girl', London *Standard*, 6 February 1997.
—. 'The King sneaks in', London *Standard*, 25 May 1989.
—. 'Putting the Ken into Frankenstein', London *Standard*, 3 November 1994.
Walker, Tim. 'Ken, Em and the "revenge thing"', *Daily Mail*, 4 January 1996.
Watson, Neal. 'Doing it for Woody', *Daily Express*, 20 November 1998.
Weber, Bruce. 'Kenneth Branagh: In Command and in Control', *New York Times*, 23 August 1991.
Weisel, Al. 'Idol Chatter: Kenneth Branagh', *Première*, December 1996.
Wells, Jane. '"Have children? I think no further than dinner or tea"', *Now*, October 1998.
Werner, Laurie. 'Playing Iago in "Othello" Helps Branagh Rebound from Bad Year', *Chicago Tribune*, 24 December 1995.
Westbrook, Bruce. 'The Many Faces of Kenneth Branagh', *Houston Chronicle*, 25 August 1991.
Westbrook, Caroline. 'Love's Labour's Lost', *Empire*, April 2000.
Whitebrook, Peter. 'Renaissance man in too much hurry', *Scotsman*, 30 September 1989.
Whitley, John. 'Mrs Dale and the Prince of Denmark', *Independent*, 23 April 1992.
Whittell, Giles. 'Branagh is backed for full-length Hamlet film', *The Times*, 8 August 1995.
Whittell, Giles, and Dalya Alberge. 'Film critics savage Branagh as Prince woos Tinseltown', *The Times*, 3 November 1994.
Wigler, Stephen. 'Imitation is Flattering to the Greats', *St Petersburg Times*, 23 August 1991.
Wiley, Mason, *et al.* (eds.). *Inside Oscar: The Unofficial History of the Academy Awards*, New York: Ballantine Books, 1986.
Wilkins, Emma. 'Competing careers split golden couple of stage and screen', *The Times*, 2 October 1995.
Williams, Jeannie. 'Branagh, DiCaprio "Celebrity" Chums', *USA Today*, 20 November 1998.

Witchell, Alex. 'How Frankenstein Has Created a Hunk', *New York Times*, 9 November 1994.
Wolcott, James. 'How Green was my Woody', *Vanity Fair*, December 1998.
Wolf, Matt. 'Hamlet? Branagh Knows Him Well', *Variety*, 1 January 1997.
—. 'Hard Act to Follow', *Listener*, 28 September 1989.
—. 'Too Much Ado Over New Olivier.', *Wall Street Journal*, 23 September 1988.
—. 'What Actors These New Men Be', *Wall Street Journal* (Europe), 23 November 1984.
Woodward, Ian. 'Branagh's other women', *Sunday Express*, 12 February 1989.
Woodward, Kate. 'Return of the Prodigal One', *O-Reading*, 16 October 2000.
Worth, Larry. 'A Chip off the Woodman', *New York Post*, 18 November 1998.
Young, Graham. 'Branagh launches Brum festival', *Birmingham Evening Mail*, 17 August 1989.
—. 'Festival first for new Henry V', *Birmingham Daily Mail*, 10 August 1989.
Young, Helen. 'Set apart?' *Radio Times*, 18 June 1983.
Zable, Arnold. 'The Boy in the Bush', *Cinema Papers*, July 1984.
Zec, Donald. 'Olivier: The greatest actor the world has ever seen', *Daily Mirror*, 12 July 1989.
Zinoman, Jason. 'Seriously Funny', *Time Out New York*, 13 March 2003.

INTERNET SOURCES

The Kenneth Branagh Compendium (www.branaghcompendium.com).

Index

'KB' indicates Kenneth Branagh